CHAOS, CATASTROPHE, AND HUMAN AFFAIRS

Applications of Nonlinear Dynamics
to Work, Organizations, and
Social Evolution

CHAOS, CATASTROPHE, AND HUMAN AFFAIRS

Applications of Nonlinear Dynamics
to Work, Organizations, and
Social Evolution

Stephen J. Guastello
Marquette University

LEA LAWRENCE ERLBAUM ASSOCIATES, PUBLISHERS
1995 Mahwah, New Jersey

Lawrence Erlbaum Associates, Inc., Publishers
10 Industrial Avenue
Mahwah, New Jersey 07430

Cover design by Mairav Salomon-Dekel

Library of Congress Cataloging-in-Publication Data

Guastello, Stephen J.
   Chaos, catastrophe, and human affairs : applications of nonlinear dynamics to work, organizations, and social evolution / Stephen J. Guastello.
      p.   cm.
   Includes bibliographical references and index.
   ISBN 0-8058-1634-8 (alk. paper)
   1. Psychology, Industrial—Mathematical models. 2. Industrial safety—Mathematical models. 3. Organizational behavior—Mathematical models. 4. Chaotic behavior in systems. I. Title.
   HF5548.8.G8 1995
   158.7—dc20
                                                          95-30865
                                                          CIP

Books published by Lawrence Erlbaum Associates are printed on acid-free paper, and their bindings are chosen for strength and durability.

Printed in the United States of America
10 9 8 7 6 5 4 3 2

To Andrea

Contents

Preface

Chaos theory, catastrophe theory, fractal geometry, and nonlinear dynamic systems theory all originated as mathematical ventures with their eyes pointed at problems in physics and engineering. Collectively, they grabbed the scientific community by the face with discoveries showing not only that their principles were all interrelated, but that the emerging theory portended to clarify a wide range of human issues and to untangle a logjam of theoretical problems in the social sciences.

This book is about some of my favorite logs that have to do with the psychology of people at work—with their machines, their management on both sides of the social hierarchy, their exposure to accidents and other health hazards, how they use their imaginations and forces that stifle them, and some of the radical shifts in the societies that they live and work in. The social theories suddenly become more organized and unified than ever before.

The topics covered in this book, apart from the core mathematical theories, are centered around my own work on catastrophe and chaos theory applications to human problems in industry since 1980. I have included mention of the work of other reseachers on the same or similar topics in hopes of pulling together a comprehensive and cohesive mosaic of theory and application. A substiantial number of the studies summarized here have been published in journals, and the descriptions of methods and details of results are available for inspection in the references cited.

As anyone might surmise, I have rethought many of my earlier ideas and I feel the same way that I initially did about most of them. In addition,

I have come to clearer insights about other ideas, or at least, I have developed better ways of explaining them. I have also included a substantial amount of new material, and the details of those studies are presented here firsthand. I have tried to use section headings that will alert the reader to the occasional pockets of detail that might be saved, for some folks, for a second reading.

ACKNOWLEDGMENTS

Before jumping into the circus ring directly, I should acknowledge my colleagues in chaos who have been remarkably supportive of this venture by commenting on the material that was eventually included or putting me in touch with information sources and sharing their viewpoints: Frederick Abraham, Kevin Dooley, Jeffrey Goldstein, Mark Michaels, Mark Rieke; and all the Citizens of Internet from Society for Chaos Theory in Psychology and the Life Sciences, Nonlin-L, and Chaos Network who were willing to do the same. I should also credit my spouse, Denise D. Guastello, for her assistance in writing the section on scientific jury selection in chapter 4, as well as her partnership in some of the research summarized in the accident chapter (7) as cited. Special acknowledgment should also go to my research assistants, John Driscoll and Mary Odak, for their tireless scoring of Island Commission videotapes (end of chapter 11) and for tracking down all those informational details I never seemed to have handy. There are more people who could be mentioned by name here, but they have all written important work too, so I will just make them part of the story.

Stephen J. Guastello

1

An Invitation to Chaos

Look out the nearest window. Is there any straight line out there that wasn't man-made? I've been asking the same question of student and professional groups for several years now, and the most common answer is a grin. Occasionally a philosophical person will comment that even the lines that look like straight lines are not straight lines if we look at them through a microscope. But even if we ignore that level of analysis, we are still stuck with the inevitable observation that natural structures are, at their core, nonlinear.

If the foregoing is true, why do social scientists insist on describing human events as if all the rules that make those events occur are based on straight lines? The probable answer is that straight lines are easier to work with. Perhaps it has been difficult enough to figure out the simple rules, and the tools to figure out the complicated rules have been in short supply.

How complicated is "complicated"? There are four characteristics that make straight lines different from each other: their slopes, intercepts, lengths (in which case we have a line *segment*), and where we put them in relationship to . . . well . . . other lines. Curves, on the other hand, can take on a myriad of shapes, ranging from gradual contours to convoluted balls of yarn. The essential challenge is to describe what all those hitherto ignored shapes, and the information implied by them, mean. If we are successful, the explanations should, in turn, have a serious impact on the way we look at the world and on the type of information we choose to seek out when we need to know something.

So how is the explanation of interesting events—such as a jury's perception of evidence, the productivity of a manufacturing organization,

1

an industrial accident or disease, urban renewal, fatigue and overwork, revolution and war—affected by the linear versus nonlinear issue? Nonlinearity impacts on our notions of cause and effect. If we have an event, or an effect, Y, that is caused by a condition X, and there is a linear relationship between X and Y, then what we are really saying is that any change in X, large or small, will have a proportional effect on Y. If there is a nonlinear relationship between X and Y, however, then a small change in X could produce a dramatic change in Y, or alternatively, a large change in X could produce no discernible change in Y. Furthermore, the amount of change in Y that we get from any change in X would have a lot to do with the initial values of X and Y that we started from.

Does any of this added complication actually get us anywhere? Are the differences between a nonlinear interpretation of an event and a linear one actually accomplishing anything? Let's put it this way: Psychology does little better than to account for 50% of any phenomenon it tries to study, particularly outside of the laboratory. As for the other 50%, we glibly call it error. Sometimes we give the unknown a long name, such as "random measurement error," or a similar concatenation of adjectives, as if all we had to do was to measure our constructs a little better and we'd have our problems licked. It couldn't be that our explanations are missing a few important parts, could it?

Of course it could! In fact, the central objective of this book is to provide a "parts catalog," some "tools" for installing those parts into theories, and an extensive array of applications where improvements are in evidence. At this early stage of the conceptual development, I will take matters a little further to say that, on the average so far, theories that are properly equipped with nonlinear and dynamic models account for twice as much of the phenomena they purport to describe compared to their linear counterparts (Guastello, 1992a). Sometimes the benefit is larger.

CHAOS BY ANY OTHER NAME

Many seemingly random events are actually more predictable than people have usually thought. The tools of prediction are differential equations, and there is a relatively small set of general models that we can apply to events that we observe changing over time. In this book we have no need to agonize over the basic theory of differential equations, advanced topology, and other mathematical contributions. We use the products of those mathematics instead.

Chaos theory is the shortest common name of the theory that we unfold and elaborate here. It is actually a charming misnomer. There is indeed a phenomenon known as "deterministic chaos," and it is an important part of chaos theory. But the underlying theory that gives the chaos part of the story meaning is much broader in scope. The repertoire of nonlinear change processes that we now have available ranges in complexity from single-point dynamics, to waves and cycles, to the seemingly random world of chaotic events. Furthermore, there are explanations for why change processes are sometimes simple, sometimes complex, and sometimes change from simple to complex or vice versa.

Nonlinear dynamical systems theory is, therefore, perhaps the most accurate label for the subject matter at hand. It's a handful of words to be processed, so the acronym *NDS* is adopted. *Complex systems theory*, sometimes called complexity theory, is closely related in meaning to NDS, but the shift is away from the mathematical tools of analysis and description to the qualitative understanding of the systems to which the new concepts are applied, of the complexity of those systems, and of how nonlinear dynamic processes could be aggregated within a complex system. *Catastrophe theory* is a special topic within the broader domain of NDS that pertains to sudden, discontinuous changes of events. In other words, catastrophe theory is all about the proverbial "straw that broke the camel's back."

The next objective for this chapter is to delineate eight central propositions of NDS or the ideas that developed from it.

1. Many seemingly random events are actually predictable with a set of nonlinear differential equations.
2. The so-called chaotic processes that produce apparent randomness and uncertainty vary in complexity and level of turbulence.
3. All discontinuous changes of events can be modeled by one of seven elementary topological forms, which are hierarchically ordered by level of complexity.
4. Complexities of systems are indicated by the dimensionality of their behaviors.
5. Conventional notions of four-dimensional space–time are inadequate to explain many phenomena; dimensionalities greater than four and fractional dimensionalities are common in natural systems.
6. The classical notions of cause and effect are replaced by concepts involving control (in the engineering sense), bifurcation, energy, and turbulence.
7. Within the discipline of psychology, and within several of its subdisciplines, many of the rudiments of chaos and catastrophe theories can be observed in research reports as far back as the turn of the last century.
8. Where there has been an opportunity to test a well-developed application of NDS against a conventional linear alternative, NDS described phenomena twice as well as its linear competitor.

The tool kit of NDS consists of attractor forces and repeller forces, stabilities and instabilities, bifurcation and self-organization, fractal geometry, the distinction between evolutionary and revolutionary change, and catastrophes and discontinuous change. Chapter 2 is devoted to the expansion on the central concepts. A new theory inevitably brings with it some new analytic techniques centered around the question, "How do we know what we know?" How can we run tests on data to determine whether one or another process is taking place, assess the level of complexity, and so forth? Chapter 2 concludes with an overview of analytic strategies that have become common in NDS research (oxymoron not intended!), and Chapter 3 is devoted to the structural equations approach to data analysis that has become most influential to applications contained in this book.

Having stated the overarching premises of NDS, this chapter continues with the concept of a general systems theory, and why the word *system* is used so often! This chapter concludes with an overview of the applications themselves, and the interrelationship among them before they were confronted with NDS. Chapter 2 discusses the basic NDS theory with frequent mention of where the applications would involve a NDS concept, whereas chapters 4 through 13 reverse the priorities and tell their stories from the point of view of the application, therein detailing how NDS concepts made improvements on specific theories and how we knew we were successful.

GENERAL SYSTEMS THEORY

A general systems theory is an interdisciplinary theory. In other words, it contains rules and propositions that extend beyond their initial application to at least one other field of study. A theory that successfully solves a problem in political economics with principles of evolutionary biology would qualify as a general systems theory. As one might anticipate, some general systems theories are more intensive and extensive than others. A theory that is intensive explains a lot about a particular phenomenon. A theory that is extensive applies to a wide variety of situations, where the more disparate and apparently unrelated the applications are, the better.

There are two traditions in general systems theory that are pertinent to NDS. One is the mathematical approach, and the other is the living systems approach. The mathematical approach, usually attributed to von Bertalanffy (1968) and Wymore (1967), uses mathematical relationships as the central set of premises. Applications would utilize the mathematical formula to solve particular problems or to model particular relationships. A good working set of mathematical models would carry with it qualitative relationships by which an application might be recognized. An application is thus an example of the generally stated prototype system.

Living systems theory (Miller, 1978) is the second tradition relevant to NDS and consists of three central premises. First, every living system contains 20 subsystems that can be divided into three groups: those that process both matter and information, those that process matter and energy, and those that process information (Miller & Miller, 1990; Miller & Miller, 1992, 1993a, 1993b). Particular subsystems are elaborated in subsequent chapters within the context of the specific applications of NDS. The second key point of living systems theory that affects the NDS applications is level of system complexity. The levels are the cell, organ, organism (sometimes differentiated between human and other), group (with the same possible subdivision), organization, community, society, and supranational system. The great preponderance of applications covered in this book involve the human organism, group, and organization, and some involve relationships between humans and groups and organizations. There are, nonetheless, a few excursions into community, societal, and supranational levels of system organization. The third key point of living systems theory is the principle of fray-out (Miller & Miller, 1990). As systems grow in complexity from cells to supranational systems, the systems and subsystems become more differentiated and complex.

General systems theories can be further thought of as metatheories, methodologies, and possibly a whole way of viewing the world. A metatheory is a theory that organizes concepts, objects, or relationships inherent in several local (or specific) theories. Thus specific objects can be interchanged from one application to another, but the relationships among those objects could remain approximately the same. Another approach might show interchangeability of objects and relationships, but the "blueprint" that defines the metatheory would tell the scientist where to look for objects and relationships that could be useful.

When viewed as a methodology, a general systems approach would proceed to analyze and describe phenomena, beginning with the tenets of a working general systems theory. The next step would be to create a *model* of a phenomenon, which would compile a representation of a system using the tools of the general theory plus additional information that is specific to the application. The model-making process typically draws on the past successes and failures encountered with applications of the general theory. If a general theory is new in the sense that working applications are few and far between, the best thing that could happen to such a theory is the discovery of an application that utilizes as much of the general theory as possible with a minimum of situational alterations. Such an application would serve as a prototype for new applications.

If a general systems theory is truly meritorious, the knowledge gained from a successful application would increase the knowledge about the core principles of theory, and thus facilitate the hunt for further applications. One good application thus serves as a metaphor for another. Limitations to applicability will inevitably be encountered, and may suggest ways to improve the general theory with, hopefully, a minimum of new propositions. A general systems theory will eventually reach its limits of generalizability, and we would hope that it would in fact do so. A theory that is so general that it explains everything explains nothing. The trick is to build a theory that explains a lot and that has tentacles linking it to other general theories, where one domain begins and another ends, and to local theories whose main purpose is to describe a particular class of phenomena typically encountered within a particular discipline.

Another aspect to the idea of general systems theory as methodology concerns how one might go about proving the truth of the general principles. Although considerable effort goes into developing a cogent metaphor for a new system based on a known system, the validity of the metaphor requires empirical testing. New theories often involve special propositions that distinguish the theory in question from alternative explanations. Unique ideas often result in the need for unique equipment, experimental designs, and protocols of data analysis. New methodologies often evolve as new questions are asked, and generate additional new questions.

The last point to make is about how general systems theory could be viewed as an entire way to view the world, as Bahg (1990) observed. No doubt, if one has a general systems theory that reliably solves a wide range of problems, using it to assimilate new information and experience becomes a habit; in that sense it is a world view. If a theory is new, contains many novel ideas, and is powerful in application, that theory would eventually become a matter of philosophical discussion. One does not need to buy into any particular philosophy (of science or of anything else), however, in order to comprehend the theory, to interpret the result of its applications, or to use it successfully for further work. Philosophy could flow from the scientific work, but NDS is not predicated on a philosophy.

AN OVERVIEW OF INDUSTRIAL PSYCHOLOGY

Industrial psychology is concerned with applying any viable idea drawn from theoretical psychology to answer questions or solve problems concerning people at work. The theoretical content is complemented by field research where the research questions are defined by the needs of real people doing real work. The topic areas are typically broken into three broad groups: personnel selection, training, job analysis, and other individual issues; organizational psychology and group dynamics; and human factors engineering and ergonomics. There is a small amount of overlap across the three topic groups. The first ideological movement emerged around 1911. "Scientific management" was concerned with analyzing jobs and time-motion studies and redesigning work to be more efficient. Advances in the field of psychological testing supported the growth of personnel selection research and application, especially during World War I.

The second major movement was the "human relations school," which emerged about 1930. A series of poorly controlled studies of the effect of work environment (in those days, who knew?) led to an enlightening observation that people were more productive when management paid attention to them as people. The subject matter placed new emphasis on leadership, group formation, and the relationship between individuals and groups. Kurt Lewin was a principal theorist during the human relations period and continued to be influential through the 1950s. Lewin contributed an important practitioner model for organizational change and development, and field theory (Lewin, 1951) was the first psychological theory to be based on topological concepts.

Contemporary human factors engineering continues to be concerned with theories of psychophysics and perception, skill acquisition, the design of controls and displays, measurements of the human body (e.g., psychomotor skill, physical strength and endurance, height, length of arms, etc.), and environmental influences in performance (e.g., heat, cold, weightlessness, noise). The advances in the computer industry had the effect of redesigning old machines as computer-based machines, and presented many new human performance issues that were not readily addressed by the existing theories. As a result, the field expanded in several directions concerned with human–computer interaction, decision making, and theories in cognition and perception.

"Ergonomics" is a European version of "human factors engineering." When the idea first arrived in the United States, it reflected a subject matter that was more concerned with environmental effects on human performance, and less on machine interfaces. Today the two terms are regarded as interchangeable. Accident analysis and prevention does not fit squarely into any of the three categories of subject matter, although ergonomics or human factors appears to be the closest link.

Advances in organizational psychology led Division 14 of the American Psychological Association to change its name to the *Society for Industrial and Organizational Psychology* in 1969. They often shorten the name of the subject matter to "I/O."

THE RANGE OF APPLICATIONS OF NDS
TO I/O PSYCHOLOGY

The series of applications begins at the interface between the living (people) and the nonliving parts of systems. Chapter 4 covers the applications of NDS to psychophysics, perception, and learning. NDS principles have been inherent in "conventional" theory, and the new approach is a logical outgrowth of existing ones. The reinterpreted theories lead to further applications that are covered in the subsequent three chapters.

Figure 1.1 depicts the relationships among the metatheory, local theory, and end applications. Relative to the metatheory, local theories are themselves applications, however. In other words, metatheory : local theory :: local theory : applications. At the same time, four different kinds of linkages can be imagined. Application 1 in Fig. 1.1 is a direct implementation of local theory; local theory has been altered or reinterpreted in terms of the metatheory. Application 2 is a situation where no satisfactory local theory existed. Metatheory principles are applied directly. Application 3 is a situation that involves two or more local theories, each of which has been influenced by the metatheory. Application 4 is one of many (two shown) possible applications that have been liberated by applying the metatheory to applications.

Chapter 5 develops a range of NDS applications to personnel selection, motivation theory, and conflict resolution. Personnel selection is conceptualized as a two-stage process in which the joint effects of ability and motivation on performance can be assessed. The personnel selection model can be extended into a full model of work performance that is dynamic in nature. The scope of motivation concepts includes organization issues that are considered further in chapters 7 and 8 on occupational accidents and

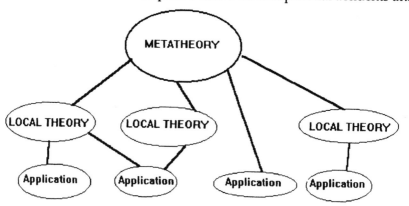

FIG. 1.1. The relationships among metatheory, local theories, and applications.

health and in chapter 11 on organizational development. The dynamics in the motivation model lend themselves to further adaptation to conflict and conflict resolution where additional dynamics are also involved.

Chapter 6 differentiates three separate models for stress and performance, all of which are based on the cusp catastrophe structure. They are the diathesis-stress model, buckling model for work load, and models for both mental and physical fatigue. A fourth approach, based on a five-dimensional model, bears some similarity with the general model for motivation in organizations developed in chapter 5.

Chapter 7 develops NDS models for occupational accidents that are largely based on qualitative concepts drawn from both organizational psychology and ergonomics. Both conventional and nonlinear theories of stress are also relevant.

Chapter 8 develops an analogy between accident epidemiology and health or disease epidemiology, and nonlinear dynamics are integral to the process. The internal security subsystem is introduced at the organ level of living systems analysis. The security model is expanded in chapters 11 and 12, and foreshadowed in chapter 5.

Chapter 9 represents some subject matter that is relatively new to organizational psychology. Contemporary applications of NDS to evolutionary laws and population dynamics have churned up some new ideas of concern to I/O psychologists: personnel selection and training programs when they are affected by a shortage of qualified talent, managerial decision making as a chaotic controller, coalition formation and cooperation. Cooperation is relevant to previous chapter sections on conflict resolution, and subsequent work in chapters 11 and 12. It would not be unreasonable to suggest that the evolutionary modeling work has itself reached the status of a general systems theory.

By one line of reasoning, chaos causes creativity, and by another, creativity causes chaos. This newly developing theory is based to some extent on population dynamics work. The curious frequency distributions associated with creative behavior are strikingly similar to accident rate distributions observed in large, diverse databases. Creativity dynamics, which are addressed in chapter 10, have a central place in organizational change processes.

Chapter 11 contains applications of NDS theory to organizational development and group dynamics. This chapter builds on previous material on motivation, conflict resolution, population dynamics, and creativity. It concludes by challenging some basic assumptions about organizations and change, by giving new meanings to other well-known ideas, and by offering a few more concerning organizational change processes.

Chapter 12 is the final extrapolation as theories developed in earlier chapters are applied to revolutions, war, and issues connected to cooperation and conflict between supranational systems. NDS theory developed in the political arena is introduced as well.

SUMMARY

Although social science may have been productive by channeling its attention to tractable straight-line relationships, considerable information about human social systems has been ignored by the inattention to nonlinearities. New information requires new theories for correct interpretation, and NDS is all about interpreting change processes that are known to be the result of nonlinear relationships among variables. NDS is characterized as a general systems theory because it involves the application of mathematical concepts to the study of systems encountered in several scientific disciplines; it represents a new way to compare the behaviors of living systems of varying levels of complexity; and it facilitates the study of a broad class of issues encountered in one discipline, namely, industrial and organizational psychology and its neighboring discipline, ergonomics.

2

Nonlinear Dynamical Systems Theory

Nonlinear dynamical systems (NDS) theory is an agglomeration of several lines of mathematical thinking. The principal ideas concerning stability, instability, and chaos can be traced to the work of French mathematician Henri Poincaré, who worked in the late 19th and early 20th century. Poincaré's contributions necessarily built on the work of the greatest earlier giants of mathematics, Newton and Leibnitz, who developed calculus in the middle 17th century, and Laplace, who extended Newton's concepts of determinism in the early 19th century.

Laplace's ideas deserve mention here as much for the contrast with Poincaré's work as for their foundational value. In Laplace's view, all behavior of physical objects (human behavior was not a subject of rudimentary scientific study until 1879) could be expressed by equations. We would no longer need graphs, geometry, or similar visual substitutes. A class of characteristic deterministic equations took the form:

$$y = e^{xt} \tag{1}$$

If we know x and how much time t has elapsed then we know y. A recursive function of y, that is especially important in dynamics is

$$y_2 = e^{y_1 t} \tag{2}$$

If we know y at time 1, and how much time has elapsed, then we know y at time 2.

Poincaré's work centered around dynamical topology, or the motion of objects in three-dimensional or higher dimensional nonlinear surfaces.

His core contribution was *qualitative analysis,* which necessitated the return of visual imagery to mathematical study. The pattern of inquiry was to study the visual topology of the function first, and then to develop equations later. His insights produced the first examples of deterministic chaos and a solution to the three-body problem in astrophysics that defied Newton's laws of motion. The essence of the three-body problem was to determine the path of an object that was under the influence of three gravitational forces.

The full impact of Poincaré's work was not realized until the late 1960s. Early 20th century physics had by many paths explored statistical concepts to explain uncertainty. Conventional statistics are strongly tied to linear models of reality, and it is no small wonder that Stewart (1989) observed that by the 1940s and 1950s, the linear habit was so ingrained that little attention was paid to any relationships of potentially greater complexity. Fortunately, the linear paralysis was only temporary.

This chapter unfolds the concepts of attractors, bifurcation, equilibria and stability, fractals, catastrophes, catastrophic changes in a dynamic field, and self-organization, all of which are core concepts in NDS. The global picture describes how chaotic processes fit into a greater world of equilibria and stability. Fractals are geometric forms in fractional dimensionalities. Catastrophe theory concerns sudden, discontinuous changes of events and global patterns of attractors, instabilities, and bifurcations. Self-organization is a natural process whereby feedback loops within a complex system give rise to nonlinear behavior. The last section provides a summary of some contemporary issues and controversies in chaos numerics that lead, almost gracefully, into the statistical issues and methods in chapter 3.

Of necessity, decades of intense work by many people are condensed to strike a balance between a picture of the field that is broad enough to capture its most important vicissitudes, and one tailored enough to emphasize the concepts of greatest use to applied psychology. Some NDS concepts are more heavily used than others in the application chapters. That, I believe, is a temporary state of affairs arising from this early stage of theoretical development and proof. At the same time, however, the substantive developments are not so primitive that they can be dusted off as provocative speculations. Rather, they are growing together in a way that permits a comprehensive social science theory.

ATTRACTORS

An *attractor* is a mathematical structure that describes some types of motion for an object in space, which is generically defined as a *vector field.* If an attractor structure is present, the object will enter a region of space and not leave it, except under specific conditions. An underlying property of *equilibrium* is often ascribed to the object remaining in the limited space. A closer look at the equilibrium concept as it has been used in the past century in biology, chemistry, and social science, however, shows that it is less specific than the attractor concept. As the following story unfolds, attractors come in different varieties, and many of them represent dynamics that are anything but motionless over time. The taxonomy of attractors ranges from the simple fixed-point types to the complex chaotic varieties. R. H. Abraham and C. Shaw (1992), F. D. Abraham, R. H. Abraham, and C. Shaw (1990), Nicolis and Prigogine (1989), Thompson and H. B. Stewart (1986), and I. N. Stewart (1989) serve as general references for this section and the next.

Fixed Points

Attractor is to behavior as magnet is to iron filings, at least in the case of the simplest attractor dynamics. With *fixed-point* attractors, a behavior will gravitate toward a steady state or a constant value. When the attractor concept first crossed into physical chemistry and biology it was known as an *equilibrium*. Although it is sometimes useful to continue to think of equilibrium states, which imply a balance of some sort, alongside the concept of attractor, it is also a good idea to keep the two concepts separate when making the distinction between a mathematical abstraction and a physical realization of the abstraction.

Figure 2.1 shows two types of fixed-point attractor. The *radial* type of fixed point attracts objects, or control points, from all directions to its center. With the *spiral* type of fixed point, the control points spiral inward toward the center, where they eventually rest. The attractor has finite strength, and it will not act on objects positioned beyond a certain distance from the center. The range of an attractor's influence is its *basin*.

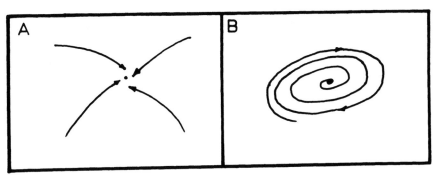

FIG. 2.1. Phase portrait for (A) radial and (B) spiral point attractors.

The paths that lead into an attractor's center need not be symmetrical radial or spiral paths. For instance, imagine that panel B of Fig. 2.1 is a rubber sheet. Hold the upper right and lower right corners with your right hand. Next, pinch the left side in the middle with your thumb and forefinger and pull. The result is a *homeomorphism* of the original spiral path, or a transformation that is produced by stretching a rubber sheet, which produces a path configuration that is *topologically equivalent* to the initial spiral.

Limit Cycles

A *limit cycle* is an attractor that holds objects in an orbit around the attractor center. A limit cycle can be created by taking several magnets and arranging them in a closely packed circle such that their basins are contiguous. When a control point is fired into their joint basin, its path stabilizes to a limit cycle around the entire configuration. A limit cycle would characterize the path of moons around a planet, or a planet around a sun. Biological events, such as circadian rhythm (elaborated in chapter 6; also see Abraham et al., 1990), that we observe as a steady oscillation or regular wave pattern over time are, in essence, limit cycles.

An example of a limit cycle appears in Fig. 2.2, panel A. The graphic of the control points' paths in the neighborhood of one or more attractors is called its phase portrait. Phase portraits can be drawn by plotting a behavior value at time t on the Y axis against the value of the same behavior at time $t - 1$ on the X axis. For more complex dynamics, the change in behavior from time $t - 1$ to t can be plotted on the Y axis against the value of behavior differences at a previous pair of time frames $(t - 2, t - 1)$ on the X axis. A phase portrait of a fixed point attractor would show trajectories into the center. A limit cycle would be round or elliptic.

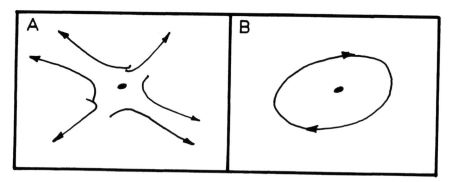

FIG. 2.2.   Phase portrait for (A) a hyperbolic repellor and (B) a limit cycle attractor.

Repellors

Repellor forces have the opposite effect on control points. Objects that get too close to a repellor force are ejected from the center to somewhere outside the repellor's *separatrix*, which is special name for a repellor's basin. Repellors can generate spiral or radial-hyperbolic paths. A radial repellor is shown in Fig. 2.2 along with a limit cycle.

Repellors and limit cycles can be readily confused at first glance, but there are distinguishing subtleties. Historically, science used to believe that there was a dynamic called centrifugal force: If we swing a bucket of water around our head the water stays in the bucket (more or less) until we stop swinging. Centrifugal force was thought to explain the water remaining in the bucket by positing a force that propels objects away from a center. Newton later showed, however, that the real dynamic was centripetal force, or a lack of an attractor in the center. Centripetal behavior is essentially a limit cycle. Objects placed in the vacant center spiral out toward the orbit. Objects outside the orbit are drawn into the same orbit.

Limit cycles are potentially confusable with *hysteresis*, which is the oscillation between two attractors that are separated by a repellor. Hysteresis dynamics are considered in a later section in the context of catastrophe theory.

Saddle Points

Saddle points have characteristics of both repellors and attractors (Fig. 2.3). An object is drawn into the saddle, but once it arrives, it is repelled into places unknown. A saddle dynamic can be generated by perturbing the motion of a pendulum. When unperturbed, a pendulum will swing an arc, forming a limit cycle pattern over time. If we perturb the path by interjecting a force transversal to the main arc, the pendulum swings in a figure-8, as shown in the middle panel of Fig. 2.3. The pinch point between the lobes of the "8" is the saddle point. In the perturbed pendulum dynamic, the lobes of the "8" represent attractors; virtual separatrices appear in the far field.

Saddle points are commonly observed in human negotiations or other game theory applications (chapter 9). Two players are faced with a range of situations, represented by the various neighborhoods of the phase portrait in the lower panel of Fig. 2.3. Some of the outcomes are favorable to one player, and other outcomes are favorable to the other player; favorable outcomes are represented by attractor basins. Undesirable outcomes for both players are represented by the separatrices. The saddle point occurs where the two attractor basins meet, and represents a possible deal between the two parties. In real human terms, the trick is to define the terms of agreement that comprise the saddle. In less difficult

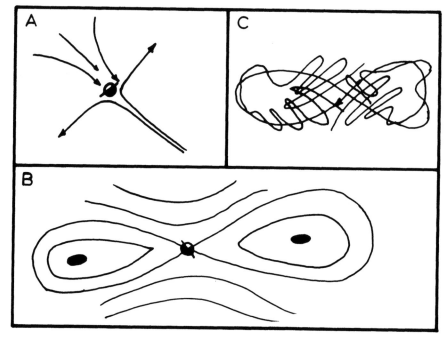

FIG. 2.3. Phase portraits for (A) a saddle point, (B) a perturbed pendulum, and (C) a homoclinic tangle.

negotiations, the saddle point is a "thick" point, which negotiation specialists call a "gray area"; for an example, see Oliva et al. (1981).

Quasi-Periodic Attractors

A *quasi-periodic* attractor looks like a limit cycle, except that it is perturbed by another limit cycle. Time series data that are indicative of quasi-periodicity are regularly observed in signal processing laboratories where the wave pattern from one sound is superimposed on another, producing an irregular waveform that repeats itself regularly.

Quasi-periodic oscillators are interesting in their own right, but they also represent a path toward chaotic behavior. By coupling the right number of sufficiently complex function, chaotic behavior can be induced. For instance, if an object is introduced into a field of three oscillating attractors, its behavior throughout phase space is chaotic.

Chaotic Attractors

Chaotic attractors are composed of trajectories that do not repeat themselves. The lack of repetition contributes to their unpredictable character. At the same time, however, chaotic functions can be generated by simple deterministic equations, which are usually coupled together in some manner. The following elaboration begins with the notion of coupled periodic dynamics in three-dimensional space as one possible route to chaos. Some of the other well-studied chaotic attractors are considered afterward.

In the first examples of deterministic chaos, Poincaré drove a periodic function across the surface of a torus (bagel-shaped object), causing a spiral-like rotation around the outside of the torus. He examined the paths of the trajectories by taking transversal sections of one point in thickness (*Poincaré sections*). The places where trajectories passed through the sections could then be compared from section to section and were often shown to change position in two-dimensional space in no predictable pattern. Birkhoff extended the toroidal forcing concept by imagining that the torus was more similar to a bagel composed of rolled dough that was twisted into its toroidal form. A forced periodic function then became still more complex from section to section, and other topological forms were similarly explored. Some specific examples of Poincaré sections are discussed in conjunction with the Henon–Heiles and Duffing–Ueda attractors.

Trajectories that passed through the same point twice were identified as a *homoclinic tangles*; those that did not were identified as *heteroclinic tangles*. An example of a homoclinic tangle is shown in the lower panel of Fig. 2.3, and represents the trajectory of a control point in a neighborhood containing a saddle point and a repellor in close proximity. Although a social science application is officially unknown at this time, I would speculate that it could represent a pattern of work performance where a person is faced with two tasks such that one is tedious and boring (repellor for many people), and the other is interesting but terribly stressful (saddle). Many of the known dynamics of work performance are addressed in chapters 5 and 6. The nonintersecting pathways, on the other hand, are trademarks of true chaotic attractors.

Smale (1964) generalized the toroidal forcing concept as the limit of periodic functions driving periodic functions; that concept became a prototype of the chaotic attractor. His now famous illustration of the horseshoe dynamic utilizes a repeated stretching and folding dynamic. Begin with a straight strip of "dough," stretch it, and fold it into three parts, tucking the end third between the first and second. Next, stretch it again transverse to the long axis of the first folding and repeat the wrapping move; then continue the pattern *ad infinitum*. If one were to mark a point on the initial strip of dough and follow it along in three dimensional space, its path would be chaotic by the nonrepeating path definition.

Lorenz's (1963) discovery of the strange attractor, shown in Fig. 2.4, was a landmark in modern chaos theory. Lorenz was experimenting with a system of three interrelated equations for describing weather patterns. The equation set required iterative calculations, meaning that initial val-

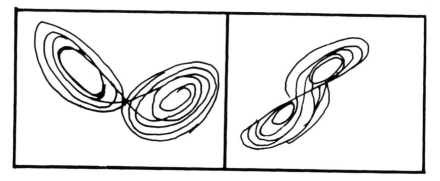

FIG. 2.4. Two views of the phase portrait for the Lorenz chaotic attractor.

ues of a variable were fed through the equations, then the outcome was fed through the equation again, and so on repeatedly. Lorenz stopped his little computer to take a work break. When he returned he restarted the sequence with the last output value. When the calculations resumed, he noticed that their time-series pattern was completely different from the sequence that he had interrupted.

The explanation turned out to be that the computer was figuring the calculations to six decimal places, but only printing out to three decimal places. All the critical activity was taking place in the unseen decimal places. This discovery led Lorenz to identify an important and distinctive characteristic of chaotic attractors, *sensitivity to initial conditions*, or *sensitive dependence*. Small changes in initial values of a variable lead to large differences in later outcomes. Thus if any small measurement errors occur when measuring the initial conditions, the final results from successive iterations of the equations would not match the actual behavior of the system; thus there is an inherent link between chaos and uncertainty or some definitions of randomness.

The principle of sensitive dependence is also known as the *butterfly effect*, meaning that a butterfly flapping its wings in Argentina could result in a tidal wave in Asia. Small perturbation in weather patterns at one place in the world compound and enlarge as they flow through a complex system. The sensitive dependence concept has become overstated, according to some dynamicists such as Abraham et al. (1990). Once a control point enters the basin of an attractor it follows the regime of the attractor, and it no longer matters what the control point was doing before entering the basin.

Lorenz Attractor. Two views of the Lorenz attractor appear in Fig. 2.4. Its system of three equations denotes coordinates on the x, y, and z spatial axes:

$$\delta x/\delta t = a(y - x) \tag{3}$$

$$\delta y/\delta t = -xz + cx - y \tag{4}$$

$$\delta z/\delta t = xy - bz \tag{5}$$

Variables a, b, and c are control parameters that govern the specific behavior of the system, and are usually set to constant values for simulations of a strange attractor dynamic. The Lorenz attractor can also be interpreted as a cubic function:

$$f(x) = (\delta^2 x/\delta t^2) - k(\delta x/\delta t) - x^3 \tag{6}$$

(Thompson & Stewart, 1986), where k controls the amount of separation between the two shells. The trajectories on the Lorenz attractor begin as nonrepeating periodic paths on one "mussel shell" of the attractor. The point then suddenly jumps to the other shell, spins around in a similar fashion for a while, then jumps back again.

Rossler Attractor.   Four other examples of chaotic attractors are shown in Figs. 2.5–2.10. The Rossler attractor (Fig. 2.5) is also a function of three interlaced equations (Nicolis & Prigogine, 1989):

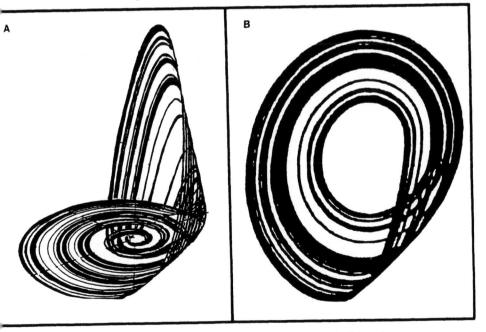

FIG. 2.5. The Rossler attractor showing view from the side (A) and top down (B).

$$\delta x/\delta t = -y - z \qquad (7)$$

$$\delta y/\delta t = x + ay \qquad (8)$$

$$\delta z/\delta t = bz - cz + xz \qquad (9)$$

The path of the control point begins on the turntable or lower shell, and proceeds in a nonrepeating periodic motion until it reaches a critical set of numerical values, at which time it blips up along a path on the upper shell, then returns. As with the Lorenz attractor, the set of functions is interlaced in the sense that change on one outcome variable, or *order parameter*, can be expressed in terms of one or both of the other two. For a general proof of the relationship between secondary behaviors in a dynamical system and lag functions of primary behavior see Packard et al. (1980).

The Henon Attractor Group. The Henon attractor is particularly complex and was developed as model for the organization of galaxies (Henon & Heiles, 1964; Rollins, 1990). The pattern in its decorative faceplate is repeated in smaller panels around the edge of the center simplex. In its outermost zones, disordered "stardust" surrounds the ordered galactic centers (Figs. 2.6 and 2.7). The equation set for the Henon–Heiles attractor is:

$$\delta y/\delta t = p(x) \qquad (10)$$

$$\delta y/\delta t = p(y) \qquad (11)$$

$$\delta p(x)/\delta t = -x - 2xy \qquad (12)$$

$$\delta p(y)/\delta t = -y - x^2 - 3ay^2 \qquad (13)$$

Figure 2.6 shows two of the many possible configurations of the Henon–Heiles attractor, based on different initial values of x and y. A Poincaré section for the scenario in the upper panel of Fig. 2.6 appears in the center panel. Each successive slice adds a few more dots to the pattern shown. The Poincaré section of the lower panel of Fig. 2.6, however, is not substantially different from the view already shown.

The Henon (1976) horseshoe is a two-dimensional chaotic attractor such that:

$$x_2 = 1 + y_1 - ax_1^2 \qquad (14)$$

$$y_2 = bx_1 \qquad (15)$$

The attractor can be alternatively represented as a lagged function such that

$$x_3 = 1 - ax_2^2 + bx_1 \qquad (16)$$

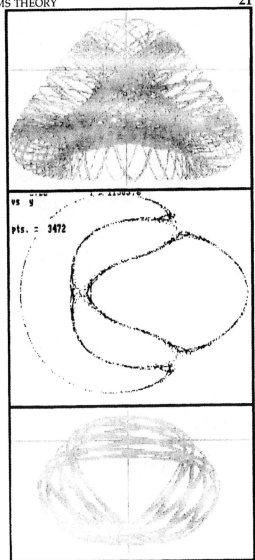

FIG. 2.6. The Henon–Heiles attractor: (a) phase portrait where $x = 0.00$, $y = -0.1475$; (b) Poincaré section of upper panel; (c) phase portrait where $x = -0.20$, $y = 0.15$.

The Henon horseshoe is shown in Fig. 2.8 in full view and with a close-up showing the folding and refolding of trajectories within the horseshoe.

STABILITY, INSTABILITY, AND BIFURCATION

This section describes the concepts of stability and instability that are implicit in the foregoing attractor concept. Bifurcation theory is itself a branch or subtopic of topology that goes a great distance toward

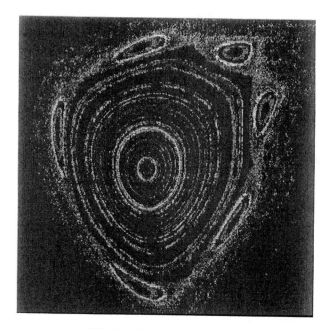

FIG. 2.7. The Henon attractor.

FIG. 2.8. The Henon horseshoe attractor.

explaining why chaos and discontinuous changes of behavior occur. The section concludes with a description of two bifurcation sequences that are known to result in chaotic behavior.

Structural Stability

Systems that are *stable* are unlikely to change in any appreciable way, if at all. An *instability* implies that a change will take place, that the results are not predictable, and that a particular result is not likely to occur again in repeated experiments. The classical topological definition, due to Andronov and Pontryagin from the 1930s, is that "[A] dynamical system (vector field or map) is structurally stable if nearby systems have qualitatively the same dynamics" (Wiggins, 1988, p. 58). The introduction of probability words such as "likely," "unlikely," and "same" is done here with the goal of connecting issues of certainty, or statistical concepts as a whole, with topological concepts. According to Berliner (1992), uncertainty is, essentially, in the mind of the system's beholder. A good topological definition of a dynamical system will arise when two replications of the same experiment will produce the same data.

Fixed-point attractors are structurally stable, as are limit cycles. Repellors and saddles are unstable. The chaotic attractors described earlier, with the exception of the toroidals, are structurally stable also, if we take a *global* view of the dynamics—that is, we view the attractor's basin as a whole. At the local level of analysis close-up within the attractor basin itself, however, there is a myriad of instabilities taking place (Ueda, 1993). Ueda showed, furthermore, that it was possible to contrive chaotic attractors by coupling instability dynamics.

Figure 2.9 shows two phase portraits from the Duffing–Ueda attractor (Ueda, 1993). The equation set involves three order parameters, x, y, and z, and four control parameters, a, b, F, and w:

$$\delta x / \delta t = y \tag{17}$$

$$\delta y / \delta t = -bx^3 - cy - F \cos(z) \tag{18}$$

$$\delta z / \delta t = w \tag{19}$$

The two panels of Fig. 2.9 describe the result of iterating the model with different initial values of F, w, and c. Curiously, the scenario in the lower panel results in an asymptotic stability where continued iterations produce no new trajectory segments; the motion picture, so to speak, freezes.

A Poincaré section of the upper panel of Fig. 2.9 is shown in the left-hand panel of Fig. 2.10. Once again, successive sectionings from continued interaction add additional dots to the pattern that is already established. (The right-hand edge of the left panel of Fig. 2.10 truncates the pattern because the numerical values were oriented off the edge of the computer screen.) By contrast, the scenario on the lower panel of Fig. 2.9 produces Poincaré sections that are virtual repetitions of four or five dots (thick points). The right-hand panel of Fig. 2.10 is a Poincaré section for the Duffing–Ueda attractor iterated with yet another set of initial values, and a similar but different pattern is produced.

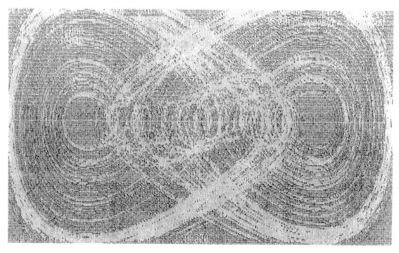

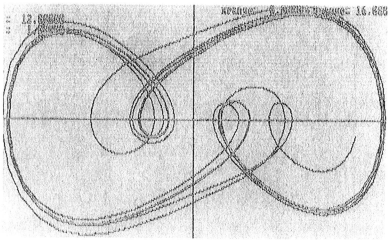

FIG. 2.9. The Duffing–Ueda attractor: (a) phase portrait with initial values of $F = 14.5$, $w = 1.1$, $c = 0.1$, $b = 1.0$; (b) phase portrait with initial values of $F = 12.0$, $w = 1.0$, $c = 0.5$, $b = 1.0$.

Bifurcation

Abraham and Shaw (1992) classified bifurcations into three categories: *subtle, catastrophic,* and *explosive.* In a dynamical scheme, a bifurcation is typically observed when control points begin to follow a common pathway, but diverge into two or more directions. Alternatively, one might observe a distinct change in the whole dynamical scheme and the attrac-

FIG. 2.10. Poincaré sectioning of Duffing–Ueda attractor for (a) upper panel of Fig. 2.9 and (b) where initial values are $F = 12.0$, $w = 1.0$, $c = 1.0$, $b = 1.0$.

tors represented within it. Abraham and Shaw noted that initially they thought that there were only two types of bifurcations, subtle and catastrophic, but further thought led them to separate catastrophic from explosive types. Because of the limited number of well-studied examples of each, they are included together in a section of this chapter. I could easily make a case for subtyping the subtle bifurcations as well, and the following paragraphs and the section on catastrophe theory explain.

Subtle bifurcations appear to fall into two broad categories. One involves the transformation of an attractor from one type to another. For instance, if we take a weak limit cycle and perturb it, or stretch the "rubber," so that we pull the extreme corners away from the center, the attractor is transformed into a spiral repeller. If the direction of the perturbation is reversed, such that dynamic vectors are introduced that point toward the center rather than away from it, the limit cycle becomes a point attractor.

Another example of a subtle bifurcation is the *Hopf bifurcation*, in which a point attractor evolves into a repellor. Additionally, in the *Neimark bifurcation*, the speed of a periodic attractor suddenly doubles; if the periodic function were a sound, the sound would be heard to jump an octave in pitch. The multiple-periodic forcing of toroidal braids, which was discussed earlier as a path to chaos, is another example. All bifurcations share a common trademark, which is the existence of a critical point, or *bifurcation point*, beyond which the effect of the bifurcation structure begins to take place. The bifurcation point itself is highly unstable; a control point located exactly at the bifurcation point could go almost anywhere in the phase space. The value of an accurate dynamical scheme for a real system would be its ability to specify conditions to predict where the control point will actually go at those uncertain moments.

The location of a bifurcation point in phase space is measured by a *control parameter*, which, when taken literally, implies a handle by which one might control a dynamical system. The bifurcation point is thus a critical value of a control parameter. Control parameters, furthermore, are distinguishable from *order parameters*. Order parameters represent multiple behavioral outcomes from the same dynamical process. Although multiple-order parameters were intimated in the previous section (e.g., Lorenz attractor), we might remain happy campers by continuing to think in terms of single-order parameters until midway through catastrophe theory.

A second form of subtle bifurcation is the type where a dynamical field becomes parsed between regions occupied by attractor basins and separatrices. The bifurcation in that context does not refer to the transformation of attractor complexity or stability, but to the direction of possible paths that control point might take. Again, catastrophe theory addresses that class of situations.

Logistic Map

Figure 2.11 shows the logistic map that can be viewed as the master plan underlying dynamic processes as they make the transition from global stability to full-blown chaos (May, 1976). In the region of the diagram labeled Period 1, the system is globally stable with dynamics characteristic of a single-point attractor.

The bifurcation point marks the transition between Periods 1 and 2. In Period 2, the terrain of the system is marked by a bifurcation and separatrix whereby the system is divided into two attractor basins. The two attractors are located above and below the "pitchfork." A virtual separatrix is located between the prongs. A control parameter is governing the transition of the system from one period to another. The behavior of a system in Period 2 could take the form of a saw-toothed oscillation between the attractors. Alternatively, trajectories of behavior that is under the influence of increases in bifurcation parameter values would diverge toward attractors on either side of the separatrix.

Toward the end of Period 2, where the control parameter has increased further in value, the bifurcation pattern bifurcates again, dividing the system into four smaller attractor regions. There is a third bifurcation as well, which divided the topography into eight attractor regions. This is

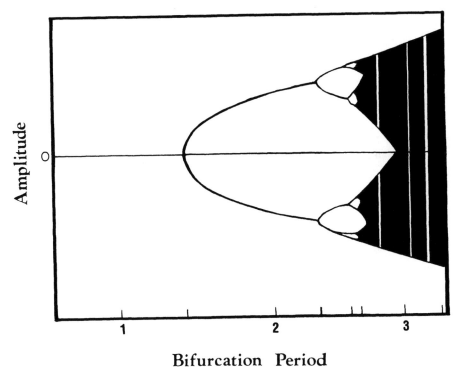

Bifurcation   Period

FIG. 2.11. The logistic map bifurcation diagram: a path to chaos.

the *period doubling* regime. The dynamics of period doubling show oscillations within oscillations. Examples of Period 1, Period 2, and period doubling time series appear in chapter 9 with a population dynamics application.

Period 3 is the region of full-scale chaos (Li & Yorke, 1975). The topography bears little resemblance to the relative order of Periods 1 or 2, or even the period doubling configuration. Of particular interest, however, are the windows of relative order that striate the chaotic region. The windows contain ordered trajectories that create a path, with additional bifurcations, from one chaotic period to another.

The equation for the logistic map is relatively simple, and usually represented as:

$$y_2 = cy_1(1 - y_1) \tag{20}$$

Alternatively, the model may be algebraically rearranged as:

$$y_2 = cy_1 - cy_1^2 \tag{21}$$

where c is the bifurcation parameter. The logistic map function can be expanded to reflect a dynamic that has the option of going into period doubling or not, such as

$$y_2 = cy_1(1 - y_1)(1 - y_1) \tag{22}$$

which is a cubic function that allows substitution of coupled dynamics into one or the other y_1 term. The function generalizes as an exponential function,

$$y_2 = cy_1 e^{ay_t} \tag{23}$$

where a in Equation 23 is another free parameter that governs the complexity of function (May, 1976; May & Oster, 1976).

Instant Chaos

Conditions are now known where a system can slip from periodic behavior to chaos without passing through the progressive regime of increased bifurcation and period doubling. Apparently the entire transition to chaos occurs in an infinitesimal range of the bifurcation parameter (Guckenheimer & Worfolk, 1992). It is unclear whether the effect of such a bifurcation parameter would be discovered through the same means as other bifurcation experiments, although the model for arms race dynamics associated with the Space Defense Initiative appears to be an example of instant chaos (Mayer-Kress, 1992; discussed in chapter 12).

Conservative and Dissipative Systems

At this juncture it is valuable to introduce the entropy concepts that characterize physical realizations of chaos and bifurcation (Nicolis & Progogine, 1989). In the case of Period 1 dynamics, the system is at rest. As an energy force is applied, such as heat to water, we observe nothing at first, until bubbles that mark the beginning of the boiling process begin to occur. The bubble rise from the bottom of the beaker, to which heat is usually applied; a convection process is now taking place where the hot water and air bubbles rise to the top and the cool water from the top is pushed to the bottom. The process continues until the water is boiling throughout the container, the water turns to gaseous water vapor, and heat is *dissipated* into the environment.

Virtually all terrestrial physical systems are dissipative systems like the common one just described. A conservative system is just the opposite: no energy transfers from the system to its environment. If the motion of a pendulum were a true conservative system, the pendulum would swing forever, once it was started. In reality, there is a small amount of friction in the system that dissipates energy. Thus the pendulum eventually slows to rest at a fixed point. Conservative systems are convenient abstractions for topological studies, but dissipative processes need to be introduced to define real-world systems that might be based on properties of particular conservative systems.

Systems containing increasing amounts of energy increase in entropy of internal randomness. Bifurcations serve the purpose of reducing entropy by allowing the system to split into two or more local topologies, each with lower entropy (Agu, 1983; Thompson, 1982). In the case of boiling water, the phase transition from liquid to gas is the result of a bifurcation that underlies a catastrophe manifold (see section on catastrophe theory).

FRACTALS

Fractals are geometric structures with fractional dimensionality. The were studied most intensely by Mandelbrot (1983) beginning in the early 1950s, although there was an early line of relevant work due to Cantor, Koch, and Hausdorff in the 1880–1920 period. The following summarizes the concepts of scale, fractal dimensional structure, and their relationships to chaotic attractors.

Scale

Mandelbrot observed that simple geometric questions such as "How long is the coast of Britain?" do not have necessarily simple answers. The coast of Britain, as with other real land forms, is ragged. If we make a crude ellipse around the periphery of the island, one measure of perimeter is obtained. If we choose to measure around the zigs and zags of the land form in 1-km units, a larger measure is obtained. If we measure the same coast in 1-m units, capturing all the subtle nonlinearities, the measurement is longer still.

The underlying theme is the measure of *scale*. Working with a particular level of scale produces a particular measure. Mandelbrot further observed that boundaries between pairs of countries in Europe have been reported to be different lengths even though the actual boundaries did not change between the reports. Different scales were used at different times of measurement, with the smaller country tending to use smaller scales of measurement.

Fractal Structure and Dimensionality

The essential fractal structure is a self-referential or recursive function. Not only does it repeat itself across space, but the resulting geometric forms build on the same spatial structure at different levels of scale. It is an essential premise of Mandelbrot's work that naturally occurring geometries are not the results of chance or randomness. According to Mandelbrot, the concept of randomness entered the English language through a medieval French idiom meaning "the motions of a horse that the rider cannot control." The essence of randomness is, therefore, that the observer is not controlling motions or activities of some sort, and has little to do with whether the actual process is actual chance.

The first historical example of such a recursive fractal function is Cantor's dust, which emulates the distribution of cosmic dust particles. The dust can be created by taking a straight line, dividing it into thirds, throwing the middle third away, and repeating the process for the remaining line segments *ad infinitum* (Fig. 2.12). The "thirds" do not need to be of equal size. Additional complexity can be introduced by middle-third-decimating several lines in several directions at once, or perhaps folding the decimated lines over like Smale horseshoes. The result will be a space full of dust that could easily resemble the "snow" on a badly tuned television.

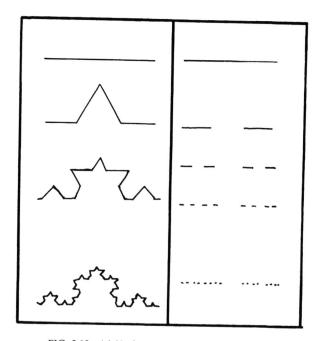

FIG. 2.12. (a) Koch curve and (b) Cantor dust.

The Koch curve is another construction based on a middle-third principle. Begin with a straight line, and divide it into three parts. Push the
end thirds inward so that the middle third buckles and folds. Repeat the
process for all line segments ad infinitum. The result is a crinkly line that
is no longer straight. The Koch curve occupies more than a single linear
dimension, but does not occupy the entire two-dimensional space of a
plane. Its dimensionality is actually equal to 1.26.

The process of making a Koch curve can be generalized to operations
performed on a triangle, or other regular closed geometric form, to produce Koch islands. The islands serve a prototypes for real land formations
and the topological analysis thereof. But why stop with planar islands?
Entire landscapes can be produced in two to three dimensions. Landscapes occupy at least two dimensions, but do not uniformly utilize the
third, which is why we have mountains and plains. Negative dimensionalities will render canyons. Figure 2.13 illustrates fractal landscapes that
are drawn in 2.7, 2.4, and 2.1 dimensions.

Fractal structure does not stop with landscapes. Trees, leaves, seashells,
lightning, cell structures, plus many other fascinating geometries can be
defined as fractals, and can be computer-generated through "forgeries."
With fractal forgeries, a computer does not need to store the entire bitmap
image of the geometric form, only the algorithm for generating the image.
A wide range of fractal images can be found in Mandelbrot (1983), Peitgen
and Saupe (1988), and Pickover (1990).

Figure 2.14 displays a particularly provocative image, the Mandelbrot
set, which has become an icon of fractal geometry and chaos theory
generally. It is also a driving metaphor for Stacey's (1992) theory of
organizational behavior and development, which is elaborated in chapters
10 and 11. It is generated from iterates of

$$z_2 = z_1{}^2 - \mu \qquad z_1 = 0 \qquad -0.25 < \mu < 2.00 \tag{24}$$

(Mandelbrot, 1983). The section on chaos numerics returns to issues
connected to the calculation of dimensionality.

Fractals and Chaos

Fractal geometry and nonlinear dynamics were eventually connected when
Feigenbaum (1978) discovered an important principle of the logistic map.
The pattern of bifurcations comprises a self-similar geometry that qualifies
the whole pattern as a fractal. The bifurcations within the period doubling
regime differ from each other and from the main bifurcation on the basis
of their scale only. That property allowed Feigenbaum to isolate universal
constants that marked critical values of the bifurcation parameter at which
a bifurcation could be assured to take place. For instance, chaos would
always set in when $c > 3.6$ in Equation 20 for the logistic map.

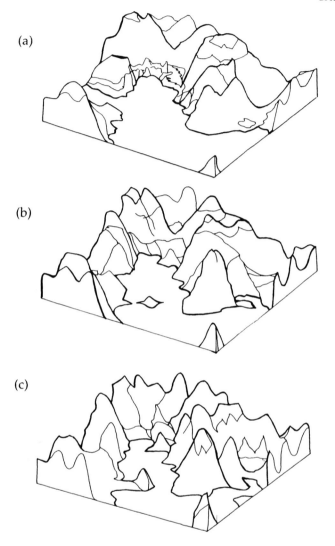

FIG. 2.13. Fractal landscape in (a) 2.7, (b) 2.4, and (c) 2.1 dimensions.

The fractal nature of the logistic map soon inspired additional work directed at describing the fractal nature of basins containing chaotic attractors (Farmer et al., 1983; Girault, 1991; Mandelbrot, 1977, 1983). The Lorenz attractor, for instance, is thought to have a dimensionality of 2.06. According to Mandelbrot, the appellation "strange attractor" is no longer appropriate; because of the widespread distribution of fractal forms in nature, there is nothing strange about chaotic attractors. In any event, the dimensionality of an attractor is now regarded as a measure of the

Detail of Mandelbrot Set

Full View

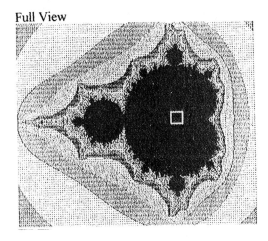

FIG. 2.14. The Mandelbrot set.

attractor's complexity and the complexity of the process that generated it. The relationship between dimensionality and the complexity of a process is, unfortunately, not exact. Catastrophe theory, because of its strong relationship to bifurcation theory, nonetheless provides some heuristics for associating control parameters to the complexity of behavioral outcomes.

CATASTROPHE THEORY

The central proposition of catastrophe theory is the classification theorem (Thom, 1975), which states (with qualifications) that, given a maximum of four control parameters, all discontinuous changes of events can be modeled by one of seven elementary topological forms. The forms are hierarchical and vary in the complexity of the behavior spectrum they encompass. The models describe change between (or among) qualitatively distinct forms for behavior, such as remaining on a job versus quitting; they do not necessarily infer any notion of desirable or undesirable outcome.

Steady states and changes in behavior are governed by one to four control parameters, depending on the complexity of the behavior spectrum under consideration. In NDS, a control parameter denotes an independent variable that has a particular function in the change process. In research, the investigator would identify one or more psychological measurements that would correspond to a particular function. To hammer this latter point for social scientists, I coined the term *latent control parameter* (Guastello, 1987) to denote the parameter in the canonical mathematical model, which is to be distinguished from *research variables*, which may, singly or in combination, contribute to the latent control parameter.

The elementary catastrophe models are classified into two groups: the cuspoids and the umbilics. The elementary cuspoids involve one dependent measure, have potential functions in three to six dimensions, and have response surfaces in two to five dimensions. They are the fold, cusp, swallowtail, and butterfly. The names reflect fanciful interpretations of what parts of their geometry resemble. The elementary umbilics involve two dependent outcomes measures, three or four control parameters, and response surfaces in five or six codimensions. The umbilics are the wave crest (or hyperbolic umbilic), hair (or elliptic umbilic), and mushroom (or parabolic umbilic) models.

The term *codimension* has multiple meanings in topology, depending on where it is being used (Poston & Stewart, 1978a). Option 1: It is an elision of "control dimension" meaning number of control parameters. Option 2: It refers to the sum of control parameters and behavioral outcome, or order, parameters. Option 3: It refers to the sum of geometric dimensions for the behavioral spectra, especially when systems are being compared that contain varying numbers of behavioral spectra. Throughout this book I refer to control parameters as control parameters, and use codimensionality of a model to mean Option 2. There is no contradiction between Option 2 and Option 3 if cuspoid models are involved, but complications arise when umbilic models are involved. In the latter case, I use the modified term *surface codimensionality* to denote the condition of Option 3.

The descriptions of the elementary models and sundry others are considered next. Thom (1975), Zeeman (1977), Poston and Stewart (1978a), Woodcock and Davis (1978), Gilmore (1981), Thompson (1982), and Arnold (1974) serve as general references for the structure of catastrophe models and provide numerous applications outside the social sciences.

Elementary Models

Fold. The potential function for the fold catastrophe is:

$$f(y) = y^3/3 - ay \qquad (25)$$

and its response surface is defined as the set of points where

$$\delta f(y)/\delta y = y^2 - a \qquad (26)$$

where y is the dependent measure and a is the control parameter. The fold model is the basic geometric building block of the seven elementary models and beyond. It describes a change in behavior from a stable steady state or attractor to an unstable state as a function of a. The relationship between a and y is a common threshold model. The behavior is observed to remain steady, even though a is changing. Once a hits a critical value, however, behavior changes abruptly. Because the change is in the direction of an instability, the trajectory of y leaves the basin of the attractor and flies outward, never to return. The equilibrium values of y are determined by setting Equation 26 equal to 0. The negative value is the center of the stable attractor, and the positive value is the unstable center.

Cusp. The cusp surface is three-dimensional and features a two-dimensional manifold (unfolding). It describes two stable states of behavior. Change between the two states is a function of two controls, *asymmetry* (*a*) and *bifurcation* (*b*). At low values of *b*, change is smooth, and at high values of *b* it is potentially discontinuous, depending on the values of *a*. At low values of *a* when *b* is high, changes occur around the lower mode and are relatively small in size. At middle values of *a*, changes occur between modes and are relatively large, assuming *b* is also large. At high values of *a*, changes occur around the upper mode and are again small.

The cusp response surface is the set of points where

$$\delta f(y)/\delta y = y^3 - by - a \qquad (27)$$

The cusp surface appears in the upper portion of Fig. 2.15. Change in behavior is denoted by the path of a control point over time (dotted line). The point begins on the upper sheet denoting behavior of one type, and is observed in that behavioral modality for a period of time. During that time its coordinates on *a* and *b* are changing when suddenly it reaches a fold line and drops to the lower value of the behavior, which is qualitatively different where it remains. Reversing direction, the point is observed in the lower mode until coordinates change to a critical pair of values, at which

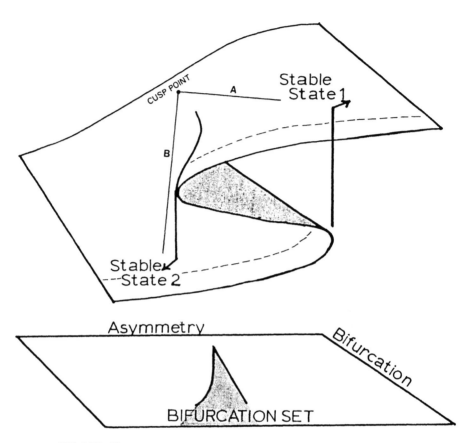

FIG. 2.15. The cusp catastrophe response surface (upper) and bifurcation set (lower).

moment the point jumps back to the upper mode. There are two thresholds for behavior change, one ascending and one descending. The shaded area of the surface is the region of inaccessibility in which very few points fall. Statistically, one would observe an antimode between the two stable states that would correspond to the shaded region of the surface.

The cusp and higher order models also have a control surface on which the bifurcation set is drawn, mapping the unfolding of the surface in (for the cusp) two dimensions. When highlighted on the response surface itself, the cusp bifurcation set induces two diverging response gradients, which are joined at a *cusp point*. The diverging gradients are labeled *A* and *B* on the cusp surface in Fig. 2.15. Behavior at the cusp point is ambiguous. The cusp point is known as the *point of degenerate singularity* and is the most unstable point on the surface. Analogous points exist in other catastrophe models as well.

In a dynamic system, the behavioral variable (y) changes values. Static systems are not change oriented; rather, the observed behavior takes a few qualitatively different forms, often with gradations. Static bifurcations are readily seen to underlie discontinuous or multimodal probability density functions (chapter 3). Bifurcation structure may be less apparent by visual inspection of data for some dynamic applications, particularly where a distribution of points centers around one mode before a change process and around a second mode after the change. It should be noted, however, that the catastrophe functions are not inherently static or dynamic; it is the application and data that give a model a static or dynamic character.

The attractor centers of the response surface can be found by setting Equation 27 equal to 0. The solution will produce three roots. The two negative roots represent attractor centers, and the positive root represents the repellor center. Critical values of y where instability takes place can be found by taking the first derivative of Equation 27, setting it to 0, and solving. The same analytic principles apply to the other models below.

Swallowtail. The swallowtail catastrophe model describes a behavior spectrum consisting of two stable states plus two unstable areas. The surface, which is shown in Fig. 2.16, is defined as the set of points where

$$\delta f(y)/\delta y = y^4 - cy^2 - by - a \qquad (28)$$

The new control parameter is c and is the bias, swallowtail, or second asymmetry parameter.

The surface is four-dimensional and requires sectioning for cases where $a = 0.0$ and cases where $a > 0.0$. Its bifurcation set is three-dimensional. For the cases where $a = 0$, behavior can take on two forms, stable and unstable in a dynamic similar to the fold catastrophe. For the more interesting case, the behavior can change between two adjacent stable states, or fall through a twist and gap in the surface into oblivion. "Oblivion" might be captured by the lower structures that are folded under the stable sheets in the event they represent a boundary condition of y for a particular application.

Butterfly. The butterfly catastrophe model describes a spectrum of three qualitatively different behavioral outcomes. Once again there are regions of inaccessibility between the sheets representing repellor forces or antimodes. The function is five-dimensional, and what appears in Fig. 2.17 is the most interesting three-dimensional sectioning. Other sectionings appear in chapter 5 with an application to work motivation. The surface features a pocket, which allows the control point to slip through

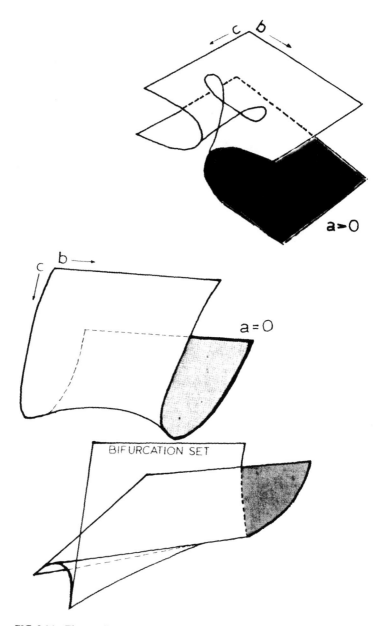

FIG. 2.16. The swallowtail catastrophe response surface (upper and center) and bifurcation set (lower).

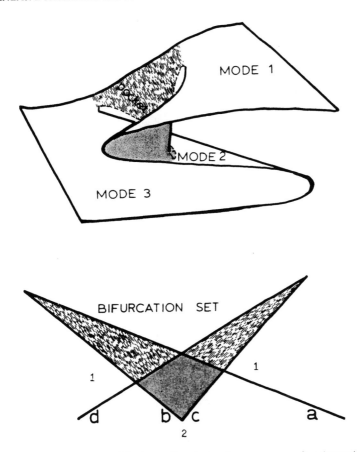

FIG. 2.17. Sectioning of the butterfly catastrophe response surface (upper) and its bifurcation set (lower).

to the middle mode, or oscillate between the top and bottom modes. The butterfly response surface is defined as the set of points where

$$\delta f(y)/\delta y = y^5 - dy^3 - cy^2 - by - a \tag{29}$$

The new control parameter, d, is the butterfly or second bifurcation parameter. It governs the joint action of control parameters b and c, such that b and c can work together to permit behavior change across successive behavior modality, or alternatively, b and c can work interactively to permit behavior change between the extreme modalities.

The manifold and bifurcation set for the butterfly catastrophe model is four-dimensional, and a two-dimensional sectioning is shown in the lower portion of Fig. 2.17. It contains four gradients. The heavily shaded area on the bifurcation plane is the zone of trimodality. Grained portions are the zones of bimodality between adjacent modes. The white area marked "2" is a zone of bimodality between extreme modes. The white areas marked "1" are unimodal.

The sets of points comprising the cusp surface exist in Cartesian space defined by axes y, a, b. As more variables are added to form the butterfly however, the five axes become organized at 60° to each other, rather than at 90° (Lu, 1976). Bifurcation axes for the umbilic models, considered next, are organized at 120° to each other.

Wave Crest. The wave crest catastrophe model (Fig. 2.18) describes a phenomenon involving two dependent measures (x, y) and three control parameters $(a, b,$ and $c)$. The two dependent measures vary separately,

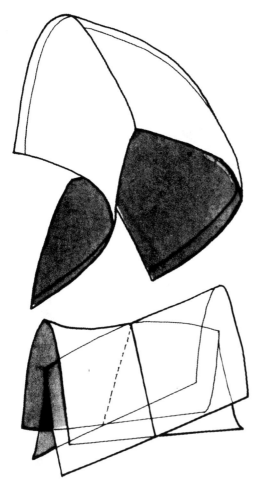

FIG. 2.18. The wave crest catastrophe response surface (upper) and bifurcation set (lower).

each having the level of complexity of the fold model, which is quadratic with one stable and one unstable state. The model got its name when it was first discovered that the crest of every wave breaks at a 120° angle (Lu, 1976). It was later discovered, however, that wave crest geometry did not adequately describe waveforms. Nonetheless, the potential function for the wave crest model is:

$$f(x, y) = x^3 + y^3 + ax + by + cxy \tag{30}$$

The response surface is composed of the two partial first derivatives of the potential function:

$$\delta f(x)/\delta x = 3x^2 + a + cy \tag{31}$$

$$\delta f(y)/\delta y = 3y^2 + b + cx \tag{32}$$

The wave crest function contains two asymmetry parameters, one for each behavior. The two behaviors share a common bifurcation factor. Note that the bifurcation of y affects changes in x and vice versa.

Hair. The hair catastrophe model (Fig. 2.19) got its name from its bifurcation set, which tapers to a single thread that connects two swallowtail points. This model also contains two dependent measures and three control parameters. Both dependent measures function separately, and each has one stable and one unstable state. The surface is composed of two partial first derivatives of the potential function:

$$\delta f(y)/\delta y = 3y^2 - x^2 + a + 2cy \tag{33}$$

$$\delta f(x)/\delta x = -2xy + b + 2cx \tag{34}$$

The hair model contains two asymmetry parameters, one for each behavior, and the two behaviors share a common bifurcation parameter. The quadratic function of x, however, affects changes in y. Also interesting is the modulus term, xy, which represents an interaction that takes place between the two dependent measures.

Mushroom. The mushroom catastrophe model (Fig. 2.20) is composed of two dependent measures and four control parameters. One dependent variable is characterized by two stable states because of its cubic germ, and the other has one stable and one unstable state because of its quadratic germ. There is an interaction taking place between the two dependent measures. The mushroom response surface is given by:

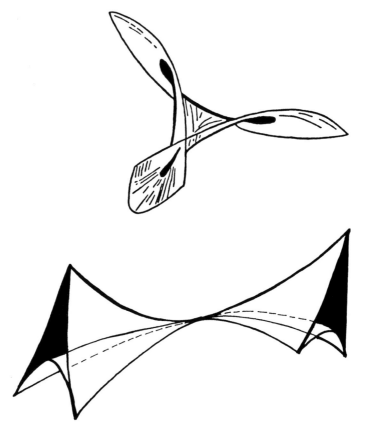

FIG. 2.19. The hair catastrophe response surface (upper) and bifurcation set (lower).

$$\delta f(y)/\delta y = 4y^3 + 2dy + x^2 + b \qquad (35)$$

$$\delta f(x)/\delta x = 2xy + 2cx + a \qquad (36)$$

The model contains separate bifurcation and asymmetry terms for each dependent measure. Its bifurcation set requires two sectionings, which are also shown in Fig. 2.20.

Beyond the Elementary Seven. According to the *singularity rule*, which is a major portion of the classification theorem (Thom, 1975), for a given bifurcation set, there is only one possible response surface. The singularity rule actually holds true for catastrophe models with five control parameters, as well as for those models with four or fewer controls. There are four catastrophe models with five control parameters. One model,

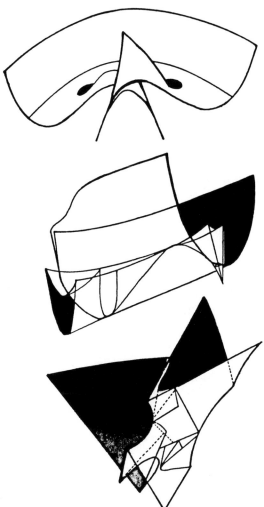

FIG. 2.20. The mushroom catastrophe response surface (upper) and two sections of its bifurcation set (center and lower).

the *wigwam*, is a six-dimensional cuspoid. There are three umbilics with five control parameters, each of which has a model codimensionality of seven. Their names are the *second hyperbolic, second elliptic*, and *symbolic umbilic* models. They differ in the number of modulus terms they contain. For a glimpse at the complex geometry associated with some of those models, see Callahan (1980, 1982).

Additional catastrophe models exist that do not conform to the singularity rule. The simplest of those is the double cusp. The double cusp consists of two dependent measures and six control parameters. Each dependent outcome oscillates between two stable states of behavior. There are four eight-dimensional response surfaces associated with the double cusp. Mathematical work connected to the double cusp and other nonsingular catastrophe models can be found in Zeeman (1977) and Arnold (1974).

Modeling Concepts

Classification. The elementary cuspoids, as well as other nonelementary models, vary in complexity. Complexity is signified by the highest exponent for the behavioral variable in the surface equation, for example, the quadratic term for the fold, the cubic for the cusp, and so forth. The leading exponent denotes the number of control parameters in the model, each with its own unique function, and the complexity of the behavioral array they perpetrate.

The taxonomy of models, together with the singularity rule, allows us to reduce the plethora of possible discontinuous change functions to a paltry few. Since topological models are rubberized rather than rigid, catastrophe models can withstand perturbations without changing their classification, so long as a tear in the surface is not introduced. This principle is known as *diffeomorphism up to transversality.*

Random Force. A random force occurs when a system is exposed to any entropy-inducing events, in which each element of the system (e.g., subjects in an experiment) has an equal probability of exposure (Agu, 1983). As elements increase in entropy, the probable location of each element in the space expands to the limits of its confinement. Bifurcation serves to reduce entropy by partitioning energized elements into neighborhoods of relative stability or equilibrium (Thompson, 1982).

One can next define situations where elements are not equally exposed to random force, but instead are systematically exposed. The level of exposure becomes the b parameter of a cusp model. Where there is more than one parameter of exposure, c is introduced, and the resulting behavioral spectrum becomes swallowtail. In a swallowtail, b and c can coact only additively or subtractively. If both can occur, then the butterfly factor d governs the degree to which b and c are additive or subtractive. In all cases, control a governs the proximity of the control point to the critical manifold.

Causality. The traditional concept of causality holds that if we do A today and obtain B tomorrow, and obtain the same pattern on a few replications just to be sure, then A causes B. Some simplistic systems work that way, no doubt, but NDS theory shows that the causation of phenomena can be much more complex. In the case of the catastrophe models, when random force and bifurcation are considered jointly, the coaction of the two may be said to cause a phenomenon. The concept of *cause* is now replaced by a combination of *control*, which implies a bifurcation mechanism, entropy, and autonomous process.

An *autonomous process* is the sequence of behaviors that emanate from the underlying structure of a system. A system with a particular bifurcation set will exhibit a distinct pattern of behavior, given a sufficient random force. Entropy itself is not sufficient, as other control parameters, notably asymmetry, affect the process. The nature of the attractors themselves is an important contributor to the end result. General NDS shows that there are several classic cases of attractors, each of which produces different patterns of behavior over time. Self-organized systems and coupled dynamics are essentially concatenations of elementary processes considered thus far.

So far, the attractors within the catastrophe models themselves have only been characterized as stable and unstable, where the unstable points have been identified as repellors, and the stable points given a generalized name *equilibrium*. The catastrophe models were developed as having smooth mappings in the neighborhood of the attractor. As such, change in behavior in the close proximity of an attractor appears linear. It is only when the global, or total, space of the model is considered that the nonlinear functions become obvious.

Control points can approach catastrophe attractors asymptotically, in which case we have fixed-point attractors, or else orbit around the fixed point, in which case we have limit cycles. The width of the limit cycle is a matter of degree, and thus we can allow a continuity between fixed-point and limit cycles in a generalized definition of an attractor in a catastrophe model.

Boundaries can introduce an attractor-like structure into a model also. For instance, if we were to crash automobiles into a very solid brick wall, the distribution of wreckage would be dense around the wall and less dense away from the wall. This is an imperfect example, of course, but it makes the point that a boundary can produce a structure on the density of control points that can analyzed as if it were a stable state in a global model.

Chaotic attractors are more problematic for catastrophe modeling because of the bifurcation structure that is thought to underlie each chaotic attractor. The catastrophe model might well define the global structure, but the goodness-of-fit associated with the mathematical or statistical analysis will be compromised by the presence of additional structures that could give the impression that the model does not work. The alternative approach, of course, would be to plan for such contingencies in advance and to build a mathematical model for a phenomenon accordingly. The issue of chaotic attractors within catastrophes can be considered as a special case of the coupled dynamics problem introduced more formally in the section on self-organization and coupled dynamics.

One of the close points of contact between catastrophe and chaos theories is seen in the similarities between the cusp model and chaotic bifurcation in Period 2 of the logistic map. Although the two entities are not synonymous, chaotic functions in Period 2 can be reasonably approximated by a cubic polynomial function (Thompson & Stewart, 1986). Thom (1983) viewed chaos theory as a generalization of catastrophe theory, whereas other writers might prefer to view catastrophe theory and chaos theory as close relatives within the domain of NDS theory.

The last point to make in this section is the distinction between global and local dynamics. This distinction extends beyond catastrophe models to virtually any other complex dynamical scheme; dynamical schemes are elaborated in the section on self-organization and coupled dynamics. A *globally stable* situation is one in which asymptotic stability occurs no matter how far from the equilibrium the control point is allowed to deflect. A *locally stable* situation is observed in a catastrophe model when the control point jumps from one attractor basin to another and remains in the latter basin. Changes in behavior along a catastrophe model surface are reversible. Hysteresis is the phenomenon by which behavior oscillates between stable states and also denotes the double threshold effect.

CATASTROPHIC AND EXPLOSIVE BIFURCATIONS

This section considers three particularly interesting situations where entire configurations of attractors and basins can change into other attractors. The models are the annihilation model, the blue sky, and the blue loop.

Annihilation Dynamic

The annihilation dynamic is an explosive bifurcation wherein the collision between a limit cycle and a repellor creates a point attractor. The model is shown in Fig. 2.21, with labels for an application that is developed in chapter 9 for urban renewal. At the first stage of the process, a limit cycle surrounds a small repellor. Anything repelled from the inside is assimilated into the limit cycle. At the second stage, the repellor is allowed to expand. The expansion is result of a changing value of a control parameter of the bifurcating type. It gains in strength and area, forcing more objects into the limit cycle. At the third stage, the repellor has expanded so much that it collides with limit cycle. The collision results in a simple point attractor in the interior of what used to be the repellor separatrix.

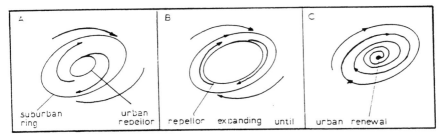

FIG. 2.21. Annihilation bifurcation dynamic labeled for the urban renewal problem (chapter 9). A repellor is surrounded by a limit cycle (A). The repellor expands (B) and collides with the limit cycle, producing a fixed point attractor (C).

The annihilation model is not reversible by itself. It can be made to repeat itself by coupling a Hopf bifurcation into the system. In that case, the fixed point would expand into a repellor. Two control parameters would be needed to produce a repeating model. One is needed to instantiate the growth of the limit cycle. The second is needed to modulate the growth of the repellor force.

Blue Sky Catastrophe

The blue sky catastrophe is a dynamic where a limit cycle attractor appears "out of the clear blue." The process begins with a terrain containing a repellor and a saddle. Objects are drawn into the saddle, but are ejected in the customary fashion. Once ejected, however, the force of the repellor sends them around the terrain "the long way" until they are drawn near to the saddle again (Fig. 2.22). Objects caught in the region between the saddle and the repellor exhibit the homoclinic tangle shown in Fig. 2.3.

At the second stage of the blue sky, a change in a control parameter value causes the saddle to steer its repelling trajectores into the separatrix. Because saddles attract the points back again, the arc around the repellor becomes tighter, with the result that a limit cycle forms around the repellor, creating a boundary around its separatrix. If the control parameter were to reverse direction, the limit cycle would disappear as suddenly as it appeared. The catastrophe dynamic that underlies the blue sky phenomenon is a fold model.

Blue Loop Annihilation

The blue loop annihilation, like the blue sky, is a ballet for saddle and repellor, but the nuance is that the terrain also contains a fixed-point attractor. Objects bounced by the saddle and repellor are collected by the

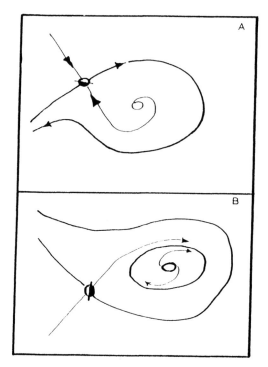

FIG. 2.22. Blue sky cata-
strophic bifurcation. A saddle
point is located in the vacinity
of a repellor (A). When a shift
in a control parameter changes
the direction of the saddle, a
limit cycle attractor suddenly
forms around the repellor (B);
this process is reversible.

fixed-point attractor (Fig. 2.23). A control point governs the proximity of
the fixed point to the saddle–repellor area. As its values change and the
fixed point is drawn into the saddle region, the two attractors collide.
The result of the explosion is that the saddle and fixed point disappear,
and a limit cycle forms around the repellor. The blue sky catastrophe is
not a reversible mechanism. Applications of blue sky and blue loop
dynamics to conflict resolution strategies are considered in chapter 6.

SELF-ORGANIZATION AND COUPLED DYNAMICS

A self-organized system is one that contains several subsystems that are
interconnected by feedback loops. Figure 2.24 shows a dynamical scheme
representing three interconnected subsystems. A *dynamical scheme* is simply a representation of complex dynamics in a self-organized or coupled-
dynamic system. The three subsystems could be hooked together in other
ways as well, but the important point is that the output parameter for
one of the subsystems becomes the input parameter for another. Also
critical is the circularity in the feedback loop; this form of reciprocal
causation is what changes a dynamical scheme from fundamentally linear

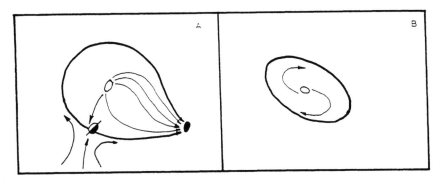

FIG. 2.23. Blue sky annihilation bifurcation. A saddle point and a fixed point attractor are located in the vicinity of a repellor (A). A shift in a control parameter moves the fixed point so that it collides with the saddle, producing a limit cycle attractor around the repellor (B); this process is not reversible.

to nonlinear. The concept of self-organization expands in three directions: coupled dynamics, replicator equations, and systems at the edge of chaos.

Coupled Dynamics

The coupled dynamics motif is grounded largely in mechanical systems, but is not confined there. Another simple example of a coupled dynamic was considered earlier when a free-swinging pendulum was perturbed on its path to create a figure-8 limit cycle with a saddle point. Another simple dynamic is the dampened pendulum. A free-swinging pendulum will slow to a stop eventually, but we can introduce a mechanical aid in the form of a fixed-point attractor to dampen the process much sooner.

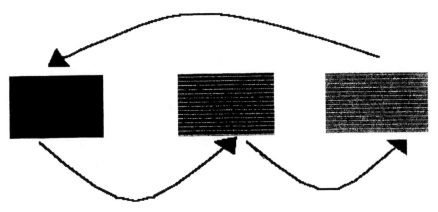

FIG. 2.24. A simple self-organized system with three components.

The time-series graph of the pendulum's motion under deliberately dampened conditions appears in Fig. 2.25, panel A.

The major work on coupled dynamics is attributed to Haken's (1984) *synergetics*, which is the study of interacting subsystems that, in turn, gave rise to the alternative name for nonlinear dynamics, *complex systems*. The springboard concept is the driver–slave relationship. A driver is usually observed as a relatively slow dynamic that modulates the behavior of a faster-moving slave. Figure 2.25 compares two phase portraits showing the coupling of two oscillators, one slow and one fast. In panel B, the driver is slow and the slave is fast. The result is a tight curlicue that rotates around a wide limit cycle. In panel C, the driver is fast, but the slave is slow. The result is different dynamic whereby an oscillation phase portrait moves slightly in and out of phase with successive cycles.

Another example appears in panel D of Fig. 2.25, suggested by Gregson (1992). The graph shows a time series of a periodic oscillator driving a chaotic slave. The result is a broadly periodic function that, when it reaches a certain point, turns on the fast-moving chaotic behavior.

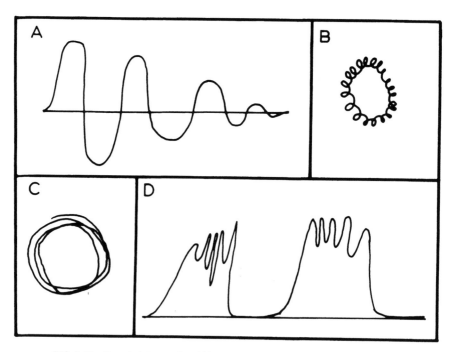

FIG. 2.25. Coupled dynamics: (A) a time series for a dampened oscillator, (B) phase portrait of a slow periodic oscillator driving a fast periodic slave, (C) phase portrait of a fast periodic oscillator driving a slow periodic slave, and (D) time series of a periodic driver and a chaotic slave.

Unfortunately, there are no real rules to specify what dynamics will result from particular coupled dynamics. I can only pass on a few rules in addition to the graphics already shown that work once in a while, maybe. *Two coupled dynamics of the same level of complexity will produce a dynamic of the same complexity.* That will work if the two functions are completely in phase with each other. *Two coupled dynamics will produce a linear time series.* That could occur if the two oscillators have the same frequency and are perfectly out of phase with each other. The more general rule is to run simulations of possible conditions and then compare results from real experiments with those of the simulations. The pattern that produces the best match wins.

Compound oscillation problems are particularly problematic in economics where the goal is often to isolate business cycles, which could be compound embedded cycles. The problem of forecasting from any dynamic model becomes more difficult when model parameters drift over time. The latest insight into the problem is worth mentioning for conceptual purposes, even though applications are not forthcoming in the chapters that follow. Ramsey (1992; Ramsey & Keenan, 1993) conceptualized the time series as a result of a weighted combination of a force affecting change and a different force affecting acceleration:

$$f(y) = d^2y/dt^2 + \alpha(dy/dt)_{t-1} + \beta y_t$$
$$= \sum_{i=1}^{4} [a_i \cos(\omega_i t) + b_i \sin(\omega_i t)] \tag{37}$$

where y is the behavior, t is elapsed time, and α, β, a_i, b_i, and ω are empirical weights. The resulting behavior is a function of dynamics that need to be observed over four successive observations at any one point in time. The assumption of oscillation leads to the use of sinusoidal functions. Sinusoidal functions are the basis of spectral analysis, which is commonplace in auditory signal processing work.

Replicator Equations

Replicator equations express self-organizational properties in the form of systems of equations. Like the Lorenz and Henon attractor models, the output of one behavioral outcome plugs into the calculation of another behavioral outcome. In mathematical ecology, the Volterra–Lotka functions and the general form of the replicator equation, Equation 38 are topologically equivalent, here meaning that they produce identical phase portraits:

$$dy/dt = y_i [\sum_{j=0}^{n} (a_{ij} x_j) - \sum_{k=0}^{n} \sum_{j=0}^{n} (z_k a_{kj} x_j)] \tag{38}$$

(Orishimo et al., 1990). In Equation 38, change in behavior y is a function of y, and two other behaviors x and z. The proportionality constants a are based on the principle that values of x, y, and z take on a total value over time, and only a portion of that total is expired on any particular iteration, hence the summation functions that capture past history.

Systems at the Edge of Chaos

Systems at the edge of chaos are predominately living systems that slip in and out of a chaotic regime through self-organization. In contemporary evolution theory it now appears that selection principles operate on populations that have a high degree of diversity such that their numbers over time or space, or their distributions of genetic qualities, are close to chaotic. Because genetic qualities are correlated, the genetic structure of a population is self-organized, and reorganizes when confronted with a selection dynamic. The self-organization ensures the future stability of that population. In contrast, populations that are isolated in stable niches, and stable therein, become greatly unstabilized when an environmental event disrupts their niche (Kauffman, 1993).

At a more general level of analysis, which would not be confined to population dynamics, complex systems co-evolve with their environment and other species. A few generalizable principles emerge. An attempt to control a complex system, perhaps through natural selection or an organizational or political policy, by operating on only one feature of the system will not eradicate or otherwise nullify the system. The system will mutate and evolve to compensate for the environmental assault. The secret of real system change is to locate the dynamical key that supports or unravels the entire system. The next policy move would be to reorganize the entire system around a new dynamical key (Hubler, 1992). The verb I use, *to reorganize*, is a poor choice of words here; the system will reconstruct itself in a more stable fashion if the elements are scrambled (I hesitate to use the word *randomize*) and allowed to self-organize in a new fashion.

CHAOS NUMERICS

A complete examination of the analytic techniques that have been used to study complex systems or nonlinear dynamics is well beyond the scope of this book. At best, this section provides only a brief overview of the essential concepts. Those techniques that have been important for testing hypotheses in the application chapters are discussed in sufficient detail in Chapter 3. This section mentions, therefore, cellular automata, genetic algorithms and evolutionary computations, and measures of fractal dimension. The first two items are simulation techniques that are separate from the coupled dynamics simulations discussed earlier.

Cellular Automata

Cellular automata were first conceptualized in the early 1950s shortly after the first electronic computers were built. Cellular automata actually served as computational models for a computer, including those that would be capable of parallel processing, which were not realized until the late 1980s. Cellular automata surfaced under different names in different areas of mathematics, physics, and biology. They are iterative calculations defined according to Boolean algebra rules by which information related to one cell, or pixel in a computer image, affects the behavior of each adjacent cell at the next discrete step in time. The simplest concept of a cellular automaton begins with coloring in a single square on a sheet of graph paper. The second step is to color in the 3 × 3 matrix of squares around the first square (a *neighborhood*). The third step repeats the process, and so forth. The result would look like Fig. 2.26, which shows the results of four iterations of the "nine-cell square" rule (Toffoli & Margolus, 1987, 1990). Also shown in Fig. 2.26 for comparison are four iterations of the "five-cell square" rule (Packard & Wolfram, 1985).

Other rules can be devised to emulate biological cells that "die" or "come to life" when juxtaposed to two live cells or too many live cells. Another rule might be based on a "voting" rule where a cells turns on or off if a sufficient proportion of surrounding cells are "on." The dynamics can be complexified by introducing multiple rules, which might possibly signify competitive voting, or different rates of diffusion of cell characteristics (Toffoli & Margolus, 1987). Two frames from a more complex cellular automata function are shown in Fig. 2.27.

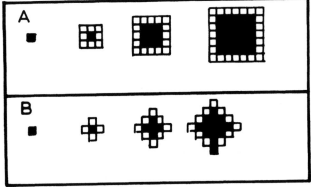

FIG. 2.26. Four iterations of simple cellular automata functions: (A) the nine-cell rule, and (B) the five-cell rule.

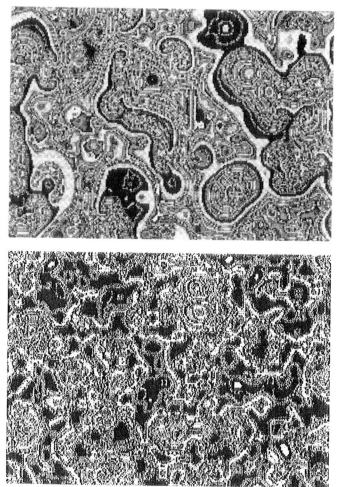

FIG. 2.27. Two frames from a relatively complex cellular automata function.

Cellular automata have several distinguishing characteristics. They can acquire only a finite number of states. They change discretely in time in a stepwise manner. Each cell has discrete boundaries. The rules that precipitate changes in each cell's behavior are deterministic, although it is possible to imagine hybridized programs containing a probabilistic component. Automata rules are *spatially local*, meaning that the behavior of a cell is dependent on the behavior of only the cells immediately surrounding it. Rules are also *temporally local*, meaning that the system typically has no memory beyond the previous step in the iterative process; that rule is often broken (Wolfram, 1986).

Cellular automata connect to nonlinear dynamics in several important ways. Some simple rules result in sudden or quickly stabilizing discontinuous changes in a global configuration in the sense of the catastrophe models (Wolfram, 1983). Other work shows that simple rules can produce fixed-point stabilization or limit cycles, while more complex rules can produce chaotic results (Ott, 1981). Given the appropriate rule structure, cellular automata draw fractal images. Instead of iterating along a one-dimensional axis of measurement, the iterations are extended in eight directions (Wolfram, 1983).

Genetic Algorithms and Evolutionary Programs

Genetic algorithms are models of machine learning that are heavily inspired by biological processes. Characteristics of a population are ascribed to "genes," which are recombined within the population, according to a rule base concerning the patterns of reproduction possible, the instantiation of mutations, and the degree of fitness associated with the resulting organism. Some relevant applications appear in chapter 9. Some algorithms involve compromises between genetic rules and problem-specific constraints. Hybridized models are known as *evolutionary programs*. Pure genetic algorithms have the advantage of theoretical support and wide applicability, but have been known to produce absurd results in some applications. Evolutionary programs, on the other hand, tend to be more viable tools for specific problems, but are narrower in generalizability (Michaelewicz, 1993). For some studies comparing genetic algorithm and evolutionary program structures, see Back and Schwefel (1993) and Muhlenbein and Schlierkamp-Voosen (1993).

Fractal Dimensions

The calculation of fractal dimension is important not only for understanding and utilizing fractal geometry but also for assessing the complexity of an attractor. The concept of fractal dimension dates back to Hausdorff (1919), later modified by Mandelbrot (1983) as described earlier in this chapter. The fractal dimension is defined as:

$$D_f = \lim_{l \to 0} \frac{\log[1/M(l)]}{\log l} \tag{40}$$

Imagine that a fractal image is covered with cubes with sides of length l. $M(l)$ is a function of the *embedding dimension*, ε. A true line will require $\varepsilon = 0$, a surface $\varepsilon = 1$, volume $\varepsilon = 3$, and so forth. The number of squares required to cover a point is proportional to $M(l)$, where

$$M(l) = l^{-\epsilon} \tag{41}$$

The *correlation dimension* has led to a well-used algorithm for calculating attractor dimension (Grassberger & Procaccia, 1983), defining dimension as:

$$D_c = \lim_{l \to 0} \frac{\log \|u_i\|_y}{\log l} \tag{42}$$

where l represents the diameter of a circle rather than the side of a square, and $\|u_i\|_y$ denotes the average value of $1/M(l)$ over all points in a time or spatial series of points. Although D_c was meant to approximate D_f, it is now known that D_c D_f (Girault, 1991; Kugiumtzis et al., 1994).

Although chaotic attractors are more complex than points, lines, or limit cycles, and exhibit fractional dimensionality, at least to a small degree, the presence of a fractional D_f is not a sufficient test of chaos. Missing is the property of sensitivity to initial conditions. The *Lyapunov dimension* is based on a concept of entropy, which is the rate at which information is lost concerning the forecastability of a variable y. *Lyapunov exponents*, λ_i, are computed for all values of y such that $y = e^{\lambda t}$, which is insensitive to initial conditions. Dimension D_L becomes a function of the largest value of λ in the series (Frederickson et al., 1983; Kugiumtzis et al., 1994; Wiggins, 1988). A positive value of D_L indicates an expanding function, which is to say, chaos. A negative D_L indicates a contracting process, which could be fixed-point or limit cycle. The best algorithm for calculating D_L to date was given by Wolf et al. (1985), but that algorithm is based only on positive values of λ, which might make it less than satisfactory as a "test for chaos" (Chatterjee & Yilmaz, 1992).

Another problem that pervades data analysis is the choice of time interval between successive measures of the behavior of interest. Recall that smooth mapping exist in the near neighborhood of an attractor; overly short time intervals would lead to a bias toward the linearity conclusion. Choice of time interval can seriously affect the definitions of attractors that one might extract from an analysis (Yee et al., 1991). The nonstatistical algorithms for identifying chaotic attractors appear to require huge amounts of data, in the order of 10^D data points (Casdagli, 1992). Sampling too close in time to attain the required database size could lead to linear bias, or a definition of attractor at a level of scale that is inappropriate to the phenomenon being addressed.

Statistical approaches for identifying chaos have been at least promising. Two methods that are currently under investigation are nonparametric techniques for determining whether there is a nonlinear component in an autoregressive time series (Brock, 1986; Brock et al., 1991; Chatterjee &

Yilmaz, 1992), and are based on the analysis of residuals from a linear time series. There is another nonparametric approach as well that is based on a different principle (Cheng & Tong, 1992). The catastrophes and discontinuous change dynamics appear to have been forgotten, meanwhile.

The next chapter addresses the conceptual issues underlying hypothesis testing for both chaos and catastrophe models. Methods are also presented for detecting chaos, dimensionality, and catastrophes, and for extracting model equations that are based on a strong parametric foundation for multimodal frequency distributions. The choice of time intervals is drawn from the substance or content of the application. As one might anticipate, there are issues to address concerning the counterpoint among chance, randomness, and determinism. Many, but not all, of the applications contained in Chapters 4–12 are based on those techniques.

SUMMARY

This chapter introduced the central concepts of nonlinear dynamics. Attractors range in complexity from fixed points to chaotic attractors. Attractors are structurally stable, while repellors and saddles are unstable. Chaotic attractors are stable in a global sense, but unstable in a local sense. Bifurcation mechanisms can transform attractors from fixed points to a chaotic regime, and the logistic map is a frequently observed route to chaos. Multiple couplings of period attractors are also frequently responsible for producing chaotic behavior.

Fractals are geometric forms in fractional dimensions. Although they were initially studied as independent lines of thought, it was eventually recognized that fractal geometry and nonlinear dynamics concerning chaos offered similar deterministic explanations for apparently random behavior. The basin of chaotic attractors was later found to be fractal.

Catastrophes are sudden discontinuous changes of events. The classification theorem for catastrophe models shows that there are 11 singular models, which range in complexity from one to five control parameters with one or two behavioral output variables. The topology of their response surfaces show that a complex manifold produces a continuity between apparently discontinuous states. Catastrophe models are configurations of stability and instability dynamics and usually involve fixed-point or limit cycle attractors, although boundary and chaotic attractors can be accommodated within the same framework. Catastrophe dynamics can be applied to understanding sudden changes in entire dynamical schemes as well.

Self-organization is a principle by which a living system in the state of chaos reorganizes its elements to produce a more stable structure and a less resource-costly existence. Self-organization can be observed from the standpoint of coupled dynamics, replicator and other interlocked sets of equations, and biological evolutionary phenomena. Other instances in human social systems are introduced in later chapters.

Cellular automata were initially developed as a concept of a computer, but became a part of the NDS fabric when catastrophic behavior of algorithms and other nonlinear dynamic processes were observed. They are one of several simulation techniques used to study mathematical phenomena or living systems that can be formalized by certain mathematical rules; genetic algorithms and evolutionary programs are two other such techniques. Computational tests for chaos or other nonlinear dynamic events are controversial, and several lines of work are currently underway to provide efficient computational methods. One such method that is based on a strong statistical theory is presented in the next chapter and is utilized in many of the applications that follow throughout the book.

3

Metaphors, Easter Bunnies, Modeling, and Verification

Nonlinear dynamical systems theory, as with any new paradigm in science, implies new ways of framing questions and analyzing phenomena, new topics to investigate, and new rules for determining how we know what we think we know about a phenomenon. Chaos and catastrophe theories are two central contributions to the new scientific outlook. Both stem more broadly from Poincaré's notions of qualitative analysis of mathematical functions. Both arrive at a drastically different concept of randomness compared to what social scientists and other consumers of statistics are accustomed to.

The new paradigm has several implications. First, many phenomena can be viewed with some heuristic advantage as autoregressive phenomena (variables that dependent of their own values from a previous point in time) that are *controlled* rather than caused. Second, changes in a system's behavior are governed by the amount of system entropy and the configuration of attractor and repellor forces. Third, many phenomena that appear adequately explained from an older paradigm can be reexamined. Gilmore (1981) showed that by reframing phase transitions (e.g., solid to liquid) and stability phenomena as a catastrophe model, it was possible to invoke another property of catastrophe—that of unfolding one model into another—to solve erstwhile unsolvable problems in irregular phase transitions, such as sublimation (solid directly to gas), and the stability of aircraft. The broad scope of NDS applications was outlined in the previous chapter.

The objective of this chapter is describe how one might so about discovering an application of NDS to an interesting social phenomenon. Applications begin with a cogent metaphor between the general rule and an application and between applications. It would be a legitimate debate whether NDS is a true paradigm of social science or a metaphor run amuck. There is some truth to both sides of the debate. On the one hand, metaphorical thinking is a major component of creative thought (discussed in chapter 10). If an idea truly represents a new paradigm, it is likely that scientists will see applications of it everywhere; numerous phenomena will look different from what they had always looked like. On the other hand, metaphors can be notoriously misleading. Thus the next section necessarily begins with two stories about metaphors. One is a relatively recent personal experience. The other is a classical historical saga of nonlinear dynamics. The chapter continues with both qualitative and quantitative issues involved with developing and testing a new theoretical innovation.

If NDS can have a major impact on theory in the physical, biological, and social sciences, as it appears to have had already, it should logically follow that it should have an equally significant impact on statistical reasoning as well. Indeed, the two following sections assemble a toolkit for the social scientist. The techniques involve relatively familiar methods, and some novel configurations of ideas that are unique to NDS issues. The central concern is with techniques for structural model building and testing, which have formed the basis of the applications that follow in Chapters 4–11. (Chapter 12 research is more eclectic in its repertoire.) The primary groups of hypotheses that are now testable using statistical techniques are (a) polynomial structure for catastrophe models, (b) polynomial structure for logistic map bifurcation structures, (c) nonlinear regression for estimating dimension, and (d) nonlinear regression for bifurcation and control parameter hypotheses. A few principles of coupled dynamics are introduced insofar as they affect the applications developed in the remainder of the book.

In the development of the hypothesis testing methods, it is necessary to assume a general familiarity with ordinary multiple regression for testing hypotheses connected to the general linear model:

$$Y = B_0 + B_1X_1 + B_2X_2 + B_3X_3 + \ldots + B_nX_n \quad \text{(raw score definition)} \quad (1)$$

$$y = \beta_1X_1 + \beta_2X_2 + \beta_3X_3 + \ldots + \beta_nX_n \quad \text{(standard score version)} \quad (2)$$

with the common methods of entering variables into a multiple regression model, such as forward, simultaneous, backward, and stepwise methods; and with methods for assessing the generalizability of a sample to a population, such as shrinkage, split sample, bootstrapping, jackknife, and unit weighting procedures. The polynomial regression variant is particularly important to testing structural hypotheses:

$$y = \beta_1 X^1 + \beta_2 X^2 + \beta_3 X^3 + \ldots + \beta_n X^n \qquad (3)$$

where powers of X_1 are substituted for separate independent variables X_i. There are many wonderful textbooks on linear regression that could serve as a basic reference. I should, however, express a bit of favoritism toward Darlington (1990) for his treatment of some special topics that are specifically relevant to procedures for structural hypothesis testing.

The standard notation in ordinary textbooks on multiple regression is to designate the dependent measure as Y, and the independent variables as X_i. It is necessary to depart from the nomenclature because it is often necessary to define two or more dependent measures. Independent variables named from the beginning of the alphabet, a, b, c, d. If these occur in groups, then they may be known as a_i, b_i, c_i, d_i. Dependent measures are Y and X (X is usually subordinate to Y in some way).

It is another convention of standard notation to use capital letters X and Y to denote a raw score and lower case italics to denote standard scores (score minus mean, quantity divided by standard deviation). In this development, the necessary distinction is between raw scores such as y and its transformed counterpart, such as z. The transformation is with respect to location and scale parameters, which are critical to the modeling system; the result looks similar to a standard score, but is a more general transformation. If additional transformed dependent measures are needed, u and v will step into the dance.

Another conventional item of notation is to define regression weights for raw score equations as capital Roman B_i, but regression weights for standard score equations as capital Greek β_i. Here there is a need for a different set of latent regression weights, those associated with transformed scores, rather than standard scores; those are designated as β_i, and may specify a constant β_0, which would not have appeared in an ordinary standard score regression equation. Furthermore, the Greek form is used to designate a model in its theoretical form. I revert to Roman B's when designating a specific model that is about to be tested.

Nonlinear regression is a technique that is much less common at the moment in the social sciences than ordinary linear regression. Nonlinear regression models allow us to estimate coefficients associated with any aspect of a curve. The simplest configuration is

$$y = e^{at} \qquad (4)$$

where y is the dependent measure, t is time, e is the Naperian constant $2.71828 \ldots$, and a is a regression weight. Although one conventional notation designates nonlinear regression weights as Roman characters from the beginning of the alphabet, plans have already been made to use those characters as predictor variables. Therefore an alternative convention will be used whereby nonlinear regression weights are designated as θ_i.

The specification of a structural equation in nonlinear regression is not as routine as the procedure in ordinary multiple linear regression. The researcher needs to specify the entire structural model, the placement of regression weights, and the placement of a dangling constant. For instance, Equation 4 is substantially different from Equation 5 or 6:

$$y = \theta_1 e^{\theta_2 t} \tag{5}$$

$$y = e^{\theta_2 t} + \theta_3 \tag{6}$$

The calculation procedures and options are different from those involved in multiple linear regression in several respects; Seber and Wild (1989) and Ratkowsky (1990) serve as useful general references.

Having unfolded the structural equations approach to hypothesis testing, we are confronted with not only a group of models, but models that describe functions that occur over time. Social scientists have had some prolonged moments of clumsiness in assessing change, and here the new paradigm clashes with old. Psychometric theory is the statistical theory of psychological measurements, what constitutes measurement reliability, and the types of error that could contaminate a measurement. Several classic principles of psychometrics are, unfortunately, based on some notions of the relationship between time and measurement that are overly simplistic and no longer warranted in light of NDS. Three such paradoxes are outlined that are encountered in later applications.

The chapter concludes with an overview of the applications. The goal in each case is to develop a qualitative theory that incorporates NDS principles against a background of conventional ideas. Some continuity among the theories inevitably emerges.

METAPHORS, EASTER BUNNIES, AND MODEL BUILDING

I exchanged letters with a colleague about an article that appeared in a recent issue of a famous psychology journal that I will not name here. My colleague wrote to me by hand, and his handwriting is marginally legible. One important sentence I read from his letter was, "I spoke with a top [researcher] who thought that [Whatsisname's] article was 'Easter rabbits.'" The letter continued with technical remarks and an expressed view that my colleague's subject area had fallen into the hands of amateurs.

I spent the better part of a day pondering what it meant for a high-profile article to be an *Easter rabbit*. I put the metaphor together with the remark about amateurs and came up with "a fuzzy little bunny for the children of psychologyland to play with." Or, in other words, it was something harmless, superficial but enchanting, and just a tad insipid on the side. It all fit, that is, until I showed the letter to one of my graduate students, who read that the top researcher thought the article in question was *utter rubbish*. Clear, unambiguous, and metaphor-transparent. The only funny bunnies were in my head. Fortunately, I did not write the target article, nor did it have anything to do with NDS.

A Catastrophe for Catastrophe Theory

The next story is a classic nonlinear saga. Chaos theory as it is experienced now is not the first example of a nonlinear dynamic general systems theory grabbing the scientific community by the face. In fact, it was predated by about 10 years by René Thom's (1975) catastrophe theory, which revolves around the principle that all discontinuous changes of events can be described by one of seven elementary topological forms. It became famous within the community of scientists as a result of extensive work by Zeeman (1976a, 1977), a mathematician, who applied its principles widely from the buckling of an elastic beam and the stability of ships to the fight-or-flight reaction, war, anorexia nervosa, the stock market, drunk driving, and prison riots. Many writers carried the applications much further in the social sciences.

The cataclysm came in the form of a critical review by Sussmann and Zahler (1978a, 1978b). They made several points worth remembering.

Triviality: Some of the applications were based on only superficial rationale, and merely stated that discontinuity did occur. The deep mathematics of the theory were seldom used.

Absurd prediction: Some of the proposed models made predictions that were counterintuitive and not wholly believable, and they were presented without empirical proof.

Parsimony: Some applications appeared to be merely threshold models or equilibrium models, which were restated in the form of functions that were more complex than what the situation would have ordinarily required.

Verifiability: Sussmann and Zahler responded to a claim in the mathematical modeling papers on catastrophe that global structure can be inferred from knowledge of local aspects of the model's geometry. They argued that the claim was not valid, that any set of points could be fitted by a surface, and there was no way to determine whether a model obtained from data was actually a member of the Thom series.

There were rejoinders to the criticisms. First, triviality was reasoned to be an outcome of deficiencies in the qualitative aspects of the modeling process, where deeper understanding of the social events was limited to begin with. Regarding the deep mathematics, in the social sciences we use the products of the mathematics, not the proofs that gave rise to the useful theorems: the classification concepts, attractors, bifurcation, and stability or instability, and the characteristic surface equations (Guastello, 1981).

Parsimony is a matter of viewpoint. A simple fold model *is* a simple threshold model. The fold concept becomes interesting when we consider that it is a building block for the more complex models. If a system changes state around one threshold when moving in one direction, but changes around another threshold in the reverse direction, then a cusp model is implied. Alternatively, if stability is observed after passing a threshold, a cusp is warranted; a fold would provide no local stability past that threshold. A catastrophe model would be a parsimonious interpretation of events insofar as it served as an organizing concept for what would be a disjointed group of mini-theories. In other words, parsimony is all relative (Guastello, 1981, 1992a).

Absurd predictions fall into two categories: those that are predicted by a theory but conflict with real observations, and those that are predicted from theory but conflict with someone's notion of common sense. Models of the first type should simply return to the drawing board. Models of the second type could generate some exciting hypotheses (Guastello, 1981).

Regarding surfaces and such, Oliva and Capdevielle (1980) responded by noting that the same problems existed for linear regression surfaces, and that it would be throwing the proverbial baby out with the bathwater to discard catastrophe theory or regression analysis from the repertoire of analytic techniques for the social sciences. Guastello (1981) continued by noting that the problem of overfitting a curve, or even a straight line, can be prevented through use of cross-validation techniques and adequate sample sizes. Perhaps, more importantly, the emphasis in empirical analysis, as with qualitative analysis, should be on modeling, not curve fitting. The success of the effort begins with a well-developed hypothesis. Although it is not mathematically possible to know one region of a surface from knowledge of another, an experimenter can capture more of the surface by testing a wider range of values for the important variables in the model. The pattern will emerge or it won't. Fortunately, NDS hypotheses are testable in ways that were not possible in early 1978.

Chaos in Chaos Theory

An important analytic objective of chaos-related experiments is the calculation of the Lyapunov exponent for the dimension of an attractor. The calculation of dimension allows a test of the hypothesis as to whether an attractor is a fixed point or a limit cycle, and thereby nonchaotic, in which case the exponent is negative, or whether the attractor is aperiodic or chaotic, in which case the exponent is positive (Casti, 1989; Peters, 1991; Wiggins, 1988), as elaborated in the previous chapter along with the complications associated with defining a dimension or an attractor. The very thought of estimating dimension by statistical methods confronts another layer of controversy, that having to do with whether deterministic chaos and statistics can ever have any common ground.

Historically, there has been an approach–avoidance relationship between NDS and statistics. The use of statistics for testing topological hypotheses was pronounced a contradiction in terms by Stevens (1951), who commented specifically about Lewin's social psychology, and by Woodcock and Davis (1978), who wrote about catastrophe theory and its applications. The thinking was that topological models are rubberized rather than rigid, and thus a response surface known by its mathematical formula could not possibly be verified as explaining or not explaining an empirical finding.

A new round of controversy on this matter came from Stewart (1989), Casti (1991), Peters (1991), and Priesmeyer (1992). Stewart's book began with a history of major paradigmatic development in physics, including a statistical era that was later to be upstaged by nonlinear dynamics, which used differential equations as its primary analytic toolkit in the natural sciences. Casti (1991) took Stewart's remarks a step further by claiming that statistics were now becoming obsolete methods for testing and developing theory, a point with which I obviously disagree. Peters (1991) took a more balanced view and reported that nonstatistical methods for estimating Lyapunov exponents were not especially reliable for some types of data; a portion of his work centered on developing new statistical indices to capture nonlinear features in financial data. Priesmeyer (1992) claimed that traditional statistics were inadequate for appropriately describing phenomena because of their reliance on linear models that discard deviations from linearity as error. It is critical not to lose sight of the key word *traditional*.

MULTIMODAL PROBABILITY DENSITY FUNCTIONS

The barriers to statistical modeling became nonproblems for catastrophe theory with the advent of Cobb's (1978, 1981a, 1981b) work on multimodal probability density functions (pdfs). The core proposition is that, based on prior work in the 1930s by Ito and Wright, any mathematical function can be transformed into a probability density function by the transformation:

$$pdf(z) = \xi e^{-\int f(z)} \tag{7}$$

where x is a constant introduced to ensure unit density, and z is a dependent measure that has been corrected for location (λ) and scale (σ'):

$$z = (y - \lambda)/\sigma' \tag{8}$$

A correction for location is needed whenever the range of data does not fully cover the bends of the underlying curve. Thus for a simple polynomial hypotheses:

$$Y = B_0 + B_1 X^3 \tag{9}$$

the common corrections are the addition of $B_2 X^2$ and $B_3 X^1$ to the predictor set and a subtraction of the mean of Y (M_Y) from Y:

$$Y - M_Y = B_0 + B_1 X^3 + B_2 X^2 + B_3 X \tag{10}$$

(Darlington, 1990). Other estimates of location are sometimes useful and are discussed later in this chapter. Also, when the estimate of location is imperfect, the correlations between X^2 and X^1 with X^3 are increased.

The scale parameter represents variability around a mode rather than variation around a mean. The ordinary standard deviation (SD_Y) is a fairly good estimate of scale when data points cluster around a single mode, such as the cusp point or a bifurcation point in a logistic map, more than they cluster around other modes in the complex distribution. As the distribution becomes increasingly multimodal, as when strong nonlinear dynamics are taking place, two types of variability are observed: variability within modes and variability between modes. SD_Y becomes a much poorer estimate of scale in that instance. Alternatives are discussed later in this chapter also, where the estimation problem shifts to determining the modes instead of σ'.

Parameter Estimation for Cusp pdfs

The cusp pdf is represented by the function

$$pdf(y) = \xi e^{(-z^4/4 + bz^2/2 + az)} \tag{11}$$

(Cobb, 1978, 1981a, 1981b). The function is three-dimensional (Fig. 3.1). At low values of b it is unimodal, resembling a normal distribution. At higher values, the pdf becomes increasingly bimodal. Two techniques have been developed for applying Equation 11 directly into hypothesis,

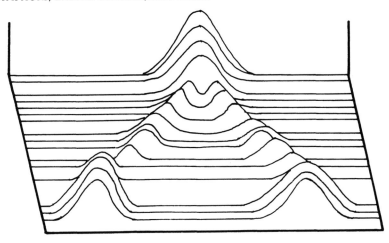

FIG. 3.1. The cusp probability density functions.

one based on least squares theory and the other based on maximum likelihood. Although those techniques have seen only occasional use in the psychological literature, they illustrate an important bridge between the cusp pdf and the dynamic difference equations. Thus a brief description is warranted.

The two methods for evaluating whether a given distribution of behavior scores is truly cusp catastrophic in nature both involve iterative calculation procedures. In the method of moments (least squares theory; Cobb, 1980, 1981a; Cobb & Watson, 1980), there are $2k + 4$ parameters to be estimated (8 for the cusp), which result in values for the variables in the stochatic cusp equation (Equation 12), plus location and scale of y:

$$0 = (a_1 - a_0) + (b_1 - b_0)z - z^3 \qquad (12)$$

In Equation 12, z is defined as before, a_1 and a_0 denote the range of the latent asymmetry parameter, and b_1 and b_0 the range of the latent bifurcation parameter. Having estimated the parameters of the latent pdf, one can then compute an r^2 coefficient for goodness of fit.

The use of r^2 for goodness of fit was named *pseudo-r^2* (Cobb, 1981b) because it does not permit hypothesis testing in the usual sense. Pseudo-r^2 by itself evaluated the cusp structure only. To test the hypotheses concerning experimental variables in the control parameter positions, one must proceed a step further by correlating latent a and b parameters with exogenous experimental variables. If these correlations are statistically significant, then it is concluded that the experimental variable contributed to the latent parameter. As a final step, R^2 is calculated for the explicit regression equation

68

CHAPTER THREE

$$y = \beta_0 + \beta_1 a + \beta_2 b \tag{13}$$

to compare the linear-only hypothesis with pseudo-r^2 for the cusp hypothesis.

A published example (Cobb, 1981a) of this technique illustrated the relationship between alcohol consumption and automobile driving speed in a simulator. The original data had been published by Zeeman (1976b), and originated from yet another study from 20 years earlier. Subjects performed a simulated driving task under varying degrees of alcohol intoxication. All had completed a test measuring the introversion–extraversion personality trait. It was found that extraverts did not change their driving speed under the influence of alcohol, but introverts either gained speed or slowed down dramatically. The cusp hypothesis was that the driving speed changes were cusp distributed such that introversion–extraversion contributed to the bifurcation parameter. There was no asymmetry hypothesis in that experiment. The pseudo-r^2 obtained for the model was .60, whereas an R^2 value of .00 was obtained for the linear alternative model.

The maximum likelihood model is based on the formulation

$$\delta y = \delta(y^4/4 - by^2/2 - ay)\, \delta t/\delta y + \sigma'_y\, \delta w_t \tag{14}$$

where δw_t is a random error term and σ'_y is a scale parameter; a multiplicative error function is thereby assumed. There are four stages to the hypothesis testing process. First, parameter estimates for Equation 14 are set equal to 0.0 (on left side of the equation), and pseudo-r^2 is calculated. Second, experimental variables are correlated with latent parameters which are estimated for each case in the sample. Third, an ordinary R^2 is found between variables a and b, with y or Δy to represent the linear alternative model. Fourth, a special χ^2 test is calculated to compare the fit of the cusp and linear models (Cobb, 1981c; Cobb et al., 1983; Cobb & Zacks, 1985). The final cusp model takes the form:

$$0 = z^3 - \theta_1(\theta_2 a_1 + \theta_3 a_2)z - \theta_4(\theta_5 a_1 + \theta_6 a_2) \tag{15}$$

where a_1 and a_2 are experimental variables that are automatically tested (by the computer program) in both parameter positions. Empirical applications of the technique are included in chapters 4 and 5.

The parameter estimation techniques just described have six major assets. First, the maximum likelihood method works better than the moments technique for estimating an entire cusp response surface from trajectories at the outer rim of the manifold. Second, the techniques separate results for the overall cusp structure and the experimental variables. Third, it is possible to test both static and dynamic hypotheses. A static hypothesis would be one where a distribution of behavior scores that are not difference scores appears to disperse in a cusp-shaped fashion. A dynamic hypothesis would be one where actual changes are observed in behavior and the set of trajectories forms all the major pathways on a cusp surface.

Fourth, the maximum likelihood method includes a significance test for comparing cusp and alternative linear hypotheses. Fifth, the technique generalizes to a limited set of chaotic, rather than catastrophic, changes where there system is essentially cubic (Cobb & Zacks, 1988). And finally, location and scale are estimated directly.

The parameter estimation procedures have five major limitations. First, they treat dynamic hypotheses as minor variations of static hypotheses; this modeling assumption is not entirely appealing. Second, pseudo-r^2 and R^2 for a linear model are not really comparable except in the limiting case where there is only one experimental variable being tested as a control. Third, there are too many parameters to estimate compared to the dynamic difference equations considered in the next section, and compared to any linear regression standard. This circumstance undermines the generalizability of the results obtained with the technique, making them twice as likely to capitalize on chance perturbations in the sample (sampling error in the usual sense). The χ^2 test does not take into account the different numbers of parameters appearing in cusp and linear alternative model, or provide any clues as to which experimental variables did more work; a set of bivariate regression coefficients is required for that purpose.

Fourth, although the procedures can, in principle, be used for other cuspoid models, such algorithms have not been developed or demonstrated. If they were available, however, testing a butterfly would involve an exorbitant number of parameters to estimate, particularly if the research involved excavating a set of many potential variables. Finally, there is no organized approach for estimating lag length for dynamic processes, which makes any numerical model hard to operationalize on any new observations where behavior and control variables can be measured.

Generalized Multivariate Method

The generalized multivariate method for estimating catastrophe models (GEMCAT; Oliva et al., 1987) addressed the matter of identifying cusp structure from a database containing a large number of experimental variables. The cusp function is defined in terms of latent constructs A_t^*, B_t^*, and Z_t^*, which are weighted composites of research variables that might contribute to asymmetry, bifurcation, and behavior, respectively, at time t:

$$\delta f(A_t{}^*, B_t{}^*, Z_t{}^*)/\delta Z_t{}^* = 0 = Z_t{}^{*3} - A_t{}^* - B_t{}^* Z_t{}^* \qquad (16)$$

A controlled random search procedure is used to identify latent variables that satisfy Equation 16. Possible models are selected on a criterion of minimum Φ, which is the lack of fit between the latent variable and raw data:

$$\text{Min } \Phi = \| \varepsilon_t{}^2 \| = \Sigma_{t=1}^{T} (Z_t{}^{*3} - A_t{}^* - B_t{}^* Z_t{}^*)^2 \qquad (17)$$

(Oliva et al., 1987, p. 128). In principle it is possible to test competing hypotheses about contents of cusp models.

The GEMCAT technique appears to be valuable as an exploratory technique, where data are rich but theory is thin. There is also a possibility of determining a desired lag length if the data are sufficiently detailed. One drawback is the possibility of Type I error because of the large number of models that are calculated and the large number of parameters that are estimated. Because criteria as well as predictors are aggregated into latent variables, GEMCAT results may be susceptible to a problem often encountered in canonical correlation analysis: Predictor and criterion composites may be highly correlated, but at the same time bear little redundancy with the original results.

DYNAMIC DIFFERENCE EQUATIONS
FOR CATASTROPHES

The dynamic difference equations proceed from parameter estimation theory, and apply where a behavior is measured at two points in time. During the time that elapses between measurements, it is assumed that a random force has been applied to the system under observation, and that the random force is strong enough to excite trajectories across the fullest possible range of the catastrophe manifold. The dynamic difference equations were the primary method of testing many of the applications of NDS to work-related phenomena. The technique evolved over a series of papers with decidedly procedural goals and covering a variety of applications (Guastello, 1982a, 1982b, 1987a, 1987b, 1988a, 1992a, 1992b, 1993a, 1993b). It can be used to evaluate hypotheses concerning all seven elementary catastrophes and extends to other structures suggested from chaos theory.

The technique is intended for testing theory-driven hypotheses, rather than for an adventure in curve fitting. The emphasis on theory was further intended to build theoetical bridges between core concepts of NDS and qualitative theory in psychology and organizational behavior. There are several steps to building a conceptual model:

1. Identify the behavioral output variable, the number and type of stable system states.
2. Identify hysteresis, multiple threshold events, or other instabilities that might be present.
3. Select a model that accounts for the observed dynamics. When in doubt, try something simple.
4. Identify real-world variables that behave as asymmetry, bifurcation, swallowtail, butterfly, or other parameters.
5. Identify any surface gradients if possible.
6. Compare the proposed function with any known functions for the same phenomenon.

Classification plays an important role in the design of analyses, experiments, and the interpretation of experimental results. Thom's classification theorem was a powerful heuristic because it narrowed the range of possible discontinuous change functions to only a few. The seven models vary in complexity, where complexity is signified by the highest exponent term that represents the behavioral variable in the surface equation, for example, y^3 for the cusp. The leading exponent denotes the number of control parameters, each with its own unique function, and the complexity of the behavioral array they perpetrate. To reverse the logic, if a bifurcation parameter is identified, then the model that includes it must be at least a cusp in complexity. (Note: There are other nonlinear dynamic models that lie outside the set of elementary catastrophes that need to be considered. The most prominent models are discussed in the next section.)

Canonical is equivalent in meaning to prototypic. Because topological models are rubberized rather than rigid, catastrophe models can withstand perturbations without changing their classification, as long as a tear in the surface is not introduced. Some types of allowable perturbations would be the addition of a term y^{R-1}, the expression of bifurcation and asymmetry parameters as more than one experimental variable, interaction between control parameters (such as $b_i a_i$), or differential weights among the contributing parts of the model (e.g., power potential, bifurcation, asymmetry).

The dynamic difference equation for the cusp catastrophe is explained next, and considers the hitherto most common case where difference scores are discrete, and two points in time are observed for a sample of people. The model is then easily extended to cover repeated time series where one or perhaps a small number of entities is observed over a long series of time intervals. The two subsequent extensions pertain to the other cuspoid catastrophe models and the umbilic models.

Cusp Model

The specification of a regression equation for a cusp begins with a definition of a function that takes place over time:

$$\delta z = (z^3 - bz - a)\, \delta t + \varepsilon \tag{18}$$

where ε is an error term that is only assumed to be additive in nature, and z is the behavioral outcome that has been corrected for location and scale. The term δt is set equal to 1, meaning that it is constant for all time intervals. Equation 18 becomes fully operationalized by replacing the differential term δt with the difference operator Δz, and inserting empirical weights among the terms:

$$\Delta z = \beta_0 + \beta_1 z_1^3 + \beta_2 z_1^2 + \beta_3 b z_1 + \beta_4 a \tag{19}$$

where z is the behavioral outcome, corrected for location and scale per Equation 8, and measured at two points in time.

A network of hypotheses is contained in Equation 19. First there is the overall statistical significance of the model, and size of R^2. The R^2 coefficient from multiple regression, with variables specified by Equation 19, describes how well the data approximate a true cusp model. F (or t) tests on the regression weights denote the contribution of each term in the model. In optimal situations, each term in the model accounts for a unique portion of criterion variance. The power potential denotes and implies a particular bifurcation structure. Under less than optimal conditions, bivariate correlations between the individual terms and the difference equation may be significant, but empirical weight may not all be significant in the multiple regression model. Here the validity of the structural model would still be upheld, and a cross-validation strategy could confirm the conclusion. Additional investigation would be required to determine whether the qualitative variables that were thought to represent control variables indeed contributed to the model; one might look at collinearity among control variables and behavior measures, bivariate correlations between elements of the model and the difference scores. Misestimates of location or scale (see later discussion) could obfuscate the contributions of the hypothesized control variables.

If a behavior y is cusp-distributed, as defined in the preceding section, then difference scores are also cusp-distributed. As the model loses accuracy for whatever reason, R^2 appears to decline in a difference model somewhat faster than it might for a static polynomial model (Guastello, 1982a). Accurate models come from good theories. Assuming the structure of the model is correct, correct definitions of control variables could account for as much variance in Δz as the power potentials. As control variables become perfectly known, R^2 approaches 1.00 (Guastello, 1992a). On the other hand, the structural model and control variables may be well selected, but need a little help to finesse some possible purturbations in the model structure that might be introduced through sampling errors. Possible options for improving a model include redefining location and scale in a particular model, and perhaps testing for structural modifications for fold degeneracy, skew, and dampening or retardation.

Figure 3.2 shows three scatterplots of Δz versus the asymmetry parameter in data where increasing bimodality was introduced. The term R^2 increased from .37 to .71 to .95 in panels A, B, and C, respectively. Because they are two-dimensional plots, they represent mixtures of top-down and head-on views. The solid line represents the placement of a slice from the outer rim of the cusp surface. The broken line represents the bifurcation gradients that are usually seen drawn on the cusp's bifurcation set plane. Ironically, the condition where R^2 was the highest did not show as much modal separation as panels A or B. The reason is that a good fit reflects not only the modal separation, but a smoother portion of the surface where the bifurcation parameter approaches zero. Points falling in around the cusp point and fanning out are seen filling the two-dimensional space between the two modes that characterize the unfolded region of the surface.

Scale. The scale parameter is particularly important in nonlinear models, and its importance was recently recognized in bilinear models where there is a multiplicative interaction between two or more variables. In the bilinear case, large differences in standard deviation between the two multiplied variables produce a term that is biased in favor of the variable with the larger standard deviation (Evans, 1991). In other words, the correlation between a single behavior measure y and the multiplicative complex xy approaches 1.00, and it is impossible to ascertain whether the interactive relationship is true at all.

This situation may not appear to be a problem in a polynomial where a variable is multiplied by itself, but in fact it is a problem when we are modeling change processes of quadratic order or higher, which would emanate from potential functions of cubic order or higher. When the change function is nonlinear, for example, quadratic, then the differential will be small for near-zero values of y but large otherwise. Scale-inflated measures of y will therefore take on smaller empirical weights than would

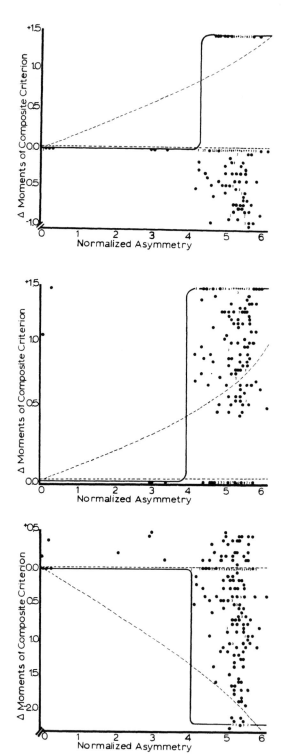

FIG. 3.2. Scatterplots showing increased cuspoid bimodality with increasing R^2. From Guastello (1982a). Reprinted with permission.

otherwise have been the case. Accordingly, the regression weight for the polynomial would approach zero, as would R, leading to the false conclusion that no polynomial events were taking place.

Scale, defined as variability around a statistical mode, is distinguished from variability between modes, or in and out of attractor basins. Thus, as the full variance of a dependent measure greatly exceeds its within-mode variability, the weight for its polynomial function increases. For the chaotic functions, where dimensionality itself is a parameter to be estimated, dimensionality will be large to the extent that the ordinary standard deviation exceeds scale.

The first task of statistical analysis is, therefore, to transform all experimental variables by scale (and location). The sample standard deviation is often used as the measure of dispersion around a mode. SD_y is a fair estimate for one-attractor problems or for cusp and bifurcation dynamics that are taking place in the neighborhood of the bifurcation point. As the dynamic becomes more catastrophic, or the underlying bifurcation increases, the standard deviation is a less adequate estimation of scale. Another approach, therefore, would be to calculate scale directly by partitioning the frequency distribution of y into modes and antimodes. Then

$$\sigma' = [\sqrt{\sum_{y=1} \sum_{m=1} y_{m-}^{m+} - m_i)^2} \,]/N - M \qquad (20)$$

(Guastello, 1992b). The N in the denominator of Equation 20 is the total number of observations. M represents the number of statistical modes around which points are actually observed to vary. For instance, M could equal 2 for many cusp applications if there were no points in the antimode. If there were points in the antimode, dispersion around the antimode should be included also; thus $M = 3$ (in a cusp). To continue, y is the raw score for behavior, and m_i is the modal value of y. Squared differences between y and m_i are summed over the range of y ($m-$ to $m+$) within the neighborhood of m_i, and then the sums are summed over modal regions.

The estimation goal in Equation 20 has now shifted from estimating scale to estimating the modes and their boundaries. One successful technique for estimating modes is to eyeball a frequency distribution of y to determine the boundary values of $m-$ and $m+$, and then observe the local mode. If the mode is not clear (perhaps because of sampling fluctuations) then the local median is the next choice.

Boundary values of $m-$ and $m+$ should be obvious in a well-defined distribution. Nearly no points at all would fall in the antimode of a well-defined cusp. If the region around the antimode is not sufficiently clear, then a rule of thumb is that no more than one-third of the cases should fall within the antimode (Jiobu & Lundgren, 1978). Alternatively, a scatterplot of the bifurcation variable against y might show better defined boundaries for the more extreme values of b. Examples where the definition of scale from Equation 20 improved a model's accuracy appear in chapters 7 and 8. In Equations 19 and 20, λ and σ' are usually preestimated separately at each point in time. In the case of scale, social science researchers have recognized that the events that produced a change in behavior could also be responsible for the change in variance from one point in time to another. An illustration appears later, following some remarks about location.

Location. The definition of location issue was given at the outset of the preceding section. In Equation 19, the dependent measure is corrected for location and scale using Equation 8. The mean of y is often used as an estimate of λ, according to Darlington (1990), who did not betray any special reference to NDS models. The operational definition of λ in most NDS models is the lower limit of y (Guastello, 1982a, 1987a; Rawlings, 1990).

In many cases, location, as defined by the lower limit of y, can change across the two behavior measurements from Time 1 to Time 2. In one class of circumstances, the drift in λ may be the result of the real change resulting from the dynamic process. In those cases, λ should be the same value in both cases.

In other situations, however, λ may change over two points in time for reasons that are produced artificially by the research situation. For instance, in a sample of people who are being studied with respect to their transition from high school to college, the lower limit of y can drop by as much as 2.5 GPA points. Consider how location and scale work together to change the meaning of a behavioral measure. A college may select students with GPAs greater than 2.5, but once matriculated, some students fail for any of a number of well-known reasons. Hence the location parameter for the sample drops from 2.5 to 0.00 from high school to college. College GPA scores would be spread over a wider range and possibly become polarized or trichotomized (butterfly distribution), and hence there would be an increase in variance. The upper limit of GPA remains the same, however. As a numerical illustration, let $\lambda_1 = 2.5$, $\sigma'_1 = 0.50$, $\lambda_2 = 0.00$, and $\sigma'_2 = 0.75$. A high school GPA of 4.00 thus becomes $z_1 = 3.00$, and a college 4.00 becomes $z_2 = 5.33$. Hence $\Delta z = +2.33$ by maintaining a 4.00 GPA. If scale did not change, then $z_2 = 8.00$ and $\Delta z = +5.00$.

Fold Degeneracy. The quadratic term in Equation 19 appears as a correction for misestimation of scale. It also serves another purpose, which is to account for a particular type of defect in the observed cusp response surface. By definition, change in behavior shows cubic potential in the cusp, which has one bifurcation variable. Also, because of the structure of catastrophes determined by Thom (1975), each model of the catastrophe series includes lower order geometries. Thus, the fold is nested within the cusp, so to speak. The cusp also has two thresholds. When one threshold is represented in the data more the other fold, degeneracy of the pure canonical shape occurs. Degeneracy is remedied by introducing a quadratic term into Equation 19.

Skewed Surfaces and Gradients. It is possible that the hypothesized bifurcation factor will emerge as a true bifurcation factor and as an asymmetry factor. In that circumstance, the hypothetical variable loads on both the latent a and b parameters. It loads in the same sense that variables are said to load on factors in factor analysis, which is to say that the variables are correlated with latent factors, as in Cobb's (1981a) parameter estimation procedure.

The empirical surface signified by this skew condition would not show unfolding directly over the bifurcation axis. The cusp point could be located in the same place, but the unfolding would be squashed a little to one side. Topological models are better thought of as rubberized rather than rigid, and skewed surfaces are examples of what that is true. Equation 19 can be amended for skew by adding another asymmetry addend:

$$\Delta z = \beta_0 + \beta_1 z_1^3 + \beta_2 z_1^2 + \beta_3 b z_1 + \beta_4 a + \beta_5 b \qquad (21)$$

Another variation of results that would not affect the structural hypothesis is one where both control variables contribute to both latent control parameters. In those cases, the variable set $[a,b]$ is a nonlinear transformation of latent control parameters $[a,b]$. Their place in the model is well approximated by modifying Equation 19 as:

$$\Delta z = \beta_0 + \beta_1 z_1^3 + \beta_2 z_1^2 + \beta_3 b z_1 + \beta_4 a z_1 + \beta_5 a + \beta_6 b \qquad (22)$$

If all terms in the model are significant, then it is reasonable to conclude that the hypothesized variables a and b contribute to the *gradients* in the cusp surface that run between the cusp point and the attractor centers.

The Markov Assumption. The structural regression models for catastrophe surfaces assume that a perfect Markov process is operating, meaning that the control point has no memory of where it came from beyond the prior instant. Depending on the specifics, violation of the assumption could result in flattening the surface (dampening catastrophic fluctuations) or expanding the dimensionality (retardation) of the surface by introducing additional convolutions. If the surface is being dampened, then the results of the regression analysis would, in combination with the experimental design procedure discussed next, show major signs of linearity. If dimensionality has been expanded, it is possible to account for the extra ruffles in the surface by adding additional polynomial terms to the end of the model, such as the following modified cusp:

$$\Delta z = \beta_0 + \beta_1 z_1^3 + \beta_2 z_1^2 + \beta_3 b z_1 + \beta_4 a + \beta_5 z_1^4 + \beta_6 z_1^5 \qquad (23)$$

Prototype Experimental Design. In a classical experiment, there are objects or people that we measure and manipulate in a theoretically interesting way. Those results are compared with those obtained from control groups where no such manipulation has taken place, or perhaps a reverse manipulation, depending on the nature of the theory. A similar principle applies to the testing of NDS hypotheses, only the contrast is made between the results of equations: the structural equation for the NDS model, and two control equations that are structurally linear and include the same qualitative variables [a,b]. The *linear-difference* model for the cusp is:

$$\Delta y = B_0 + B_1 a + B_2 b \qquad (24)$$

If more than one experimental variable is hypothesized for either of the controls, additional terms containing those variables would be added to Equation 24. The *linear pre–post* model is essentially the same model as the linear-difference model, except that y_1 has been moved to the right side of the equation:

$$y_2 = B_0 + B_1 y_1 + B_2 a + B_3 b \qquad (25)$$

The dependent variable, y, needs no correction for location or scale because ordinary linear models are robust with respect to those transformations.

The R^2 coefficient for the nonlinear model should exceed the R^2 for the two linear alternatives. The value of R^2 for Equation 25 is often larger than R^2 for Equation 24, but not always. In the studies on record through July 1991 that tested catastrophe hypotheses using the polynomial method and behavior measured at two points in time, the R^2 for the catastrophe hypothesis was larger than R^2 for the next best linear model by a ratio of 2.01 : 1 (Guastello, 1992a). The epilogue to this book contains a revised estimate based on all the applications of NDS that have involved the same or comparable techniques.

Cusps in Time Series

The next extension of the dynamic difference technique is for situations where one object or person is observed repeatedly over time. The random force that propelled, in a sense, the catastrophic functions in the previously discussed models is still operating. Bifurcation parameters will still trigger the change in behavior from one attractor neighborhood to another, and asymmetry parameters will still have their usual role as well. Location and scale are the same annoyances they always were, but a new error concept needs to be introduced, that of dependent error.

The dependent error concept has existed in conventional regression theory in three ways. First, the standard analysis of variance for split plot experimental designs (one or more factors are repeated measures whereas one or more factors are fixed and not repeated) routinely separates variance into between-subject variance and within-subject variance; both types of variance are separated a second time between experimental effects and error, which is everything else. Between-subject error is unexplained differences in behavior among people in the study. Within-subject error is unexplained differences in behavior for a single person over repeated observations. So far nothing is new except to call attention to a well-accepted idea.

The second traditional theme concerning dependent error is seen in program evaluation studies where an experimental group and a control group change (or do not change) behavior after a training, therapy, or policy exposure. Often enough, the variance in behavior changes from one time period to another as do the mean scores on behavior. That problem alone made reliance on difference score criteria, suc'. as Δy, unworkable, and led to the common query in analysis of variance of how can one tell if the means for a set of groups are truly different if the variances are also different (Labouvie, 1980).

This program evaluation example is one where the variance of y is dependent on an experimental condition (predictor x). The next situation is one where the variance of y is dependent on itself. It is often tempting to use ordinary linear regression in situations where an x and a y are both observed repeatedly over time from the same entity. The problem is, however, that x_1 may appear correlated with y_2, but only because they are confounded in time together, and not because one is causing the other or that there is reciprocal causation at play. Rather, x is correlated with itself over time, as is y; in other words, x and y are autocorrelated.

In time-series regression, therefore, the next analytic step after conducting an ordinary least squares regression is to determine whether dependent error is present. Thus one calculates the residuals of y after subtracting the predicted values of y (which are linear functions of x), which is followed by the Durbin–Watson statistic, which registers the presence of serial dependency among residuals. If the Durbin–Watson statistic is significant, then the ordinary least squares regression is invalid, and one must proceed to a generalized least squares technique that was developed especially for time series (Box & Jenkins, 1970; Ostrom, 1978).

The question we are leading toward is whether such a conversion is necessary in the case of time-series NDS. The answer appears to be "no" on the basis of three demonstrations (Guastello, 1982c, 1992c; Larrain, 1991). In the first attempt, a cusp model conducted in time series for prison riot data (described in chapter 5) was compared against the linear control equations. Durbin–Watson statistics for the linear model were significant, but they were not significant for the cusp model. Larrain (1991) made the same negative observation for residuals of a cubic polynomial calculated on econometric data; unfortunately, no linear comparisons were conducted. The third example actually involved a case of a nonlinear bifurcation model (defined in the next section) for population dynamics (described in chapter 9). Again, dependency among residuals in the linear model disappeared in the nonlinear case.

The disappearance of dependent error is a symptom of why the NDS models work so well if they are applied in a theoretically viable model. Part of what used to be known as dependent error is now variance accounted for by the polynomial or other nonlinear terms in the structural equation. Nonlinear structure accounts for a major piece of variance often enough and reflects an autonomous process taking place over time. The system has a natural course of action, or evolution, that occurs naturally and without the influence of any control variable. As we also know, however, systems often encounter control variables that model their behavior, but the pattern by which that modification occurs is again natural and dependent on the level of complexity of the system. The topic now turns to models of lesser or greater complexity than the cusp.

Fold, Swallowtail, and Butterfly Models

Hypotheses concerning the fold, swallowtail, and butterfly models can be tested in the same manner as the cusp. Their characteristic regression equations are, respectively:

$$\Delta z = \beta_0 + \beta_1 z_1^2 + \beta_2 a \tag{26}$$

$$\Delta z = \beta_0 + \beta_1 z_1^4 + \beta_2 z_1^3 + \beta_3 c z_1^2 + \beta_4 b z_1 + \beta_5 a \tag{27}$$

$$\Delta z = \beta_0 + \beta_1 z_1^5 + \beta_2 z_1^4 + \beta_3 d z_1^3 + \beta_4 c z_1^2 + \beta_5 b z_1 + \beta_6 a \tag{28}$$

The R^2 coefficients for Equations 26–28 would be compared with those obtained from their respective linear difference and linear pre–post equations.

Figure 3.3 shows slices from fold, swallowtail, and butterfly pdfs. The fold distribution contains a single mode, and antimode, and a dense region shown at the zero point, which reflects an instability. The swallowtail pdf shows two stable modes, an antimode, and an instability. The butterfly pdf shows three stable modes that are separated by antimodes.

The fold, swallowtail, and butterfly models have not received the same attention in the social sciences as the cusp, perhaps because in the natural order of things cusps are more frequent, and they are more frequent because they are relatively simple. The fold has not been especially interesting except perhaps to contrast with other models. It is unclear, however, how many examples of quadratic functions, which are reported every so often in psychology, are really functions of nonlinear dynamical systems that we already know something about.

An example of an empirically tested swallowtail appears in chapter 6, and empirically tested butterflies appear in chapters 5 and 6. Figure 3.4 shows scatterplots of Δz against asymmetry for a butterfly catastrophe study (Guastello, 1987a); they are two-dimensional slices from a five-dimensional surface. The value of R^2 increased from .35 to .47 to .70 as greater trimodality was introduced into the data.

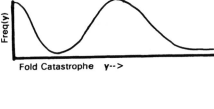

Fold Catastrophe   y-->

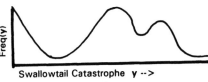

Swallowtail Catastrophe   y -->

FIG. 3.3. Slices from unfolded manifold regions of fold, swallowtail, and butterfly probability density functions.

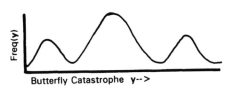

Butterfly Catastrophe   y-->

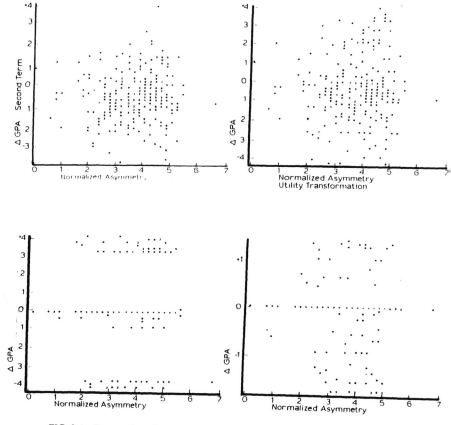

FIG. 3.4. Scatterplots showing increased butterfly trimodality with increasing R^2. From Guastello (1987a). Reprinted with permission.

Umbilic Catastrophe Models

The umbilic catastrophe models contain two dependent variables and thus present a new analytic challenge. The ideas, nonetheless, parallel those already developed. In the case of the wave crest, the two differential functions result in a pair of polynomial difference equations:

$$\Delta u = \beta_0 + \beta_1 u_1^2 + \beta_2 a + \beta_3 cv \tag{29}$$

$$\Delta v = \beta_0 + \beta_1 v_1^2 + \beta_2 b + \beta_3 cu \tag{30}$$

where u and v are dependent measures x and y, respectively, after they have been corrected for location and scale. The control parameters are a, b, and c. The modulus term (constant 3) that appears in the deterministic formula is now absorbed into the empirical weight for the variable associated with it; the same manipulation has been made in the statistical models for the hair and mushroom catastrophes as well. The theoretical presence of the modulus terms suggests that some empirical weights are meant to be three or four times larger for some terms of the statistical umbilic catastrophe models. Not enough is known about the umbilic functions in social science to guarantee that such ratios in weight size would actually be observed. The known empirical cuspoid models that are discussed throughout the book frequently show sharply different weight sizes, and the largest weights are often associated with power polynomials.

There are two choices of procedure for testing an umbilic hypothesis such as a wave crest model. One is to treat the two functions as two separate models, each with its own pair of linear difference control models,

$$\Delta x = \beta_0 + \beta_1 a + \beta_2 c + \beta_3 y \tag{31}$$

$$\Delta y = \beta_0 + \beta_1 b + \beta_3 c + \beta_4 x \tag{32}$$

respectively, and its own pair of linear pre–post control models,

$$x_2 = \beta_0 + \beta_1 x_1 + \beta_2 a + \beta_3 c + \beta_4 y \tag{33}$$

$$y_2 = \beta_0 + \beta_1 y_1 + \beta_2 b + \beta_3 c + \beta_4 x \tag{34}$$

The R^2 coefficients for the various equations can be compared in the usual fashion.

The second option is to add Equations 29 and 30 together to form a canonical regression model where the two partial derivatives can acquire empirical weights and their relative contributions can be assessed:

$$\gamma_1 \Delta u + \gamma_2 \Delta v = \beta_0 + \beta_1 u_1^2 + \beta_2 a + \beta_3 cv + \beta_4 v_1^2 + \beta_5 b + \beta_6 cu \tag{35}$$

where γ_i are empirical canonical weights (Guastello, 1982a, 1987b).

Similarly, the hair catastrophe model can be expressed as a pair of regular polynomial regression functions, or as a canonical model,

$$\gamma_1 \Delta u + \gamma_2 \Delta v = \beta_0 + \beta_1 u_1^2 + \beta_2 v_1^2 + \beta_3 u_1 v_1 + \beta_4 cv + \beta_5 cu + \beta_6 a + \beta_7 b \tag{36}$$

as can the mushroom catastrophe model,

$$\gamma_1 \Delta u + \gamma_2 \Delta v = \beta_0 + \beta_1 v_1^3 + \beta_2 u_1^2 + \beta_3 u_1 v_1 + \beta_4 cu + \beta_5 dv + \beta_6 a + \beta_7 b \tag{37}$$

For any of the umbilic structural models, canonical correlation analysis will produce two weighted functions of Δu and Δv that are optimally correlated with weighted functions of u, v, a, b, c, and sometimes d. Hence two *canonical* r^2 coefficients are produced. In the known uses of the mushroom (chapters 7 and 11), the structure of the model was determined on the basis of comparing the first (and larger) canonical r^2 for the mushroom against the R^2 for a cusp. The well-recognized problem with any canonical correlation analysis is that the weighted functions of predictors and criteria may be highly associated with each other, but at the same time they may have a low direct relationship to the actual underlying measurements. A redundancy analysis would quantify the degree of relationship between the canonical variates and the original variables.

A mushroom catastrophe pdf appears in Fig. 3.5. It was prepared from a study of accident claim statistics (presented in chapter 7) in which the canonical r^2 was .99 for the first canonical variate. Although it was hypothesized that two canonical functions would emerge that contained exactly the same terms as the respective partial derivatives for the mathematical mushroom model, the results showed instead that the whole mushroom model was contained in the first canonical variate. One part of the model was represented by the second canonical variate.

The mushroom pdf has a very interesting shape. Although it appears to be a skewed distribution with a long positive tail, there is actually more detail taking place. The distribution begins with a sharp primary mode, which I refer to as a *blast*. The blast is followed by a *cascade*, a *plateau* showing a secondary mode, an *antimode*, and an *aftershock*. A scatterplot of the same data that appear in the pdf is shown in Fig. 3.5. Mushroom surface contours are overdrawn. The mushroom pdf emerges also in creativity research, which is discussed in chapter 10.

LOGISTIC-TYPE MODELS, CHAOS, AND DIMENSION ANALYSIS

This section covers NDS hypotheses that are not catastrophe models. The catastrophe modeling techniques apply to some of the models encountered here. Dimension analysis for determining the presence of chaos and related models require nonlinear regression analysis. As before, the modeling process begins with a structural hypothesis. A structural statistical model is selected, and its results are compared with those for one or more alternative linear models.

The topics in this section are organized around the continuity that exists between potentially useful chaotic structures and structures already discussed in the preceding section. The first item is the general logistic model,

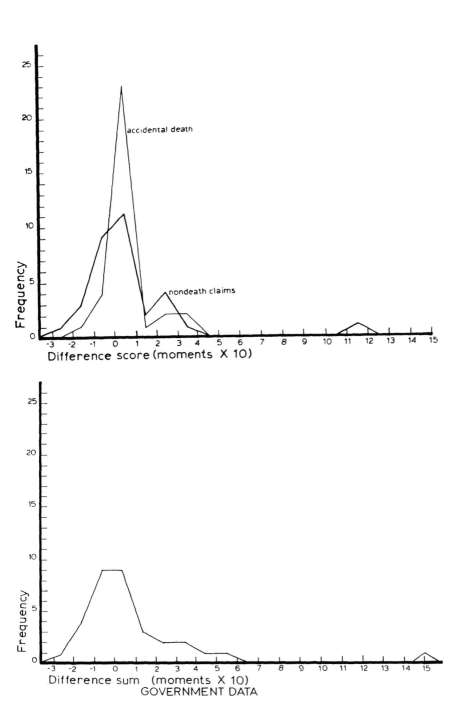

FIG. 3.5. Probability density function for the mushroom catastrophe model.

which has quadratic and polynomial forms. The second item is an exploration of the relationship between the quadratic logistic map, the wave crest catastrophe, and complex lag structures. Complex lag structures are symptomatic of complex coupling of subsystems. If three oscillating subsystems interact (cross-coupling), then a chaotic system result will take place. The relationship that is explored between complex lag functions and the wave crest thus opens an important window to the study of coupled dynamics such as those that occur in self-organized systems.

The exposition next turns to models containing fractional dimensionalities and more complex functions of time, which parallel the simplex logic map structure, but at another level of complexity where nonlinear regression is the central technique for testing hypotheses. The section concludes with a description of how nonlinear regression results can be used to estimate dimension.

Polynomial Models for the Logistic Map

The prototype situation to which the logistic map model would apply is one where trajectories pass through Periods 1, 2, the period doubling, and on into chaos at Period 3. Equation 20 from chapter 2,

$$y_2 = cy(1 - y) = cy^2 - cy$$

which is the deterministic equation for the logistic map, would convert to a polynomial regression equation:

$$z_2 = \beta_0 + \beta_1 c z_1^2 + \beta_2 c z_1 \tag{38}$$

where z is once again a behavioral outcome measure that has been transformed for location and scale, and c is the bifurcation parameter. A variant of Equation 38 would be a difference function of the same level of complexity:

$$\Delta z = \beta_0 + \beta_1 c z_1^2 + \beta_2 c z_1 \tag{39}$$

If period doubling is responsible for a greater level of complexity, then adding a cubic component might be appropriate:

$$z_2 = \beta_0 + \beta_1 c z_1^3 + \beta_2 c z_1^2 + \beta_3 c z_1 \tag{40}$$

In each case, R^2 for the nonlinear structural model is compared with that obtained for the linear difference control model,

$$\Delta y = \beta_0 + \beta_1 c \tag{41}$$

and the linear pre–post model,

$$y_2 = \beta_0 + \beta_1 y_1 + \beta_1 c \tag{42}$$

An application of this polynomial series appears in chapter 10.

Wave Crests and Lag Relationships. At the next level of complexity, the logistic map dynamic contains two behavioral outcomes that occupy different regions above and below the bifurcation pitchfork. The two behavioral outcomes are synchronized by sharing the same bifurcation parameter. The resulting model bears a close resemblance to the wave crest catastrophe function. The relationship is discussed next in terms of the structural statistical models.

The partial functions of u and v in the wave crest would display dynamics similar to that of fold catastrophes, with the nuance that the two functions are synchronized by a common bifurcation parameter, c, which governs the magnitude of the system's instability, or its propensity toward dramatic sudden change from stability to instability. It is of further interest that the interaction term c is associated with the opposite behavior; cv appears in $f(\Delta u)$ and cu appears in $f(\Delta v)$ in Equations 29 and 30. Note further the similarity between the wave crest partial functions and the structure of the logistic map in Equation 39 when z_1^1 is moved from the left side to the right side of the equation:

$$z_2 = \beta_0 + \beta_1 c z_1^2 + \beta_2 c z_1 + \beta_3 z_1 \tag{43}$$

The signs of the components are unimportant for purposes of classifying the complexity of the function. Note that control parameters a and b in the wave crest substitute for u_1 and v_1, respectively. The wave crest is thus a close variation of the logistic map model.

The two functions become more similar when they are viewed as functions of time. Let control parameter a in Equation 29 be substituted by a lag function of u. Also, if u is a coupled dynamic of v, we can *slave* the variable u to v and obtain:

$$u_3 = \beta_0 + \beta_1 u_2^2 + \beta_2 u_2 + \beta_3 u_1 \tag{44}$$

The foregoing represents a thumbnail sketch of the relationship between logic map and bifurcation dynamics, lag relationships, and coupled dynamics. The ramifications have yet to be explored thoroughly. The first steps in that direction appear in the remainder of this chapter and in chapter 10.

Exponential Forms of the Logistic Map

Exponential functions are particularly good for modeling curves that do not have dramatic discontinuities, and nonlinear regression is well suited to estimating exponents statistically. The exponential models that follow have the additional property of capturing a curve with fractional dimensionality, such as the fractal nature of a chaotic attractor. The model is produced by a Laplace transformation of Equation 21 of chapter 2 for the logistic map. Define a function of P as:

$$f(P) = 1/(P - Q) \quad P = cy^2 \quad Q = cy \tag{45}$$

The Laplace transform of $f(P)$ would be

$$L[f(S)] = e^{Qt} = e^{cyt} \tag{46}$$

Because $f(P)$ is actually the reciprocal of Equation 21 of chapter 2 for the logistic map, the logistic function would be transformed in

$$y^2 = e^{-cyt} \tag{47}$$

where t is time, which would vary from 1 to T days. The first day of observation would be noted as y_1. Equation 47 would be the same if $3y^2$ were substituted for cy^2 in Equation 45.

Equation 47 can be expressed in statistical form as

$$z_2 = \theta_1 e^{\theta_2 czt} \tag{48}$$

where θ_1 and θ_2 are parameters to be estimated through nonlinear regression analysis; z is the result of transforming y by location and scale as defined earlier.

Equation 48 allows the time intervals between measurements of behavior to take on varying lengths. The statistical expression can be simplified by keeping the time intervals constant, in which case t drops out of the model. This simplification of the time parameter is retained throughout the remainder of this section of the chapter. Another possible simplification of Equation 48 would be to drop θ_1, thereby reducing the number of empirical regression parameters; this modification is not made in the more complex model that follows.

The model of behavior depicted by Equation 48 is not totally insensitive to initial conditions of z, because, after all, $z_2 = f(z_1)$. On the other hand, a more sensitive model would incorporate a mechanism whereby random shocks to z_2 are carried through the time series, rather than treated as error deviations from the main function. The modification of Equation 48 is accomplished by splitting z into two components, one that remains on the course of the core function and another that is sensitive to random shocks. The result is:

$$z_2 = \theta_1 z_1 e^{\theta_2 c z_1} \tag{49}$$

Equation 49 is essentially the same model that May and Oster (1976) applied to population dynamics and that was later reapplied to workforce population dynamics (Guastello, 1992c). In the population dynamic models (discussed in chapter 9), a variant of Equation 49 was hypothesized to be the end result of a coupled dynamic of two subprocesses. In the May and Oster variation of the model, the bifurcation parameter c was removed from the exponent and absorbed into the empirical estimates of θ_1. This regorganization of terms produced a scale-free index of bifurcation (θ_1), which signifies periods of the logistic map:

$$z_2 = \theta_1 z_1 e^{\theta_2 z_1} + \theta_3 \tag{50}$$

Estimating Dimension

It is possible to specify a statistical calculation of dimension based on the foregoing development of exponential forms of the logistic map. The method is simplified by the assumption that turbulence is held constant throughout the time series. That assumption is convenient, potentially treacherous, and fortunately optional. The goal is to determine dimension D, which is a Lyapunov value:

$$D = \lim_{t \to \infty} \| e^{-at} \|^{1/t} = e^{-a} \tag{51}$$

(Wiggins, 1988, p. 54), where $\| e^{-at} \|$ is normatively evaluated and t is time. Equation 51 can be solved statistically as

$$z_2 = \theta_1 e^{\theta_2 z_1} + \theta_3 \tag{52}$$

In Equation 52, the obtained value of θ_2 is the Lyapunov exponent, which we inspect for its positive or negative direction. The dangling constant

θ_3 represents a correction for location beyond what was already estimated when y was converted to z. Finally,

$$D = e^{\theta_2} \qquad (53)$$

If $D < 1$, trajectory $\|z\|$ converges to a fixed point; a fixed point has a dimension of 0. If $D > 1$, a chaotic process of some type is taking place.

If varying levels of turbulence and fast-acting responsiveness to shock are reintroduced to the system, we calculate Equation 49 for measuring the model's goodness of fit, but drop c to estimate dimension:

$$D = e^{\theta_2} + 1 \qquad (54)$$

The constant 1 is added to make up for one dimension of z that was left outside the exponentiation term in Equation 49 for the bifurcated model. Whether or not c is measured, or known to exist before studying the problem, the analysis of dimensionality provides some information about the complexity of a behavior. Successful identification of the qualitative variables responsible for complex change requires a sound theory base.

The foregoing interpretations of dimension do not generalize to repellor forces or saddle points. In those situations, the direction of flow must be taken into account. Dimension for a saddle point becomes the ratio of two Lyapunov exponents, where one exponent characterizes outflow and the other characterizes inflow. Because applications of saddle dynamics are not well developed in psychological applications, the dimensionality of saddles is not considered further.

Hierarchy of Models and Dimension Estimates

Up to this point, we have identified three simple chaotic models, each of which returns a measure of dimension. The simplest is the unbifurcated model:

$$z_2 = \theta_1 + e^{\theta_2 z_1} \qquad (55)$$

which is simplified further from Equation 52, and for which dimensionality is measured according to Equation 53.

The second simplest model is the bifurcated model with c unknown, which was encountered in Equation 50:

$$z_2 = \theta_1 z_1 e^{\theta_2 z_1} + \theta_3$$

The third in the series is the bifurcated model of Equation 49 where c is a variable that is explicitly tested:

$$z_2 = \theta_1 z_1 e^{\theta_2 cz_1} + \theta_3$$

which is equivalent to

$$z_2 = \theta_1 cz_1 e^{\theta_2 z_1} \tag{56}$$

Dimensionality for Equations 48–50 and 56 is figured using Equation 54.

The fourth model is a case where there are two dependent measures resulting from a pair of partial functions, such as the umbilic catastrophe structures:

$$u_2 + v_2 = \theta_1 + e^{\theta_2 u_1} + e^{\theta_3 v_1} \tag{57}$$

Dimension would be the sum of partial dimension estimates:

$$D = e^{\theta_2} + e^{\theta_3} \tag{58}$$

The fifth case is the lagged function of one dependent variable, such as

$$z_3 = \theta_1 + e^{\theta_2 z_2} + e^{\theta_3 z_1} \tag{59}$$

Equation 59 can be generally stated as:

$$z_T = \theta_1 + e^{\theta_2 z(T-1)} + e^{\theta_3 z(T-2)} + \ldots + e^{\theta(L+1) z(T-L)} \tag{60}$$

In Equation 60, a dependent measure z at time T is a function of several lags of itself, $T-1$, $T-2$, and so forth, and L is total number of lag terms. The dimension of a system structured in this fashion is:

$$D = e^{\theta_2} + e^{\theta_3} + \ldots + e^{\theta(L+1)} - L + 1 \tag{61}$$

The reason for subtracting L and adding 1 in Equation 61 is based on the value of D under conditions of the null hypotheses. For the simplest cases, such as Equation 55, the null hypothesis is that $\theta_2 = 0$, in which case $D = 1$, and the time series has a linear structure. When adding additional terms, θ_i, the null hypothesis is that θ_i makes no additional contribution to the estimate of predicted value of z_i, nor any additional contribution to the estimated value of D. If nonsignificant terms were added, then D would increase even if the null hypothesis were true. Thus it is necessary to remove these lower limits of D, adding back only the first dimension to preserve the condition of linearity under the null hypothesis.

Comparison of Nonlinear Statistical Approaches

Additional work is in progress to determine how the nonlinear regression modeling approach might behave with chaotic attractors of various types, such as the Lorenz, Rossler, and Henon horseshoe attractors. It now appears that other nonlinear regression modeling approaches such as Equation 62 (from Tong, 1990),

$$y_2 = \theta_1 y_1 + \theta_2 \exp(-\theta_3 y_1{}^2) \qquad (62)$$

could provide at least as high R^2 coefficients for Lorenz and Rossler attractors as the series of nonlinear regression models just presented in Equations 48–50, 55–56, and 59–60 (Johnson & Dooley, 1994). The trade-off, however, is that models such as Equation 62 provide no estimate of dimensionality, and fall short on qualitative interpretation of the phenomena under study. The dimension measurement system presented here (Equations 53–54, 58, and 61) provided close estimates of the actual dimensionalities of the Lorenz and Rossler attractors. The Henon horseshoe, however, was more accurately represented as a polynomial of chapter 2, Equations 42–43 type. Further comparative studies should examine the roles of the additional linear term in Equation 62, lag length, and presence of qualitative variables.

DRAWING PHASE PORTRAITS

Priesmeyer (1992) explained some techniques for graphing phase portraits of attractors that may be operating in a system. The general idea for producing a phase portrait proceeds as follows. The first task is to identify variables X and Y (such as one organization's market share for a product vs. a competitor's share) that have more or less inverse cycles over time. The second task is to create a marginal history of each variable which is a series of changes in X and Y (ΔX and ΔY) as they occur over time. The third task is to plot the values of ΔX and ΔY on a two-dimensional grid. Each point will be a pair of ΔX and ΔY values taken at the same point in time. The fourth step is to interpret the plot.

The method of phase portrait construction just described is actually one of three possible methods of construction. It is based on the analogy that $X : Y :: X : (1 - X)$, in which case we have a regular oscillating (sinusoidal) function that is characteristic of a limit cycle. In the two-way plot of

ΔX versus ΔY, the plotted trajectory will zigzag diagonally, vertically, horizontally, or erratically across the quadrants (chaotic behavior) depending on the degree to which X and Y are in phase with each other.

Priesmeyer's (1992) second possibility for an $X : Y$ relationship is where X and Y have an interactive relationship to each other such as in the case of the relationship between price and demand for that product. A third possibility for $X : Y$ is for ΔX for one pair of points in time to be plotted against ΔX for the previous pair of points in time. When this method should be used and how it may deliver different conclusions from what would have been the case in the $X : (1 - X)$ condition was not explained. The mathematical convention, however, is to draw a phase portrait by plotting ΔX as a function of X. Plots of ΔX at two lagged intervals are also used when higher dimensional functions are suspected. Examples appear in chapters 9 and 11.

Finally, a cute phase portrait does not prove the existence of chaos. The more erratic portraits may not distinguishable from meaningless noise, particularly if they are based on a very small number of data points.

THREE PARADOXES OF PSYCHOMETRIC THEORY

This chapter would not be complete without playing a few rounds of "What's wrong with this picture?" Actually, the picture of NDS and its statistical methods looks just fine, but there are three portraits in the attic where the faces grow freakish every day. Those portraits are the concepts of regression to the mean, measurement reliability, and the generalizability of a test validity coefficient over time. All three ideas have been familiar to psychologists and measurement theorists for most of the last century.

Regression to the Mean

There are two phenomena that are classically known as regression to the mean. The first is the observation that if two scores X and Y are correlated, the predicted score on Y is always less extreme than the score on X. That is because the predicted value of the standard score of Y, z_Y', is equal to $r z_X$, where r is the correlation between X and Y. Because $|r|$ *is almost universally less than 1.00*, $|z_Y'| < |z_X|$. It is this example of regression to the mean that gave the regression technique its name.

The second phenomenon that is also known as regression to the mean occurs in situations where people in a group are measured on the same test twice, or two related tests, after an interval of time. In an often-cited textbook example, a class full of students takes two subject-matter tests and the teacher correlates the two sets of scores. If the correlation is positive, the teacher concludes that the same people who did well the first time did well later on, and the rest of the class retained its relative rank ordering of students; no one complains about this interpretation.

On the other hand, if a negative correlation between the two tests is found, then the teacher is tempted to conclude that the better students didn't study as hard the second time, so their scores dropped, and those that did not do well the first time finally caught on. "Oh no," say the statisticians, "you can't conclude that about the students' performance; all you have is *regression to the mean!*" As a professor myself, I have seen slacking off and failure avoidance firsthand, and corroborated the same through discussions with the students. The statisticians, however, defined the interpretation of the correlation so that rank ordering could be preserved, but slacking and failure avoidance would never occur, and classical statisticians make no suggestion about what a correlation between two scores should look like if they did occur.

The problem, as I see it, is that the two examples of regression to the mean, discussed back-to-back in many textbooks, are two completely different phenomena. In the first example, the less extreme nature of predicted scores is a result of the mathematics, purely and simply; that is real regression to the mean. The second example has nothing to do with the mathematics and everything to do with the behavior of the people being measured. NDS would reinterpret the class performance example as *gravitation toward an attractor*. Furthermore, in a complex system with a bifurcation taking place, it should be possible to observe some dispersion away from an attractor, to another attractor basin, under certain conditions.

Reliability of Measurement

The prototype conceptual definition of test score reliability runs as follows: "If I can measure your X today, erase all memory of test testing experience, and measure your X tomorrow, reliability is the degree to which I am likely to obtain the same score." The absurdity of memory erasure is obvious. The task of getting 100 people together to take the same test twice at a short time interval, particularly when they have no reason to take the test again, is also formidable if anyone has ever tried to do that outside the classroom setting. Indeed, the better part of psychometric theory has been devoted to finessing the limitations of the classical definition. Or so it would appear.

The currently standard true score theory of mental measurements runs as follows: A test score (X) is composed of two elements, true score (T) plus error (ε). Errors have means of 0.0 and standard deviation σ_ε. Errors are uncorrelated with true scores of the same test, uncorrelated with true scores of other tests, uncorrelated with other errors on the same test, and uncorrelated with measurement errors from any other source. Reliability is the ratio of true score variance to total score variance (Lord & Novick, 1968). Because of the uncorrelatedness of errors with everything else, reliability is necessary but not sufficient for validity. Validity here is taken to mean the correlation of a test score with some behavior or other measure that the test in theory was meant to be correlated with in the first place; an expansion on this concept occurs in chapter 5.

So how is reliability calculated? The *test–retest* reliability method, of course, where the examinees are given the test twice at some time interval—anywhere from 2 days to 2 years—and the correlation between the two sets of scores is the reliability coefficient. Reliability coefficients range from 0.00 to 1.00; there are no negative values. What! Regression to the mean never happens? Without actually addressing that question, psychometric theory has danced around the test–retest method since 1910: The parade of methods included *split-half* reliability, by which the test was split into two parts, the scores on the two parts were correlated, and a formula was applied to the correlation to retrieve a reliability coefficient that would be based on the total number of test questions; the *odd–even* variant of split-half, whereby odd-numbered questions were correlated with even-numbered questions to prevent fatigue from the beginning to the end of the testing session; the *parallel form reliability*, whereby the examinees took two versions of the same test, the scores on which were correlated, and the correlation was repaired to emulate test–retest on the same test; and so on until the *Kuder-Richardson Formula 20* (KR-20), which was the generalization (average) of all split-half pairs. That brings us up to 1939 (Lord & Novick, 1968).

The next landmark innovation in reliability theory was Cronbach's (1951) alpha reliability coefficient. Alpha was based on the principle that test questions should all be well correlated with the total test score. The reliability concept departed from temporal stability in favor of *internal consistency*, or *test homogeneity*, which is the extent to which all test questions are drawn from the same universe of items. Because the alpha formula was the same as KR-20, it too was interpreted as a substitute for test–retest reliability. Novick and Lewis (1967) showed that alpha was more correctly the lower limit of test–retest reliability, but test developers and most other researchers who needed a reliability coefficient continued to interpret alpha as a substitute for test–retest reliability (Cortina, 1993).

The principal concepts of reliability continue to revolve around temporal stability. Now what if the *construct* that was being measured really did change over a short period of time? In other words, what if the person really changed? Reliability theory would ignore that possibility by saying that the test score was unreliable, meaning that the test was loaded with error variance. People could not possibly change, right? Suppose a dramatic social event took place that changed respondents' responses on a measure, such as an attitude, and the effect on the respondents was complex: Did change occur? Reliability theory might say that real events do not count, and then raise a question about regression to the mean.

Against the backdrop of a fractured theory of reliability came the proof about the inherent unreliability of difference scores that is of direct concern to NDS. When two tests are uncorrelated, the variance of the sum of the two measures is the same as the variance of the differences between the two measures. When the two measures are positively correlated, however, adding the two tests together increases the reliability, but difference scores decrease in reliability. What essentially happens with difference scores is that the true scores are subtracted from each other and the error scores are added together, thus lowering the ratio of true score variance to total score variance (Lord & Novick, 1968).

The supposed inherent unreliability of difference scores forms the basis of long-standing admonitions against using difference scores in research. According to Labouvie (1980), the doctrine of uncorrelated error is not always true. The theme of dependent error was discussed earlier. Indeed much of what was regarded as psychometric error appears to be dependent error, and dependent error is actually a function of a dynamical process, and thus should no longer be regarded as error. Rather, it is important variance that can now be accounted for by the nonlinear components in NDS structural models. When in doubt, however, behavioral measures should be as objective and reliable (in the true sense) as possible, so that a little piling of error variance does not amount to any trouble.

Stability of Validity Coefficients

The last saga of this trilogy is an example of, "If it ain't broke, don't fix it." For eons since the first dawn, industrial psychologists advised that if a mental measurement showed a significant correlation with work performance in one situation, there was no guarantee that the same test would work as well in another situation; similarities of job descriptions could not be relied on (there's that word again) to prove job comparability. Furthermore, validity coefficients should be rechecked every so often to determine if the test is still valid in a particular setting.

By the early 1980s, the validity generalization theory changed the philosophy by showing that, for a large number of studies involving the same class of tests (e.g., all measuring mechanical ability) and the same type of work (e.g., all operating complex machinery), up to 90% of the variability in correlation coefficients and their tests of significance could be accounted for by artifacts such as differences in reliability among the different tests used, differences in reliability in measures of work performance, restriction of range on the predictors, restriction of range on the criteria, differences in sample size, subtleties in the internal composition of the tests, and keypunch errors in the data sets (Schmidt, 1992). The wave of research that ensued sought to identify a population validity coefficient that was widely generalizable over closely related tests and jobs, and corrected (always in the upward direction) for the forms of error just mentioned.

Because the wide array of validity coefficients contributing to a generalized value inevitably covered many years, the question arose regarding the old axiom about the temporal stability of validity coefficients, and a brief controversy ensued. Barrett et al. (1985) collected all the validity studies published in the *Journal of Applied Psychology* and *Personnel Psychology* since those journals were first published. After eliminating all the studies in which the researchers had made a deliberate attempt to change something in the work environment, there remained approximately 50 studies where a validity coefficient was tested at two points in time. Barrett et al. then compared the pairs of coefficients, and reported that significant changes in validity occurred only in 8% of the situations; the latter, they concluded, had to be the result of some sort of unreliability in the validity process.

The reply from Austin et al. (1989) cited several important flaws in the review. The statistic that was used to compare pairs of coefficients was known to be too stringent. Under those conditions, the surviving 8% of differences in coefficients was too large to be dusted away as unreliability. Also, the review missed some important work by Rambo et al. (1983) concerning the temporal dynamics of work (which is covered in chapter 5).

The reply to the reply (Barrett & Alexander, 1989) did not change anything. Instead, there began a major organized effort to study dynamic performance criteria (Hofmann et al., 1993). Beneath the more obvious concern for validity coefficients was a further theoretical concern, as expressed by the debate participants, as to whether work performance can possibly change over time when management is not taking a deliberate action to change the work behavior. To date, the debate participants have not said "boo" about NDS or its implications for work performance, although quadratic functions are starting to poke their noses into the light (Hofmann et al., 1993; Rambo et al., 1983).

SUMMARY

This chapter began with the premise that a cogent metaphor between a principle of NDS, or one of its known applications, and a new application in the social sciences constitutes a firm beginning for the development of a new theory. Metaphor is not proof, however, and social science applications are not immune from that burden. Proof has not come easily, as it did appear, once upon a time, that NDS concepts defied statistical methods that social scientists have relied on to test their theories.

It was argued, however, that if NDS is as powerful a paradigm as it was alleged to be, than it would have a strong impact on statistical theory as well. Three sections of this chapter catalog the progress in hypothesis testing for NDS models. The result is a set of theory-driven structural models that cover all the categories of hypothesis that social theorists appear to require. The structural models are rooted in a theory of complex probability density functions, and fall into several broad classes: polynomial regression for cuspoid catastrophes, canonical polynomial regression models for separating partial differential functions associated with the umbilic catastrophes, polynomial regression for functions of the logistic map, nonlinear regression models for logistic map functions and estimating fractional dimensionality, and variants of these for analyzing coupled dynamics. Techniques for coupled dynamics are on the vanguard of development at the present time. A further section explained some useful techniques for displaying phase portraits of chaotic and some less complex data once the appropriate models have been verified.

The final section returned to the counterpoint between NDS and statistical theory, this time with specific concern for error functions in mental measurements. Three long-standing paradoxes were uncovered that NDS appears to resolve. First, not all phenomena thought to reflect regression to the mean actually do so. Many are really gravitation toward attractors, and the analysis and interpretation of pertinent data needs an NDS overhaul.

Second, reliability in measurement has been, for nearly a century, closely equated with freedom from temporal change, an assumption that flagrantly ignores the possibility that people and their psychological properties often do change in the short-term or long-term time horizon. NDS has contributed here by showing that not all errors are created equal, and that some of them are epiphenomena of dynamical processes and not error.

Third, there is the debate as to whether work performance can change over time without deliberate action from management, which is pertinent to another claim that the relationship between a human attribute and work performance does not change over time. Although a true dynamicist might regard the debate as something less interesting than whether water is wet, those who have taken it seriously have unearthed some findings that lie on the edge of being recognized as chaos. Those discoveries and many more are embedded in the chapters ahead.

4

NDS, Human Decision Making,
and Cognitive Processes

This chapter considers the application of NDS principles to a broad spectrum of theories in cognitive psychology. The exposition begins with psychophysics, which is the relationship between the strengths of physical stimuli and the psychological perception thereof. Classical theories of how people perceive patterns of stimuli and integrate them into patterns of what they actually see and hear follow. The conventional experimental paradigm has been based largely on reaction time, or the time delay between the presentation of a stimulus or pattern and either the recognition of the pattern or the making of a decision related to the content of those patterns. Reaction time itself is subject to many influences, and reaction-time studies are particularly germane to human factors engineering where information flows between people and their machines. Somewhere between stimulus and response is another world of information processing and learning; the key ideas from pre-NDS psychology are thus presented subsequently to reaction time.

The first section presents the pre-NDS theories in encapsuled form. The goal is to capture the major movements in thinking for purposes of moving onward, rather than to write a compact introductory psychology textbook. The next four sections discuss the NDS applications to those key theory groups that seemed to be lying dormant for a long time. Psychophysics and learning are given proportionately more attention in light of the amount of work that has been done in those areas, and because of their relevance to the applications the follow in the subsequent chapters.

The final section draws on everything that preceded it under the heading of decision making. The concept is introduced of a chaotic controller, which organizes and explains what is really thought to be taking place when people make decisions in a dynamic environment. The ideas of this section are developed in further chapters, particularly when game theory is introduced in chapter 9.

SOME CONVENTIONAL BUT CENTRAL THEORIES OF COGNITIVE PSYCHOLOGY

Psychophysics

Psychophysics is the relationship between physical stimuli and the human perception of those stimuli. For instance, how bright does a light appear to be, or how loud is a loud noise? There are two important movements in pre-NDS psychophysics: the classical model that dates from the middle 1800s, and signal detection theory, which coalesced in the early 1950s.

Classical Model. The classical approach begins with two definitions. The *absolute threshold* of a stimulus is the minimum value of a stimulus intensity by which it can be detected. A *difference threshold* is the minimum change in stimulus intensity that can be detected. Minimum change is also known as a "just noticeable difference" or JND.

In the classical paradigm, the absolute threshold for detecting a sound (loudness) would be determined in a simple experiments. Human subjects would be presented with sounds of increasing loudness. When the subject first indicates that a sound is present, an estimate of the absolute threshold is obtained. Next, the subject is presented with sounds of decreasing loudness. When the subject first indicates that the sound has disappeared, then the second estimate of the absolute threshold is obtained. Typically, the two estimates differ such that the first estimate is physically louder than the second; thus the average of the two estimates is taken as the real value (Fig. 4.1).

Difference thresholds in the classical paradigm were obtained in a similar fashion, except that subjects would be presented with a standard stimulus and a second stimulus. The minimum value of the second stimulus that produces a response from the subject saying that the two stimuli are different is taken as the JND.

Classical psychophysics produced two important laws. According to Weber's law, the ratio of the change in intensity to initial intensity is a constant,

$$\Delta I / I = C \quad \text{or} \quad \Delta I = CI \tag{1}$$

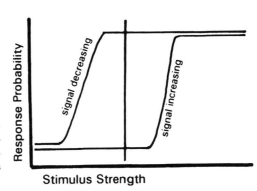

FIG. 4.1. The relationship between signal strength, response criterion, and the absolute threshold in the classical psychophysics paradigm.

or, alternatively, that change in perceived intensity is proportional to the initial intensity, where ΔI is the JND, and I is initial intensity. C is constant for all values of a particular type of stimulus, such as loudness of a tone, brightness of a conventional light bulb, and so forth.

According to Fechner's law, psychological signal strength is a logarithmic function of physical signal strength:

$$\Psi_s = k \log(\Phi_s) \qquad (2)$$

where Ψ_s is the psychological magnitude, k is a constant, and Φ_s is physical magnitude. Once again, k is specific to the type of stimulus (D'Amato, 1973). The Weber–Fechner laws lose accuracy for extreme values of I. Nonetheless, they are often used with success for mid-range stimulus values in one dimension. The classical model breaks down considerably when multidimensional stimuli are involved, such as in the perception of small color differences (Wandell, 1982).

Signal Detection Theory. Signal detection theory (Stevens, 1951) was developed to address several sources of artifact in the classical psychophysics experiments. Specifically, subjects in signal detection experiments make judgments based not only on the nature of the stimuli themselves, but also on the basis of the sensitivity of their sensory apparatus, motivation to respond in the experiment (gains and penalties associated with certain responses), and knowledge of the likelihood that a certain stimulus will appear. All of these affect discriminative behavior, and thus subjects' threshold to respond to a stimulus. Signal detection theory separates those influences.

Signal detection theory introduced three fundamental new concepts that distinguished it from the classical paradigm. The first major change from classical psychophysics was to redefine the threshold. Instead of an absolute definition of the absolute and difference thresholds, there is a relativistic definition. *Absolute threshold* in signal detection theory is defined as the point where 50% of the subjects perceive the stimulus. The *difference threshold* is similarly redefined as the point where 50% of the subjects detect a difference. The frequency distribution of the number of people detecting a stimulus value as the threshold is thought to be normal (or Gaussian; Fig. 4.2.).

The second major change was to redefine the task of perceiving a signal: We do not detect simply a signal, we detect a *signal relative to noise*. Figure 4.2 shows two normal density functions on an axis defined by signal strength. The left distribution represents the absolute threshold for perceiving a standard noise, and the distribution on the right is the total strength of a target signal embedded in the noise. The difference in means is known as the discrimination index, or *d'*. With increasing signal strength, *d'* increases. When signal strength is held constant, *d'* represents the keenness of one's sensory apparatus.

The third major change was in the presentation of stimuli to a subject during a signal detection experiment. Instead of presenting stimuli in a fixed, graduated sequence, stimuli were presented randomly with respect to the distinguishing physical feature of the stimulus (e.g., stimuli were randomized with respect to loudness). It was found that the double-threshold effect was the result of a response set on the part of the subject, and the double-threshold effect disappeared when the stimuli were presented in random order.

A response set, more generally stated, is a habit of responding that the subject acquired within an experiment. Such a habit is explicable as a learned response and an artifact of the experimental process, and is

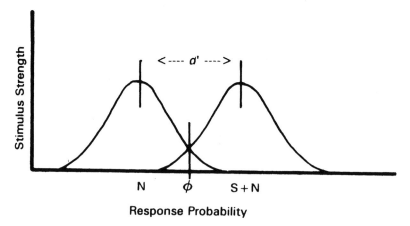

FIG. 4.2. The relationship between signal strength, response criterion, and the absolute threshold of a signal detected relative to noise in signal detection theory.

TABLE 4.1
2 × 2 Contingency Table of Psychophysical Judgments and Error Types

	Responses	
Stimuli	*Signal + Noise*	*Noise Only*
S + N	"Hit" $P(S \mid S+N) =$ $\dfrac{\text{(number of hits)}}{\text{(number of S+N trials)}}$	"False rejection" $P(N \mid S+N) =$ $\dfrac{\text{(number of false rejections)}}{\text{(number of S+N trials)}}$
N	"False alarm" $P(S \mid N) =$ $\dfrac{\text{(number of false alarms)}}{\text{(number of N trials)}}$	"Correct rejection" $P(N \mid N) =$ $\dfrac{\text{(number of correct rejections)}}{\text{(number of N trials)}}$

thus not a part of a real relationship between physical events and human processing thereof. (Or so it would appear: NDS interprets the double threshold as *hysteresis*.)

Having defined signal detection as a statistical phenomenon, it was possible to express the results of a signal detection experiment in the form of a 2 × 2 contingency table. Table 4.1 expresses the probabilities of a subject, or a group of subjects, giving the right and wrong answers. The 2 × 2 contingency table forms the basis of several types of statistical tests that draw inferences about the overall percentage of right–wrong judgments. The table also forms the basis of decision theory where the decisions in question are far more complex than determining presence or absence of a tonal signal.

The *likelihood ratio* is defined as the ratio of the probability of a hit to the probability of a false alarm. The likelihood ratio is optimal at a point where the two normal curves cross (ϕ, Fig. 4.2). The point of optimal likelihood is the point of optimal signal detection. Points such as ϕ occur in game theory (chapter 9), where they are known as saddle points.

Probabilities, as defined in Table 4.1, take into account subjects' response behavior under conditions where the noise and signal-plus-noise are equally likely. If the experiment were devised such that there was a 90% chance of a signal being present, a subject might be inclined to respond as if there were a signal on every trial, thereby obtaining a total accuracy of 90%; errors would be biased toward false alarms.

Subjects would respond differently, however, when there were different payoffs attached to each type of response. For example, if a miner were panning for gold, a correct hit could be valuable, but a false alarm error would have a trivial impact. In medical decision making, however, a rejection of a disease diagnosis without confirmatory testing could be very costly, and thus it would be better to err on the side of overly sensitive testing, using follow-up tests to confirm the diagnosis and so on.

A *receiver operating characteristic curve* is a plot of the proportion of correct hits to false alarms for all subjects in an experiment (Fig. 4.3). The data points configure as a set of arc, where each arc represents a value of d'. Thus subjects of a given discrimination ability would respond anywhere along their arc. Position along the arc is the result of a response set. The points falling in the lower left of the arc would denote subjects who tend not to respond, and who accumulate many false rejections and correct rejections. The points falling in the upper right would denote subjects who have a low threshold to response to any stimulus, and would accumulate a large number of correct hits and false alarms.

Finally, the Stevens power law describes the relationship between the strength of a physical signal and the psychological perception thereof:

$$\Psi_s = k \, (\Phi_s - \Phi_0)^C \tag{3}$$

where Ψ_s is the psychological rating of signal strength; k is a constant for the idiosyncrasies of the experiment, such as procedural errors that often appear minor or trivial or a particular payoff function; Φ_s is physical signal strength as before; Φ_0 is the absolute threshold value of Φ for each human subject; and C is the characteristic exponent for each type of stimulus. Examples of C include loudness of a sound, 0.6; brightness of a light, 0.33; smell of coffee, 0.55; and electric shock, 60 Hz through the fingers, 3.5 (Stevens, 1951).

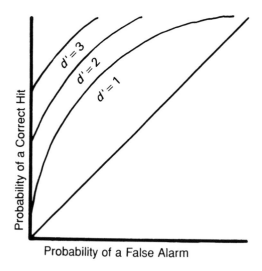

FIG. 4.3. Receiver operating characteristic curve.

The power law seems to hold for every type of signal detection except the detection of vibration, which seems to require a more complex function. Situations requiring multidimensional inputs and outputs also require more complex treatments. A few signal detection experiments related to telephone communications have crossed into the domain of the situations addressed by NDS. Auditory experiments involving two sinusoidal pulses as inputs, for instance, show that absolute thresholds for the underlying stimuli do not change under those stimulus delivery conditions (Green et al., 1988).

Psychomotor Skill

The first studies of psychomotor skill had to do with *reaction time* (RT, or response time). Reaction time is the real-time delay between the presence of a stimulus and the subject's response to it. In the early days of psychology, RT was thought to be a function of the complexity of a cognitive process. The cognitive process would include both physical time to make a control action, and mental work time. The longer the RT, the more complex the process.

Cattell (1886) found that it takes twice as long to recognize and name a color, given a patch of color as a stimulus, than to recognize and name a word representing the name of a color. Stroop (1935) found that it took even longer to recognize and name a color when the stimulus was a word written in colored ink and the response was the name of the color in which the word was printed. The phenomenon was explained as a form of interference caused by the simultaneous activation of (at least) two mental processes that were processing conflicting information.

The first studies of RT pertinent here were conducted in the 1850s by Donders (Kantowitz & Sorkin, 1983). Donders developed a general method for establishing RT by dividing it into two components: *stimulus identification time* and *response selection time*. In the prototype experiment, RT was measured under three conditions. In Condition A, subjects were presented with one target stimulus and were required to make one response when that stimulus was present. In Condition B, subjects were presented with two or more stimuli and were required to make any of two or more responses, where respondents must choose a reaction suitable to a particular stimulus. In Condition C, subjects were presented with several types of stimulus, but only one stimulus mapped onto a response. The difference in RT(C − A) was thus the identification time. The difference in RT(B − C) was the response selection time.

Determinants of RT. Reaction time increases with the amount of information needing processing. The relationship between RT and amount of information is linear when the information is composed of digits. The relationship is logarithmic if other types of information are used (Kantowitz & Sorkin, 1983).

There are many other known determinants of RT, including physical characteristic of stimulus, such as size, shape, and color; type of response, such as the use of a switch, lever, knob, wheel, voice; stimulus–response compatibility; and amount of practice. Stimulus–response compatibility issues fall largely into two categories. Population stereotypes are ways in which people believe a machine control should operate in order to obtain a desired response. For instance, screws are turned clockwise to screw in or tighten, but counterclockwise to loosen. Airline pilots who perceive they are going to crash head-on with another plane should turn right to avoid collision, according to a rule of maritime law dating from the mid-1700s. Unfortunately, a simulator study once showed that 25% of pilots turned left instead of right (Berringer, 1978).

The second aspect of stimulus-response compatibility pertains to the consistency between the control and display designs. For instance, if an operator desires to change the system so that the pointer on a display will move to the right, the knob controlling the system should be turned to the right as well. Reaction time is fastest when the stimulus and response are compatible. Reaction time is slower when the stimulus and response are opposite each other, but not as slow as when the stimulus and responses are arbitrarily connected.

Practice improves RT according to the function

$$RT = k \log_{10}(NT) + c \tag{4}$$

where NT is number of trials in a practice session and c is a constant. The resulting function is an inverse learning curve that gravitates to an asymptotic minimum. In contemporary applications to human–computer interaction, the response time related to psychomotor skill is separated from mental response time:

$$RT = nku^{-a} + c^f(mu^{-b}) \tag{5}$$

where n is the number of keystrokes, k is the time per keystroke, u is the number of units of practice, a is an exponent of speed-up for the physical process, f is the coefficient of time decrease associated with a particular combination of mental operations, c is the number of such repeated operations (McKendree & Anderson, 1987).

The c^f function in Equation 5 represents *consolidation* of knowledge, or the *automatization* of a mental process. Consolidation or automatization was first reported by Bryan and Harter (1897, 1899) in studies of telegraph operators. Bryan and Harter offered two basic conclusions. First, sending information is faster than receiving information. When receiving, a skilled operator can hold a whole sentence in short-term memory while transcribing the previous sentence. Second, transmission time improved with training; plateau functions or successive learning curves were obtained when letters, then words, then phrases, then sentences become the cognitive units of analysis.

Although faster RT is a desirable system engineering criterion, accuracy is another! Human operators can gain control over their mistakes by working at a slower speed. Figure 4.4 shows a typical speed–accuracy trade-off function, where optimal speed is located at the upper bend in the curve.

Learning

Several implications of learning theory were discussed already, and it was convenient to assume common knowledge of what was meant by learning. This section summarizes some of the key movements in learning that are germane to what follows in this and subsequent chapters. The basic principles of learning are applicable to both humans and other animals. Some processes, such as social learning, only appear to apply to humans and primates.

Stimulus–Response Bonds. The first comprehensive approach to learning is attributed to Thorndike (1911), who conceptualized learning as a process in which stimuli were associated with responses to form an S–R bond. The S–R bond was strengthened by reinforcement, which, loosely speaking, is reward and punishment. Not so loosely, positive reinforcers such as food strengthen S–R associations, whereas negative reinforcements can be used to break an S–R bond by selectively applying, for instance, electric shock when the animal does a naughty deed. Alternatively, nega-

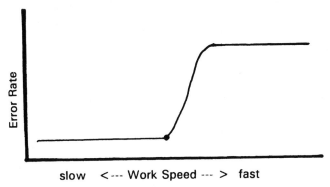

FIG. 4.4. The speed–accuracy trade-off.

tive reinforcement can be applied until the animal makes the "correct" response, at which time the noxious stimulus is removed.

Thorndike also introduced the learning curve, which is a plot of the amount of learning as a function of reinforced trials. Examples of learning curves appear in Fig. 4.5, where the shape of the curve is expressed as the asymptotic function:

$$P_2 = k(M - P_1) + P_1 \qquad (6)$$

where P_2 is performance on a subsequent trial, M is maximum performance on the task, P_1 is performance on a previous trial, and k represents the inflection of the curve (Deese & Hulse, 1967).

Extinction is a process of unlearning, during which reinforcement is not given. Lack of reinforcement weakens the S–R bond such that the behavior disappears. The effectiveness of extinction can be deceiving, because spontaneous recovery is often observed in the absence of rewards. Extinction curves are roughly the inverse of learning curves, and can be modeled by a logarithmic function such as Equation 4.

Conditioned Reflexes. Pavlov (1927) and his dog are responsible for the *classical conditioning* or *conditioned reflex* model of learning, which was strongly influenced by physiological processes. Learning began with a natural reflex (*unconditional response*) behavior, such as drooling, which the organism (dog) makes in response to a stimulus (*unconditional stimulus*),

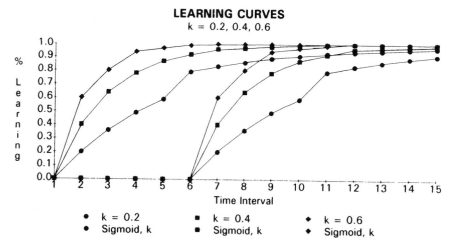

FIG. 4.5. Learning curves. Three examples were generated with Equation 6 for different values of k. Three examples (shifted right) are sigmoid extensions of same curves and reflect stability before the onset of a learning process.

such as raw meat. The experimenter then intervenes by ringing a bell (*conditioned stimulus*) a second or two before presenting the dog with the meat. When drooling has occurred, the dog is allowed to eat the meat (*reinforcement*). After several trials, the experimenter only has to ring the bell in order to induce the dog to drool. The drooling now becomes a *conditioned response* to the bell.

The dog will continue to drool when he hears the bell so long as a reinforcement follows his response. Extinction sets in after too many trials without reinforcement.

Operant Conditioning. Skinner (1938) observed that not all learning occurs in a conditioned reflex situation. The operant conditioning model began with a rat being allowed to wander freely in its cage. Interesting random behaviors of the rat (operants), such as pressing a level located in the cage, would be selectively reinforced. The effect of reinforcement was to strengthen the operant; no concept of S–R bond or reflex needed to be assumed. This general model led to voluminous studies on schedules of reinforcement, generalization and discrimination, skill acquisition, and complex forms of human learning where information concerning one's behavioral progress (*feedback*) served as a reinforcer. Complex human and animal behaviors could be conditioned through *shaping*, where a primitive form of the desired behavior was reinforced, then reinforcement was withheld until the next most complex version of the behavior was emitted, and so on until the desired outcome was attained.

Programmatic applications of operant conditioning principles to human behavior patterns became known as behavior modification, which in turn gave rise to some useful therapies for "behavior problems," and a fictional utopic community called Walden Two (Skinner, 1948), which dramatized the pervasiveness of behaviorist principles in society at large. The atheoretical stance was extreme. There were no cognitive structures, nor any special learning rules germane to humans. Concepts such as freedom or dignity were illusions because all behaviors were the result of shaping from societal forces that give out reinforcers (Skinner, 1971).

The rejoinder to the freedom and dignity argument is that much of human learning is the result of self-directed behaviors. People often learn and accomplish things quite without the reinforcing interference of other people (Geiser, 1976). This theme dominates several contrary views of learning and motivation which are discussed next.

Cognitive Maps. Tolman (1932) hypothesized that learning physical spaces involves more than strengthening operants. Rather, the rat knows where the cheese is. The method of study involved running rats in a radial maze. The cheese would be located at the end of the same branch of the maze each trial, but the rat would be allowed to enter the maze from a different branch on each trial. If reinforcement only strengthened the pattern of left turns or right turns, the rat would always make the same turns, but would attain the cheese on only a chance number of occasions. Instead, the rat appeared to respond to the different entry points and reached the cheese on a far greater number of occasions. The conclusion was that the rat gained a *cognitive map* of the maze during the learning set.

Further experiments showed that the rat was capable of responding to the probability that the cheese would be located in one or another branch of the maze. The principle of learning probabilities contributed to statistical learning theory, considered later in this section, and the expectancy theory of motivation, which is considered in Chapter 5.

Motivation and Learning. Hull (1943) noticed that food reinforcers worked better on hungry rats than they did on rats who had just finished a meal. Similar effects were found for water as a reinforcers to a thirsty or nonthirsty rat. Hull's work thus centered around the role of motivation in learning as an explanation for why reinforcement should work. Motivation was conceptualized as a *drive* that had a *force* and a *direction* in the sense that a vector has a length and a direction. Force would be expressed in terms of hours of food deprivation. Direction would be the substance of the motivation, such as food or water. Behavior, therefore, served the purpose of *drive reduction.*

Primary reinforcers were those associated with biological drives such as food or water. *Secondary reinforcers* were those that were conditioned to a biological drive. The secondary reinforcement concept explained why people do things for nonbiological reinforcers such as money, fame, or attention. One of the more important ideas to emerge from this line of work was that motivation affects learning, and learning affects motivation. The linkage between motivation and learning is explored further in Chapter 5.

Statistical Learning Theory. Estes (1950) built on the work of Skinner and Tolman to answer the question of whether learning was an all-or-none phenomenon, or whether partial learning can occur. The first clue that partial learning could occur might be drawn from the shape of the learning curve itself; the inflection is not completely vertical. Another clue comes from the rat knowing the odds of where the cheese is located, and the expectancy concept. A third clue came from the transfer of training research by Osgood (1949), which showed that learning will transfer from one situation to another to the extent that the stimuli are the same, the behaviors being reinforced as the same, and the reinforcement rules are the same between the two situations.

Statistical learning theory explained that learning was the result of bits of information about the behavior, setting, and desired response. With each reinforcement, more bits are acquired until the entire array of stimulus, setting, and behavior are learned. Furthermore, when reinforcement is variable or intermittent, animals and people learn the probabilities with which events occur and behave accordingly.

Social Learning Theory. Bandura (1977) showed that a substantial amount of primate behavior could not be explained simply in terms of Pavlovian or operant conditioning. There were three additional mechanisms involved. Primates learn through vicarious reinforcement. When a monkey sees another being reinforced, positively or negatively, for a given behavior, the voyeur monkey changes behavior without having experienced the reinforcer directly.

The second mechanism is imitation. A monkey will copy the behavior of another monkey without having seen the target monkey receiving any sort of reinforcer; in other words, "monkey see, monkey do." Imitation occurs naturally in human infants, and is thought to be a key feature of learning and cognitive development (Piaget, 1952). The imitation mechanism gave rise to the hypothesis, which is not conclusively established, that children learn violent behavior by watching it on television. Some role models are more influential than others (Bandura, 1977).

Once a behavior has been learned, the primate carries out the behavior without the presence of a reinforcing party. Thus the contingencies of reinforcement are said to be internalized, which is the third mechanism of social learning theory. The internalization principle was once thought to contradict cognitive developmental models of moral development, which have stability and instability themes, but has not been successful in doing so. Developmental schemes are considered briefly in Chapter 12.

NDS AND PSYCHOPHYSICS

The first attempt to apply NDS to psychophysical phenomena began with the habituation response set encountered in classical psychophysics and presumably corrected in signal detection theory. Yelen (1980) hypothesized that the double-threshold hysteresis effect would result from an underlying cusp manifold. He presented subjects with two lights, of which one was a standard and the other displayed variable intensity. There were two such standards used in the experiment, one brighter than the other. The subjects' task was to view the pair of lights and determine whether the test light was brighter than the standard. Stimuli were presented in ascending and descending order of test bulb brightness. The dependent measure was the number of responses given by the subjects that the test bulb was brighter than the standard.

Yelen found the hysteresis effect for the bright standard but not for the dim standard. Thus the cusp manifold was concluded to underlie the habituation response set such that data for the bright standard occupied the unfolded rim of the cusp surface, and data for the dim standard occupied a ribbon behind the cusp point. The brightness of the variable bulb, measured in volts, functioned as the asymmetry variable.

Ayres (1981) argued that it might be more psychologically appropriate to calibrate the test bulb in terms of $\Delta I/I$, expressed in percent of the standard. Using that transformation he reanalyzed the published data points and observed that the hysteresis effect was present for both the dim and bright standard conditions. He concluded that his results refuted the cusp interpretation.

In spite of the rocky start, there is now a fairly comprehensive theory of psychophysics built on NDS theory. Gregson (1988) began with the limitation of preexisting theory to handle multidimensional inputs and outputs. He further noted that olfactory stimuli, which are generally regarded as multidimensional, have a two-stage decay in effectiveness that is well known but not incorporated in standard theory. The gamma recursive function was developed, therefore, to provide such an expandable model of psychophysical processes that is based on the logistic map:

$$\Gamma: Y_{j+1} = -a\ (Y_j - 1)(Y_j - ie)(Y_j + ie) \tag{7}$$

(Gregson, 1992, p. 20). Equation 7 states that the strength of a response, Y, at time $j + 1$ is a function of the response at a previous point in time, j, a control parameter representing physical signal strength (a), a situational control parameter e, and the imaginary number $(-1)^{1/2}$. Note that as the signal strength becomes sufficiently weak, the response is thrown into a chaotic regime.

Equation 7 can be expanded to two response parameters that may be useful for modeling cross-modality responses, such as interpreting a hue of a colored light from the perception of its brightness only, or studying the size–weight illusion. Two-dimensional outcome expansion is accomplished by substituting a real number, x, for i:

$$X_{j+1} = a\ (e^2 - e^2X_j + X_j^2 - Y_j^2 - 3X_jY_j^2 - X_j^3) \tag{8}$$

$$Y_{j+1} = aY_j\ (-e^2 + 2X_j - 3X_j^2 + Y_j^2) \tag{9}$$

(Gregson, 1992, p. 27). The structure of Equation 8 is roughly an umbilic form with two separate power potentials and a modulus term. The function Γ is further expandable into multidimensional inputs and outputs, which were applied to real situations such as perceiving the taste of wine. For superimposed stimuli, Γ has the convenient property:

$$Y_{TOT} = \Gamma(a_1 + a_2) = \Gamma(a_1) + \Gamma(a_2) \tag{10}$$

in the parts of Γ involving real numbers (p. 165). The Γ functions are hypoadditive in some regions of $<a_1,a_2>$ space, and hyperadditive in others, suggesting an interaction between the two processes. The probability of hypo- or hyperadditivity is normally distributed around Equation 10. This Gaussian function is unrelated to any noise or error functions that could be inherent in the data.

A relevant premise of the new psychophysics is that distinctions between psychophysical perception, pattern recognition, memory, and other cognitive functions are largely artificial. Perhaps those distinctions facilitated a scientific division of labor in days gone by, but currently they undermine the holistic understanding of the cognitive system.

Every psychophysical process, according to Gregson (1992), is the result of at least two functions, one involving the proximal connection between stimulus and response, and one pertaining to the delivery of the stimuli over time. Virtually all the stimuli in conventional experiments utilize a fixed interval stimulus delivery time. No such regularity can be assumed in the real world. Rather, coupled oscillators should be prevalent. For instance, if a system consists of a chaotic slave, which is proximal to the perceiver's response, coupled to a periodic driver that delivers the stimuli, the overall pattern of response should appear as a periodic function that is peppered with burst of chaosticity. Such functions currently defy any analyses directed at isolating and identifying nonlinear components. For the time being, a viable method of analysis is to simulate coupled dynamics of various sorts and to match a particular outcome against the known prototypes.

PERCEPTION MODELS AND EXPERIMENTS

Two groups of perception studies are particularly interesting. The first group is concerned with the perception of optical illusions, which, in turn, makes a viable case for studying social judgment processes as well. The second group is concerned with the human perception of fractal forms.

Reversible Figures

An *invariant process* is a fundamental perceptual process that is based, at least in part, on neurological preprogramming. Optical illusions are thought to work the way they do because they somehow trip an underlying invariant perceptual process. Studies of optical illusions have led to explanations for depth and motion perception, both of which are sustained by multiple mechanisms. Auditory illusions are now known that arise from invariant processes related to the perception of total patterns, some of which are closely analogous to the Gestalt laws of visual perception and the spatial location of sound (Narmour, 1992).

Depending on how one squints one's eyes, some specially prepared pictograms can look like either of two different images. Some of those reversible figures illusions are quite famous, such as the vase–face illusion, which is often used as a poster logo for events having something to do with psychology, or My Wife, My Mother-in-Law. The latter can look like a youngish woman wearing a necklace with her face turned away from the viewer, or an older woman with a large nose wearing a babushka and looking sideways toward the viewer. Reversible figures, such as those just described, work the way they do because they play a trick on yet another Gestalt law of perception, that of the *figure–ground* distinction. When the portion of the picture that represents the figure, which should ordinarily command central attention, is in precarious balance with the background, either portion of the figure could be perceived as figure or ground.

Two other such illusions have attracted the attention of dynamicists. The first was a figure that could look like a man's face by one view, or a woman seated by another view. The reversible figure illusion was renamed multistable perception to reflect the idea that two qualitatively distinct perceptual organizations were taking place (Poston & Stewart, 1978b). Poston and Stewart prepared additional versions of the man–woman figure that had systematically deleted lines and curves in the drawing. Their thesis was that as the total quantity of detail was reinstated to the drawing, the perception of the figure would change from unstable to bistable; the total quantity of detail thus represented a bifurcation parameter of a cusp manifold. The particular nature of the details, which could be selectively reinstated to favor either the man or woman interpretation, comprised the asymmetry parameter.

The model was eventually tested empirically by Stewart and Peregoy (1983). The data were analyzed with Cobb's maximum likelihood parameter estimation procedure. The pseudo-R^2 for the cusp model was .62, and the R^2 for the linear comparison model was .48. The roles of the hypothesized control parameters were substantiated as well.

The second reversible figure of nonlinear note is the Necker cube. The Necker cube is a line drawing of a cube that, at one glance, appears to thrust forward from the page to the viewer but, at another glance, drops backward from the page away from the viewer. The Necker cube plays on the linear perspective cue for depth perception. The perception of the cube was also hypothesized to be multistable in the sense of cusp dynamics (Ta'eed et al., 1988). The amount of shading was tested as the bifurcation parameter, and bias in the shaded portions of the figure was tested as the asymmetry parameter. The pseudo-R^2 for the cusp hypothesis was .72 and exceeded the R^2 that was obtained for the linear control model (.62). The Necker cube stimulus was used in some of the fatigue experiments reported in chapter 6.

Social Judgment Processes

The foregoing work on multistable perception lends itself readily to an understanding of decisions made on the basis of perceptual organization. One the one hand, cusp structure has been implicated in binary choice decisions where amount and substance of information coact to predispose a person to one or the other choice (Keown, 1980; Wright, 1983; Zeiler & Solano, 1982). Although social judgments involve abstractions and complex data rather than lines or squiggles, the dynamics of social decisions are thought to be similar. Two such examples are discussed next, followed by a different type of person perception experiment that is more closely related to the psychophysical models.

Zoning Board Decisions. Keown (1980) developed a cusp catastrophe model for zoning board decisions as a tool to assist lawyers in establishing the viability of cases presented to them by clients. The model was based on the U.S. legal system and actual zoning board decisions in the state of Connecticut. The cusp response surface defined "judgment for the plaintiff" and "judgment for the defendant" as the two attractor states. Control parameters were defined in terms of the two surface gradients, which run between the cusp point and the plaintiff's attractor or the defendant's attractor. Gradients were developed empirically, beginning with Equation 11, which was derived through ordinary multiple regression:

$$E = 0.57 + 0.16V_1 - 0.55V_2 - 0.26V_3$$
$$+ 0.21V_4 - 0.19V_5 + 0.12V_6 + 0.05V_7 \qquad (11)$$

In Equation 11, E is the probability of judgment in favor of the plaintiff; V_1 is the prior decision of the common court to approve or deny similar zoning changes in the past; V_2 is the prior decision of the zoning authority to approve or deny similar changes in the past; V_3 is the adequate physical planning involved with the proposed zoning item; V_4 is the compatibility of the proposed project with the immediate vicinity as indicated by large uniform blocks; V_5 is whether a zoning change would be detrimental to the environment; V_6 is whether large area zoning is used; V_7 is whether the characteristics of the area support change; and $V_1, \ldots, V_7$ are dichotomously valued.

The positively and negatively weighted variables were separated into two gradients and the weights were adjusted to further reflect cusp geometry. Unfortunately, there has been no follow-up on the zoning model, and thus it is not possible to discern whether the cusp interpretation predicted future zoning decisions better than Equation 11. The cusp concept, however, is consistent with other expressed ideas concerning dichotomous decision making.

Jury Decisions. The next model is more speculative still, but is based on one special signature of nonlinearity, that small changes in control parameter values can result in large changes in outcomes in the neighborhood of critical values. Scientific jury selection is the application of social science methodology to aid in the jury selection process. Its methods have been used in three distinct phases of jury selection. One phase has been to determine the biases of a particular venue so that the venue could be changed if prejudice toward either side is demonstrated. Another phase has been to investigate jury panel composition to assess whether a jury panel represents a cross section of the community in which the court is situated. The third, and most controversial, application is the actual selection of jurors favorable or not unfavorable toward a particular side of the argument.

The third type of selection involves surveying a sample of the potential jurors on a variety of relevant questions and demographics. A profile of a likely pro-defense or anti-defense juror can be developed from that information. Proponents of scientific jury selection have argued that the method is useful as evidenced by acquittals and hung juries in cases where it has been used. On the other hand, some critics have argued that the particular cases studied were weak to begin with, whereas others argued that the method was not tested correctly. Saks (1976) concluded that the effects of juror attitudes and demographics on jury verdicts were less important than the weight of actual trial evidence. I should add further that very strong or very weak cases tend to be settled before the trial. Trials are more likely when evidence is ambiguous or somewhat even, at least in the defendant's view of the situation.

Tindale and Nagao (1986) illustrated the impact of one juror's biases in a thought experiment. They composed juries of 6 or 12 experimental subjects and presented them with hypothetical case evidence. For very weak or very strong cases against the defendant, the addition of one not-guilty juror made little difference in conviction rates. However, for moderately strong cases, the addition of one favorable juror lessened the conviction rate by 30% for a 6-person jury, and 19% for a 12-person jury.

The issues in scientific jury selection studies lend themselves to a cusp model that is analogous to the cusps presented for reversible figures and the zoning board. The attractors on the response surface would be the guilty or not guilty verdict. The bifurcation parameter would be composed of the total volume of the evidence facing the jurors. Jurors' certainty levels about the meaning of that evidence would additionally contribute to the bifurcation parameter, where uncertain jurors would be positioned around the cusp point.

The Maxwell convention in catastrophe modeling would be applicable in two ways. The general rule states that if the two modalities have unequal a priori probabilities of occurrence, any behavioral changes will be more frequently observed in the direction of the more frequent modality (Fararo, 1978). The legal disposition of "innocent until proven guilty" is one example of the principle. A second application would emerge in the course of jury deliberations. In the event that the group is initially split between guilty and not guilty verdicts, the majority more often convinces the minority of their point of view (Penrod & Hastie, 1980).

The packets of evidence favoring the defendant's case or the State's case would take the form of gradients, in the same manner as the gradients in the zoning situation. Juror biases would contribute to the asymmetry parameter. When the gradients are of near-equal strength, a small amount of juror bias could determine whether the group's decision falls on the guilty or not guilty side of the critical threshold.

The Maxwell convention would further suggest that the opposite dynamics would occur in an appeal process. The appealing defendant is working against the weight of a past guilty decision. New evidence and arguments need to be sufficiently strong to move the new court well past the first critical point to the second, where the not guilty status would be restored.

Performance Appraisals. The ritual of appraising performance in industry, which is usually done for purposes of salary administration or training and development, is a process of people perception. Hanges et al. (1991) investigated the possibility that the appeasers' view of workers' performance formed a stable gestalt. The stable perception does not change, even though slow drifts in workers' performance may be occurring. When the actual performance level reaches a critical threshold, then the perceptual gestalt would change. Hanges et al. formalized their concept in a cusp catastrophe model where the amount of incongruence between the old and new performance information was treated as the bifurcation parameter. The favorability of prior information was hypothesized as the asymmetry parameter.

In their experiment, human subjects were presented with a series of descriptions of a worker's performance. After reading each, the experiment participants rating the performance on a standardized scale. Stimuli were presented in ascending and descending orders, as in the old-time psychophysics experiments. Data were analyzed with the maximum likelihood parameter estimation procedure, and a pseudo-R^2 of .31 (average value of two data treatments) was obtained for the cusp hypothesis, and an R^2 of 20. Both hypothesized control variables contributed to both latent control parameters, suggesting that they formed gradients.

The first conclusion that can legitimately drawn from the study is that person perception is a stable configuration, at least insofar as work performance commands the center of attention, and that the transition between stable configurations is cusp catastrophic. The second conclusion is that the apparent stability in work performance over time, which Barrett et al. (1985) insisted on and which other have refuted, is the result of a perception stability artifact in situations where performance ratings were used as dependent measures. Other evidence against the performance stability argument is considered in the next chapter.

Perception of Fractals

Landscape Contours. Because it is now known that fractals characterize the geometric structure of natural objects and landscapes, Gilden et al. (1993) investigated the possibility that human perceptual organization is naturally capable of extracting fractals. Prior studies showed that human observers can successfully rank order fractals in terms of their complexity based on visual cues (Cutting & Garvin, 1987). People can also distinguish fractal contours of the same dimensionality when the governing parameters of those fractals are drawn from different statistical distributions (Westheimer, 1991).

Gilden et al. (1993) compared the efficacies of two theories of perception, the signal-to-noise theory and the fractal theory. According to the signal-to-noise theory, the perception of landscapes would be based on separating the visual image into two components, the contour and the noise; noise would subsume any irregularities that we now associate with the fractal shape. The fractal theory, however, posited that the peaks and troughs would be meaningful, and the recursive and hierarchical structures of fractals would be meaningful as well.

The experimental stimuli consisted of fractal shapes and nonfractal contours, which had to be discriminated from contours created from a hybrid of target stimuli. The human participants were actually computer algorithms that were built with "precisely the same sensitivities as human observers" (p. 460). Pairs of stimuli were fed to the program, which then discriminated them from the hybrid. Receiver operating characteristic (ROC) curves were plotted for fractal and nonfractal stimuli, and the area under the ROC curve was used as the index of accuracy. The results showed that perception was based on a signal-to-noise rule, and that the recursive and hierarchical structures that distinguished fractals were generally ignored.

Chaotic Music. Gregson and Harvey (1992) conducted an auditory perception experiment to determine if human listeners (not simulated) could distinguish quasi-musical tonal sequences that were totally random from those that were sampled from a chaotic attractor function, such as the Lorenz, Kaplan and Yorke, Henon, Zaslavskii, Baker, logistic, logistic Period 1, and Γ functions. Numerical sequences from each of the attractor functions were discretized at intervals of the 12-tone piano scale. Subjects were presented with pairs of stimuli, one of which was random and the other chaotic. The task was to identify the random sequence.

Results showed that all the auditory attractor patterns were definitely distinguished from random sequences. Gregson and Harvey (1992) noticed, furthermore, that attractor functions with multimodal distributions were the most distinguishable from random. Because common linear statistics cannot distinguish chaos from randomness, the fact the human observers are capable of doing so suggests that auditory pattern perception is a more complex process than any captured by a linear model.

MATHEMATICAL MODELING OF LEARNING PROCESSES

Nonlinear dynamical systems theory has generated innovations to learning theory in three areas. The first was the relationship between the cusp catastrophe model and learning curves. The second concerned neural networks, and the third concerned chaotic learning.

Cusp Functions and Learning Curves

Rescorla and Wagner (1972) launched an influential line of research that was directed at parameterizing a learning curve and defining precisely what properties of reinforcement, stimuli, or situation are responsible for values of learning curve parameters. Although no such cookbook has come to fruition, that structuralist line of study led to some useful insights. Frey and Sears (1978) noticed that Rescorla and Wagner's (1972) mathematical model for classical conditioning would predict that extinction curves are mirror images of acquisition. They discovered that was not the case, and that a double-threshold, or hysteresis, effect could be identified at which the number of unreinforced trials would result in the animal withholding the behavior that was being extinguished. A more correct mathematical model required an ingredient drawn from the cusp catastrophe model, which in turn led to some further work connecting learning and extinction to cusp dynamics (Baker & Frey, 1980).

Although Equation 6 suggests that learning curves conform to a definite mathematical function, that is not the case. Other mathematical models can be used effectively also. For instance, the learning curve can be viewed as a sigmoid. The lower panel of Fig. 4.5 shows the same learning curves that appear in the upper panel, but with two alterations. The horizonal axis is defined as real time, into which units of reinforcement may be confounded. The second alteration is an extension of the learning curve backward into time; the extension displays the amount of learning taking place before the deliberate experimental learning intervention has been reduced. The result is a function that is bistable. Stewart (1980) showed that sigmoid curves are trajectories, or little slices, of a cusp response surface. Experimental factors that affect k (per Equation 6) contribute to the bifurcation axis, and exposure time contributes to the asymmetry parameter (Guastello, 1986).

Neural Networks

Neural networks are models for machine learning that are based on learning and association dynamics in living systems. There is no claim that these algorithms are true definitions of human learning, however, but just the observation that the virtual system can mimic the results of the real system. "Neural nets" are often used to program a machine to recognize a visual or other pattern. The algorithm "looks" at the data and systematically searches for patterns, which it then stores and tries to match against more data until the algorithm converges to a pattern it can extract. Sometimes the algorithms are "guided" or "supervised" by preloading the program with possible patterns for which to search; supervising is sometime necessary to prevent the algorithm from reaching an absurd conclusion (Greenwood, 1991).

Another interesting feature of neural networks is the pattern of linkages or associations that emerge among virtual neurons. Neurons may belong to several patterns or nets; unique and separate pathways for information channeling would actually be a special circumstance. The "reuse" of neurons in varying combinations provides an efficient explanation for the vast number of mental and physical functions that could be controlled by neurological activity, and for the well-known phenomenon where the function of a damaged neuron or area of the brain can be taken over by an adjacent neuron. The basic nature of neural nets lends itself to an analogy to human communication networks that is considered in chapter 12.

Chaotic Learning

Neuringer and Voss (1993) extended Estes' work on statistical learning theory to assess whether humans can learn to recognize chaotic patterns and to forecast the next element in a series of chaotic stimuli. They presented three experiments. In the first, four subjects were presented with points that eventually formed a line graph of a chaotic function based on Equation 12 for the logistic map:

$$y_2 = 4y_1(1 - y_1) \tag{12}$$

The task was to place a cursor at the position for next point before it arrived from the program. After successive trials, the difference between the positioned and actual values decreased to an asymptotic minimum in a skill acquisition learning curve (Equation 4 type). During the first block of 120 trials, the subjects' values for the time series of y_2 predicted from y_1 fit a linear-assisted quadratic function with an average R^2 of .37, with a range between .20 and .57. The average value of R^2 increased to .93 for the final block of 120 trials, with a range from .74 to .997.

The second experiment required the subjects to predict digits rather than points on a trajectory. Similar results were obtained: The average R^2 from the first 120 trials improved from .31 (range .19 to .56) to .80 for the final block of 120 trials (range .36 to .99). The third experiment was a continuation of second. Subjects received another block of trials, but with feedback withheld occasionally. The average R^2 for trials with feedback was .72, and .79 without feedback. The results from the third experiment were odd; two subjects improved performance without feedback, one's performance degraded, and one did not change appreciably. It is possible that the intermittent reinforcement schedule had a powerful conditioning effect, which is well known in other types of experiments, rather than inducing an extinction effect.

Ward and West (1994) noticed that the subjects in Neuringer and Voss's experiment were given logistic map numbers that were truncated to three decimal places, which had the effect of generating a seven-number repeated sequence. In contrast, a digit sequence of several thousand numbers would be generated from iterates with seven-digit precision. The implication was that Neuringer and Voss's subjects could not be generating chaotic functions. Metzger (1994) made a similar observation about digit precision, adding that there was no proof that subjects had learned a chaotic sequence; they could have been using a different heuristic that approximated the same predictions. In my opinion, the subjects' use of a particular heuristic is not a central issue; the important point is whether they could learn to *control* chaos.

Ward and West (1994), by using more precise calculations of logistic map iterates, showed that their subjects "learned to reproduce a quadratic equation noisily" (p. 325). Graphs from two representative subjects showed that one subject could generate a clear bifurcation arc pattern, while the other distorted the arc beyond recognition. Unfortunately, R^2 coefficients were not reported for comparison. After the main experiment, subjects were asked how they arrived at their predicted values. They could describe the (different) rules they had used, but none were the logistic map.

There appear to be individual differences at work here, but the current state of research has only scratched the surface of what they might be. Perhaps one is the complexity of the heuristic that a subject is likely to invoke. Perhaps another has more to do with the degree to which precise detail is filtered.

DECISION MAKING AND CHAOTIC CONTROLLERS

Decision making takes many forms and its literature is scattered among a variety of subtopics and applications. Some types of dichotomous social decisions can be expressed as examples of cusp catastrophe dynamics, as suggested in an earlier section. Decision making under risk or uncertainty is considered in chapter 5. Decision making under strategic, competitive, or cooperative conditions is considered in chapter 9. Creative thinking involves a different type of thought process and is considered in chapter 10.

A new concept in decision making that has been receiving much attention lately is the *chaotic controller*. Chaotic controllers are based on the *law of requisite variety*, which is an engineering principle that posits that the controller of a system needs to be at least as complex as the system it intends to control. Chaotic systems obviously need something special. Chaotic control works counterintuitively by first *adding* a small amount of low-dimensional noise into the system. The reasoning is that the amount of sensitivity to initial conditions is not uniform throughout the attractor's space; sensitivity is less in the basin of the attractor and least in its center. The level of sensitive dependence may be affected by the attractor's proximity to another attractor. Adding noise to the system allows the attractor to expand to its fullest range (Breeden et al., 1990; Jackson, 1991a, 1991b; Ohle et al., 1990).

The controlled can then respond in one of two ways. One is to apply a filter that allows a special range of values to pass through. The noise reduction system on many common tape recorders works on this principle, although the noise reduction systems were developed almost 20 years before the chaotic controller concept. The signal processor parses the (musical or other) sound into frequencies above and below 12,500 Hz, which is the point where tape hiss generally begins. The high-frequency material is then amplified, noise and all, and then filtered to remove the noise. The signal portion is then reintegrated with the lower frequency sound groups.

The second option is to mimic the chaotic motion of a point, predict where it is going, and respond in a strategic manner. One industry I am familiar with is using this latter type of controller for automated intelligent manufacturing systems. When one part of the system fails for whatever reason, which will be a random or chaotic occurrence, the remaining parts of the system need to respond accordingly to keep as much of the system operating properly as possible.

Some aspects of chaotic control of systems by humans have been considered already in this chapter. Signal detection is a simple decision about the presence of a stimulus, or a comparison of properties. Chaotically generated signals require an equivalently limber detection strategy. Of further interest, the noise that was always believed to be independent of the signal may, in some circumstances, be inextricably linked to the dynamics of the chaotic attractor (Abraham, 1985; Gregson, 1988). The interpretations of chaosticity in some situations may not be natural (Gilden et al., 1993), but at least they might be learned or reasonably approximated (Neuringer & Voss, 1993; Ward & West, 1994). Applications of the chaotic controller concept to human social situations are considered in chapters 9, 10 , and 11.

SUMMARY

Although it may have been convenient to study psychophysical processes, perception, learning, response time, decision making, and control as separate entities, the processes are all interrelated. Nonlinear dynamical systems theory is beginning to address the self-organization of these subsystems and propose new principles for understanding the detection of information, perceptual organization of stimuli, and learning and adaptive systems. The noise that was once thought to be an extraneous annoyance may be an important part of the perception and decision process.

5

Dynamics of Motivation and Conflict

This chapter begins with some classical thinking on personnel selection and work motivation. Classic work on personnel selection has been, in turn, based on concepts of human abilities and the use of the correlation coefficient. Motivation theories were derived initially from more basic theories of animal and human motivation, which were in turn adapted with other innovations to explain individuals at work. Individual motivation theories later contributed to organizationally based theories of management, climate, and culture.

The classical material is voluminous, and there has been little in the way of conceptual groundbreaking in the past decade, at least not within the old paradigm. I therefore present the ideas in a novel way, by running the "movie" on fast-forward, where some highly interesting patterns emerge. The emerging thesis that lends itself to NDS interpretation and research is that theoretical aspects of personnel selection, motivation, learning, and training evaluation are intimately entwined in real processes. Breaking those concepts apart in the past undoubtedly served the purposes of getting many people started on figuring things out about every aspect of the organizational system. The contemporary systems scientist would observe, however, that the divide and conquer approach was an outgrowth of Newtonian thinking: Understanding the parts of the system will add up to knowledge of the whole. The contrary view, which should become evident soon, is that our understanding of the parts leads us to an opposite condition: a conspicuously absent knowledge of the whole.

The exposition of NDS concepts begins with the development of two-stage personnel selection and training evaluation. Here roles of abilities in the selection process and learning in the training process are merged into one integrated model of people entering an organization.

Job retention and desirable levels of performance do not sustain themselves for long without motivational aspects of work playing a role. Thus the butterfly catastrophe model of motivation in organization is a logical expansion of the selection-training dynamics and incorporates all the features of motivation and work behavior that became central within the conventional paradigm. The empirical illustrations and tests of the model begin with a relatively mundane but readily accessible application to academic performance, which is followed by two studies of learning and motivational dynamics. The saga continues with additional applied work on the absenteeism and turnover aspects of the butterfly motivation model.

Where there is motivation, there is a potential for conflict, particularly where the parties concerned view the same situation differently, or prefer actions that conflict with the intentions of other people or groups. Thus the first installment of the conflict resolution theme follows, based on approach-avoidance dynamics. The second installment appears in chapter 9, where cooperation and competition dynamics are considered.

The chapter concludes with an enigma that is left for subsequent chapters to unravel, that of defining the full meaning of butterfly control parameter d in the motivation model. Throughout this chapter, the dynamics of motivation and performance are individualistically centered, although group and organizational influences are considered relative to the individual experience. The focus throughout the book slowly shifts, in a rather nonlinear path, toward organizationally centered themes.

CONVENTIONAL THEORY FOR PERSONNEL SELECTION, WORK MOTIVATION, AND JOB SATISFACTION

The goal of personnel selection was to answer two questions about a job applicant: *Can* the applicant do the job? And *will* the applicant do the job? The two questions form a viable place to start now as they did years ago, but with a touch of irony. Mainstream theory in personnel selection remains largely confined to the "can" question. The "will" question is usually left outside the picture as someone else's job to figure out—unless motivation can be measured in a paper-and-pencil test and treated like a "can" item. Curiously, there is theory from both the direction of personnel selection and that of motivation that shows how the two groups of ideas link up. In keeping with long-standing tradition, however, the proverbial left hand does not always pay attention to what the right hand is doing.

Personnel Selection

The selection process involves four basic steps. The first is the choice of predictors and criteria. Typical predictors include tests of ability, job knowledge, achievement, personality, and biographical data. Personality traits can be considered as social skills in many respects, but they are also related to motivational dynamics, particularly as to whether a person will be suited to the demands of a particular occupation (Conn & Rieke, 1994). Criterion measurements are variably subjective ratings or objective measures of work performance.

The second step is the validity study. Validity is assessed in terms of both the conceptual and empirical relationship between the prediction device and the performance outcome. Empirical strength of the predictor–criterion relationship is characteristically measured by a zero-order correlation or multiple regression coefficient. If the multiple regression equation itself is to be used for future selection in an actuarial sense, then a cross-validation study is performed. The history of validity studies conducted with a set of jobs or with a set of tests strengthens any new hypotheses concerning the role of any tests for predicting performance in other applications.

The third step in the process is to determine the utility of a decision based on the validated selection device. Taylor and Russell (1939) developed tables to determine the percentage of successful candidates that would be selected by the device when three pieces of information are known: the proportion of employes considered satisfactory before testing (*base rate of success*), the percentage of the applicant pool that will be hired (*selection ratio*), and the validity coefficient for the device. The Taylor–Russell approach to utility uses a discrete payoff function, that is, the person is successful or not, with no middle ground. Later approaches utilized continuous payoff functions such that the viability of an employee is converted to a dollar measure.

Adverse Impact. The fourth step in the process of personnel selection research is the assessment of adverse impact. Personnel selection in the 1970s was complicated with concerns about racial bias in tests used in personnel selection and in the selection process itself. Pursuant to Title VII of the Civil Rights Act of 1964, and the landmark case of *Griggs v. Duke Power* (1971), there were numerous federal lawsuits charging racial and gender discrimination by employers who used personnel selection testing with adverse impact against the power minorities. The essential defense in those circumstances was for the defending employer to demonstrate that the selection devices, alleged to incur adverse impact, were bona fide occupational qualifications. Such proof required a validity study, and it was further valuable to challenge whether adverse impact actually did occur.

A number of bias concepts were, as a result, introduced to the educational and psychological testing literature. The regression model proposed by Cleary (1968) became the most popular in the courts. According to the Cleary model, bias occurs if the regression equation for the two groups has either different slopes, hence different correlation magnitudes, or different intercepts. Other models based on a combination of regression and discrete utility were also proposed, along with multidimensional utility models (Linn, 1986). The essence of the multidimensional utility models was that the benefits to the employer must be weighted against the damage to the job applicant or to society as a whole (Cronbach, 1976). Similar concepts emerged in the arenas of public policymaking (Edwards, 1981; Novick, 1980; Thrall et al., 1981).

The Cleary model of adverse impact was essentially the concept of differential or single group validity. According to that line of reasoning, a test may be valid for one ethnic group but not for another. Alternatively, a test may be more valid for one group that it is for another. According to the oppositional view, the single and differential group validity concept and the empirical evidence related to it were artifacts introduced by restriction of range and insufficient sample sizes. After statistical correction, it could be shown that people who scored better on the test scored better on the performance measure (Schmidt & Hunter, 1981).

The Civil Rights Act of 1991 reaffirmed plaintiff's rights under *Griggs*, addressed new issues in racial and gender discrimination that emerged over the decade, and placed a clear prohibition on the use of racial- or gender-specific norms on cognitive ability tests for employment. The question of whether racial or gender corrections are warranted for noncognitive tests remains controversial (Guastello, 1993c).

Moderator Relationships. In light of the resurgent interest in racial and gender policy issues as well as the demise of the differential validity framework for studying those issues, the moderator regression framework has emerged as a preferred method of study. It is presented next, not only to continue the bias in selection theme, but also as a method of studying other variables, such as motivation, that could complicate the relationship between ability and performance. The moderator regression model is the point of contact between conventional and NDS approaches to the study of the same phenomena: it takes the following form:

$$Y = B_0 + B_1X + B_2M + B_3MX \qquad (1)$$

where Y is the performance measure, X is the predictor test, M is the moderator variable, and MX is an interaction between the moderator variable and the ordinary predictor.

For a racial bias study using Equation 1, group membership would be used as the moderator variable. The overall R^2 coefficient would give the proportion of criterion variance accounted for by the predictor and by subgroup differences. A significant weight for the interaction term would denote differences in slopes for the two groups, which would, in turn, indicate different subgroup correlation coefficients. A significant group membership term would indicate differences in intercepts for the subgroup correlations, and also gross differences in performance that could be attributable to group membership but that are not accounted for by ordinary predictors in the model.

Motivation variables are also strong candidates for moderator variables. The dynamics could work out in one of two ways. In one scenario, highly motivated people are working to the best of their abilities. Thus the relationship between motivation and performance would be stronger than would be the case when motivation is low (Edwards & Waters, 1981; Locke et al., 1978). People with low motivation would not push themselves, and the more capable performance would not be distinguished from those less capable but more highly motivated to perform. Alternatively, highly motivated people would all perform maximally, and thus neutralize any individual differences in innate ability. Persons of lower levels of motivation would perform well if it were easy for them to do so, but not otherwise.

Job Satisfaction and Related Attitudes

Job satisfaction and work motivation are not the same phenomenon, although some theories have done their best to twist the two together. Motivation pertains to what a person wants to do in the near future. Satisfaction is a response to what took place in the recent past. Nonetheless, there are a few key ideas embedded in the satisfaction literature that are directly pertinent to the NDS theories that follow.

Motivator–Hygiene Theory. Job satisfaction is an inferred affectual state that is somehow linked to behavior in organizations, or caused by conditions in organizations (Locke, 1976). Locke traced the concept of job satisfaction from scientific management, through the human relations movement, to a boom in research in the 1950s, which culminated in the two-factor theory of job satisfaction (Herzberg et al., 1959). According to Herzberg et al., job satisfaction elements can be classified into two categories, motivators and hygiene or maintenance items. Deficiency of hygiene elements can lead to dissatisfaction, but an overabundance of them does not contribute to satisfaction. Motivators, on the other hand, lead to satisfaction when enough are present, but lack of motivators does not contribute to dissatisfaction. When hygiene elements are in place and motivators are increased, therefore, increased productivity and satisfaction will result.

Hygiene elements are groups into six categories: physical, economic, social, security, status, and orientation. The list of physical elements would include work layout, job demands, work rules, equipment, company location and grounds, parking facilities, ventilation, lighting, and noise. Social elements include work groups, coffee groups, lunch groups, social groups, and interest groups. Status elements include job classification, job titles, furnishings, use of company newsletters, bulletins and handbooks, and inclusion in that network known as the grapevine. Security elements include fairness, consistency, reassurance, friendliness, seniority rights, and grievance procedures. Economic elements include wages and salaries, automatic increases, profit sharing, social security, workman's compensation, unemployment compensation, retirement programs, paid leave, insurance, and tuition discounts.

Motivation elements appeal to individual needs for growth, achievement, responsibility, and recognition. The list includes delegation of meaningful tasks, access to information, freedom to act, an atmosphere of approval, involvement, goal setting, opportunities to make plans and to solve problems, work simplification, performance appraisal, merit increases, discretionary awards, profit sharing, utilizing one's skills, interesting work, opportunities for inventions and publications, company growth, promotions, job transfers and rotations, and educational opportunities.

The work simplification element has a specific interpretation as a motivator. Simplification is a motivation insofar as an employee can find easier and better ways of performing a task. It does not mean that jobs are more motivating when they are atomized into short-cycle assembly line tasks, as in the scientific management paradigm. Quite the opposite is true. One of the basic tenets of motivation–hygiene theory is that satisfaction and productivity can be increased by enlarging and enriching jobs according to the principles just outlined. The job enrichment principle is known as *vertical loading*. It is distinguished from *horizontal loading*, which is to give a person a wide range of disconnected, and rather dumb, tasks to perform.

Satisfaction and Performance. Satisfaction, or lack of it, has been found to have some robust relationships to behavior in industry. Job satisfaction has a generally low correlation with productivity, for example, about .14 (Vroom, 1964), or $R^2 = .02$. Validity generalization with newer measurement devices has updated the R^2 to .03 (Iaffaldano & Muchinsky, 1985). Correlation is not causation, however, and it is well known in social psychology that behavior predicts attitude more often than the other way around. Thus Lawler and Porter (1967) hypothesized that performance leads to rewards of both a motivator and hygiene variety. (Note: The labels "motivator" and "hygiene" were actually stated as "extrinsic" and "intrinsic," respectively, after some concurrently developed theories of motivation, which are considered later in this chapter.) If the rewards were perceived as fair (invoking equity theory, discussed later), then satisfaction results (Lawler, 1973; Lawler & Porter, 1967). Supporting research remains controversial, according to one recent analysis (Muchinsky, 1990).

Behavioral Intention, Satisfaction, Absenteeism, and Turnover. In spite of the attitude–performance relationship just cited, folks have continued to work on attitude-to-performance models. According to Fishbein (1967), it is possible to predict overt behavior using a multiple regression equation:

$$B \cong BI = (A_{act})w_0 + (NB_s \times MC)w_1 \qquad (2)$$

where B is overt behavior, BI is behavioral intention, A_{act} is the subject's attitude toward the behavior, NB_s represents social norms as perceived by the person, MC is the person's motivation to comply with norms, and w_0 and w_1 are empirical regression weights. Laboratory studies showed that the multiple regression equation predicts a range of behaviors with R^2 around .65 (Newman, 1974) and as high as .92 (Smetana & Adler, 1980).

Newman (1974) compared the relative efficiency of the behavioral intention model with the Job Description Index (JDI) satisfaction measures for predicting absenteeism and turnover. Neither model was found to be constantly superior. Job satisfaction ($R^2 = .36$) outpredicted behavioral intention for absenteeism ($R^2 = .14$), but behavioral intention ($R^2 = .14$) outpredicted turnover ($R^2 = .21$). Hom and Hulin (1981), however, reported an R^2 of .64 for a turnover hypothesis.

Organizational Commitment. Porter et al. (1974) proposed that attitude toward the job should be separated from attitude toward the organization. For instance, a person may leave one organization to do similar work for another organization. Thus organizational commitment would be a better predictor of withdrawal than job satisfaction. Sheridan and Vredenburgh (1978) found empirical support for that idea. Hom et al. (1979) discovered, however, that neither job satisfaction nor organizational commitment was superior to the other, and neither was better than a behavioral intention model ($R^2 = .42$).

Mobley Turnover Process. According to Mobley (1977), the relationship between dissatisfaction and turnover is consistent but not always strong, and a more detailed model was required. He reconceptualized the turnover process as consisting of a series of cognitive stages: evaluation of the existing job (the job satisfaction framework would apply here), followed by the experience of job dissatisfaction, thoughts of quitting, evaluation of the expected utility of searching for another job and the cost of quitting, intention to search for alternatives, the actual search for alternatives, comparison of same with the existing job, intention to quit or remain with the present job, followed by the final outcome of staying or leaving. Unlike a true stage theory, the employee may skip stages or repeat stage sequences. Highly visible job alternatives may preempt the role of job dissatisfaction. Economic conditions and the employee's age may prevent a successful job change.

Research on the Mobley process has been supportive (Miller et al., 1979; Mobley et al., 1978; Waters & Roach, 1979). A noteworthy point relative to NDS is the contrast between the Mobley process and the behavioral intention model: The antecedents of *BI* are static, but time-sequential or dynamic in the Mobley process.

Satisfaction and an Absenteeism Process Model. Nicholson et al. (1976) sought to dispel the popular belief that job dissatisfaction causes absenteeism. According to Nicholson et al., the belief was popular because it "made sense." It was easy to confuse the fact of withdrawal with the motivation for withdrawal. The hypothetical relationship vindicated job satisfaction research in light of its very small relationship with productivity. It also provided an economic incentive for employers to improve the quality of work, because some studies claimed a reliable relationship between employee attitudes and absenteeism. When they investigated the reliability of the relationship, Nicholson et al. found that anomalies of method, findings, and interpretation confounded the general interpretation of the empirical studies. In their own empirical investigation, they found evidence contrary to the causation hypothesis and concluded that the relationship between satisfaction and absenteeism was tenuous at best. They suggested transposing Lawler and Porter's idea (1967) to say that attendance causes satisfaction, and utilizing a research paradigm that focused on motivation to attend, rather than motivation to withdraw.

In light of the foregoing, Steers and Rhodes (1978) conducted a review of 104 empirical absenteeism studies and concluded that attendance is influenced by two basic factors: ability to attend and motivation to attend. The latter is influenced in turn by various external and internal pressures to attend and job satisfaction. Unlike the Mobley (1977) turnover model, their absenteeism model took the form of a multilinear flow chart, with circles and arrows connecting 13 categories of variables. Watson (1981) conducted an empirical investigation of the Steers and Rhodes (1978) model, using a static correlational analysis, rather than a time-sequential or dynamic method. He found support for the full model; R^2 was relatively low (.22) in spite of the large number of variables involved. Job satisfaction had raised the R^2 by an increment of only .01, suggesting that job satisfaction is a fair surrogate for all the other variables thought to be involved in the process.

Opponent Process Model. Landy (1978) offered an opponent process model of job satisfaction and work motivation. The job satisfaction model is strongly analogous to an opponent process model for addiction proposed by Solomon and Corbit (1973, 1974). A diagram of the model appears in Fig. 5.1.

The cycle begins with the initiation of a primary process (drug injection in the addiction model), which is followed by a period of positive subjective experience. Shortly after the onset of the primary process, however, the onset of the opponent process (physical dependence in the addiction model) occurs. The opponent process, which is growing stronger during the primary process phase, is not perceived until the primary process wears off. The opponent process is perceived as a negative subjective experience, which can only be counteracted by a new onset of the primary process. With repeated onsets of primary process with equal intensity, the peak subjective experience steadily decreases in intensity. Eventually, additional onsets of primary process will only serve to neutralize the opponent process.

In the satisfaction-performance application (Landy, 1978), intrinsic factors, in the sense of Herzberg's motivators, form the primary process,

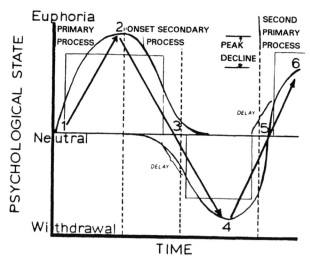

FIG. 5.1. Opponent process model of motivation. From Guastello (1984a, 1987a). Reprinted with permission.

and extrinsic factors form the opponent process, such that "intrinsic factors have the capacity to yield neutral hedonic states in their presence and positive hedonic aftereffects; extrinsic factors produce neutral hedonic states in their presence and negative hedonic aftereffects" (p. 541). The model is thought to explain quasi-periodic changes in behavior over time. A person starts a phase of work in a highly motivated fashion and indeed performs excellently. Both intrinsic and extrinsic rewards result. The mishap, however, occurs after repeated units of performance; the novelty and intrinsic motivation value of the task wear off, and work continues in order to maintain the flow of extrinsic rewards. The intrinsic motivation to perform declines, and does not return until the old program of work activities is exchanged for a new program of work activities.

According to Landy, it is possible to deduce the Herzberg et al. (1959) two-factor theory of job satisfaction and the Lawler–Porter (1967) process from the opponent process model. To date, there has been no recorded attempt to verify the truth or falsehood of the opponent process model. It was shown, however, that opponent processes underlie virtually all forms of motivation (Solomon, 1980). The opponent process model was later incorporated into NDS models of motivation in a more or less wholesale fashion (Guastello, 1984a, 1987a).

Intrinsic Work Motivation

The concept of intrinsic and extrinsic needs or outcomes was first introduced here in the context of motivator–hygiene theory. The concept did not actually appear in the theoretical motivation literature until a decade later, and when it did it appeared in several variations. That saga is considered next, followed by some important work on specific types of intrinsic work motivation. Note the transition that eventually takes place where the topic of study evolves from understanding motivation in individuals to what leaders can do to enhance motivation in a group.

The distinction between intrinsic and extrinsic motivation was initially based on animal research that was centered on learning theory. Premack (1971) showed that animals will perform a behavior, Task A, in order to receive permission to perform a Task B, if the probability of performing B is low. Behavior can reward behavior. He further showed that if he reversed the rules for the same animal such that performing Task A was rare, the animals would perform B in order to have an opportunity to perform A. It really did not matter what the tasks were, only that relative rarity of the behavior distinguished between work and reward.

Mawhinney (1979) extrapolated the Premack principle to work motivation and suggested that being allowed to engage in rare behaviors was rewarding. People would find their jobs "rewarding" if the opportunity to do that sort of work was relatively rare. Similarly, the forms of participation in decision making advocated by Herzberg et al. (1959) as sources of motivation were indeed sources of motivation because such opportunities were infrequent. As all jobs situations evolved toward the favorable end of the motivator spectrum, the motivational quality of enriched jobs could dissipate.

Deci (1972) proposed a definition that centered around the principle of where the rewards came from. Extrinsic rewards were those that required a third party to deliver. Intrinsic rewards did not require a third party to deliver; rather, the intrinsic rewards came from the task itself. Intrinsically motivated people are, for example, those who obtain their principal motivation from the opportunity to achieve, wield power, or do something that reflects some sort of personal values. Extrinsically motivated people think of the money first, if not also last and foremost. Saleh and Grygier (1969) and Slocum (1971) offered similar definitions. Wernimont (1972) added an emotional component: "All the intrinsic factors are internal feelings, while extrinsic factors are external situations" (p. 173; also see Dyer & Parker, 1975).

There is some fairly consistent evidence that intrinsic and extrinsic rewards interact in an odd way. In studies of both humans and monkeys, the introduction of an extrinsic reward to a task situation where the worker was already intrinsically motivated resulted in a decrease in output, rather than an increase. (Pritchard et al., 1977; Enzle & Ross, 1978). The obvious problem here is that if human at real work do not receive their raisins and bananas every so often, they do not work at all.

Three avenues out of the dilemma have been proposed. In one view, the introduction of extrinsic rewards causes a temporary primitivization of one's motivation whereby the presence of the extrinsic reward shifts the focus of attention away from the intrinsic qualities of the task to the more obvious and elementary extrinsic reward (McCullers et al., 1987). In another view, the explanation was rooted in why a person went to work at all. Most people have basic human existence needs to fulfill, and a job that does not fulfill those needs is unacceptable. Yet at the same time, those who seek to develop their careers, denoting a concern with the interest value of their tasks, will be more concerned with career development as long as basic human needs are being met; they frequently enough take major cuts in salary to change from dull jobs to something more exciting (Guastello, 1981). The third view is that money, a major extrinsic reward, has considerable symbolic value, as do most other aspects of reward in organizations. The culture of the organization shapes the relative importance of intrinsic and extrinsic features of the rewards, and the manipulation of this is under the control of management (Maehr & Braskamp, 1986).

Social Approaches to Motivation. According to social motivation theory, there is only one type of motivation, and that is arousal. Any further differentiation of motivation is a result of learning. Social motivations are no exception, and all social motivations can be placed in one of three categories: achievement, affiliation, and power (McClelland et al., 1953). All healthy adults are thought to have a reservoir of potential energy, which flows out through the expression of those three needs or motives, the relative strength of which varies across individuals (Atkinson, 1964). Note the dynamical language implicit in this view of motivation. The motives for achievement, affiliation, and power are all forms of intrinsic motivation.

Achievement motivation is the concern with standards of excellence, or unique accomplishments and long-term goals (McClelland, 1961). Achievement-motivated people like to set goals, make plans to reach them, and take action. The goal-setting aspect of achievement motivation has become a major line of motivation research itself (Locke & Latham, 1990). Affiliation is the interest in establishing or maintaining positive emotional relationships with other people. Affiliation motivation tends to be low among entrepreneurs and managers in organizations (McClelland & Boyatsis, 1982). Power is the concern about getting or maintaining control of the means for influencing people (McClelland, 1975). Power motivation is an important motivation for entrepreneurs, and the dominant motivation for executives in organizations. McClelland (1970) differentiated two expressions of power: Personalized power directs the goals of power toward the self, and is sometimes expressed by concerns for one's reputation, winning an argument with another person, or other types of interpersonal competition. A manager whose power motive is directed primarily toward personal goals will be seen as manipulative, exploitive, and having a win–lose attitude toward subordinates. Socialized power directs the goals of power toward other people, and is sometimes expressed by giving help to people who need it but do not request it, and taking action to mobilize people around a worthwhile activity. A manager whose power motive is directed primarily toward other people is concerned with making others feel more powerful and in control of their behavior and outcomes. Power motivation can also be enhanced though training .

The Origin–Pawn Concept. Personal causation is the experience of personal control over one's behavior even though environmental factors may be primary determinants of behavior (deCharms, 1968, 1976). At the individual level, *origins* show greater responsibility for action, commitment to the task, greater creativity, better impulse control, and goal setting than pawns. *Pawns*, at the other extreme, show more overt symptoms of anxiety, helplessness, and less achievement-oriented behavior. Interpersonally, origins, especially in leadership capacities, create a climate that enhances origin characteristics in group members. Similarly, pawns as leaders inspire group members to pawn behavior. Origin characteristics may be enhanced through training.

It is possible to distinguish between origins and pawns once one learns the differences (deCharms et al., 1965). Additionally, subjects in the deCharms et al. experiment who were measured as more like origins themselves viewed vignette protagonists as more like origins. The latter finding is generally consistent with the person perception literature, and in turn suggests a mechanism by which origins and pawns impact on other group members.

Nicholson et al. (1977) investigated notions of personal causation in a study of British steel workers. The researchers found job absence and turnover to be related to the existing control the individual workers had over the task and social environment. They considered both existing levels of influence and desired levels of influence at the local, medium, and distant levels of the organization. Existing local level influence was the most predictive of job absence, more so than for propensity to leave the organization. Desired levels of influence on equipment maintenance (local), quality of work (local), job procedure (local), buying materials (medium), and hiring recruits (medium) were significantly correlated with absenteeism.

Argyris (1976) incorporated the personal causation and origin–pawn concepts into the concepts of Model I and Model II problem-solving environment. The shift in focus to problem-solving applications gave rise to the concepts of double-loop learning and organizational learning. Organizational learning is elaborated later in this chapter as a nonlinear dynamical process.

Equity Theory

Equity theory (Adams, 1965) is a concept of motivation that centers on social exchange. The central idea is that equity and inequity underlie the stability or instability of personal and employment relationships. A state of equity, which implies relative stability, is a situation where Person's ratio of outcomes to inputs is equal to that of Other. If inequity is perceived by Person, Person will take action to restore equity. Possible responses for Person are to put less into a relationship, to put something new into the relationship, or to terminate the relationship.

Deviations in the input–output ratios are tolerated to some extent. The threshold of inequity for Person to respond to an overpayment is usually larger than the threshold of inequity for Person to respond to a shortage

(Adams, 1965). In many situations, Other is making decisions about the relationship also. Person and Other may adjust the relationship several times in order to reach the stability they prefer. If there are multiple others and the relationships are in a state of flux, a chaotic set of relationships is likely to ensue, according to NDS theory.

Equity theory has explained a wide range of human relationships found in industry, penology, marital therapy, and elsewhere (Walster et al., 1973). The general trend in industry was as follows: Piece-rate workers responded to inequitable overpayment by producing the same amount of work at higher quality, and responded to inequitable underpayment by producing more units of lesser quality. Hourly workers responded to inequitable underpayment by producing fewer units, and responded to inequitable overpayment by increasing quality rather than quantity (Goodman & Friedman, 1971). Other research suggests that hourly workers would respond to either form of inequity by adjusting either quantity or quality levels, depending on which was easier to adjust (Campbell & Pritchard, 1976). Equity principles also appear to explain coalition formation, bargaining, and consumer behavior (Guastello, 1981). Adams and Friedman (1976) wrote that the range of applications of equity theory has grown so large that it should be regarded as a general theory of social relationships.

Our hypothetical Person evaluates equity not only with respect to pay but also with respect to intrinsic or intangible features of a relationship, such as supervision (Katzell, 1980), absenteeism and turnover (Dittrich & Carrell, 1979), and effort as another form of input (Anderson & Farkas, 1975). Labor relations studies illustrated the importance of fairness of a decision process. People are usually willing to forego some personal gain to ensure that the process of distribution of rewards or wealth is fair (Sheppard & Minton, 1986).

Expectancy Theory

According to Vroom (1964), motivation is the amount of effort, or force (F), a person will expend on the job:

$$F = \Sigma(E_{ij}V_j) \qquad (3)$$

where E_{ij} is the *expected probability* of the behavior i being followed by an outcome of a given type, and V_j is the *valence* of the outcome, that is, its potential satisfaction value. Vroom's was not the first theoretical proposition to specify a formula such as Equation 3. According to Wahba and House (1974), it was at least the 11th, where the first dated back to 17th century economics. In psychology, the concept can be traced back to Tolman (1932), who further claimed that

$$\text{Behavior} = \text{drive} \times \text{habit strength} \tag{4}$$

and perhaps more importantly, that the rat knew where the cheese was located. A rat would thus run to the branch of a radial maze that had a higher E_{ij} of containing cheese, rather than follow a sequence of turns learned through operant conditioning.

Expectancy theory continued with two additional propositions. First, valence V_j is itself a product of instrumentalities I_{jk}, which are beliefs that outcome j leads to other outcomes k, and V_k is the valence associated with those additional outcomes:

$$V_j = \Sigma(I_{jk}V_k) \tag{5}$$

(Vroom, 1964). Textbooks now commonly condense Equations 3 and 5 to:

$$F = \Sigma(EVI) \tag{6}$$

with no loss of meaning. Valences can consist of both extrinsic and intrinsic outcomes (Wahba & House, 1974). Second, and most pointedly for the NDS applications to follow,

$$P = f(FA) \tag{7}$$

where A is ability (Vroom, 1964). Equation 7 is the same result as Equation 1, and states that motivation moderates the relationship between ability and performance.

Research designed to test expectancy theory has generally reported favorable results, although the median R^2 between measures of E, I, and V with performance hovered around .09. One problem with most of the work, however, was that the theory called for a multiplicative relationship between E, I, and V, and only additive relationships were tested. One study that multiplied appropriately obtained an R^2 of .16 with a composite of 10 performance criteria (Heneman & Schwab, 1972). Expectancy theory also makes the same predictions as equity theory regarding how a person would respond to conditions of overpayment and underpayment (Campbell & Pritchard, 1976).

Another problem with the empirical applications was that the theory was designed as a within-person choice theory, meaning that one person chooses between Door Number 1 and Door Number 2 in a variety of situations, rather than a between-person choice theory, where many people make the same choice between the same two doors on in the same situation. Different people may assign very different values to E, I, and V to the same door, and may integrate those values differently when making a decision. Zedeck (1977) later showed that R^2 for a predictive model can increase from .21–.23 to .53–.67 as the participants are progressively clustered (bifurcated) into 2 to 91 clusters.

Summary of Conventional Theories

The exposition of conventional theories of motivation, ability, and work performance began with the rudiments of personnel selection, the potentially moderating influence of racial factors, and the potentially moderating effect of motivation. The models of job satisfaction and theories of work motivation all make a similar distinction between intrinsic and extrinsic forms of motivation, but at the same time apply to both forms of potential reward, motivation, or outcome. Intrinsic and extrinsic rewards appear to have a peculiar impact on work performance when they appear in combination.

Two other unifying themes of motivation theory are the pervasiveness of equity and the opponent process model. Fairness issues have systematic effects on relationships of all sorts, and many occupationally relevant examples have been illustrated. The opponent process model of motivation is further thought to underlie all forms of motivation, and the application to work performance discussed earlier is strongly analogous to the dynamics of drug addiction. The opponent process model of job satisfaction, or motivation, is further thought to subsume the dynamics of motivator–hygiene theory and the Lawler–Porter process for satisfaction and performance.

Finally, equity and expectancy theories can both be regarded as "balance theories," which is a noncommittal way of calling them theories of stability and instability. They began with different theoretical roots but arrived at similar predictions. Most pointedly, expectancy theory posited a relationship between motivation, ability, and performance that was exactly the same as what would be expected from personnel selection research.

The foregoing commonalities among theories were coupled with low overall predictive accuracies and unresolved details. The differential results for applications to work performance, absenteeism, and turnover require explanation as well. It would be only a small and visible next step to suggest that a still more comprehensive theory could be synthesized from the available raw materials. The most theoretically powerful tools are those that contain dynamical concepts, such as stability and instability, and processes such as the Mobley turnover model that specifically address events that occur over time.

TWO-STAGE PERSONNEL SELECTION

The cusp catastrophe model for two-stage personnel selection and training evaluation begins with a premise similar to one that Gregson (1992) invoked regarding cognitive processes: Although it is convenient to study psychophysics, perception, memory, and reaction time as separate phenomena, all those processes work together in the real world and might not be as readily separated without a significant loss of meaning. Similarly, the relationships between ability, motivation, training, and performance are convenient to separate, but the actual process of people going to work is a wholistic event where several subprocesses could be operating in synchrony.

In the case of personnel selection, the vast majority of the literature concerns decisions made about job applicants at the time of hiring. The real process of integrating those people into the organization's workforce only begins with the hiring decision. Hiring is typically followed by a succession of training programs, formal or otherwise, the development of links with other employees, work-related or otherwise, and the development of an understanding of the subtleties of the organization's life and culture. This integrative view is not unfamiliar (Organ, 1988; Wanous, 1980), but has not yet integrated any major chunks of theory either.

Organizations often construct two-stage hiring systems without resorting to any particular use of psychology. In some of the skilled trades, there is a 30- to 60-day trial period before which the organization can check out the contributions of the new hire, and after which the employee joins the labor union, when new rules concerning job dismissal take effect. For university faculty the time period can extend for 7 years; those rites of passage are known as the tenure application. In contemporary work life, organizations are skirting the initial hiring process altogether. Rather, new employees are selected by temporary employment agencies that service numerous organizational clients. The only people who are really hired by the organization are those who performed well in the temporary system and who exhibited talents that organization wants to acquire. The temporary system not only dumps the risks of poor hiring decisions onto agencies that spread the risk in a different manner, but allows the organization to remain uncommitted to long-term agreements, to avoid paying benefits to the employees, and to keep the rate of pay low (which is still lower after the temporary agency takes its chunk).

Racial or cultural subgroup differences in assimilation into an organization need not be confined to discrimination during the initial hiring process. They could occur during the socialization period, and may reflect differences in adjustment patterns. If personality characteristics are used as predictors of success, perhaps to denote some interest pattern or social skill, the personality measurement may not have the same meaning for every cultural group relative to the performance objective. Similarly, there could be male–female differences that are not well understood now.

Cusp Model

The cusp model for organizational entry is defined as having two stable states of outcome (Fig. 5.2). On the lower sheet of the response surface the person is not a member of the organization, and on the upper sheet the person is employed by the organization. Between two attractors, along the vertical axis, is a continuous measure of performance, which ranges from "not working here" to "maximum output that could be expected from anyone." At the time of making selections, the personnel manager must be content with predicted values of the performance continuum for the job applicants, which would be based on selection test scores or job application information. The fold line that creates the sudden shift in status from not hired to hired is the organization's minimum acceptable level of performance, or predicted performance.

Job knowledge, aptitudes, abilities, and skills contribute to the asymmetry parameter. Motivation contributes to the bifurcation parameter. Those applicants with weak qualifications in those areas remain not hired. Those with strong qualifications have a high likelihood of being hired and remaining hired. Applicants with moderate skill levels for the job could experience either fate. Those who placed greater effort into their

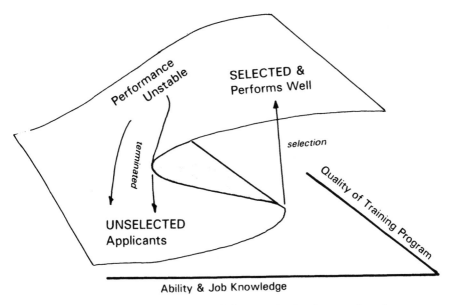

FIG. 5.2. Cusp catastrophe model for organizational entry, two-stage personnel selection, or training evaluation.

application materials and into their work once hired may be indistinguishable from those with greater natural talent or previously acquired knowledge. Moderately qualified applicants who do not expend the extra effort may run the risk of short-term employment if they are to be even casually compared against other incumbents.

Moving in the opposite direction along the surface from "hired" to "not hired," those new people who find that the job does not motivate them will be likely to seek other employment when the next available opportunity arises. If the poor motivation is not coupled with the skills needed to coast through the job and to not look blatantly bad at it, the employee runs the risk of involuntary termination. Notice that the critical level of performance needed for hiring is greater than the critical level to provoke a firing; this is the double threshold effect.

In the cases where demographic variables could be moderators of the ability–performance relationship or bifurcation variables in a dynamic process, the groups who adapt more flexibly to the new environment would follow trajectories on the low bifurcation side of the response surface. Those who are less flexible will acclimate suddenly or not do so at all; their trajectories would be found on the unfolded side of the response surface. The dynamics of flexibility are expanded on further in Chapter 6.

If the model is to be taken literally, which is the intention here, performance needs to be measured at two points in time. The first measurement would be taken during the earliest weeks of employment. The second measurement would be taken around the time when the training and socialization period has been completed. The control variables are ideally measured at or before the time of the first performance measure. The real time delay between measurements is dependent on the complexity of the socialization process; some organizations will require more time than others.

The next step is to apply the dynamic difference equation for the cusp and to calculate R^2, and to compare the results with those obtained from conventional models and analysis. If all features of the cusp model are well defined, then R^2 will be higher than that obtained for competing models. A bifurcation effect would be identified, along with asymmetry variables, on the basis of significance tests for the separate terms in the model.

Example

The following case analysis was prepared as an example of the cusp model for two-stage personnel selection and as a demonstration that the dynamic difference equation for the cusp would perform its intended function (Guastello, 1982a). Data for Time 2 were real; data for Time 1 were simulated by altering the Time 2 data.

The participants were 272 salespeople for business accounts from a midwestern firm. The sample consisted of 17 Spanish-speaking Americans (SSA) and 255 non-SSA subjects. Group membership was the bifurcation variable in the cusp analysis and the moderator variable in a special control comparison model (Equation 1). The asymmetry variable was a unit-weighted composite of scales from the Gordon Personal Profile and a measure of "adaptability" composed of items that were similar to intelligence test items. The criterion was a composite score on a variety of job-related behaviors, such as accuracy of paperwork, management of sales calls, and the use of safety procedures.

The simulated data for Time 1 were prepared according to what would be expected if the cusp concept had been used to collect data. First, criterion scores were converted to standard (z) scores. Second, negative standard scores were recoded to zero. The resulting distribution was positively skewed, which would be characteristic of performance scores taken close to the first day on the job. The mode would perform at real zero, with the more proficient ones performing at the higher level. The situation was defined such that no one could perform at a value less than zero.

For the ordinary moderator regression model (Time 2 data only), the obtained value of R^2 was .04 ($p < .01$). A significant weight was obtained for the personality–adaptability composite, but not for the interactive moderator term or group membership. For the cusp model, the obtained R^2 was .37 ($p < .001$). Only weights for the cubic and quadratic terms were significant, however. A check for retardation was also made; the quartic term was significant and was included in the final model. The quintic term was tested, but could not be retained in the model due to insufficient tolerance.

Additional data treatments were pursued to determine if R^2 for the model would increase as further bimodality was introduced into the model. Indeed that did occur, and those results were shown in Fig. 3.2 and discussed in the accompanying text. Of particular interest was the data preparation whereby the lowest performing 16% of people at Time 2 were contrasted against all other participants. The R^2 was .95, and significant weights were obtained for the bifurcation and asymmetry variables. No quartic effect was found.

There were several important conclusions from the analysis. First, the statistical model worked as intended. Second, a two-stage personnel selection model based on the cusp catastrophe could provide a substantially more accurate assessment of behavior dynamics. Third, there is a difference between selecting people out of a system compared to selecting them into a system. The two approaches do not produce equal statistical models, which would be assumed by an ordinary linear function. Fourth, bifurcation on the basis of cultural group membership may indeed occur in the process of assimilating new employees into an organization.

BUTTERFLY CATASTROPHE MODEL
OF MOTIVATION IN ORGANIZATIONS

The butterfly catastrophe model of motivation in organizations is developed next, beginning with cusp subspaces of the butterfly model. The full model is unfolded in stages.

Motivation–Performance Subspaces

The modeling process builds on the cusp for two-stage personnel selection just described. There were two stable outcomes: staying with the job or termination. Abilities contribute to the asymmetry parameter. The bifurcation parameter could be represented by demographic group membership or, more pertinently here, motivation variables. The next subtopics address the Yerkes–Dodson function for motivation and performance, studies in the stability of performance, and the opponent process model.

Yerkes–Dodson Function. According to Yerkes and Dodson (1908), there is an inverted-U relationship between motivation, arousal or anxiety, and performance. McGrath (1976) found that the relationship could be decomposed into two linear functions. First, higher level of motivation lead to higher levels of performance. Second, performance decrements follow increased task difficulty. Task difficulty can be reasoned to be a negative function of ability. These effects are modeled by trajectories from the cusp point to the locally stable attractors on the cusp surface in Fig. 5.3. (Further applications and extensions of the Yerkes–Dodson function are elaborated in chapter 6.)

Stability of Performance. Work performance in industry is more stable under some conditions than under others (Rambo et al., 1983). For instance, performance is more variable when rewards are not tied to performance than when they are tied to performance. Also, performance is more variable when the job requires a greater task difficulty compared to simple task conditions. These effects are modeled by orbits drawn on the cusp bifurcation set in Fig. 5.3, which indicate the path of the control point on the response surface.

For the situation of pay tied to performance, let pay be somewhat motivating, that is, $b > 0$ in the cusp, and the ability of employees be adequate. Next, let motivation decompose into bifurcation gradients—positive toward the upper performance level when performance is obviously rewarded, and negative when it is not. When pay is tied to performance, performance varies only a small amount over time, orbiting

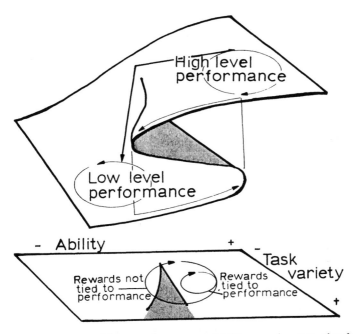

FIG. 5.3. Cusp model for performance variability as a function of task complexity. From Guastello (1987a). Reprinted with permission.

the upper attractor. When it is not tied to performance, variability between attractors occurs.

Task variety can be positively or negatively motivating. In the positive case, task variety enhances motivation by providing the employee with a range of responsibilities that add up to a whole job rather than just fragment of the operation. On the other hand, if the employee is given a group of "dumb jobs," the impact would be demotivating since "they just want more work out of me."

Rambo et al. (1983) showed that performance stability approaches an asymptotic limit. They adopted a formula from Kessler and Greenberg (1981) for "structured change." The covariance of performance between two time periods is equal to the sum of two components: performance at Time 1 squared, and the covariance of performance at Time 1 with change in performance. That is:

$$S_{(y_1 y_2)} = S^2_{(y_1)} + S_{(y_1 \, \Delta y)} \tag{8}$$

Equation 8 essentially states that the optimal relationship between performance at Time 1 and Time 2 is:

$$\Delta y = \beta_1 y_1^2 + \beta_2 y_1 \tag{9}$$

Job performance is typically represented by a linear function, albeit an imperfect one, of job-related ability, when motivation factors are not introducing and purturbances. Thus it is possible to substitute ability, a, for y_1, and the result is the fold catastrophe model.

Rambo et al. (1983) found that the correlation between performance measures taken from two points in time reached an asymptotic lower limit as the number of weeks between measurements increased from 1 to 178 weeks. During that time, working and incentive conditions (in a sewing factory) did not change. Computed values of structured change were found to be fairly constant throughout the time series. Their plot of correlation versus lag time resulted in an elbow curve that started with correlations in excess of .90, dropped fairly rapidly to the elbow of the curve at 20 weeks, and dropped more gradually to the asymptote at 30 weeks. The asymptotic correlation between performance measures was .62 for sewing jobs and .85 for nonsewing jobs.

The simplest NDS interpretation of the results, therefore, is that the work situation was globally stable, deviations are fold catastrophic, and the orbital period is about is 30 weeks. Although Rambo et al. did not specify an equilibrium value of performance, some sort of equilibrium was approached. Not much change occurred between consecutive performance weeks; hence high correlations were observed. The elbow function showed that all the change that was likely to occur transpired in a relatively fixed amount of time. Global stability could be inferred because the asymptote was calculated for all possible pairs of performance scores, given lag length. Global stability is additionally reinforced by knowing that the work situation was not manipulated during that time horizon.

From an inverse viewpoint, however, a correlation of .62 indicates that close to 60% of performance variance between measurement periods is not accounted for. It is uncertain whether waves of turnover and training new workers could account for that variation or whether the stable attractor is structurally simple but chaotic nonetheless.

A later study involving grinders and chippers in a foundry (Vinchur et al., 1991) produced results that were similar but different from the results of the Rambo et al. (1983) study. Performance measures on several specific tasks were correlated at intervals of up to 6 years. Correlations dropped from an average of .70 at 1 or 2 weeks of delay to .50 after 3 years, but increased to .60 afterward. Vinchur et al. concluded that performance, in some jobs, was less stable than previous results appeared to indicate. Of particular interest here was their analysis showing that the relationship between correlation and lag time was not a simple elbow curve, but a cubic polynomial function. The most parsimonious NDS interpretation would be that some sort of coupled dynamic was taking place. Unfortunately, the study was not sufficiently detailed to provide a clue as to what constituted the driving subsystem. Whatever it was, the driver was acting as a bifurcation factor, causing greater and lesser variability in performance over time. Some of the instability in performance, once again, could possibly have been the result of employee turnover and training of new employees; although there were 155 people in the study altogether, only 5 persisted on the job for the entire duration of 6 years.

Hofmann et al. (1993) ventured beyond the initial question of whether performance is stable. Their goals were to perform some structural equation modeling on performance trends and to determine whether employees could be clustered in separate performance–time curves. They found that sales output for 319 insurance salespeople followed a trend over time (12 quarters of a year) that resembled the classic learning curve: a relatively linear beginning followed by an asymptote, with oscillations around the asymptote. Polynomial regression analysis showed that performance was a cubic function of time, with linear and quadratic components (R^2 = .52). Other analyses they conducted with simulated data caused them to reject the cubic term, but the cubic effect was significant in the original data.

In the next major step of their work, performance–time trends for each employee were analyzed, and the employees were clustered according to their time trend. Three clear trends emerged. All groups started at zero dollars in sales at the beginning of the time horizon. One group increased performance monotonically over the 12 quarters. Another started to increase monotonically, but declined to a mediocre level of performance by the end of 12 quarters. The third group started to increase in sales but remained below the others throughout the time horizon, which ended with some apparent net losses in sales. The curves are shown in Fig. 5.4. A complex bifurcation process was clearly taking place. Explanations for how those bifurcating effects originated were beyond the scope of their study, although they did make reference to motivation and learning dynamics as a plausible category of explanations.

Opponent Processes. The opponent process theory of job satisfaction describes an oscillation between two qualitatively different levels of performance (Landy, 1978), thus suggesting, at first blush, a cusp catastrophe model. The bifurcation gradients may be the motivator and hygiene factors, or intrinsic and extrinsic forms of motivation, which are in turn thought to be linked to the sympathetic and parasympathetic nervous system processes. The greater the number of hygiene and motivator elements, the larger the possible variation in performance. The second part of the process calls for a peak decline in peak performance over time, which is caused by boredom. Where ability is held constant, peak decline contributes to the asymmetry parameter. Six steps in the

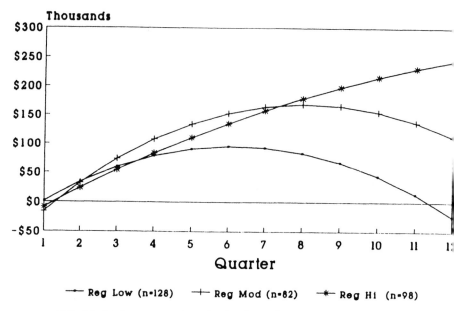

FIG. 5.4. Performance trajectories for three clusters of sales employees. From Hofmann et al. (1993). Reprinted with permission.

opponent process phenomenon are modeled as trajectories in Fig. 5.5; the six numbered points correspond to analogous points marked in Fig. 5.1.

When ability is free to vary, moderately high-ability persons would show the peak decline, or boredom effect. Low-ability subjects would simply show poor performance with only small variability. Persons of high ability, though they may experience vast amounts of boredom, can more easily keep their performance levels from dropping too low. Boredom can be considered as native intrinsic motivation. It has the effect of shifting the peaks to a new mode as an asymmetry parameter would do.

The effects of ability, hygiene factors (extrinsic motivation), and boredom (intrinsic motivation) can be combined next into a swallowtail model. The surface has two stable modes for acceptable but uninspired performance, and one for superior feats. The unstable zone represents organizationally unacceptable performance. The control parameters are as follows: a is ability, b is hygiene, and c is cycle number or boredom (Fig. 5.5). The six steps in the opponent process appear on the swallowtail surface. At step 4, the control point drops through the inaccessible region to the unstable mode and returns to the lower stable mode at step 5.

Turnover and Absenteeism. Motivation and satisfaction theories are also relevant to absenteeism and turnover as discussed in the first section. It is generally true that absenteeism is precipitated by a lack of intrinsic

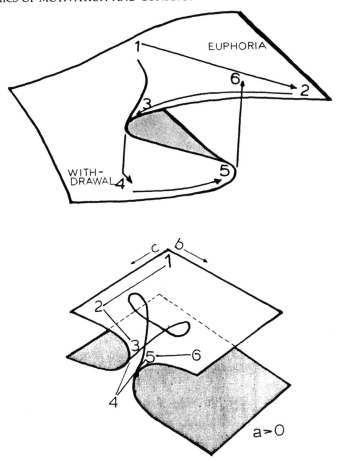

FIG. 5.5. Opponent process model of satisfaction or motivation depicted as cusp and swallowtail catastrophe models. From Guastello (1984a). Reprinted with permission.

satisfaction, and turnover is precipitated by a lack of both intrinsic and extrinsic elements. Because these forms of motivation and satisfaction are already implicated, a fully developed model should account for absenteeism and turnover as well. Indeed, cusp catastrophe models for absenteeism and turnover have withstood preliminary tests (Guastello, 1984b; Sheridan, 1980, 1985; Sheridan & Abelson, 1983). Abelson (1982) expanded on the cusp concept by identifying stages of the Mobley (1977) turnover process as positions along the cusp surface.

Approach–Avoidance. If one were to view the cusp surface divergence gradients in two dimensions, they would be equal in length but different in their slopes. The downward gradient is steeper. This relationship describes the differential approach and avoidance gradients that have long been observed in animal and human social behavior. The subject avoids a negative stimulus faster than it approaches a positive one (Brown, 1948). The approach–avoidance gradients are implicit in all motivation–performance subspaces, and account for the differential impact of positive and negative utilities in expectancy and financial decision making (Kahneman & Tversky, 1979; Leon, 1981). To give a simple example, suppose we were to present an unseasoned investor with a series of possible business transactions, all with varying probabilities of gaining and earning varying amounts of money, our investors would avoid the possibility of losing $500 considerably faster than they would accept a possibility of earning $500; in others words, $500 lost is bigger than $500 gained.

Butterfly Model

Surface. Two stable, qualitatively different modalities of work performance were described in the foregoing cusp interpretation of the opponent process model. An unstable third mode was hinted at in the swallowtail unfolding of same. The cusp models for turnover (Sheridan, 1980, 1985; Sheridan & Abelson, 1983; elaborated subsequently) and two-stage personnel selection simply contrasted staying on the job and quitting. Merging the two ideas, there are three distinct modes of performance: high, good enough to get by, and poor enough to warrant termination. A butterfly surface would be required to describe change in behavior, or the distribution of behavior among the three modes. The butterfly also allows for voluntary turnover from good performers. In studying change in behavior among the two work modalities and turnover, turnover would be scored 0.00 on a performance scale ranging from 0.00 to some positive value.

Absenteeism can be thought of as a hysteresis between staying on the job and quitting. Frequent absence can become a stable mode of behavior in its own right. Although it is not often mentioned in the literature (but I have observed it first hand), three modes of absenteeism can be typically identified from personnel records: those persons who gravitate toward no absences at all, those who gravitate toward what they perceive as an average level, and the chronic absentees. The modalities for absenteeism, performance, and turnover can be organized into a butterfly surface as follows.

On the upper sheet of the surface, subjects would show self-directed, internally committed behavior: high output and high-quality work. Innovation, which would be partially based on prerequisite abilities (and considered at great length in chapter 10), would occur at the extreme end of this subdivision. Absenteeism rates would gravitate toward virtually none, although, conceivably, internally directed and competent people might organize their work to permit an occasional day off. Some people in the neighborhood of this attractor would harbor a strong intent to leave the organization, whereas others would harbor none. No discernible difference in the work behavior between the two groups would be expected, however.

The attractor on the middle sheet of the response surface is thought to be characterized by externally motivated behavior at low levels of commitment. Innovation would not be forthcoming from high-ability employees. Quantity and quality of work would be merely adequate. Absenteeism would occur at the average level for the organization or work group. Turnover intentions would be greater than what would be expected from the upper sheet overall; there would be less disparity among employees on this issue.

The lower mode would describe people who leave the organization voluntarily or are fired for chronic absenteeism or poor performance. In organizations that do not have an organized absenteeism policy, chronic absentees would be noted at this level. Strikes and riots are expected in extreme conditions. Turnover is the asymmetric reverse of organizational entry, as explained earlier.

Control Parameters. Control parameters in the hypothesized model are a, ability, b, extrinsic motivation, c, intrinsic motivation, and d, organizational climate. Ability is broadly defined and may consist of cognitive measures of ability, job-specific personality measures or social skills, or ability to attend work as defined in the Steers and Rhodes (1978) process model for absenteeism. Extrinsic and intrinsic motivation are defined as broadly as they were in the conventional motivation theories. Additionally, demographic variables that are otherwise known as moderators of ability would contribute to parameter b.

Organizational climate appears for the first time in the butterfly model. Climate itself is a complex concept that has given way in recent years to notions of organizational culture (Schneider & Reichers, 1983), on the one hand, and specific social climate concepts such as a climate for achievement (deCharms, 1976; Litwin & Stringer, 1966) or a climate for innovation (Siegel & Kaemmerer, 1978). Climate may, in many instances, be a matter social conditions and social perceptions, but may in other instances be linked to objective features of an organization's structure such as its size (Heller et al., 1982; James & Jones, 1974; Porter & Lawler, 1965).

Relative to motivation, however, the general rule is that d governs the coaction of intrinsic and extrinsic motivation; the culture that management propels determines what is a motivator and what the salient motivational conditions of an organization happen to be (Maehr & Braskamp,

1986). Parameter *d* may vary across gross types of organizations, (e.g., work, volunteer, academic), across organizations with type, or across subunits within an organization (Drexler, 1977).

Figure 5.6 shows a sectioning of the butterfly surface over parameter *d*. For low values of *d*, intrinsic and extrinsic motivation are additive, and a relatively greater number of behavior changes would occur between adjacent modalities. For higher values of *d*, intrinsic and extrinsic motivation are interactive, and a relatively greater number of behavior changes would occur between extreme modalities. Because *d* is continuously defined, it would follow that the additivity or interactivity of intrinsic and extrinsic motivation is actually a matter of degree. Leadership style and organizational policies and practices would determine the specific relative contributions of intrinsic and extrinsic motivation to the behavior spectrum.

Gradients. The surface gradients of the butterfly surface describe changes in behavior from an ambiguous (unstable) state to one of the stable modalities, often illustrating interesting theoretical properties. Gradients in the motivation model describe satisfaction, equity, tension, and commitment constructs. The role of satisfaction in the opponent process subspace model was described earlier.

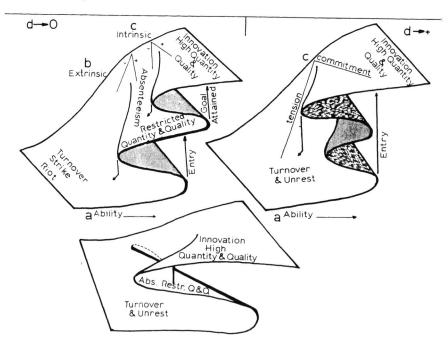

FIG. 5.6. The butterfly catastrophe model of motivation in organizations. From Guastello (1987a). Reprinted with permission.

Equity theory, as proposed by Adams (1965) and embellished by many, can be thought of as a statistical concept (Guastello, 1981). Although a person has a reasonably clear notion of what constitutes fair or unfair exchanges, some deviation is tolerated. This approximating process occurs in a single exchange, but more so in repeated exchanges. Equity judgments are made relative to something, and involve a social comparison process. If a person's outcome to input ratio exceeds that of a comparison person or other reference point, a relative reward is experienced. If the ratio is less than the reference, a relative cost is experienced.

In a work relationship, the repeated exchanges integrate into a long continuous pattern of exchange. The exchange itself can become quite complex, consisting of numerous intrinsic and extrinsic facets, some of which are inevitably valued by some people more than other quantities. The social comparison and judgment process are thought to apply to each important facet of the exchange. Each facet is perceived and judged in approximately the same way as a signal is detected relative to noise in a psychophysical process. According to most theories, people process intrinsic and extrinsic rewards (or promises of same) differently. It is required, therefore that they be separated in the model. In a job relationship, therefore, the individual is judging four varieties of signal that comprise the surface gradients: extrinsic rewards, extrinsic costs, intrinsic rewards, and intrinsic costs.

Some exchanges involve higher stakes than others, in which case something akin to d' in a psychophysical process becomes larger. High-stakes situations, in this context, are those where large potential outcomes are paired with large inputs, and larger potential losses exist as well. According to the butterfly mechanism, the stakes need to be sufficiently high for the individual to reach the basin of one of the performance attractors.

Low-stakes exchanges, by contrast, occur around the butterfly point and are inherently unstable. There is not much exchanged, so there is little to gain or to lose. Performance would reflect mid-range output on the average, but would be unstable and susceptible to strong signals coming in from another source, such as a better job. On the other hand, should the motivation to work be suddenly enhanced by a new approach to management, a trajectory to a middle- or high-performance attractor would be observed.

Tensions and commitment were initially presented as rotated control parameters in a cusp model for turnover (Sheridan & Abelson, 1983) and represented the positive and negative aspects of intrinsic motivation. Tension arises from a job that is interesting, arousing, and novel in an unpleasant way. Commitment is the positive side and is a hybrid composed of the interest value of the task, job involvement, and the motivational qualities of the employee and the surrounding work environment.

Steps within the Mobley (1977) turnover process can be identified as points along the cusp surface. Behavioral intention, which is the step closest to turnover, is anchored next to the fold line at which the behavior change occurs.

Some empirical tests of the butterfly model or its subsets are considered next. They are followed by additional empirical work on extensions of the butterfly motivation theory to learning dynamics.

Academic Performance

The application of the butterfly model of motivation to academic performance (Guastello, 1987a) addressed a common situation. Consider unsuccessful freshmen where their level of success is measured by grade point average (GPA). Students may perform poorly because of insufficient ability, poor study habits, negative attitudes about grades, disinterest, or unfocused interest in the subject matter studies. Psychological adjustment problems may frequently be responsible for poor adjustment. The design of the study further assumed that the period of adjustment that affects nearly all students would be completed by the end of the freshman year.

Subjects in the study were 272 freshmen males and females from a midwestern technical university who participated in a voluntary counseling program; they represented 27% of two freshmen classes. The following measurements were extracted from counseling records: American College Test (ACT) scores; realistic, investigative, and enterprising themes and academic orientation scores from the Strong–Campbell Interest Inventory (Campbell, 1977); and the GPA from the last year of high school. High-school GPA was computed from grades into a scale equivalent to the 4-point college GPA.

The ACT composite score was adopted as ability parameter a in the butterfly model. For extrinsic motivation, the cost of education and financial aid are not analogous to pay in work situations. A closer analogy can be found, however, by separating motivation into two aspects: interest value of the subject matter, and motivation to perform the external features of college study. The latter would include studying hard, working for grades, and selecting courses that would ensure a successful completion of a major, which would imply a linkage to desirable jobs or entrance to graduate school later on. The external feature of academic motivation were thus represented by the academic orientation scores (parameter b).

The interest theme scores are generally lower at the beginning of the college career than later on. Patterns of career interests crystallize over time. It would be expected that a freshman with highly developed interests would be intrinsically motivated to do well; a negative reaction might appear in a student of high motivation and low ability. It was also conceivable that low-interest students would comprise the multimodal or high-variance end of the relationship, in which case the high-interest theme students would show a unimodal performance-difference distribution.

Realistic, enterprising, and investigative theme scores were all hypothesized to contributed to parameter c in the butterfly model. The realistic theme pertains to practical interests and to outdoor activities, with subscales for agriculture, nature, adventure, military, and mechanical activities. It is thought to be similar to the interests of engineers. The enterprising theme represents interest in public speaking, law and politics, merchandising, sales, and business management; it would be pertinent to business majors and engineers preparing for engineering management. The investigative theme is an aggregate of medical and other science, mathematics, and service interests and would be characteristic of science majors and engineers. The Strong–Campbell contains other theme scores, but those interest groups were not well represented by the majors available to the students in the study.

Freshmen tend to take a variety of introductory courses; thus their exposures are distributed among many of the departments of the institution by the end of the school year. In addition, they are exposed to certain commonalities among department. With regard to climate, the school's idiosyncrasies suggest that it is at greater variance with colleges in general than there is variance among subunits. For those reasons, d was replaced by a constant 1.00 in the analytic model, which was the dynamic difference equation for the butterfly catastrophe.

The data analysis showed that R^2 for the butterfly catastrophe model (.35) was much greater than values obtained for the control difference (.02) or pre–post linear (.09) models. The weights for the quintic and cubic terms in the butterfly model were significant, but no significant weights were observed for the terms containing control variables. The nonsignificant terms did display large bivariate correlations with the criterion, suggesting some strong collinearity with the power potentials that indicated the structure of the surface.

One significant weight was observed for realistic theme in the control difference model ($p < .05$). Students scoring high in realistic theme tended to improve their relative academic standing. That bivariate correlation was rather low ($r = .11$), however. The only significant weight observed in the pre–post control model was high school GPA ($p < .001$; bivariate $r = .26$).

Split-sample cross-validation analysis showed that the butterfly model actually gained accuracy from the validation subsample ($N = 191$, $R^2 = .34$) to the hold-out sample ($N = 81$, $R^2 = .37$). The accuracy of the control difference model did not change. The R^2 for the linear pre–post model dropped from .10 to .05.

The results of the study showed, overall, that butterfly structure was an accurate depiction of academic performance. The role of the motivation variables was tenuous at best, and the question remained as to whether the selection of motivation measurements was at fault or whether motivation was not the answer at all. Later research, fortunately, supported the former interpretation and ruled out the latter.

Turnover and Absenteeism

A cusp model for turnover among nursing staff that was proposed and tested by Sheridan and Abelson (1983) showed one of the highest correct classification rates on record (84–86%) for determining which employees would stay and which would quit their jobs. In his review, Mobley (1982) encouraged management scientists to discover catastrophe theory in light of those results. Sheridan and Abelson utilized a qualitative technique first proposed by Jiobu and Lundgren (1978) to analyze their data. Their two control variables were tension and alienation. Their procedure began with a scatterplot of cases on the two control variables, and each case was labeled as a "stay" or a "quit." The next step was to hand-fit a bifurcation set through the scatterplot; in a good application the data points should separate clearly into a V configuration, with points to either side of the V. The third step was to calculate a chi-square showing that stays and quits were localized to opposite sides of the V.

The success of the turnover application was replicated in a later study where job tension and work group cohesion were the control variables (Sheridan, 1985). Sheridan also investigated absenteeism under the same stable conditions of work and found that the cusp-difference model afforded a model improvement over the linear alternative ($R^2 = .21$ compared to .17).

In a different approach to absenteeism, absence rates for 19 work groups were studied as a function of a changing organizational policy about absenteeism (Guastello, 1984b). The sample contained a total of 460 employees from two factory facilities. One plant was located in a commercialized zone of a suburb and the other in a more rural location 20 miles distant from the suburban plant. The same types of work took place in both divisions, but some support departments existed only at the suburban location.

Every year employees received cash bonuses for good attendance based on the average number of absences per year for the year at hand and 2 years previous to that. From 4 hours to 3 days of continuous absence was counted as a single absence. If a person were absent 5 days in a row, two absences were scored, and so forth. The usual allowances were made for vacation, jury duty, inclement weather, and major family emergencies.

The former policy on absenteeism allowed for 32 hours of bonus pay per year for less than two absences, and lesser amounts of bonus for up to five absences. Graphs of company attendance records showed that the attendance level had stabilized by the time the new policy was put into effect.

The revised policy allowed for a larger top reward of 40 hours of pay for no absences, but had more demanding rules for lesser bonuses, where the smallest bonus was 8 hours of pay for up to four absences. In addition, the new plan allowed employees to review their attendance records each month for feedback as to how well they were doing.

When the new plan went into effect, there was a 23.5% drop in absences during the first 6 months compared to the first 6 months from the year before ($p < .05$). When the results were figured in terms of percentages of lost work time, the suburban plant dropped from 2.6% to 2.0%, the rural plant showed a gain from 1.6% to 1.8%, and the office (counted as 1 of the 19 groups) showed a drop from 1.7% to 0.9%. The national average at that time was 3.3%. Of additional interest, departments where the average age of employees was older responded better to the new plan than younger departments (rank order $r = .44$, $p < .05$).

A cusp model for the events was defined as a subset of the butterfly model where the upper two sheets of the surface were studied. The rural–suburban distinction was defined as the bifurcation parameter, and department age was treated as parameter a. The rationale for including age was that older workers were less intrinsically motivated than younger ones, according to Meltzer and Ludwig (1968), who had conducted their studies in the same corporation a decade before. Because only a cusp subset was involved, the bias variable c was treated as a primary asymmetry variable. Results showed that the dynamic difference equation for the cusp was more accurate ($R^2 = .58$) than the next best linear alternative ($R^2 = .30$). Significant weights were obtained for the cubic potential, bifurcation, and asymmetry terms in the cusp model. Results are depicted in Fig. 5.7.

MOTIVATION AND LEARNING

The next two applications of the NDS motivation theory concern learning in classroom settings. The first focuses on the performance of college students, mostly freshmen, in an introductory psychology course (Guastello, 1986). Although the application may look pretty banal, the situation allowed the investigator to observe butterfly structure, and to assess the role of gender differences and teacher effects as control variables. The second application of the NDS motivation theory concerned the devel-

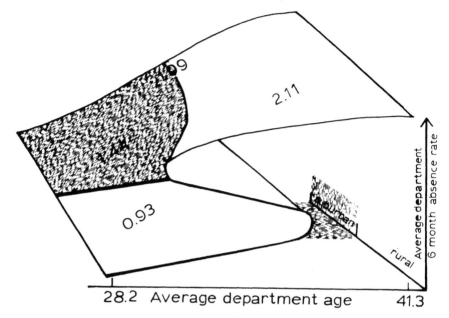

FIG. 5.7. Effect of a new policy to control absenteeism. From Guastello (1984b). Reprinted with permission.

opment of human relations knowledge as the criterion. The application allowed some different tests of motivation hypotheses.

Introductory Psychology

The study participants were 455 students enrolled in four consecutive administrations of an introductory psychology course, which was taught in both spring and fall semesters. The sample was approximately 60% female. The four courses were the first four introductory psychology courses ever taught by that professor.

The performance measures were based on four noncumulative exams that the students took plus extra credit points the students acquired for volunteering to participate in experiments run by psychology department faculty. The system for converting experiment participation time to extra credit points was developed independently by other members of the psychology department before the classes involved in the study began. The regular exams contained all multiple choice items, which were borrowed liberally from ancillary materials supplied by the textbook publisher. The Time 1 performance measure was the score on the first exam, which was administered approximately 4 weeks into the semester. The Time 2 performance measure was the sum of four exam scores plus the extra credit points. If a student dropped the course after the first exam, the Time 2 performance measure was 0.00. The location and scale parameters were estimated separately at each point in time. Location values of y were the total number of exam points a student could collect by random guessing on the exams. Scale values of y were the ordinary standard deviations.

For control variables, two ability-related variables were hypothesized to contribute to the a parameter; one was the number of prior semesters of college experience, and the other was whether the student had taken a statistics course prior to taking the psychology class. Gender differences comprised the b parameter as specified by the personnel selection model. All students attended the same classes and took the same exams, so there was not opportunity for any actual differential treatment of students. The version of the course was tested as a d parameter. Version represented management style, in one respect, and the teacher's improvement in another respect. There was no intrinsic motivation variable available. The butterfly model was tested in two stages; the first stage did not contain a cz_1^2 term, and the second stage introduced z_1^2 where c was a constant 1.00.

Results of the analysis showed, at the first stage, that the butterfly catastrophe model ($R^2 = .47$) was clearly superior to linear control models. Significant weights were recorded for all terms in the butterfly model except the quartic scale correction. One significant weight for semesters experience was observed for the linear difference model ($R^2 = .04$). Weight for the first test and semesters experience were significant in the control pre–post model ($R^2 = .29$). When the quadratic term was entered into the butterfly model, R^2 increased to .55.

The results of the study confirmed the butterfly structure for motivated learning where dropping out (turnover) was a possibility. The potentially bifurcating effect of gender was also confirmed. Gender differences could not have reflected bias because of the standard treatment all students received. Rather, it showed that the female students made greater progress increments than male students for reasons that need to be explored in other ways.[1]

Version of the course, which represented management's contribution to motivated learning, was a strong effect, accounting for 30% of variance by itself. That finding confirmed the central premise of the d parameter in the theoretical model. In this particular case, the results confirmed that the professor improved his act in the course, but the measurements taken in the study were not sensitive enough to decipher

---

[1]Years later it became common knowledge in the field that the proportion of women professionals in psychology had reached 50% and could be increasing to a majority.

how much of the improvement was related to clearer presentations or to funnier jokes.

Human Relations Training

Issues in Training Evaluation. Before jumping into the application directly, it would be useful to consider the relationship between the catastrophe applications and conventional wisdom regarding training evaluation. A well-controlled experimental evaluation of a training program will utilize five groups of human participants. Group 1 is pretested on the learning objective, trained, and retested. Group 2 is pretested, given a sham training program, then retested. The comparison of Group 1 and Group 2 test scores will indicate how much learning was associated with the real training program, compared to what would take place in any training environment. Group 3 is pretested, not trained, and later retested. A comparison of Group 3's results against those of Groups 1 and 2 will indicate how much change in learning was a function of maturation, or how much learning would take place without a program. Group 4 would not be pretested, not trained, but given the test at the second point in time. The comparison of Group 4 with other groups would indicate how much of the change observed in Group 3 was a result of pretesting. Group 5 would receive no pretest, but would receive training and a posttest. The comparison of Group 5 results with those from Group 1 would indicate the impact of pretesting on training.

In practice, a researcher is fortunate to have Groups 1 and 3 available. Group 2 is expensive to include, but may be available if two or more distinct training programs are to be given. Use of Group 2 provides a more stringent test of the program's effectiveness than what would be obtained through use of maturation Group 3, however. If learning is measured unobtrusively, as opposed to measurement by paper-and-pencil testing, Groups 4 and 5 are unnecessary.

In spite of all the control groups, however, the foregoing experimental design provisions do not assess the stability of learning over time. Golembiewski (1986) and Guastello (1982a) did suggest that the cusp catastrophe model would be a useful analytic tool for assessing the stability of change as a function of program implementation, because strong concepts of equilibrium and stability are part of the catastrophe functions. In a catastrophe analysis, one would expect greater change for the training Group 1 compared to control Group 2 or 3. Data points for the training group would fall on the unfolded portion of the surface (manifold region). Sham training data points would fall somewhat further toward the unruffled side of the surface, and maturation group data would fall furthest away, behind the bifurcation point.

Application. The human relations training application centered on human relations learning in university course in industrial psychology, where knowledge was measured by a standardized test, How Supervise (File & Remmers, 1971). How Supervise contains 70 items covering supervisory practices and opinions and implementation of company policies. Correct answers are keyed to opinions given by a major of managers and supervisors over the 1948–1971 period. The test is available in two alternate forms, and its authors cited 10 studies in which How Supervise was used to evaluate supervisory training programs. Of the 10 studies, 7 showed significant score improvements as a function of the training program, 1 showed mixed results, and 2 showed negative results. Only 3 of the 10 studies used control groups, of which 1 showed positive findings, 1 showed mixed results, and 1 showed negative results. Correlations between the two forms of the test, measured before and after training ranged from .34 ($p < .01$) to .81 ($p < .01$), with an average value of .63.

The dates associated with the test norms should trigger a few warning lights. Although much of the test content can be considered fundamental or harmless, the test cannot be expected to reflect any societal learning about human relations that could have transpired over the past few decades. The test was introduced to the industrial psychology courses as a learning module early in the course curriculum. Feedback on test scores was accompanied by discussions of interesting and problematic items. Indeed, some of the test content was contradictory to contemporary viewpoints. The use of the test in the study therefore reflected an opportunity not only to study a particular form of learning, but also to study the convergence toward, and divergence from, an archaic, and a somewhat-bent-out-of-shape societal norm.

The participants were 136 students enrolled in psychology courses over a 5-year period. Of that number, 20 were graduate students enrolled in an organizational development course. Those remaining were undergraduates, of whom 76 were enrolled in an advanced course in organizational development, 20 in industrial psychology, and 23 in a course in psychological testing. The psychological testing students were used as the control group, whereas the others were aggregated into the training group. The control group served as a sham training group as well as a control for learning about psychological testing. Thus, a stringent comparison was performed.

All participants completed the How Supervise, the Thematic Apperception Test (TAT), and a brief questionnaire near the beginning of the courses. The TAT provided measures of achievement, affiliation, and power motivation, as defined in the first section of this chapter. The questionnaire provided a count of the number of semester of college or graduate school the student had completed prior to the course in question, an index of extrinsic motivation. The latter was the response to one question, which was rated on a 1-7 scale: "How important is this course to your career goals, in your opinion today?" Students were retested on How Supervise near the last day of class.

Catastrophe analyses were preceded by a convention 2 × 2 split-plot analysis of variance. The fixed effect was training versus control group. Time of measurement, that is, before and after training, comprised the repeated factor. Scores on How Supervise were the repeated measure. The main effect for training versus control groups was not significant, although a significant difference on the pretest versus retest was registered ($F = 28.00$, $p < .001$). Although the training group showed slightly greater improvement on the criterion than the control group, the F test on the interaction term was not significant.

Both cusp and butterfly models for the training situation were tested. A scatterplot of Δz showed two clear modes and an antimode plus a single separate point reflecting the possible beginning of a third mode (Fig. 5.8). The hypothesized control variables were a, number of semesters college or university experience; b, extrinsic motivation; c, achievement, affiliation, and power motivation (tested separately); and d, training versus control group. A decent effect size for the butterfly dynamic difference equation was obtained ($R^2 = .38$). After eliminating nonsignificant terms in the model, four remained: the quintic term ($p < .001$), the quadratic ($p < .01$), cz_1^2 for achievement ($p < .10$), and number of semesters ($p < .01$).

The cusp model dropped the hypothesis that training and control groups might be different. The extrinsic motivation question was also dropped. The resulting control variables were b for achievement and a for number of semesters. Preliminary testing showed no impact for the quadratic location correction. A quartic term was added to capture a possible retardation effect. The resulting R^2 was .39, and all weights were statistically significant (z_1^3, $p < .01$; bz_1, $p < .05$; semesters, $p < .01$; z_1^4, $p < .05$).

The final cusp results compared favorably to the linear pre–post model ($R^2 = .23$), which showed significant weights for the pretest ($p < .01$), semesters ($p < .01$), and achievement ($p < .05$). A significant positive bivariate correlation was obtained for affiliation motivation ($r = .24$, $p < .01$). The linear difference model contained no significant weights ($R^2 = .04$).

Several conclusions can be drawn from the study. First, motivation and learning comprise a nonlinear dynamical process. Second, stable learning took place in the human relations training situation. Some students registered a stable drop in performance on the test; conversations with them indicated that they distinctly changed their minds about some of the issues represented on the test and that they meant every answer

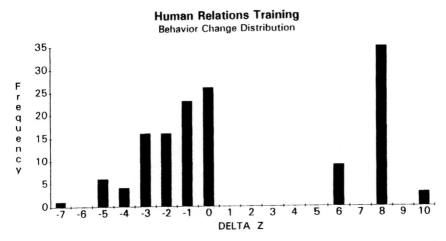

FIG. 5.8. Frequency distribution of Δz for human relations training data.

they gave. Third, there was no difference between the treatment and control groups, meaning that whatever was measured by the test was learned equally well in classes concerned with testing and classes concerned with human relations; this result was consistent with results from the ordinary evaluation statistics. Fourth, achievement motivation acted as a bifurcation effect as initially theorized.

PRISON RIOTS

One of the first empirical applications of catastrophe theory in the social sciences was a model for prison riots (Zeeman et al., 1976). Although Zeeman et al. emphasized prediction in the intuitive use of the word, their treatment of data involved graphic analysis only, with no summary statistics or measures of association between predictors and criteria. The model drew some negative criticism (Poston & Stewart, 1978; Sussmann & Zahler, 1978a, 1978b) and a revision (Smith, 1980). It was later possible to test both models with dynamic difference equations, as discussed below. The riot application also provided an opportunity to test a cusp hypothesis with serial data.

Zeeman et al. Model

According to Zeeman et al. (1976), the sequence of disturbance episodes and quiet periods leading up to a prison riot follows a cusp catastrophe rule. Tension is the asymmetry factor, and alienation is the bifurcation factor. Disturbance level increases as a function of tension. Outbreaks of disturbance were thought to be more sudden under high alienation conditions. The Zeeman et al. riot model also posited two other behavior conditions, abnormal quiet before an outbreak, and a disturbed quiet immediately following an outbreak (Fig. 5.9).

The concept of tension was encountered in previously described motivation work. Alienation is generally interpreted as a negative form of intrinsic motivation. Hence, riots were prescribed as a possible outcome on the butterfly motivation response surface. Labor riots, of course, represent the fiercest form of response to extreme inequity, and would be coupled with an inability to escape the inequitable situation.

The data set for the Zeeman et al. riot model consisted of 52 weekly measurements of tension, alienation, and disturbance. The measurements were organization-wide repeated measures. The tension variable was the sum of standardized scores for the number of inmates reporting sick or reporting sick from work, the number of welfare visits, and the number of complaints or appeals to the Governor (Smith, 1980; Zeeman et al., 1976). The alienation variable was the simple sum of persons receiving special punishment plus the number of inmates requesting segregation. The six measures have been separated into two factors by factor analysis of data from prison records. The data table reported the combined tension score plus separate scores for punishment and segregation. Control variables were reported in raw and smooth form; only the unsmoothed data were considered in this reanalysis.

The disturbance index was devised by the experimenters by assigning severity values to the actual incidents that took place in the course of the riot. The scale, which I have renamed the *rowdy index* to avoid confusing

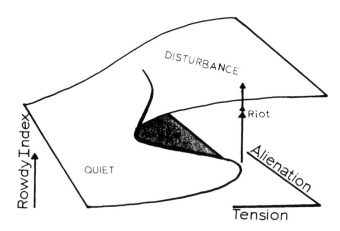

FIG. 5.9. Cusp catastrophe model for prison riots as hypothesized by Zeeman et al. (1976).

with one of Smith's (1980) variables, was valued from 0.0 to 9.9 for the full riot. Examples of rowdy incidents included hunger strikes, work strikes, fines, escape attempts, and attacks on guards. The Zeeman et al. model can be expressed as a dynamic difference equation:

$$z_t - z_{t-1} = \Delta z = \beta_0 + \beta_1 z_1^3 + \beta_2 z_1^2 + \beta_3[\text{Alienation}]z_1 + \beta_4[\text{Tension}] \quad (10)$$

Smith Model

According to Smith (1980), the Zeeman et al. model was not useful for predicting riots in a different prison or in the same prison 6 years later. The discrepancy was traced to the choice of control dimensions. Tension was considered a poor choice because its meaning is highly moderated by prison policies regarding sick reports and so forth. In its place, *support for disturbance* was suggested. The criterion was simply riot versus no riot as stable states, as no intermediary incidence occurred at Hull Prison in 1976, and only two such incidents occurred prior to the 1978 Gartree Riot (each scoring 7.0 on the Rowdy Index). Smith also replaced alienation with *antagonism*.

In regard to antagonism, Smith observed that riots are "usually preceded by a sudden influx from Punishment Block and/or exodus of inmates requesting segregation. A sudden drastic change in the overall mood of the prison" (organizational climate) "will increase frustration felt by the inmates not involved in the changes, and this will increase their pay-off aggressive action" (1980, p. 159). Antagonism A_t was defined as function of the proportion, P, of inmates in punishment block and the previous level of antagonism:

$$A_t = 0.9A_{t-1} + 0.1P_{t-1} \quad (11)$$

Support for disruptive action, D_t, was defined as

$$D_t = V_t - E_t - P_t \quad (12)$$

where V_t is the number of prisoners in voluntary segregation (passive prisoners), and E_t is enforced segregation (aggressive) prisoners; punishment block prisoners are also aggressive.

Analysis

The cusp dynamic difference equations were calculated for the two riot models along with their respective linear comparison models. Location parameters were set equal to 0.00; ordinary standard deviations were used as measures of scale. For additional comparison, data from the Smith series were analyzed once for the 1972 riot only and again with three riots together; Smith had also provided values of antagonism and support for disruption for the Zeeman et al. riot. The linear control equations for the three riots together also contained three additional variables: the Rowdy Index at a 2-week lag, and dummy-coded variables representing the 1976 Hull Prison riot and the 1978 (second) riot at Gartree.

In order to test the dependent error hypothesis, Durbin–Watson statistics for serially correlated residuals were calculated for all models. Significance was determined using the Theil–Nagar critical values for upper and lower bounds:

$$Q = \frac{(T-1)}{T-K} - \frac{2.43635}{T+2} \tag{13}$$

for the .01 significance level, where K is the number of regression parameters including the constant, and T is the length of the time series (Ostrom, 1978). For the .05 level, the value 1.64485 replaces 2.32635.

The Zeeman et al. cusp model for the 1972 Gartree riot accounted for 45% of the Δz variance. Weights for all terms in the model were significant (z_1^3, $p < .05$; z_1^2, $p < .01$; bz_1, $p < .05$; a, $p < .10$). The Smith model for the 1972 Gartree riot also accounted for 45% of the criterion variance. The only significant weight was obtained for support for disruption ($p < .05$). There was considerable multicollinearity among the terms in that regression model. Similar results were obtained when all three riots were analyzed together ($R^2 = .47$). A scatterplot of data appears in Fig. 5.10.

The best linear alternative control model (pre–post) produced an R^2 of .05. The linear control model did contain one significant term, which was the Rowdy Index at a 2-week lag. The Durbin–Watson statistic was not significant for the cusp models, but it was significant ($p < .05$) for the control model.

The conclusion from the analysis was that the Zeeman et al. and Smith models were equivalent in predictive power, but that the former variable set had the more unique set of terms. On that basis the Zeeman et al. model might be preferred.

The Zeeman et al. and Smith models complement each other qualitatively. The operationalizations of tension, alienation, antagonism, and support for disturbance were fairly realistic in light of concepts appearing in the organizational psychology literature. One model accentuated social inferences and traits of the organization, whereas the other accentuated behavioral dynamics. Neither appeared to take the inmates' views into account. The allegation that the Zeeman et al. model did not predict later riots is still perhaps valid. A better model would define the points along the Rowdy Index in such a way that values can be determined before

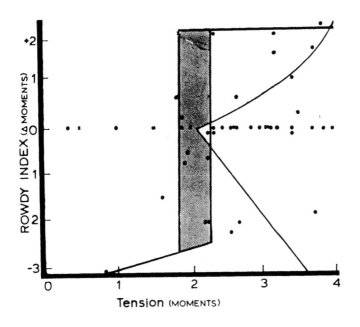

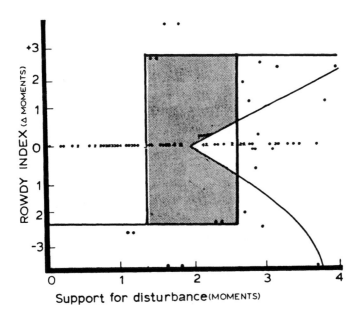

FIG. 5.10. Scatterplot of Δz versus asymmetry for three riot data series.

creating a forecast. It would have been valuable to provide evidence of the external validity of the control variables or definitions that would readily transfer to other institutions. Another finding of importance was that the dynamic difference equations for the cusp models reduced dependency among residuals and turned it into variance accounted for, which was predicted from the theory, as explained in chapter 3.

APPROACH–AVOIDANCE CONFLICTS

In an earlier section we remarked that the gradients of approach and avoidance of a goal could be expressed as gradients on a catastrophe response surface. Townsend and Busemeyer (1989) observed that approach–avoidance dynamics underlie a wide range of goal-directed behaviors and motivational conflicts. They took the notion of dynamics literally, and developed equations to represent the system. The essentials of their theory are considered next with remarks, and are followed by further developments and applications to negotiation teams.

Simple Systems

One-Goal System. A goal, in Townsend and Busemeyer's (1989) work, can be either something to approach or something to avoid. The only difference between the two types of goals is the relative strength of the forces of attraction and avoidance. In a one-goal system, a person's behavior is affected by both forces, as defined by Equations 14 and 15 for approach and avoidance, respectively:

$$F^+(t) = \delta^2 P(t)/\delta t^2 = a_0 - a_1[G - P(t)] - [(k/2)\,\delta P(t)/\delta t] \qquad (14)$$

$$F^-(t) = \delta^2 P(t)/\delta t^2 = b_0 - b_1[G - P(t)] + [(k/2)\,\delta P(t)/\delta t] \qquad (15)$$

where $P(t)$ is the position of a person at time t, G is the position of the goal, a_0 is the value or valence of the positive approach gradient, a_1 is the slope of the approach gradient, b_0 is the valence of the avoidance gradient, b_1 is the slope of the avoidance gradient, and k is an effort coefficient that exerts drag or resistance on the person as they approach the goal (Townsend & Busemeyer, 1989, p. 116).

The two slopes cross somewhere. A person who is sitting at the intersection of the two slopes would experience a considerable amount of ambivalence as to how to continue to proceed, given the balance of rewards and costs. Approach and avoidance behaviors would oscillate, such that the amplitude of the oscillation would be:

$$A(F^+, F^-) = [(a_0 - b_0) - (a_1 - b_1) G] / b_1 - a_1 \tag{16}$$

This limit cycle would break if a_0 became stronger than b_0, or vice versa.

Remark. Equation 14 can be transformed into a dynamic difference equation that is similar to those used throughout the chapter to characterize dynamical behaviors. First, Equation 14 can be simplified by setting the initial distance from the person to the goal, G, equal to 1.00 unit. Position, $P(t)$, is then a proportion. Integrate both sides of the equation with respect to P, and combine terms:

$$F^+ = \delta P/\delta t = a_0 P - a_1 P/2 - (a_1 - k)P^2 \tag{17}$$

The result, Equation 17, is a quadratic function that represents the type of instability encountered in a logistic function. There are three control parameters, however, which would suggest that the model is overspecified. Therefore, it would be useful to reflect on what the control variables actually mean. The slope of an approach is going to be the result of several real conditions. Goals with strong valences will generate steeper slopes. Goals that are difficult will generate shallower slopes. Thus a_1 can be essentially replaced by $(a_0 - k)$ in Equation 17, which becomes:

$$F^+ = \delta P/\delta t = kP/2 + a_0 P^2/2 - 2kP^2 \tag{18}$$

The same procedure can be applied to Equation 15 for the avoidance gradient. Here the negative valence of the attractor and the cost of approaching, k, are heading in the same direction, and thus b_1 is replaced by $(b_0 + k)$:

$$F^- = \delta P/\delta t = -kP/2 - b_0 P^2/2 \tag{19}$$

If we subtract pain (Equation 19) from pleasure (Equation 18),

$$\begin{aligned}\Phi = \delta P/\delta t &= kP + a_0 P^2/2 + b_0 P^2/2 - 2kP^2 \\ &= (a_0/2 - b_0/2 - 2k)P^2 - kP\end{aligned} \tag{20}$$

We can drop the annoying constants 2 by absorbing them into our definitions for the scales of a, b, and k, which we can leave unstated for the present purpose. If avoidance, b_0, and negative approach, k, are regarded as two aspects of the same latent gradient, then we can simplify further:

$$\Phi = \delta P/\delta t = a_0 P^2 - cP^2 - cP \tag{21}$$

where $c = b_0 + k$. We end up with a simple logistic model for avoidance, which represents an instability, with an additional effect aP^2 pulling the system in the opposite direction.

The foregoing construction made a few assumptions, such as whether the addition of F^+ and F^- or the substitutions of b_1 and a_1 required unequal weights. No harm has been done; the function can be expressed as a regression equation,

$$\Delta P = \beta_0 + \beta_1 cP_1 + \beta_2 cP_1^2 + \beta_3 a_0 P_1^2 \tag{22}$$

For research purposes it may be convenient to expand the equation to allow separate hypotheses to be tested concerning a, b, and k, but that would be only a convenience. The key point is that a one-goal approach–avoidance system displays a quasi-logistic function, which in turn would indicate that a two-goal system should be roughly cuspoid.

Two-Goal System. A system containing two goals that could be approached or avoided would require a total of four gradients (Fig. 5.11). "Should I play baseball or practice the violin?" was the example (Townsend & Busemeyer, 1989). Cusp dynamics strongly suggest, however, that the two negative gradients reorganize into a cusp manifold, making two diverging gradients of approach with an antimode repellor in between. Dynamics of this type were first decribed by Zeeman (1976a) to show

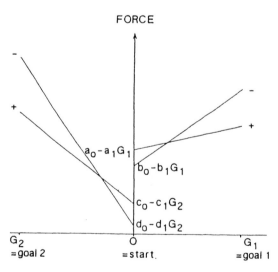

FIG. 5.11. Approach (+) and avoidance (−) gradients in a double-goal situation where each has both positive and negative attributes. From Townsend and Busemeyer (1989). Reprinted with permission.

attack–retreat response of a dog who encounters a hostile stimulus. Signal strength, which could be the proximity of the danger, comprises the bifurcation parameter. Signal strength in this application is comparable to $(a_0 + b_0)$ functions, decribed earlier. The asymmetry parameter, a, would be the relative success of an attack response, as estimated by the dog. Success or difficulty of an attack response is comparable to an ability variable in the motivation model, and is further comparable to a combination of elements from the approach–avoidance model in Equations 14–22:

$$a = (a_0 - k) - (b_0 + k) \tag{23}$$

Note that the Zeeman cusp model actually involved one apparent goal, but a second stable state, safety from the hostile stimulus, was implied throughout the process.

The foregoing applications to the baseball–violin or attack–retreat dilemma imply an either/or choice situation. If it were possible to avoid both attractors, then an unstable third option would unfold. The resulting response surface would be a swallowtail, where the "open drain" in the surface would allow a double-avoidance outcome.

Multiple Person–Goal Systems. Townsend and Busemeyer (1989) completed their exposition by extending approach–avoidance gradient systems to multiple person–goal systems. In principle it is possible to specify gradients where there are multiple goals and multiple actors, each having their own values of a_0, b_0, and k for each goal. Another important ingredient that needs to be taken into consideration, however, when multiple people are involved is the interaction among the actors (Abraham, Abraham, & Shaw, 1990; Abraham, Kugler, Xie, & Abraham, 1992; Guastello et al., 1993). One person's apprehensions (avoidance function) can affect other actors who may not have had the same experiences. Alternatively, the presence of a person who knows the roads to an interesting place can take a carload of people along.

Multiperson, multigoal situations are evident in many common business adventures. According to basic expectancy theory, salespeople follow leads and promote products that promise the quickest routes to a payoff. Investors behave similarly, as do creative people who must often choose between promising projects; the latter application is considered in depth in chapter 10. Prospect theory (Kahneman & Tversky, 1979) improved on basic expectancy theory by explaining where strict rationality rules go awry: People pay for certainty, and costs are not evaluated in the same manner as rewards. Approach–avoidance theory, coupled with NDS theory, reframed and improved those dynamics, which led to the extensions just mentioned.

The introduction of feedback loops implies that self-organizing processes are likely in complex person–goal systems. It now appears that many common social dynamics that we know as social facilitation, competition, and cooperation can be interpreted as complex self-organized person–goal systems. In the case of social facilitation, the common situation is one where Person A would venture off to a place or into a project if Person B would go along also. How many times have we heard in conversation, perhaps in reference to a social event, "I wouldn't go alone, but if you'll go, I'll go." Persons A and B only arrive in the presence of each other. Alternatively, Person A would do a better job of something (reach a more difficult goal in a field of similar goals) if Person B was paying attention. Perhaps the valences for A change when discussing them with B; a clear interactive feedback process would be taking place there.

In the case of competition, the presence of others working toward a goal, along with the prospect of besting the others, enhances the attractiveness of the goal. Alternatively, the presence of low competition for a goal that is perhaps not widely perceived or understood provides the attraction. Undoubtedly, much of basic motivation and learning theories was at play when a person's facilities for interpreting valences were shaped.

In cases of cooperation, people form coalitions to share expenses and efforts in service to a common goal that is big enough to be worthwhile for all the participants. Additionally, the comradery of working together as a team for its own sake seriously reduces the k factors, and increases the valences of a task by way of greater performance levels. On the flip side of the issue, however, is the pervasive finding that group performance is not necessarily greater than that of the most capable individual in the group. These issues are addressed in later chapters.

We arrive next at a compelling phenomenon: Where there is chaos, there is hope. Imagine that we have a system containing multiple actors and one goal. Imagine further that the actors are all interacting and their approach–avoidance gradients with respect to the goal are such that they are all stuck in the ambivalent condition where they oscillate between approach and avoidance initiative. The result is that the proximity of any one of them toward the goal over time is chaotic.

Chaos increases further when the same group of actors is working with a multiple attractor field. The results of their interactions will resemble creative problem solving in groups. In brainstorming groups, no one begins by knowing definitively what they are doing, but the actors cheer each other on (reduce k), generate and swap ideas, and thereby reduce chaos as they define worthwhile objectives (valences) and clear paths (reduce b_0 and k) to those objectives.

Finally, we can take all the foregoing approach–avoidance processes, magnify them over many actors, goals, and subgoals, and pop them into a large system we call an organization. Management self-organizes somehow as a conduit for feedback loops. Sometimes it facilitates communication, and sometimes it stifles. Sometimes it accentuates some types of valences and sometimes it shifts its emphasis. The next result is a motivational climate, such as what parameter d in the butterfly catastrophe model of motivation in organizations was meant to represent.

SUMMARY

This chapter began with a summary of key theories of job attitudes and work motivation, and proceeded to develop nonlinear dynamical theories for two-stage personnel selection, motivation and learning, riots, and approach–avoidance dynamics for conflict resolution. Common themes within the conventional lines of thought were the distinction between intrinsic and extrinsic stimuli and motivation; the relationship between abilities, motivation, and performance; and aggregation of motivational theories into cognitive (equity and expectancy), attitudinal (satisfaction, values that affect equity perception), and rational-emotive (social motivation, perception of control) concept groups. Conventional theories tended to arrive at similar conclusions with regard to the impact of their constructs on performance, absenteeism, and turnover, as well as the perceived need in the research community for improvement in the overall accuracy of all theories.

A self-organizing process appears to have taken place in the development of both the conventional and NDS theories. Theories aggregated with empirical observations into process models, which eventually subsumed each other. The Lawler–Porter performance process built on equity, and intrinsic–extrinsic theory. The opponent process model subsumed the Lawler–Porter process and the motivator–hygiene theory with added value. Cognitive theories supported each other's conclusions and some key findings in personnel selection. The cusp catastrophe model, when viewed as a subset of an NDS motivation theory, subsumed all of the foregoing, personnel selection and training evaluation, and approach–avoidance conflicts. The full butterfly catastrophe model was required to explain the dynamics of intrinsic–extrinsic motivation.

The resulting theory had broken down old boundaries between personnel and ability testing, learning and training evaluation, motivation in learning, and performance dynamics. In the complete picture, work behavior is a topology that is prominently characterized by three attractor basins, each of which is complex in its implications for performance,

performance decisions, absenteeism, organizational entry, and turnover. Change processes within the attractor field, which are often discontinuous, are governed by a coaction of a randomizing force or exposure, and four control parameters that are also complex in meaning. Empirical tests of either the full model or its subsets have been supportive of all essential principles of theory, although not all principles were verified in each application.

There are, of course many opportunities for future development of the emerging theory. The R^2 coefficients leave substantial variance in behavior change unaccounted for, in spite of their wide advantage over conventional linear alternatives. Clues to improved explanations could lie in the characterization of the dynamics of the attractors themselves. In catastrophe theory response surfaces, attractors are ideally fixed point with smooth mappings in their neighborhoods. Other evidence from the performance dynamics literature can be interpreted, however, to mean that the attractors themselves are in low-dimensional chaos, and coupled oscillations may also occur in some situations. Fortunately, the dynamic difference equations are robust with respect to the types of attractors existing in the attractor field, and other measurement models are recently available for testing other forms of hypothesis. The subsequent chapters will cover some of the better understood situations where chaos resides.

Entirely different avenues for future work are emerging from a forest of social exchange situations, in both work and nonwork situations. The extensiveness of expectancy and equity principles is already well known, and widespread improvements in any of their current applications could be imminent. Similarly, approach–avoidance dynamics appear to underlie a wide range of motivational phenomena and group dynamics, particularly when the elementary concepts are coupled with principles of self-organization, where the latter occurs in response to chaos.

6

Stress and Human Performance

This chapter describes some applications of NDS where psychophysics, perception, cognitive and physical work load, and other forms of stress combine to affect human performance. Some of the applications pertain to industrial production. Other applications involve athletics or laboratory experimentation. Four types of stress-behavior mechanisms are developed. The first is the *diathesis-stress* mechanism, in which the effects of stress are the result of an interaction between environmental influences and the individual's inherent biological weaknesses. For instance, if there was an inherent weakness in a person's digestive tract, ulcers could result from prolonged stress exposure. In the studies of industrial color matching and printing processes which are to follow, a diathesis-stress interaction between an industrial process and the biological effects of shift work translated into serious performance changes. In the diasthesis-stress applications, a logical analogy is made between the diasthesis-stress mechanism at the individual and organic levels of a living system and a similar mechanism at the organizational and group level of system level. Health-related examples of diathesis-stress relationships, which are more gemane to the original meaning of the concept, are considered in chapter 8. Most known examples share cusp catastrophe structure. An example of a swallowtail function is also described.

The second form of stress type is an *ability-stress* mechanism. The concept holds a few parallels with the butterfly catatastrophe model of motivation in organizations. The application to performance at the game of golf does not occur within an organizational context, and is thus an individual-level model.

The third type of stress-behavior relationship is the *buckling under load* model. An anology is drawn between the buckling of an elastic beam when it is put under an increased load, and performance time for an industrial laborer's task where the work load can be varied. The application thus connects the buckling mechanism for a nonliving system to the impact of work load in the organismic or individual human level of analysis. Both share a cusp catastrophe mechanism.

Fatigue models are the fourth type of stress-behavior relationship. Principles of NDS appear to have been influenced the earliest studies of fatigue, which began nearly a century ago. Fatigue is the loss of work capacity over time, and is studied in the context of physical strength (either labor or athletics) and mental RT. Data from mental fatigue studies that were first published in 1914 have now been statistically analyzed belatedly for the first time; the results are reported in this chapter for both conventional and cusp catastrophe hypotheses.

CONVENTIONAL THEORIES OF WORK LOAD, STRESS, AND PERFORMANCE

Once again, the NDS applications are built from existing theory, and some aspects of the pre-NDS knowledge base are inevitably more germane than others. Most essential here are the principles of how work load is thought to affect performance, the nature of stress and its impact on performance, and theories of fatigue.

Work Load Effects and Theories

Speed, Load, Errors. In the previous discussion of psychomotor skill, the relationship between RT and errors was observed for situations where the work load was held constant. The research summarized next considered what happens when work load is allowed to vary as well.

Conrad (1951) made a distinction between speed stress and load stress. *Speed stress* is a reaction on the part of a person working on a task that has the effect of worsening his performance beyond what might be expected from the physical characteristics of the of the work or equipment involved. *Load stress*, on the other hand, changes the character of the task. As the number of signal sources (for instance, visual displays in the experiments) is increased, more time is needed to make judgments simply because of the greater amount of information that is being processed.

In a series of studies (Conrad, 1951), subjects were engaged in a a clock-watching task in which they pressed a key as a pointer approached the 12 or 6 o'clock position on any of the clock dials used. In the various experimental conditions, two, three, or four dials were used, and speed was varied. The arithmetic product of speed × load typically shows a linear relationship with performance (McCormick, 1976).

Human Channel Capacity. Theory and empirical findings covering maximum human channel capacity revolve around two viewpoints: the limited capacity theory, and the variable allocation theory. The limited capacity theory holds that there is a rigid fixed upper limit to channel capacity. Total cognitive capacity is thought to be divided between a major channel, a minor channel, and perhaps a third channel. For instance, if maximum channel capacity is 10 bits per second and the primary task requires only 8 bits, then 2 are left over for the second task. If the primary task requires only 6 bits, and the second task requires 2, then 2 bits are left over for a third task. This is the *time-sharing* principle, which is a computer analogy (Kantowitz, 1985).

Under limited capacity time-sharing, transmission speed is slower for difficult task. For two easy tasks, there is no slowing of transmission. When the primary task is difficult and a second is added, transmission speed decreases. The time-sharing mechanism implies a bottleneck occurrence under certain conditions. The slowing of transmission under excessive load and bottlenecking, taken together, is known as the *potency principle*.

The variable allocation model is based on the principle that processing space is allocated on an intentional basis, that is, by setting priorities. The amount of channel capacity is thus thought to increase with increased demand. No bottleneck conditions are specified. Eventually an upper limit is reached, but there is flexibility as to where the upper limit occurs.

Maximum channel capacity, to some extent, depends on the nature of the information being processed and its difficulty. Difficulty is inferred by the amount of channel capacity that must be allocated to perform a task up to a given level of quality (Kantowitz, 1985). Both the limited capacity model and the variable allocation model are vague about the real maximum channel capacity, but in the limited resource model, channel capacity is fixed by nature of the channel itself. In the variable allocation model, however, the maximum capacity is fixed by situational demand characteristics. Experiments further suggest that the limit becomes fixed late in the channel's sequence of stages, rather than at the early stages.

The Nature of Stress. Stress, according to the classical definition, is the nonspecific reaction of an organism to any environmental demand (Quick & Quick, 1984). This definition is extremely broad, and suggests that any stimulation at all is a form of stress, and that the negative, undesirable consequences of stress are really a matter of degree and interpretation. Both desirable and undesirable events can be stress producing (Holmes & Rahe, 1967).

Anxiety is an irrational fear, according to classic clinical psychology. Although it could be based on real-world events, anxiety, strictly speaking, is apprehension gone out of control. Anxiety can be experimentally conditioned in animals and humans (Watson & Rayner, 1920; Wilson & Davison, 1971), and the conditioning aspect of anxiety offers a strong partial explanation for numerous psychological disorders. Anxiety is a nonspecific symptom of many psychological disorders, and could be regarded as the mind's alarm system that goes off when something is wrong. Anxiety is frequently cited as a symptom of prolonged or chronic stress. Indeed, the clinical profile of traits observed for people who have experienced chronic stress exposure is not distinguishable from the personality profiles of people suffering from clinical depression. Posttraumatic stress syndrome, on the other hand, is a severe psychological reaction to acute and intense stress, and the symptoms may be schizotypal as well as depressive (Glover, 1988; Natani, 1980; Walker & Cavanar, 1982).

Strain is the amount of deformity caused by stress. In other words, strain is a measure of damage in the sense of a material science metaphor that is explored in this chapter. The material science concept of elasticity translates into notions of psychological resistance to stress. Some personality variables, such as locus of control and Type A personality syndrome, are relevant to resistance to stress, but the broader concept of buckling and elasticity is less well developed in conventional psychology. Fatigue is the loss of work capacity over time. It is not synonymous with stress as just defined, although it can be thought of as a specific result of a specific type of stress, the type of stress being a heavy and fast-paced work load. The issues connected to fatigue, both physical and mental, are elaborated in subsequent sections of this chapter.

Types of Stress. There are many types of stress that a person can experience. Although they have common results on the person, it is convenient to classify them according to their sources because the goal is, ultimately, to reduce unnecessary stress both in the workplace and in one's personal life. The three broad categories are, therefore, physical stressors, social stressors, and speed and load stress.

Physical sources of stress would include toxins, excessive heat, excessive cold, and noise. Toxins comprise a large and varied category. As a general rule, a person is likely to experience the common stress symptoms, but with specific medical impairments peculiar to the toxin (Travis et al., 1989), and many of them are severe. Fortunately, human-computer interaction has generally little to do with environmental toxins.

Excessive heat and excessive cold can impair work performance and cause medical impairment. Studies in Antarctica have shown, however, that the discomfort of cold can be counteracted by appropriate clothing and training to perform the work under cold conditions. Excessive heat is a different matter, as there is a limit to the amount of clothing a person can remove. Performance decrements begin to appear at 86°F after 8 hr of exposure, but begin after 45 min of exposure to 100°F heat. Ventilation can ameliorate some but not all the effects of severe heat (Kantowitz & Sorkin, 1983).

Stress can be induced by social sources, and it is convenient to subdivided those into source categories: work-related and nonwork-related. Work-related social stressors would include role ambiguity ("What am I really supposed to be doing here? No one is making it clear what they want"), role conflict (trying to meet conflicting demands), obnoxious supervisors and coworkers, job insecurity, new job assignments, and insufficient authority to perform tasks necessary for work assignment, and planning for retirement, to mention a few.

A personal success can be stressful too. Not all stressors are unwanted events. Stressful events are *arousing*, which is what makes them stressful. Nonwork-related stressors include illnesses or death in the family, divorce, changing homes or hobbies, change in work patterns of family members, changes in eating or sleeping habits, financial difficulties, the holidays, and Christmas in particular (Holmes & Rahe, 1967). Crowding and isolation are sources of stress that can affect both personal and work life (Oldham & Fried, 1987).

Disregulation is a particular form of stress, characterized by a combination of changes in eating and sleeping habits and difficulties with same. It is often caused by shift work or irregular work schedules (Depue & Monroe, 1986). Shift work deserves special attention because of its relationship to periodicities of work performance. Shift work often has deleterious effects on individual work performance because it interrupts or conflicts with the daily biological (circadian) rhythm cycle, which includes the sleep–wakefulness cycle, concomitant brain-wave patterns (Andreassi, 1980), and variations in body temperature and adrenaline secretion (Akerstedt, 1977; Colquhoun, 1971; Wojtezak-Jaroszowa, 1978). Permanent night workers have been found to show out-of-phase rhythms, which, in turn, had an effect on their productivity and effectiveness (Agervold, 1976; Malaviya & Ganesh, 1976, 1977). Rotating shift workers express greater amounts of sleep inadequacy, gastrointestinal ulcer, and eating problems, irritability, and job dissatisfaction compared to nonrotating shift workers (Tasto et al., 1978).

Physiological Mechanism and Health Consequences. Stress can result from work overload and understimulation. The latter is recognized as boredom. The physiological mechanism that underlies the stress experiences is based on the two subdivisions of the peripheral nervous system. The sympathetic nervous system is responsible for bodily arousal when it is activated. Once sufficient energy has been expended, the parasympathetic nervous system is activated and the body relaxes; relaxation is a physiologically active process, not a passive process. Stress reactions occur when arousal is frequent but there is no opportunity to expend energy at the moment when it is necessary to do so; thus, prolonged arousal results.

The physical health consequences of long-term stress include hypertension, heart disease, kidney failure, alcohol and drug abuse, and medical consequences of alcohol and drug abuse. Psychological health consequences of stress include anxiety, impaired interpersonal relationships, impaired decision making, burnout, and depression; some of these consequences were already explained. The effects of stress on work behavior can take the form of errors, accidents, absenteeism, and turnover. Figure 6.1 depicts the effect of arousal on performance. Too much or too little arousal, besides being subjectively stressful, results in suboptimal work performance. Of further interest, difficult tasks require less arousal from other sources for optimal arousal, whereas easy tasks are best performed with alternative forms of arousal added (such as playing a radio in some situations). The effects of stress and work performance specifically are considered next.

Stress and Work Performance. People who work under conditions of stress typically do not work as effectively as those who can work under more hospitable conditions. Stress has a greater negative impact on performance when the stressors are uncontrollable and unpredictable (Cohen, 1980). One of the more theoretically challenging observations in the stress experiments is the aftereffects of stress phenomenon. After a stressor has been introduced, work performance decreases. When the

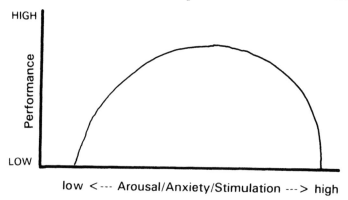

FIG. 6.1. The Yerkes–Dodson law.

stressor is removed, however, depressed performance levels continue. A viable theory about stress and performance needs to account for the aftereffects phenomenon. The three best-supported explanations for the phenomenon are, according to Cohen (1980), persistent coping, adaptive cost, and learned helplessness.

According to the persistent coping thesis, people under stress reorganize their mental efforts such that they are actively fending off the stressful stimulus in the form of a coping mechanism. The key point is that, once the coping mechanism has been initiated, it is difficult to turn it off immediately. Thus the act of coping with the stressor persists after the stressor is removed (Deutch, 1964; Epstein & Karlin, 1975).

The adaptive cost thesis (Glass & Singer, 1972) holds that the process of adaptation depletes cognitive resources, and, as a result, performance remains depressed until the individual recovers or is sure that the "coast is clear" before regrouping resources and ignoring the possibility of stressful stimuli. The depletion of resources, or cognitive shrinkage, explanation is consistent with theories of human information processing: People scan the stressful stimuli for information that could be meaningful to their health, safety, or success. By doing so, mental channel capacity is consumed, and the available capacity with which to perform the primary task becomes smaller. Once the channel capacity has been reconfigured to include the stress channel, it takes a while to reallocate that channel capacity to the main task; perhaps the person is typically waiting to be sure that the alarming condition has passed.

According to the learned helplessness thesis, people under conditions of uncontrollable stress either learn or have already learned that there is nothing they can do about the stressor or its effects on their performance, and therefore they do not try to do so (Seligman, 1975). Learned helplessness reactions have been demonstrated empirically in experiments with both people and animals. Learned helplessness is a premier theory of clinical depression, which is symptomatically similar to severe stress reactions.

Fatigue

Early theory (Ash, 1914; Starch & Ash, 1917) suggested that physical and mental fatigue processes are similar; as a result, the study of one becomes a contribution to the study of another. This section details the central concepts pertaining to fatigue curves, which are mostly related to physical work, the results of the earliest mental fatigue studies, and contemporary views on the topic.

Fatigue is operationally defined as decrement in work capacity over time; it is often inferred from decrements in performance on physical tasks (Ash, 1914; Guastello & McGee, 1987; Ioteyko, 1920; Kroll, 1981;

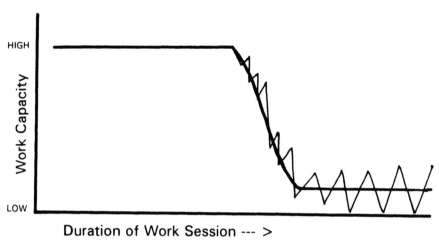

Duration of Work Session --- >

FIG. 6.2. The classical fatigue curve showing increased variability during and after the performance decline.

Mosso, 1894, 1915; Starch & Ash, 1917; Weinland, 1927). The *work curve* is a graphic plot of performance over time. It can be decomposed into two parts: the curve itself and deviations from the curve. The curve denotes a loss of work capacity and decrement of performance caused by fatigue; see Fig. 6.2. The variability from the curve increases dramatically toward the end of the work period and denotes loss of control over one's neuromuscular system (Ash, 1914; Starch & Ash, 1917; Weinland, 1927).

Seven types of work curve were identified: those that (1) dropped gradually, (2) dropped suddenly, (3) maintained stable but high performance, (4) maintained stable but low levels of performance, (5) maintained stable levels of performance prior to, and sometimes after, the output drop, (6) were highly unstable, or (7) increased suddenly (Crawley, 1926; Ioteyko, 1920; Marks, 1935).

Some subjects in the physical fatigue experiments showed an increase in strength or work capacity after having been exposed to a physical work set that would have fatigued other subjects. Two explanations emerge from the literature: exercise and scalloping. Crawley (1926) found that subjects increased work output in a subsequent test session if the same muscle groups were utilized in a previous session. More generally, exercise is known to increase work capacity by an additional 50% compared to preexisting levels (McCormick, 1976). Crawley (1926) also found that individuals who know their work period would end expended their greatest effort just before the close of the session. Subjects who were not so informed exhibit a more typical work curve.

Ioteyko (1920) determined a general formula for the work curve that satisfied all varieties of work curve that were known at the time:

$$H_2 = a + bt + ct^2 + dt^3 \qquad (1)$$

where H_2 is the height to which a weight is pulled, a is the (constant) initial height of the weight on the experimental apparatus, and t is time. According to Niefeld and Poffenberger (1928), variables b, c, and d are just empirical constants that do not have specific meanings; their interpretation was based on experiments in which they obtained values of b, c, and d that were different from those that Ioteyko found. In a later investigation, however, Marks (1935) also observed cubic structure, and interpreted b as meaningful and c and d as empirical in nature. Subjects in the latter study were classified as pykniks (high weight/height ratios) or leptosomes (low weight/height ratios). A comparison of extreme groups determined significant differences in the change in work rates, whereby pykniks fatigued faster than leptosomes.

Modeling research for fatigue disappeared for more than 20 years, then reemerged in the form of exponential modeling rather than as cubic polynomials. (Caldwell & Grossman, 1973; Clarke, 1962; Clarke & Stelmach, 1966; Grose, 1958; Kroll, 1981). Modeling research for fatigue then disappeared for another twenty years before surfacing in the context of nonlinear dynamic theory. Guastello and McGee (1987) demonstrated that the Ioteyko curve (Equation 1) was essentially the same as the cusp catastrophe model, which was a well-known model for explaining discontinuous changes of events. They further showed that Ioteyko's parameters c and d were empirical constants, but b was meaningful and related to the steepness of inflection in the work curve. Height and weight, among other variables, contributed to the b parameter.

Mental Fatigue. The early fatigue researchers reported evidence to support the claim that mental fatigue follows the same essential temporal dynamics as physical fatigue. Work capacity declines after successful intervals of demanding mental work, and recovers after a rest period (Ash, 1914; Starch & Ash, 1917). The early research, however, relied on the visual inspection of data, crude averages, and occasional graphic plots to support or refute hypotheses. The following is a reanalysis of Ash's mental fatigue experiments using analysis of variance (ANOVA) techniques.

It should be noted that, in the original text, "experiment" was used as a shorthand for "administration of an experimental procedure to a subject" as well as to refer to the set of procedures designed to test an hypothesis. The designations of Experiment 1 and Experiment 2 are my demarcations of the data sets, and are closely tied to, but not always identical with, the demarcations in the original.

Another important feature of the sequence of the early studies that is relevant to the human–computer interaction studies, which are of primary concern in this volume, was that two human performance phenomena were inevitably taking place instead of one. Although the experiments were designed to reduce work capacity, as evidenced by increasing RT, repeated testing was expected to produce a practice effect, which would have the impact of lowering RT. The experiments in mental fatigue did not utilize control groups of people who were repeatedly tested, but not fatigued during the time between testing; the apparent supposition was that practice reduces RT, so that if an intervention raised RT, then it would be safe to conclude that the fatigue effect was genuine.

Although the assumption about practice and fatigue effects was not unreasonable, some attempt was made in the reanalysis of experimental data to make experimental–control comparisons directly where possible. Some reanalyses worked through conventional ANOVA modeling to verify qualitative conclusion. Other reanalyses involved nonlinear dynamics and are detailed in the section of this volume pertaining to nonlinear dynamical theory.

Ash Experiment 1. The goal of Experiment 1 was to demonstrate loss of mental work capacity following a demanding mental task. Ten human subjects completed a figure-reversal task after 1 hr of mental work that consisted of a mental arithmetic task that was known from previous research to induce fatigue. The stimuli for the work capacity test were a cube and a pyramid (Fig. 6.3), each of which was presented in one form of the figure, and the subject was asked to make a mental reversal of the image and to press a telegraph key as soon as the reversal was made. The dependent measure was the number of seconds required to complete the task; the cube and the pyramid were timed and reported separately.

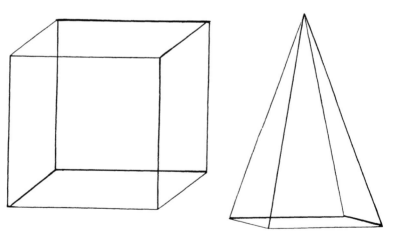

FIG. 6.3. Ambiguous figures used in Ash's (1914) mental fatigue experiments.

Each data point (Ash, 1914, p. 38, Table V) was actually an average of several trials per subject, but the number of trials was not stated.

Data were analyzed using a two-way repeated-measures analysis of variance (ANOVA) with a pooled error term. Because of the low statistical power in these experiments caused by small sample size, an alpha level of .10 was used to determine statistical significance. Results showed that the pyramid task was performed faster than the cube ($F_{1,27} = 6.63, p < .05$). More importantly, RT increased after the hour of mental work ($F_{1,27} = 24.44, p < .001$). There was no interaction between shape and time (before and after mental fatigue), which meant that the extent of fatigue was not dependent on which of the two stimuli was used ($F_{1,27} = 0.05$, NS).

Ash Experiment 2. Mental fatigue Experiment 2 illustrated the continued decline in mental work capacity after successive hours of mental work. Four university professors served as human subjects. They completed the figure reversal task (cube) four times. The first testing was done before mental work. The next three tests were made after consecutive 1-hr periods of exam grading. Data were analyzed using a one-way repeated-measures ANOVA. Results (Fig. 6.4) showed a significant increase in RT after successive rounds of mental work ($F_{3,9} = 3.35, p = .069$; an alpha level of .10 was used to compensate for the low statistical power caused by the small sample size).

Contemporary Views on Mental Fatigue. The studies of mental fatigue continue to be sparse since the time of the Ash experiments. No real landmark work emerged until Conrad (1951) reported his studies on

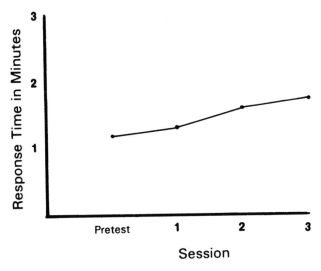

FIG. 6.4.   Increase in reaction time after successive rounds of mental work.

speed and load stress. Speed and load stress studies evolved over the next 30-year period, with the next major landmark being the cognitive engineering perspective, which directed efforts toward measuring cognitive channel capacity (Kantowitz, 1985). Strictly speaking, mental fatigue was the not the primary theme behind most cognitive performance research until two reviews surfaced in the early 1980s (Holding, 1983; Welford, 1980). The effects of fatigue on performance and stress and performance were often obscured in the way researchers defined problems and experiments (Holding, 1983; Welford, 1980). There were, nonetheless, some laboratory phenomena that clearly distinguish the two types of phenomena. Bills (1931) reported a *blocking effect* in cognitive fatigue experiments (as in "mental block") where excessive reaction times would occur after prolonged work on an aperiodic basis. Blocking effects became typically defined as an instance of RT greater than two times the mean RT (Welford, 1980). The blocking effect has been thought to dissipate the effect of fatigue. Two critical aspects of the blocking effect have been studied; one is the onset of the block, and the other is the increased number of blocks that appear as the experiment continues.

Although some studies showed that the time needed to recover from mental fatigue is less than the time needed to recover from physical fatigue, recovery time could be dependent on the specific examples of mental and physical tasks used in those experiments (Welford, 1980). In some situations, recovery requires a prolonged time and is not qualitatively different from the aftereffects of stress phenomenon discussed earlier (Holding, 1983). Aftereffects of fatigue often do not transfer to subsequent tasks, and may be related to the repetitiveness of the task and level or arousal or boredom. Boredom is particularly prominent in jobs involving vigilance tasks. Perceptual fatigue, according to Holding's interpretation, is largely related to arousal and can be manipulated by reward structures. Underarousal, on the other hand, is typically regarded as a stress phenomenon, as discussed earlier.

Experiments on mental task performance after prolonged work periods do not consistently result in a decline in performance for all people subjected to the same or similar experimental conditions (Dureman & Boden, 1972; Holding, 1983; Poffenberger, 1928). For instance, Poffenberger (1928) reported that people who perform prolonged mental work report feelings of tiredness in much the same way as they do after having performed extensive physical work. Performance on mental tasks, however, may remain stable or improve after prolonged work, in spite of reports of tiredness.

The clear differences in mental work curves produced by the same stimuli and experimental conditions for different people may be explained by a more inclusive equation and theory in much the same way as Ioteyko

(1920), Crawley (1926), and Guastello and McGee (1987) developed. Finally, two other trends in mental fatigue research suggest that nonlinear dynamic processes could be involved. First, the physical work curves show greater variability from the curve with prolonged work, and similarly, RT tends to become more erratic after prolonged mental work (Holding, 1980). Second, there is a provocative theory suggesting that at least some forms of fatigue are the result of increased noise in the neural system, rather than the failure of the neural system to transmit signals. Both the variability from the work curve over time, particularly blocking phenomena, and the neural noise concept strongly suggest that chaotic processes are operating.

DIATHESIS STRESS MODELS

The next two applications of NDS illustrate three important points. First, although conventional approaches to experimentation study perception in isolation from other cognitive processes, perceptual phenomena in the real world occur in a relatively open system where other forces affect performance simultaneously. It is often difficult, if not arbitrary and counterproductive, to determine where one process begins and the other ends. Second, there is regular periodicity to work performance that is attributable to circadian rhythm and patterns of "booking-up" or the timing of work load within an organization or work unit. Those trends readily lend themselves to NDS analysis. Third, stress phenomena introduce additional complications into the perception–performance relationship and take the form of the diathesis-stress mechanism in the industrial color vision applications that follow.

Perception in a Complex System. According to Wandell (1982), one of the possible applications of phychophysical theories for the perception of small color differences was to determine standards for manufacturing and government use for the allowable variations in color specificity for a manufactured product. The problem becomes psychological when the question becomes: How much physical difference in color constitutes a psychological difference?

The central problem for a complex systems analysis is that in commercial color matching there are not one but four criteria involved in a color match: chroma accuracy, saturation accuracy, brightness accurcy, and time to complete a match. In the commercial world the criterion of a "good" match is its acceptability to the consumer or to another organization's quality control department, which is on a par with time to complete the match. Intervening problems for perceptual accuracy include glare, ambient lighting, the substrate the test materials are printed on, and whether the customer is using the same standard ambient lighting arrangement.

Color drift is a problem associated with the concept of just noticeable differences in color brightness. More specifically, when the job order calls for long footages of printed product, color mismatch begins as a functionally perfect match becomes much less so after about 10,000 feet of print. Changes in print quality are attributable to printing cylinders wearing down, hence picking up less ink, resulting in a different print. The changes are below the human threshold to observe from any one moment to another. When cylinders are repaired they pick up as much ink, or more, as when the job began, with the result that the ink must be rematched and retinted.

Stress and Color Perception. Hartley and Shirley (1976) administered the Stroop test for color-name interference to a group of 12 subjects who were tested at 8 a.m., noon, 8 p.m., and midnight. Significant decreases in performance were observed on both the interference and noninterference tasks from 8 a.m. to noon to 8 p.m., and performance improvements from 8 p.m. to midnight. The researchers concluded that there was a significant circadian effect on color perception, but the size of the differences would not have much impact on people actually doing such work at the high-risk times of day. We see later in this section that the impact of circadian rhythm on color perception becomes considerably greater when the entire manfacturing system is considered.

Prolonged work time to complete a color match is additionally compromised by visual fatigue. Types of color vision fatigue include desensitivity to brightness and intensity, color desaturation, target disappearance, and background fade (Bartley, 1976).

Cusp Model for Color Matching and Shift Work

This study began with a midwestern printing firm that specialized in high-technology products and was experiencing financial difficulties precipitated by instabilities in the oil industry in late 1979. The change in market conditions resulted in the first layoff in the 60-year history of the company. The impact on morale was noticeable. In the 4-week accounting period following the layoff, the accounting and scheduling departments noticed the lowest rate of production efficiency that they could remember, and the financial impact of low efficiency was, by their standards, major. The cause-and-effect relationship between external financial events and productivity losses was taken for granted until two accounting periods later, when the most efficient rate of productivity occurred (again) in the memory of management. The question for the industrial psychologist was, therefore, "What did we do right?!"

In the course of the 2-month period there were some changes in operation department managers. Also, the organizational status of printing and color matching departments had been equalized. In the opinion of management, those leadship changes were expected to improve both work performance and social conditions. Productivity did, in fact, increase to a record high, even though ambient economic factors grew steadily worse after the layoff.

In the analysis of paperwork another alarming datum was found. The best work efficiency was found on the night shift (11 p.m. to 7 a.m.), followed by the day shift (7 a.m. to 3 p.m.). There was a noticeable (before statistical analysis) drop in efficiency occurring on the afternoon shift (3 p.m. to 11 p.m.). A general systems problem was unfolding where the active ingredients included physiological psychology with respect to shift work and perception, person–machine system interaction, and socio-organizational variables.

The cusp catastrophe model (Fig. 6.5) was developed around the hypothesis that there was a discontinuous change in performance throughout the day, created by the conflict between shift work and circadian rhythm. Performance would thus be polarized between two stable ex-

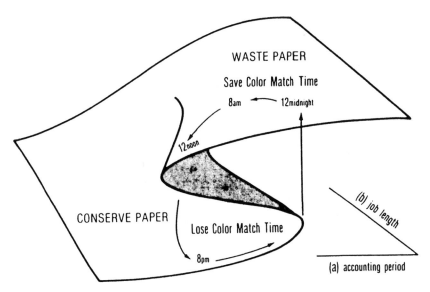

FIG. 6.5. Cusp catastrophe model for work performance in an industrial process as a function of circadian rhythm, job difficulty, and ambient stressors. From Guastello (1982b). Reprinted with permission.

tremes. The transition between the extremes would be governed by two control variables. The hypothesized bifurcation variable was job length, which would capture the color drift problem. The asymmetry factor was a time variable spanning the three accounting periods in which the jobs in questions were performed. Three dependent measures were investigated: color matching time, expressed in terms of positive and negative deviations from the production standard, the amount of printing paper saved or wasted, and printing press time.

Research Subjects and Procedure. The workforce under study consisted of 13 color matchers and 30 rotogravure printers, all of whom worked rotating shifts. The staffing was two printers per machine, and the color matchers remained the same for the duration of a particular job. Supervisors rotated with their shifts.

The unit of data analysis was the job order. Production records offered six useful pieces of data: color match time, printing press time, paper consumed, job length, date of job initiation, and time of initiation. The total data set consisted of 85 job runs. All jobs were woodgrain designs in usually three but sometimes four or five colors. Job runs were sorted into pairs in which they were matched by job length within accounting period. The value of the bifurcation factor used in the analyses was the average of the two job lengths. There were 38 possible pairs. Sixteen pairs included a job initiated on the 7 a.m. shift; 22 pairs involved jobs initiated on the 11 p.m. shift. Night-shift data were treated like day-shift data.

Difference scores for the cusp regression equation were generated by taking the dependent measure for the day shift and subtracting the comparable value for the second shift. Time 1 and Time 2 data were corrected for scale by using their respective standard deviations before differencing. Bifurcation and asymmetry variables were similarly transformed before analysis.

Analysis and Results. The cusp catastrophe model accounted for 99% of the variance in the color matching time criterion. Weights for all predictors were significant, including the skew and lag to the fourth power.

The cusp model accounted for 98% of the paper consumption variance. Weights for all terms in the regression model were signficant except for accounting period. Weights for skew and lag to the fifth power were significant also.

The cusp model accounted for 37% of the printing press time variance. None of the weights representing control variables were signficant, and the resulting model was not distinguishable from a fold catastrophe model.

The R^2 values for linear difference regression models using the same data were: color matching time, .19; paper consumed, .09; press time, .12.

Another set of linear models was compared in which shift work, accounting period, and job length were tested as predictors of performance efficiency. These linear models were chosen to represent the type of analysis that would have been used in a conventional, or pre-NDS, investigation; all 85 cases were used. The alternative linear models produced R^2 values that were somewhat larger than those obtained from the linear difference models but much less than those obtained from the cusps: color matching time, .39; paper consumed, .15; press time, .09. Details for all statistical analyses are published elsewhere (Guastello, 1982b).

The results of the analyses showed rather decisively that the cusp model does in fact describe variations in the work performance of groups on color-matching tasks throughout the course of the day. The data corroborated Hartley and Shirley's (1976) results with controlled individual testing, but the main conclusion was stronger: The differences in performance are indeed critical in industrial production. The subsystems of the production process, beyond individual color perception, amplified the effects of the underlying control variables.

There are further practical implications from the study. It would be possible and perhaps worthwhile to include shift information in scheduling and accounting procedures, such that the least affected tasks would be run on the high-risk shift. The host organization actually responded by leaving its leadership alterations in place and by restructuring its prices to customers to encourage them to accept the work in spools no greater than 10,000 feet of print. That way it would be possible to re-engrave the printing cylinders before print deterioration became critical.

Swallowtail Model and the Work Week

The next application also applies to color matching in the same factory, but with respect to fluctuations in performance throughout the work week. Weekly trends in industrial performance or accidents have received far less attention than the circadian effect. Two somewhat related effects had been recorded prior to NDS: Risk is high during the first half of the week compared to the second half, with sometimes an upturn just before a weekend or other nonwork period. ("Don't buy a car built on Friday afternoon.") Risk is also higher on booking-up day, on which weekly production scheduling begins or on which the deluge of new job orders comes in (Colquhoun, 1971).

The only other viewpoint on the weekly work cycle that I was able to discover (Guastello, 1985b) came in the form of office graffiti in which a cartoon dog acted out the attitude pattern: Sunday he was dancing. Monday he grumbled, "Don't speak to me!!" Tuesday he was lying flat on his back muttering "God get me through this day!" Wednesday he was lying flat on his stomach in a thunderstorm saying, "Please let me die!" Thursday he was sitting upright thinking, "Life slowly seeps back into my body." Friday he hummed, "Anticipation. . . ." Saturday he was dancing again.

The weekly performance cycle was hypothesized to fit a swallowtail catastrophe function, as shown in Fig. 6.6. The section of the upper sheet of the surface containing Monday is a high-performance area, but not as high as the section of the upper sheet containing Thursday and Saturday. The lower regions of the surface containing Tuesday, Wednesday, and Friday are unstable low-performance areas.

Once again, the dependent measures for this study were color matching time, paper consumed, and printing press time, as defined previously. The hypothesized control parameters were as follows. The swallowtail factor, c, was whether the job occurred in the first or second half of the work week (semicycle). The bifurcation factor, b, was job length as before, and the asymmetry factor, a, was accounting period as before.

Method and Procedure. Job orders were once again the unit of analysis. Job runs were sorted into 27 pairs in which they were matched as closely as possible by job length within accounting period and across semicycle. The value of b used in the analysis was the average of the two job lengths. The following differences were compiled: Monday versus

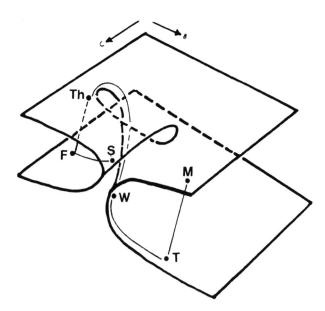

FIG. 6.6. Swallowtail catastrophe model for work performance during a work week. From Guastello (1985a). Reprinted with permission.

Tuesday jobs, Wednesday versus Tuesday (different) jobs, Thursday versus Friday, and Saturday versus Friday (different).

Analysis and Results. The swallowtail catatrophe function accounted for 55% of the variance in the color matching time criterion. Significant weights were obtained for the power potentials, accounting period (asymmetry), job length as both a bifurcation and asymmetry variable, and semicycle as an asymmetry variable. The weight for the swallowtail variable was not significant, not was its bivariate correlation with the criterion ($r = -.01$).

The swallowtail function accounted for 55% of the variance in printing press time. Significant weights were obtained for the power potentials, and for job length as both an asymmetry and bifurcation variable. No effects were observed for accounting period or bifurcation.

As a further check on the role of the semicycle variable, another set of swallowtail models was tested in which job length was tested in all three control parameter positions, and semicycle was treated as an asymmetry variable only. The revised model produced no improvement for color matching time or printing press time, but an improvement was observed for paper consumed. In the latter case, R^2 reached .83. Significant weights were obtained for the power potentials, job length as a swallowtail and bifurcation factor, and semicycle as an asymmetry variable.

Linear control difference models were tested for comparison with the swallowtail results. They accounted for 27%, 18%, and 10% of variance for color matching time, printing time, and paper consumed, respectively.

The results of the study clearly favored the swallowtail interpretation, meaning that weekly trends in production efficiency do exist. Although prior research (Colquhoun, 1971) found weekly cycles to be more often true than false at the individual level, it can now be further concluded that they exist at the group level when they are aggravated by task and social conditions. The social conditions captured by the accounting period measure emanated from the organizational level of the system.

The pervasiveness of the weekly work cycle, or at least the jokes about it, are more likely to be not an invention of the organization that is under study, but rather a cultural phenomenon. The work week has always been punctuated by a day of rest, if not a whole weekend of freedom, and thus the weekly cycle seems to have taken on a life of its own.

STRESS, ANXIETY, AND PERFORMANCE IN SPORTS

Hardy and coworkers developed a series of cusp and butterfly models to link stress, anxiety, and performance in sports such as basketball and golf (Fazey & Hardy, 1988; Hardy, 1990, 1993; Hardy & Parfitt, 1991;

Hardy et al., in press). Qualitative analysis showed that basketball performance demonstrated a hysteresis effect under high cognitive anxiety conditions, but not in low anxiety experimental conditions; thus anxiety acted as bifurcation parameter, or possibly a high-order control parameter. Furthermore, high anxiety contributed to making players' best performances better or worst performances worse than those of low anxiety players (Hardy et al., in press).

The catastrophe models were developed in a series of conceptual efforts that were supplemented by non-NDS experiments and analysis. Hardy (1993), however, provided a comparative test of a cusp and two alternative butterfly models using the polynomial structural difference equation method. The best results were obtained for a butterfly model, initially proposed by Hardy (1990), that worked as follows. There were three levels of performance (in the game of golf) on the butterfly surface. The unit of performance was the putt, which was measured as a function of the putting distance and the distance to the center of the hole.

Physiological arousal was hypothesized to contribute to the asymmetry parameter, cognitive anxiety was hypothesized as a bifurcation variable, and self-confidence was hypothesized as a bias or swallowtail factor. Physiological arousal was measured by heart rate. Cognitive anxiety (as opposed to somatic anxiety) and self-confidence were measured by questionnaire. No variable for the butterfly parameter was hypothesized in this application.

According to the model, as physiological arousal increased, the golf player was more likely to move into the manifold region of the behavior surface. Anxiety would have the effect of bringing out the best or the worst in a player, as observed in the basketball study. Self-confidence would bias the player toward higher levels of performance; self-confident people can experience the same sources and levels of arousal as other people, but their interpretation of the arousal does not allow them to be overwhelmed.

Hardy's butterfly accounted for 76% of the criterion variance, compared to 36% for the pre–post control. Although competing catastrophe models showed similar levels of accuracy, the butterfly discussed earlier exhibited the strongest results with respect to unique contributions (significant weights) for the individual regression weights. Self-confidence and cognitive anxiety behaved as expected. Physiological arousal, however, did not make a significant contribution to the model.

Hardy's (1993) final result supported not only the propositions concerning nonlinear dynamics, stress, and performance, but also the butterfly structure of motivated performance. We know from basic psychology that there is only a fine line between motivation, stress, and arousal. If the motivation theory is any guide, further work on NDS, stress, and sports performance should include a measure of individual differences in player skill, which is probably not easy to do because varsity players are already highly selected. The butterfly parameter remains unknown; perhaps variations in coaching style or team climate are responsible for the last bit of variation.

BUCKLING MODEL FOR WORK LOAD

The next application is one where the time to complete a physical labor task is affected by the work load applied to the task. The study was completed in the context of a broader project to study the effects of physical strength on performance of physically demanding work in a steel factory. Research participants were 129 employees who were either in the general labor pool (80 cases) or volunteers from staff positions (49 cases). Nonlabor employees were invited to participate because we wanted to capture the full range of the physical strength and labor experience variables.

All research subjects participated in a 2-hr work simulation in which they performed several common physical labor tasks such as shoveling, carrying heavy objects under varying conditions, navigating a loaded wheelbarrow through an obstacle course, sledge hammering, and pushing and pulling a heavy bar of steel across a greased track. Physical strength was measured before and after the 2-hr simulation, and other intake data were collected along with the pretest measures of strength. The research situation provided an opportunity to study work under varying load and physical fatigue. Fully detailed reports can be found in earlier articles (Guastello, 1985b; Guastello & McGee, 1987). The rest of this section summarizes the highlights.

The Buckling Model

The exposition that follows begins with definitions of stress and strain as they are known to material scientists. Next, the model of beam buckling is described, which is in turn transposed to living systems and, more specifically, to work performance. The resulting model is then subjected to empirical test.

Stress in material science is defined as the amount of load per unit area of a test piece of material, usually measured in pounds per square inch. There are a number of stress types, such as bending, pulling, and torque. Given a pulling stress, *strain* is the ratio of the change in length of the test piece to its original length, measured in inches per inch. The *modulus of elasticity* is the ratio of stress to strain. A plot of stress versus strain results in a curve that has both linear and nonlinear segments, with a peak known as *ultimate tensile strength*. In a fatigue test, stress is plotted against the number of stress cycles to failure, N, where a failure is a break in the test piece. The stress–N curve has an asymptotic lower limit of stress, called the *endurance limit*, which is linearly related to ultimate tensile strength and indicates the range of stress the test material can withstand before fracture. Some materials increase in strength, whereas others decrease, upon successive cycles.

In Zeeman's (1977) application of catastrophe theory to beam buckling (Euler buckling), an elastic horizontal strut is given a vertical load and a horizontal compression. The amount of buckling is the deflection of the beam under the vertical load. The system was modeled as a cusp with deflection as the dependent measure (a difference score). Compression, which is the ratio of the modulus of elasticity times π^2 to length, functions as the bifurcation factor. Vertical load is the asymmetry factor. Buckling occurs at the cusp point, which is the most unstable point in the system.

Euler buckling is actually a group of related phenomena. The situation just described was one in which both ends of the horizontal beam were pin-jointed. If both ends are fixed, buckling load is four times that of the pin-jointed example. If one end is fixed and the other pin-jointed and free to move sideways, the critical buckling load is one-fourth the value for the pinjointed example. In its original form, the problem was to determine how long one could make a thin pole before it buckled under its own weight. On the other hand, beams that are too short fail by crushing rather than buckling (Gordon, 1978).

The same tests of strength, elasticity, and so forth that are made on building materials can be made on living samples of bone, kangaroo tendon, and butterfly wing. As the systemic level shifts from nonliving to human, the task is redefined from measuring the strength of various materials to measuring the strength of composites of materials. The composites can also think, which, in turn, necessitates subdividing the problem into primarily physical and primarily psychological forms of stress. The problem at hand pertains primarily to the physical form.

Application to Work Performance

The application of Euler buckling to work performance requires a close-up study of the wheelbarrow obstacle course data from the physical abilities project (Guastello & McGee, 1987). In that simulation, subjects pushed a wheelbarrow over a 50-ft course, where the obstacles were traffic cones and barriers on the floor that were designed to simulate railroad tracks. The course was completed three times, first with a load of 100 lb (sandbags), then 200 and 300 lb. Time in seconds to complete the course was the criterion.

Subjects completed the 100-lb course with a model response time of 50 sec. The response time distributions were bimodal for both the 200-lb and 300-lb courses, with the lower modes at 40 sec. The upper modes were comprised of all those who could not complete the course; their score was set equal to the longest completion time for the sample, which was 664 sec.

Of the Euler buckling models described earlier, the act of pushing a loaded wheelbarrow (strut) over a floor obstacle is more similar to the strut that is fixed at one end and free to rock sideways at the other. The worker exerted the compression force; when buckling occurred the wheelbarrow tipped, dumping sandbags on the floor. The worker then had to right the wheelbarrow and its contents and continue if possible, thus increasing the performance time score.

Performance time differences replaced strut deflection, which shows the cubic potential denoting critical change. Vertical load was the asymmetry term as in the Zeeman (1977) model. The modulus of elasticity/height ratio (bifurcation factor) was represented by several experimental variables: body fat (as measured by calipers), exercise habits (number of hours of exercise per week outside of work), height, body balance (rail walk test), and gender (the sample of participants contained 79 men and 50 women). The cusp catastrophe model for the buckling applications appears in Fig. 6.7.

The buckling problem might be improved by taking human characteristics into account. There appeared to be learning component to the obstacle course task, although its effect and specific nature had not been isolated (either empirically or otherwise). Some participants may have learned all they needed to know about working the obstacle course in one trial, while others required two trials. As a result, a lag-1 model is appropriate for some subjects and a lag-2 structure is appropriate for others. Alternatively, complex lag may be introduced by subject differences in fatigue and recovery reactions.

Analysis and Results

In the first of two analytic experiments, the participants were assigned to one of two groups. For half, their performance times would bas based on the comparison of the 300-lb course with the 200-lb course, whereas for the other half, performance times would be based on the comparison of the 300-lb course with the 100-lb course. The cusp model produced an R^2 of .68. Significant contributors to the bifurcation parameter were balance, height, and gender. A significant weight was observed for vertical load as the asymmetry parameter.

The linear difference comparison regression equation, by contrast, produced an R^2 of .11. Linear pre–post models, which were tested to represent

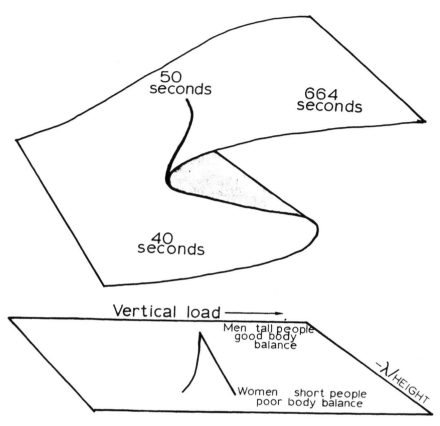

FIG. 6.7. Cusp catastrophe model for Euler buckling in a wheelbarrow obstacle course. From Guastello (1985b). Reprinted with permission.

a non-NDS point of view on the problem, contained strength variables as possible independent variables and were conducted separately for the 300–200 and 200–100 lb comparisons. The average R^2 for the two tests was .67.

In the second of two analytic experiments, additional tests were performed to determine if a complex lag effect could be operating. In that approach, polynomial regression models were built to assess a cusp catastrophe function at lag-1 (300–200 lb course), and another catastrophe function at lag-2. It was indeed possible to produce a model with a codimensionality of eight, but the extra dimensions only raised the R^2 value to .75.

It was possible to conclude from the results of the study that the buckling analogy could indeed be applied to human work performance under increased load. The validity of the model was not appreciably better than an alternative linear interpretation, but the theory was compelling nonetheless. The model showed that workers who displayed only small changes in performance time under increased load were those who had a low modulus of elasticity, indicating greater flexibility; as a group they consisted of men, tall people, and people with good body balance. Those with a high modulus of elasticity, indicating less flexibility, were more likely to display catastrophic changes in performance time; as a group they consisted of women, short people, and people with poor body balance. The lag effect was just large enough to remind us that lag effects could be more important the next time, but small enough not to complicate the interpretation of the model.

Of course, the specific physical qualities that signified elasticity in a wheelbarrow obstacle course may not be the same in other situations. The control parameters may be totally different again when mental work load problems are considered. At the moment it is left to future research to investigate quesions such as whether the buckling and modulus of elasticity concepts rectify any discrepencies between the fixed capacity and variable allocation models of mental channel capacity. In chapter 11, the buckling model is applied to organizational development and change.

PHYSICAL FATIGUE

The concepts of stress and fatigue are closely connected in material science. In analogous psychological situations, however, they are less similar. They share cusp structure, nonetheless. The next application discussed is a study of fatigue in the same physical abilities simulation (Guastello & McGee, 1987). That is, in turn, followed by a new, nonlinear look at Ash's (1914) experimental data for mental fatigue.

Model Development

In the physical abilities simulation, participants were measured on physical strength before and after the 2-hr workout. The first step in building a catastrophe model for the fatigue process was to reinterpret Ioteyko's (1920) fatigue equation as a cusp, as follows. The dependent measure H in the original equation was the height to which a person could lift a set of weights. In the physical abilities model, strength was the measure of work capacity, which was closely related to amount of work a person could perform. The constant a in the original equation was analogous to the location parameter in the in the cusp. The variable b, which denoted the steepness of the inflection point in a work curve, was analogous to the bifurcation parameter in the cusp. The variables c and d in the original equation corresponded to the the empirical weights for the cubic and quadratic power potentials in the cusp. Time in the original model was replaced by physical strength at Time 1 in the cusp, and because strength was hypothesized to vary with time, the criterion in the cusp would continue to be a difference score.

Next, it was possible to reinterpret the seven work curves identified by the early researchers as trajectories on the cusp response surface. Those relationships are shown in Fig. 6.8. Curves 1 and 2 are trajectories in the low versus high bifurcation sides of the surface, respectively. Curves 3 and 4, which reflect global stability, are high and low performance states, respectively. Curve 5 reflects local stability in which performance orbits around the upper mode, escapes, then drops suddenly to the lower attractor where it remains. Curve 6 is an orbit around a cusp point, which is the region of greatest instability on the surface. Finally, Curve 7 is the exercise or scalloping effect by which output increases over time.

Variables that were hypothesized to contribute to the bifurcation variable were those that were known to affect the rates of ascent or descent: exercise history, height, weight, and body fat. The amount of work done was additionally hypothesized as a bifurcation term: Those people who did the most work would be expected to show the most change compared to those who did none at all.

Some muscle groups were thought to compensate for loss of strength in other muscle groups. In the case where arm strength was the primary muscle group experiencing fatigue, back strength and leg strength might act as compensatory muscle groups. Compensatory strength was tested as an asymmetry factor.

Analysis and Results

The cusp catastrophe model for arm strength turned out be fairly accurate ($R^2 = .90$). Bifurcation variables with negative weights in the model,

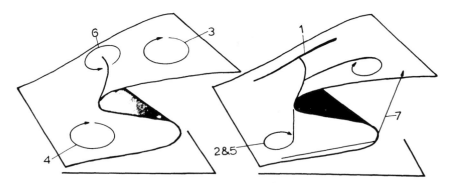

FIG. 6.8. Seven different work curves displayed as trajectories on a cusp catastrophe response surface. From Guastello and McGee (1987). Reprinted with permission.

indicating that they promoted fatigue, were the amount of work done, greater amounts of exercise outside of work, labor experience, and higher body fat percentage. Bifurcation variables with positive weights in the model were weight and motivation (as measured in a highly subjective fashion). Leg strength emerged as a strength compensation variable. The results for the cusp model compared favorably with those for the linear difference model ($R^2 = .26$) and the linear pre–post model ($R^2 = .72$). Results are organized in Fig. 6.9.

MENTAL FATIGUE

An important point about mental fatigue that appears to be have been overlooked in contemporary research is that the fatiguing process is often coupled with other events, such as practice effects (cf. Ash, 1914; Starch & Ash, 1917). Practice and extended effort would have opposite effects on performance in a fashion that is loosely analogous to the exercise–

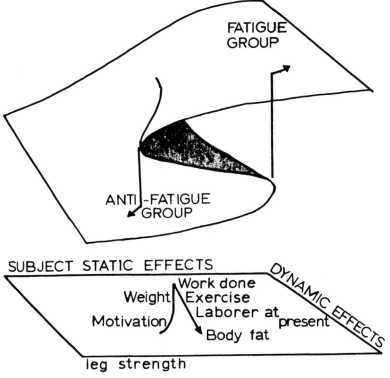

FIG. 6.9. Cusp catastrophe model for arm strength fatigue among steel-workers. From Guastello and McGee (1987). Reprinted with permission.

fatigue effect encountered in physically demanding work. Although the technology of the World War I era did not facilitate model building for conflicting effects, it is now possible to construct such a model based on the cusp catastrophe and to test it using the data published in Ash (1914, pp. 38 and 41).

Figure 6.10 defines two stable states of behavior, RT under conditions of fatigue, and RT under conditions of practice. In principle, RT in both instances gravitates toward asymptotic values, or attractors, both of which are known to exist on the basis of the learning curve and some varieties of fatigue curve, as explained earlier. The bifurcation parameter is the number of units of work performed by the human subject. A greater change in RT is expected as more opportunities accrue for measuring the RT to the figure reversal task.

The mental fatigue data from Ash's experiments sometimes involved participants who were exposed to more than one version of the experiment. In other words, they were not naive subjects when a lot of their data were generated, and they accumulated practice from their previous participations. Confounding effects of this type may have rendered those early experiments only marginally interpretable from the vantage point of contemporary conventional experimental methods. For a cusp experiment, however, those data are especially useful.

It was possible to isolate pairs of RT measures for some participants in which there was no intervening fatigue-inducing process. Those pairs of RT measures constituted instances of practice rather than fatigue plus

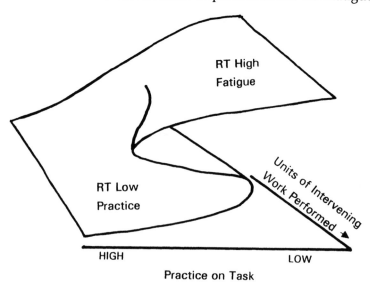

FIG. 6.10. Cusp catastrophe model for mental fatigue experiment.

practice. The asymmetry parameter of the cusp model is thus defined as a dichotomous variable that characterizes an RT pair as a pure practice effect or not. Decreases in RT would be expected in the pure practice measurement pairs, and increases would be expected in the observations collected during mentally fatiguing treatments.

Data from Ash's (1914, pp. 38 and 41) experiments, which were analyzed by conventional means earlier in this chapter, plus other small data series presented on the same pages were compiled into a common data set. Examples of pure practice conditions were created by comparing the RT for a research participant before first experience of a fatigue treatment in one experiment with RT for the same participant before the first experience of a fatigue treatment in a second experiment. RT pairs of the pure practice variety were given a value of 1.0, and RT pairs observed before and after a unit of mentally taxing work were given a value of 0.0. Units of mentally taxing work ranged, in hours, from 0.0 to 4.0, with several instances of 1.5 units. There were totals of 6 practice observations and 38 fatigue observations, which resulted in a total of 43 observations when RT differences were taken.

The cusp catastrophe model was tested using the polynomial regression method, and its R^2 coefficient was compared against those obtained for the linear alternative models. Units of mental work time was tested as the bifurcation variable, and practice trial versus fatigue trial was tested as an asymmetry variable. The type of stimulus used, cube or pyramid, was also tested as a dichotomous asymmetry variable, based on the earlier observation that there was a slightly shorter RT for the pyramid than for the cube trials. Separate measures of location and scale were used for the practice and fatigue trials.

A multiple R^2 of .72 was obtained for the cusp model ($p < .001$). Regression weights for the cubic term ($p < .05$), quadratic term ($p < .01$), and bifurcation term ($p < .01$) were all statistically significant. The weights for the practice effect and type of stimulus were not significant.

The linear comparison models showed that changes in RT were best explained by practice ($R^2 = .37$); no significant effects were observed for type of stimulus or units of mental work. For each pair of RT observations, the second RT, after fatigue or lack of same during the interexperiment interval, was best explained by practice again ($p < .01$), RT before treatment (at Time 1, $p < .001$), and the number of hours of intervening mental work ($p < .10$). The R^2 coefficient for the pre–post linear model was .63.

Both linear models showed that practice comprised the largest explanation for RT, such that decreased RT was associated with the opportunity for nonfatiguing practice. Surprisingly, however, units of mental work made a small contribution in one case and none in the other. Type of stimulus did not have an effect in either the linear or cusp models.

The cusp model accurately represented the trends in the data and was consistent with the expectations drawn from the view of the experimental situation producing both fatigue and a practice effect. The bifurcation term was an interaction between units of mental work and previous RT. As the units of mental work increased, either an increase or decrease in RT could arise.

It might have been tempting to conclude that the practice trials simply had no effect on RT, but the linear models did show a substantial effect for practice, which has to be reconciled. The lack of a direct relationship between the practice observations and changes in RT could be explained by the effect of practice being already inherent in the Time 1 RT values for some of the mental work trials.

Overall, the results of the analysis supported several principles. First, the dynamics of mental fatigue are cusp-catastrophic in nature. Second, the dynamics of mental fatigue are closely analogous to the dynamics of physical fatigue. Third, a clear picture of the phenomenon was achieved by viewing the system as a relatively open system where factors other than the deliberate fatigue-producing treatment were operating. Indeed, this viewpoint can be characterized as a primitive form of open systems theory, which was not scheduled to emerge for another 40 years.

7

Accidents and Risk Analysis

Accidents are the fourth leading cause of death in the United States, after heart conditions, cancer, and stroke. Accidental deaths currently number approximately 90,000 per year, and represent approximately 10% of annual deaths from all causes. Approximately half of all accidental deaths are vehicular in origin, and the other half are almost equally divided among home, occupational, and public settings (National Safety Council, 1989). A common rule of thumb is that for every accidental death that occurs, there are approximately 10 accidents requiring some medical attention, often of a serious nature (Heinrich, 1931). For every nonfatal accident, there are, in turn, approximately 10 near-miss encounters.

Accidents appear to happen suddenly, and often take their victims and bystanders alike by surprise. Accidents that incur a sudden impact, or a trauma, often result in a modicum of memory loss for the events that occur just moments before the impact. This imperfect recollection for events adds to that spooky "Where in world did that come from?" reaction. Their relative rarity on a day-to-day basis, sudden onset, and possibly severe consequences all contribute to an aura of unpredictability.

As every insurance company knows, however, things are more predictable than they appear when enough data are available for study. Their methods of analyzing those data have not, to date, taken advantage of NDS. Hopefully this chapter provides some compelling reason for doing so. For readers who have no attachments to the insurance industry, this chapter should demystify the accident process.

Most of the applications considered in this chapter are confined to occupational accidents. Frankly, they are easier to study than other types of accidents because the placement of people in potentially dangerous environments is relatively stable, and it is often possible to observe people in a variety of subenvironments and to ask them questions. A key problem in studying automobile accidents is that one of the vehicles that could be involved in an accident is moving, and it is anyone's guess where it came from or where it would have gone. Fortunately, where there has been opportunity to compare research findings concerning many different types of accidents, the same basic principles of causation appear to apply.

The first section of this chapter summarizes key points from conventional accident theory. Hints of nonlinear dynamics may be found in a few places. The next two sections describe and elaborate the cusp catastrophe model for the accident process with applications to factories and transit operation. The fourth section takes a societal level view of differential accident rates from the vantage point of an insurance database. There a more complex dynamic involving the mushroom catastrophe model is discovered.

CONVENTIONAL APPROACH TO ACCIDENT CAUSATION AND CONTROL

The path of this section begins with a discussion of individual accident proneness and then proceeds to structural concepts of accident phenomena, culminating with a nonlinear dynamical scheme showing numerous feedback loops among risk sources in an industrial environment. Emerging from the summary is the concept of safety climate or safety culture, whereby the responsibility for accident control is shifted from the individual level processes to group dynamic and organizational processes.

Individual Accident Proneness

The concept of accident proneness first appeared in the 1920s when insurance statisticians discovered that approximately 90% of the industrial accidents involved only 10% of the people in the workforce. That finding led to the premature conclusion that those 10% were chronically doing something wrong, and they were thus labeled "accident prone." The label provided an illusion of explanation for the mysterious probability structure. Later, however, it was shown that the 90%–10% finding could easily occur by chance if one assumes that a Poisson statistical distribution, rather than a Gaussian or normal distribution, generates accident incidence rates (Mintz & Blum, 1949). With the change in assumed distribution, several data sets no longer showed abnormal accident frequency rates. Those that continued to show deviations from Poisson expectation could not be interpreted as evidence of individual accident proneness; environmental causes could just as easily be responsible.

Mintz and Blum's (1949) conclusions appeared to fall on deaf ears or closed minds, particularly where psychological research has been involved. The past 40 years has hosted a parade of individual variables studied for purposes of advising employers how to avoid selecting accident-prone job applicants. The prevailing concepts in the past 15 years have centered around impulsivity, personal or social maladjustment, and alcohol or drug use. Unfortunately, those studies were correlational and postdictive in nature. Maladjustment could just as easily be the result of working too long, or not enough, in poorly controlled environments where ineffectual safety management reigns. Even if the correlations between individuals' personality characteristics and their accident rates were to be regarded as if they were as good as predictive values, personnel selection techniques were shown to be the least effective method of accident control of all the available options (Guastello, 1993e). Within the category of personnel selection variables, drug testing (including rare predictive studies) was the least effective variable, with an effect size of 0.0% accident rate reduction.

The emphasis on individual-level explanations for occupational accidents (and illness) continues to be fueled by claims that the same people who are involved in accidents are also those with higher absenteeism rates. Verhaegen (1993) illustrated, however, that no such correlation exists in an ergonomically suitable environment. Furthermore, it is only when the environment is ergonomically degraded that one might observe correlations between personality measurements and accidents; an ergonomically sound workplace would leave no room for such individual differences to influence risk. According to Quinlan (1988), the unwarranted individual focus is an outgrowth of practices in industrial psychology, dating back to the scientific management era, where psychologists are called in (and paid) by management to solve so-called work problems. The "right answer" for the client was one that blamed the victim in some way. Such viewpoints overlooked collective causes of accidents and management's role in same, particularly when the pace of production is stepped up beyond safe working limits.

In spite of the widespread bimbles and foozles of individually centered psychology, pockets of sanity have been known to exist. Swedish occupational safety legislation, for example, recognizes the value of ergonomic quality to the concerns of both the workforce and management. The British model is less regulatory, but the tradition has placed primary responsibility on management because management creates the hazards for every one else and reaps the largest profits from them (Shipley, 1987). In the United States, there was a sudden awareness at the federal government level that job-related stress is the third largest cause of Workman's Compensation claims (Quick et al., 1992). The topic thus turns to management's contribution to occupational safety and ergonomic sophistication in the work place, beginning with some structural concepts for accident occurrence.

Structural Risk Models

Structural risk models have been widely offered as heuristics for understanding accident occurrence. One or another of the models is implicit in virtually every form of accident control. Structural risk models vary in complexity and can be ordered as single-cause mechanisms, factorial approaches, domino mechanisms, process event sequences, fault trees, multiple linear models, deviational models, Petri nets, and catastrophe models (Benner, 1975; Guastello, 1991a; Rowe, 1977).

Single Causes and Factorial Models. Personnel selection methods and technology-based approaches to accident prevention invoke single-cause models most often. Single-cause models take the form, "If condition X is present, then Y will occur." Nothing especially complicated is taking place in the modeling sense.

Single-cause models are often predicated on linear relationships, and at other times the relationship is categorical. As another alternative, there could be a breakpoint relationship between the hypothetical cause and effect. In a breakpoint relationship, the amount of X must increase up to a critical threshold before any Y can occur (Rowe, 1977). This relationship is essentially nonlinear, and implies a transition from a stable safe state to an unstable state.

Single causes can expand into factorial models as soon as multiple X's are found to be associated with the unfortunate Y. The logic then becomes, "If X1, X2, or X3, is present in some combination, then a known level of Y will occur."

Dominos or Event Chains. Domino models are chains of events. The Chicago fire is a classic example. The cow knocked over the lantern, which ignited the hay, which ignited the barn, the fire from which spread to the next house, then to the next house, then to the next house, until it burned the last available building—with the ironic exception of the water pumping station.

Behavior modification approaches to workplace safety invoke a domino model, such that reinforcement strategies affect safe behavior, which in turn affects accident rates. Behavior modification programs, which selectively reward desired safety responses and censure undesirable behaviors, rank among the most effective means of controlling accidents (Lonero & Clinton, 1993; Guastello, 1993d), as long as the contingencies of reinforcement center on rewarding the desired behavior to a greater extent than on punishing undesirable behavior. Their chief limitations are, however, that they require constant monitoring by the agencies delivering the rewards, and only a narrow set of behaviors can be targeted effectively within a specific program. Also, they tend to view targeted behaviors in isolation, rather than as results of a complex system process. Sometimes those limitations are not problems, of course, but sometimes they are.

Process Event Sequences. The simplest form of event sequence model accords less attention to causes and more attention to the outcomes leading up to an accident. The nuance here is that an accident is a process, rather than a single discrete event. Surry (1969) conceptualized the accident process as a hazard buildup cycle. At first, the workplace is safe with no uncontrolled hazards. As people start to work, however, tools are left out in work spaces, and different people enter the work space to do different things with different tools and equipment. People and objects move around and make opportunities to bump into each other. Eventually hazards accumulate to a critical level when an accident occurs. Notice that there is a entropy concept implicit in the hazard buildup view of an accident process.

An intervention based on the hazard buildup cycle would emphasize training for good factory housekeeping. Other possible forms of training would center on the best use of tools, and procedures that would minimize the acceleration of the hazard buildup. Workers should learn to recognize the buildup cycle, and to spontaneously intervene by reorganizing their work spaces for a safer outcome. The intervention essentially kick-starts a self-organization process. Entropy, having increased unto chaos, now causes the system to self-organize into a state where there is less internal entropy, and a more controlled transferral of energy into the work environment.

Fault Tree. A fault tree is a diagram that represents a sequence of events. The sequence could represent a process or a chain of events. The distinguishing characteristic of a fault tree is that it contains one or more branching functions that denote choices, options, or opportunities for multiple outcomes. A fully defined fault tree would contain estimates of probabilities associated with each branch at a node. An example appears in Fig. 7.1. The branching feature seriously implicates bifurcation mechanisms.

The fault tree in Fig. 7.1 is my reinterpretation of the Sunshine Silver Mine Disaster (Denny et al., 1978). The disaster started several floors

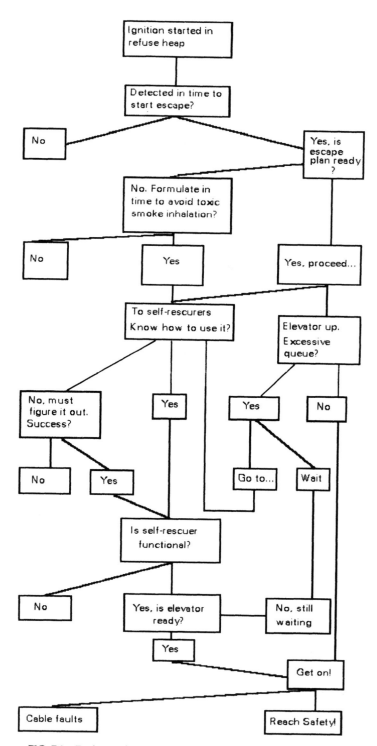

FIG. 7.1. Fault tree for survival from an underground mine fire.

underground in a trash heap in an obscure part of the working cavern. The ventilation system was inadequate, and caverns filled up with smoke. Not everyone was able to detect the smoke before it blocked their exit to the nearest escape route. Analysis showed that the mine did not have a working evacuation method, so the miners had to figure the way out extemporaneously. Those that survived to the next set of options faced insufficient elevator space and self-rescuers (respirators) that often did not work. If the devices did function properly, many other miners did not know how to use them properly. The net result was 91 deaths out of 173 miners within an hour.

A close look at the fault tree reveals that, after all the bifurcations and loops, there were two stable states of outcome: death or survival. Somewhere in between the two extremes was a fighting chance of survival. At several points there were opportunities for low-dimensional chaos, such as in figuring out an escape route or how to use the self-rescuers.

Complex Event Series. A multilinear event series (Benner, 1975) is a compilation of multiple simple event series and fault tree. The new premise is that a complex manufacturing system is composed of activity patterns that occur simultaneously. In principle, the patterns have been designed by management to maximize work output and to minimize accidents. When patterns of activity fall out of sequence, or outside the toleration limits for those sequences, risks escalate.

Kjellen and Larsson (1981; Kjellen, 1984a, 1984b) extended the multi-linear event concept by introducing the concept of deviations. The conceptual model assumes that there is a normative and functional work pattern with which to begin. When deviations from norms are introduced, they become carried through the system from subprocess to subprocess and their impact magnifies. At some point in the magnification process a burst of energy is released, which suddenly transforms the system into the second stage of the accident process. During the second stage, personnel have the opportunity—maybe—to take evasive action to either prevent the accident itself, thereby transforming it into a near-miss event, or to minimize the damage. Large accumulated deviations may interfere with successful evasive maneuvers. The third stage of the process is the actual delivery of harm to the employee; by that time, the event is final.

Sources of deviation in a work setting may pertain to the flow of materials, changes in personnel assignment, flow of information, equipment anomalies, intersecting activity patterns, and environmental disturbances (Kjellen & Hovden, 1993, p. 421). Kjellen and Hovden presented an example of how a confluence of deviations described a construction accident: A regular worker was out sick and was replaced by an apprentice. The task of the day was to erect a beam. A crane that would have been very useful was needed somewhere else. There was ice on the beam. The worker erected the beam manually, but it was crooked, so he walked out onto the beam to realign it, slipped on the ice, and fell to the floor below, breaking a rib and puncturing a lung.

The deviation principle in accident investigation is similar to the deviation principle encountered in systems for ensuring quality in manufactured goods. Kjellen and Hovden (1993) observed through experience, however, that the standards against which one might compare deviations are more rigorously defined in product quality management and involve fewer sources of deviation. Operationalization of the model requires detailed information sources. Both issues, in their opinion, explained the limited uses of the deviation principle in actual practice.

In spite of the limits to practical use, the deviation principle has some clear implications for NDS applications. The core idea is that a deviation, once it occurs, is magnified as it travels throughout the work system. When combined with additional deviations, the final outcome—an accident—is far removed from what would have been a safe and stable situation. The magnification of the deviation is an example of the sensitivity to initial conditions that characterizes chaotic systems. A deviation is an instability. Depending on its actual trajectory, or course throughout the system, its effect may be benign. But on other occasions the trajectory goes to a place in phase space that is totally undesirable.

Control systems in the work engineering could steer the trajectory back on course. Doing so would require subsystems that detect, follow, and correct the deviations as they spontaneously occur. Larsson (1993) observed that the original deviation model was lacking cognitive and decision-making aspects that could describe the onset of some forms of deviation and correct others. In light of the connection that is building between the deviational concept and NDS theory, it would appear that the decision-making mechanism should function at the level of complexity of a chaotic controller.

Flow Charts, Petri Nets, Dynamical Schemes. The social science literature is speckled with models of phenomena that are characterized by the prominent use of boxes and arrows. The contents of the boxes could indicate objects or events. The arrows convey a vague notion of causation. Such *flow charts* represent the weakest definition of what might be a dynamical scheme. If the flow of arrows heads in one direction only, the model might be verifiable through use of linear structural relational analysis. The structures undergoing analysis are patterns of linear correlations; patterns associated with a hypothetical model would be stronger than alternative patterns of correlation.

If, on the other hand, the hypothetical linkage of boxes involves some reversals or circular reactions, then the linear structural relations techniques are inapplicable. It would follow, therefore, therefore, that truly nonlinear functions and self-organized processes have defied those linear structural analyses that have become commonplace in the past 20 years. Indeed they remain problematical, although NDS scientists are working on the problem under the more formal rubric of coupled oscillation problems and driver–slave relationships.

Petri nets look like boxes and arrows also, but the definition of system elements is more literally confined to the flow of information among subsystems of person–machine networks. Marked Petri nets are embellished with big dots in the boxes that indicate that a parcel of information has reached a particular box or subsystem (Peterson, 1981). Marked nets can be found in industrial engineering work, but have not yet turned up in ergonomic or social theories. I mention them as an important, although overlooked, transitional concept between a loose flow chart and a true dynamical scheme.

The following substantive model of industrial accident causation is an attempt to organize numerous qualitative research findings research findings on the linkage between human and environmental characteristic and occupational accidents. It is intended as a transitional concept from which we can further derive a working nonlinear dynamical model of the accident process.

A Complex and Circular Causation Network

Figure 7.2 shows the apparent connections among stress, anxiety, errors, hazards, perceived danger, beliefs about accident control, and errors and accidents. The scheme was started by Guastello, Ikeda, and Connors (1985), and developed further by Guastello and Guastello (1987a) and Guastello (1991a). The network of relationships culminates in a detailed concept of safety climate, or safety culture within an organization. To begin, it is only necessary to say the definitions presented in chapter 6 of stress in its many forms and of anxiety are operational here.

Stress and Anxiety. Correlations between anxiety and accidents are known, but the relationship appears to be bidirectional (Guastello & Guastello, 1987a; Guastello, 1992b; Guastello & Guastello, 1988; Guastello et al., 1985). Leary (1990) identified two paths by which, under a broad range of circumstances, anxiety could lead to a behavioral disruption. In the first case, a person's cognitive evaluation of a situation, here a dangerous one, leads to anxiety, or the excessive fear that something bad will happen. As a result, actions are not taken that could have been taken because the person could not decide what to do. A second path is one where a person engages in a behavior, but anxiety intrudes and interrupts

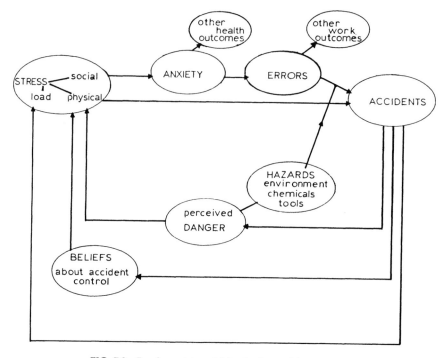

FIG. 7.2. Psychosocial variables in the accident process.

the behavior sequence. The interruption may take the form of an inopportune hesitation, or a major attempt to escape the situation without forethought to the consequences of dropping everything and making a quick exit. As an example, think of how many people climbing a mountain or working on a tall building tell each other not to look down.

Accidents, or even some near-misses, could easily trigger elevated anxiety on the part of the worker. Even if the involved person was not personally harmed or as harmed as others, the effect of seeing what happened to others can be greatly traumatic (Kasl et al., 1981; Weisaeth, 1989a, 1989b, 1989c). What we have essentially established are two mechanisms by which stress can be regarded as contagious. In one sense, there is within-person buildup caused by repeated exposures to stress and personal accident involvement. Each accident or serious near-miss serves the purpose of elevating stress beyond the threshold at which anxiety sets in. Alternatively, there need not be an experience of anxiety for stress to affect behavior, according to the cognitive explanations discussed in chapter 6.

In the second contagion mechanism, an accident experienced by one person leads to the experience of stress by another. Thus there is transpersonal stress buildup, which is the more conventional notion of contagion.

Hazards and Danger. The next two loops in Fig. 7.2 express how danger and beliefs about accident control are connected to the circular stress–anxiety–error–accident cycle. Hazards in the environment are perhaps the first prerequisite for any type of accident process. If we all worked in rubber rooms, there would be little point in discussing these concepts. Although they make unique contributions to the accident process on their own, hazards lead to perceptions of dangerousness, and that level of danger serves to modulate the person's stress level. (Dangerous is not good!). Hazards can be further separated into their sources of origin, such as environments where, for instance, fires and explosion occur; tools; or chemicals. Chemical toxins were listed as stressors in the previous chapter, and it is probably fair to say that there is a fine line sometimes as to whether a toxin represents a stressor or a hazard. Perhaps fine distinctions do not matter.

Beliefs about Accident Control. Some people believe that the good and bad things that happen to them in life are the results of their own behaviors, whereas others believe that more of less everything is a matter of luck. This polarity is well known as the *internal* versus *external locus of control* concept (Rotter, 1966). Several attempts have been made to link a variation of the locus of control construct to accident involvement. Some people believe that accidents are controllable whereas others believe that accidents are matter of bad luck. The concept of beliefs about accident control was actually hatched as an outcome of accident involvement (Guastello & Guastello, 1986), although other researchers have attempted to use it in a predictive sense (reviewed in Arthur & Doverspike, 1992) as a newfangled variety of individual accident proneness.

Safety Climate, Safety Culture. The next question to ask is, given the nexus of relationships depicted in Fig. 7.2, where does safety management fit in? The answer, as I see it, is at every connection in the diagram. Let's back up a few paces.

The concept of safety climate was first expressed by Zohar (1980), who was investigating the safety practices, and workers' views of those safety practices, that distinguished factories with good safety performance from those with poor performance. Attitudes toward the organization's safety program and its effectiveness, worker training, availability of needed tools and personal protection equipment, and the foreman's attentiveness to rule violations, all served to distinguish high and low performing groups. The set of survey questions, taken together denoted a climate for safety. The concept of climate was similar in principle to the organizational climate concepts introduced in Chapter 5, except that climate was viewed with respect to a more limited set of objectives or issues. The introduction of an organizational construct was justified because the measurements distinguished organizations rather than individuals.

Brown and Holmes (1986) discovered through factor analytic techniques that climate for safety, as measured by Zohar's (1980) questionnaire with an American sample, consisted of three factors: perceived risk, management concern, and management action. All three variables distinguished between employees who experienced a "traumatic incident" within the year prior to completing the survey and those who did not.

Later work on the same concept, but measured by a different questionnaire, replicated the associations between safety climate and accidents at the group and individual levels of analysis (Guastello & Guastello, 1987a; Guastello & Guastello, 1988). Furthermore, linkages were also present between measures of stress, anxiety, hazards, and beliefs about accident control with measures of safety climate. Thus the notion of safety climate was expanded to include all the variables depicted in Fig. 7.2. The result was a method of safety intervention that involved a diagnostic survey that addressed a comprehensive inventory of ergonomic concerns. The interpretation of the survey was based on results at the level of the work group or larger organizational subunit. Comprehensive interventions of this type appear to be the most effective means of lowering accident rates in organizations (Guastello, 1993e; Saari, 1992).

The concept of a safety climate eventually was transformed into safety culture. The transition was not a result of any pertinent research, but rather a shift in buzzwords at the level of safety practitioners. Researchers checked out the possible implications nonetheless. It appears that the semantic transition took place in the wake of the Chernobyl nuclear disaster in 1987, when it was noticed that different societies had different views of what constituted as risk and what the risk was worth in terms of societal benefits (Douglas & Wildavsky, 1982; Pidgeon, 1991).

A successful safety culture is one that has positive readings on all the variables mentioned to this point. Personal experience (mine) with measuring those constructs in a variety of settings appears to show, however, that the strength of the interconnections among variables in Fig. 7.2 shifts from organization to organization, as do the linkages between theoretical constructs and accident rates. An "average" set of linkages among constructs and accident rates would not be representative of any of the contributing organizations. Rather, safety culture appears to self-organize in a variety of ways in different work settings, and the pattern of self-organization is probably related to the type of work that takes place and the technologies involved. The topic now turns to formal assessment of NDS principles in the accident process.

ORGANIZATIONAL SUBUNIT SIZE

Organizational structure contributes to climate, as mentioned in chapter 5. The size of an organization or its subunits is probably the most active structural variable, next to division of labor or job design. The actual relationship between subunit size and behavior within the organization was unclear for many years, but it now appears that size and possibly other structural differences give an organization a propensity to behave in a variety of ways, and other variables would explain the particular outcomes that would actually occur. Three studies illustrated that size, more specifically, has a bifurcating effect on group accident rates. The first two are considered in this section, and the third is discussed in the next section, where size is considered alongside other safety climate variables.

The first study involved 435 employees, from nine sheet metal mills and foundries, who were organized into 76 work groups (Guastello & Guastello, 1987b). The work groups ranged from 3 to 30 people. Accident rates were calculated for each group and were expressed in reportable accidents (as defined by the Occupational Safety and Health Administration) per 100 person-years of exposure. There was a "pitchfork" relationship between group size and accident rates. For the larger groups, the accident rates hovered around the national average for the industry. For groups smaller than 17 people, however, there were two distinct levels of accident rate. The upper rate was again close to the national average, but the lower rate was close to zero accidents.

It appeared that small group sizes provided the opportunity for a zero accident rate, which was not always attained. The recommendation for organizations based on the findings was that large work groups should be organized such that the density of employees who are well trained in safety matters is no less than 1/15. The job of "safety contact person" could be rotated among group members and need not require additional personnel. Although there has not been a formal test of this principle, one division of a large organization that adopted this recommendation reported (personal communication) that it worked well for them. Establishing a system of safety contact persons was one of several recommendations they pursued that had the net effect of improving their safety record from average for their organization to the best of eight divisions (they avoided citing numbers).

The second opportunity to study the subunit size relationship specifically came from a large steel-making facility (Guastello, 1988a). There were 283 functional work groups, ranging in size from 3 to 60 people, that were organized into 37 departments. The criteria were changes in the OSHA-reportable accident rates over a 2.5-year period. It was hypothesized that a cusp catastrophe model could be identified, such that the two modes were accelerating and decelerating accident rates, and the bifurcation effect was group size. Asymmetry was represented by a set of dummy-coded variables that represented the departments.

Results showed that the cusp did in fact provide a decent interpretation of the accident trends. The average R^2 for two different time panels was .41, and the comparable value for the next best linear alternative was .16. A scatterplot of change in accident rate versus subunit size appears in Fig. 7.3. The bifurcation point was situated at 37 workers per group per shift. The critical value was larger than that obtained from the earlier study, but that difference could possibly be accounted for by differences in the distribution of safety-trained personnel in the two settings. There was no significant safety intervention of either a positive or negative kind during the time horizon under study. The less than perfect fit between the model and the data, however, suggests that the organization was not fully stressed to cover the entire cusp manifold.

CATASTROPHE MODEL FOR THE ACCIDENT PROCESS

Figure 7.4 shows a cusp catastrophe model for the accident process that includes a detail of the qualitative variables discussed in the first section, and subunit size. The two stable states of behavior are once again high and low accident rates, where high rates are somewhat above the national average for a particular industry, and the low rates are close to the zero accident level.

The operator load and environmental hazard parameters can be thought of as background and trigger variables, respectively. The relationship between hazards and accidents is thought to be linear in the sense of the Surry (1969) hazard buildup process. Other evidence suggests that the linear relationship is actually a log-linear relationship, such that hazards are more closely related to the log of accidents rates, rather than to accident rates directly (Guastello & Guastello, 1987a).

Variables that represent sources of stress, which in turn affect performance (chapter 6), are thought to cause a sharp inflection of risk over a short amount of time when the background hazard level is sufficiently strong. The bifurcation manifold describes risk inflection, which is greatest when anxiety and stress are high, safety management is poor, and group size is small. Good safety management is thought to produce only a relatively low

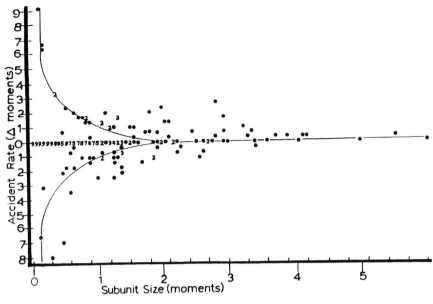

FIG. 7.3. Scatterplot of changes in accident rate for groups of various size. From Guastello (1988a). Reprinted with permission.

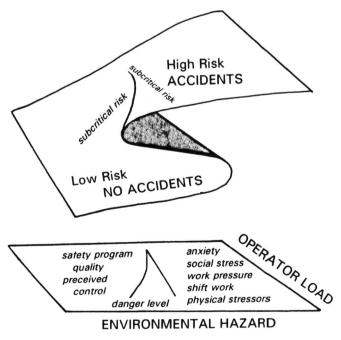

FIG. 7.4. Cusp catastrophe model of the accident process.

219

accident rate, whereas poorly managed groups are more susceptible to positive or negative change. The role of group size was discussed earlier. The gradients of the cusp response surface can be defined behaviorally. When one observes the process underlying a single accident, the surface modalities represent either the presence of an accident or a lack of one. If a person's experience were to be traced along a trajectory on the outer rim of the surface where stress is high, the experience would begin with relative safety. As hazards build up, nothing appears to happen. But when hazards reach a critical threshold, an accident results. The gradients running between the cusp point and the centers of the attractors represent underlying subcritical levels of risk that become more apparent in a group-level analysis.

Mills and Foundries

One way to test the model would be to find a sample of work groups, measure the control parameters and accident rates, wait a while, then link the changes in accident rates to the independent variables and the nonlinear function. Such an experiment for an accident model would be ghoulish at best, because corrective information could be provided to the host organizations soon after the first measurements were taken. Indeed, participants in the study of mills and foundries volunteered because they needed to receive some useful diagnostic information and their accident rates were already climbing.

The solution for an evaluation design, therefore, combined an evaluation of the accident model with a training outcome (cuspoid as discussed in chapter 5). Additionally, a training outcome study could be viewed as a limited form of organizational development intervention (discussed in broader terms in chapter 11), which would be appropriate considering the centrality of safety management in the theoretical model. In practice, therefore, the participating organizations in the study (Guastello, 1989) were measured on the control variables, and were given feedback as soon as possible. The manipulation was that they were given varying amounts of time to work on the recommendations derived from their data before the Time 2 measures of accident rate were taken.

Participants were employees of six foundries and three sheet metal mills who completed a 75-item version of the Occupational Hazards Survey. One organization dropped out of the study due to bankruptcy, leaving 68 work groups to participate. Each organization received a feedback report of their own survey results, plus a combined report detailing recommendations that were common to all participants. They were given varying amounts of time to work on their recommendations, ranging from 1 to 9 months, with an average of 6 months. A new bifurcation variable was introduced, therefore, which was the number of months holding the report before the Time 2 data were taken. A measure of experience with similar work was also collected with the survey and tested as a bifurcation variable. Change in group size was another new variable tested as a bifurcation term.

Analyses contrasted cusp, linear difference, and linear pre–post models in two forms. In one form Y was accident rate, and in the other Y was the base-10 log of accident rates. Location and scale transformations were applied to either form of Y for the cusp models. A summary of R^2 coefficients appears in Table 7.1. Results indicated that the cusps were clearly more accurate than any of the alternative models.

Different sets of bifurcation terms were prominent in the two cusp models. For the regular cusp, physical stress, anxiety, social stress, and the initial size of the work group comprised the bifurcation parameter. For the cusp-log model, experience, safety management ratings, and months holding the report comprised the bifurcation parameter. The difference in model composition is interesting but has not yet been explained. Hazards and danger ratings did not contribute to the asymmetry parameters, possibly because the environments were similar, and possibly because the easiest corrective procedures in those situations were hazard removals.

Qualitative aspects of the results showed that the groups that responded the most to the intervention where those that had initially high accident rates and were more anxious, thought safety management was doing a better job, and initially believed that accidents could be controlled. Goldberg et al. (1991) later reported similar results. Another valuable piece of information came from the log-linear difference model, which showed a −.27 correlation between months holding the feedback report and change in log accident rates. This result translated into a 58% decrease in the average accident rate over an average intervention period of 6 months (Guastello, 1993e).

Transit Operators

The application of the cusp accident model for transit operators (Guastello, 1991b) involved an individual level of analysis. In spite of the focus on group activity, bus drivers drive alone. There are, nonetheless, con-

TABLE 7.1
Summary of Regression Results (R^2) for Mills and Foundries

Model Type	Accident Rate	Log Accident Rate
Linear pre–post	.00	.15*
Linear difference	.05*	.07*
Cusp model	.42***	.36**

*$p < .05$. **$p < .01$. ***$p < .001$.

nected by common experiences and common management programs, so the concept of safety climate and all its essential measurements would apply. Transit operation is considered to be one of the most stressful occupations worldwide (Gardell et al., 1982). In the United States, the rate of loss from workday accidents for transit operation was twice the national average for all industries at the time the study was conducted. Sources of stress impinging on the bus driver include time pressure, traffic hazards, and complaining, troublesome, and abusive passengers.

Participants in the study were 290 transit operators from a major U.S. city who completed an expanded version of the Occupational Hazards Survey for transit operators. The survey contained a special scale for transit hazards such as threatening and violent passengers, and the need to reprimand passengers for radio playing, smoking, or loud talking. The survey also contained sets of questions pertaining to stress-related health disorders, which are discussed in the next chapter, and self-reports of accidents while driving the bus or in personal automobiles.

Difference scores for this application were created by differencing the level of accident involvement in the bus against accidents in one's personal automobile. This technique was based on the viewpoint that the driver is experiencing a rapidly oscillating level of risk between work and nonwork. The differencing technique also controlled for poor driving ability, which was probably not a problem among professional drivers. Initially, the ordinary standard deviation was used as a measure of scale in the cusp model.

The linear difference model contained one significant variable, which was transit hazards ($r = .38$). The R^2 increased from .14 to .20 when all survey variables were entered into the regression model. The linear pre–post model showed that the top three predictors of bus accidents were transit hazards, automobile accidents (the Time 1 measure), and anxiety ($R^2 = .22$). The R^2 increased to .26 when all survey variables were entered into the model.

The cusp model was a better fit for the data ($R^2 = .50$). Significant weights were obtained for the cubic and quadratic terms, transit hazards as an asymmetry variable (all $p < .001$), and social stressors as a bifurcation variable ($p < .05$). Shift work did not emerge as a significant variable, although it was known from past research to be an important stressor wherever it is found. Further analysis showed, however, that the transit hazards varied by shift. Nights were the worst for some hazards, but afternoons were tied with the nights for others. Additionally, "extra board" personnel experienced elevated levels of transit hazards, as they were, more often not, assigned to all the least desirable routes and shifts.

Three years after the initial analysis I discovered the alternative measure of scale shown in chapter 3 as Equation 20. The revised analysis did not alter the contents of the cusp model, but the R^2 jumped to .63, and the significance of the social stress variable registered at the .001 level (Guastello, 1992b).

RISK DISPERSION FOR 10 INDUSTRIAL CLASSES

The next part of the story is a summary of an extensive analysis of accident and death rates across virtually the full spectrum of businesses in the United States: agriculture, mining, construction, manufacturing, transportation, wholesale trade, retail trade, finance, services, and government. Here the cusp model for the accident process, developed in a section, was expanded with the mushroom catastrophe model to cover accidental death and other nondeath claims from an insurance database. Control parameters in the study were age, sex, and industrial categories, all of which are widely recognized moderators of accident rates throughout society. In an effort to make lucid reading out of what could be cruel and unusual punishment to the reader, I focus on the essential procedures and results, and save the voluminous tables of statistical results for a document on deposit with *Social and Behavioral Sciences Documents* (Guastello, 1987c).

Model Expansions for the Insurance Database

The Society of Actuaries' *1980 Transactions* provided reasonably complete and manageable data tables showing claim rates that were aggregated over the years 1974–1979. There were 89 industrial categories sorted under the 10 headings just listed. The actual number were provided for males, females, and sex-unknown data, subdivided into attained age of 65 or over, and under 65. Data for some occupational groups did not use the sex-unknown category. For persons under 65, total disability claims were reported only; the rate of accidental death was not significantly different from the medical death rate.

The *casualty ratio* is the number of actual claims divided by predicted claims. Predicted causality rates were generated by taking the claim rates for men and women, aggregated over all industrial categories and broken down by age at issue, and multiplying by the years of exposure for the subgroup. If there were no deviation in accident rate by individual category, then casualty ratios would hover around 100%. In reality, however, they varied from 0% to 739% with an outlier at 1128% (female data, fishing, hunting, and trapping, age 65 or over).

Trends in mortality from the 1965–1970 aggregate period to 1978, also reported in the *Transactions*, showed a significant lengthening of life expectancy for both men and women regarding medical death, but more so for men. One insurance analyst noted that overall differences in life expectancy for women and men narrowed to only 3 years (women living longer), compared to a 6-year gap recorded in 1958 (Mitchell, 1983). Casualty ratios vary more widely for men across industries than for women across the same industries. Similarly, wider ranges of accident claim ratios exist for persons under 65 compared to persons over 65.

Cusp Hypothesis. The cusp catastrophe hypothesis was that casualty ratios would be cusp catastrophically distributed around 100%, rather than normally distributed. Age and gender would contribute to the bifurcation parameter, indicating that the subgroups would react differently to their environmental exposures. Industrial categories would contribute to the asymmetry parameter.

In the case of males and females, it is unclear how much of the difference in reactivity to a general industry is the result of inherent biology, or how much of the effect is related to differential exposures within those occupations. In light of the societal trends toward greater percentages of women in the work force over the 1958–1983 period, and toward greater percentages of women in male-dominated occupations, the differential exposure explanation could carry some serious weight, particularly in light of the lessening differences in life expectancy over that time period.

Age was thought to function as a differential exposure variable because retired people, who would dominate the age 65 or over category, would be less likely to have an industrial accident, on the one hand, but would be more likely to register the effects of chronic exposure to environmental hazards, on the other. In other words, occupational compromises to health might not show up until the later years.

Industrial categories vary in risk level, sometimes for reasons that are not well understood. The industrial category was regarded as an asymmetry variable for the same reason that environmental hazards were thought to contribute to asymmetry in the accident models considered earlier. Hazards were thought to be precursors of medical death rates as well as precursors of accident involvement.

Gender was introduced as a dummy-coded variable with a value of 1 if female, and 0 otherwise (males and gender-unknown). Age was tested as a dummy-coded variable also, with a value of 1 to denote the age 65 or over category, and 0 otherwise. Industrial groups were tested as a set of dummy-coded variables also. For analyses involving the 10 industrial classes in their entireties, government data were the default group.

The criterion measure in the cusp model, Δz, was the difference between actual and predicted claims, expressed in values corrected for location and scale. The efficacy of the cusp model was tested along with alternative hypotheses for the mushroom catastrophe, as well as linear control difference models. Preliminary analysis showed that the cusp difference model was the more challenging test in this situation.

Mushroom Hypothesis. The hypothesized mushroom model for the insurance data was defined as follows. The dependent measures were accidental death rates (u, the quadratic function), and nondeath claims (v, the cubic function). Differences scores Δu and Δv were defined as contrasts between subgroup actual values and predicted values as for Δz in the cusp model. Age (d) and gender (c) were tested as bifurcation terms again. The industrial groups and classes were tested as asymmetry variables, such that groups contributing to a or b were distinguished on the basis on results from canonical polynomial correlation analysis. The hypotheses are expressed in terms of the mushroom response surface in Fig. 7.5.

Data Analysis Strategy

The data set consisted of 484 cases, not including 6 cases of "unclassified establishments." A total of 23,770,727 years of life exposure was represented. Cusp and control difference models were first computed for the entire set of 484 cases where the major industrial classes were tested as asymmetry variables, and age and gender groups were tested as bifurcation variables. Pilot analyses showed that power potentials no greater than the cubic were operating.

The data set was then broken down and analyzed within industrial class where industrial subgroups were used as asymmetry variables. A forward selection method of variable entry was used in the regression

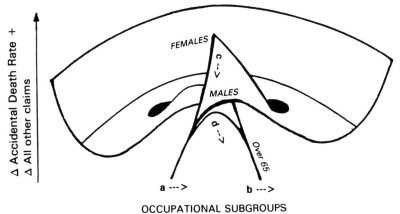

FIG. 7.5. Mushroom catastrophe model for risk dispersion.

analysis. In the event that a cusp model was difficult to interpret, non-significant terms were removed, and the model was computed again. In the event that a cubic potential was significant but age or sex did not respond as bifurcation variables, subgroups that were not significant in the asymmetry position were tested as bifurcation variables. Most of the within-class models required a revision of some sort.

The third stage of analysis repeated the first with new asymmetry variables that were uncovered in the within-class analyses. The new asymmetry terms were added to the end of the model.

Finally, canonical and noncanonical mushroom catastrophes were tested where accidental death and nondeath claims (including medical death) were the criteria. Noncanonical mushrooms were calculated for each of the 10 occupational classes. The modeling hypothesis was whether the mushroom explained the data better than the cusp. Because the mushroom is qualitatively more complex, its statistical superiority (as measured by R^2) would be cause by a greater number of terms in the regression equation. Thus, the stepwise method of variable entry was used rather than forward selection. For the noncanonical analyses, both criteria were given equal weights.

No stepwise entry option was available for the canonical correlation analysis, so the full model analysis was used. The superiority of the noncanonical versus canonical model was based on the R^2 for the first canonical variate.

Results

The results for the linear, cusp, noncanonical and canonical mushrooms appear in Table 7.2. The R^2 coefficients for the best models are given in boldface type for each data group.

Mushroom catastrophe models were supported for 6 out of 10 industrial classes. For four of the six mushrooms, both the noncanonical and canonical versions outperformed the cusp and linear models. In the case of financial organizations, the cusp and canonical mushroom models were equivalent. In the case of transportation, the noncanonical mushroom was clearly better than the canonical mushroom, cusp, or linear models.

For manufacturing data, the effect sizes for the cusp and canonical mushroom models were equivalent, and both were better than the linear alternative; the cusp would be the more parsimonious interpretation. For service organizations, the cusp was better than either the linear or mushroom models. Mushroom models could not be calculated for construction or wholesale trades because of the very small sample sizes; cusp models outperformed linear models in those cases. Cusp models

TABLE 7.2
Summary of Regression Results for 10 Industrial Classes

| | R^2 | | R^2 Mushroom | | |
Industry Group	Linear	Cusp	Noncanonical	Canonical	N
All 10 classes—initial	.10***	.12***			434
Agriculture	.16	.66***	.90***	.99***	30
Mining	.12	.55**	.61***	.75***	28
Construction	.34	.74***	a	a	18
Manufacturing	.27	.60***	.51***	.60***	120
Transportation	.26	.38*	.86***	.31	57
Wholesale trades	.32	.85*	a	a	12
Retail trades	.18	.48**	.57***	.63***	48
Financial organizations	.15	.20*	.20***	.55***	48
Service organizations	.43***	.87***	.79***	.81***	90
Government	.22	.86***	.90***	.90***	33
All 10 classes—final	.27***	.35***	.33***	.37***	434

aNot calculated because of small sample size.
*$p < .05$. **$p < .01$. ***$p < .001$.

outperformed linear models in all 10 cases. A detail of the winning models is presented next.

Agriculture. Two significant canonical variates for agricultural data were found. The criterion for the first was simply accidental death. The second criterion was the difference between accidental death and nondeath claims. All principal mushroom terms except bifurcation by gender were judged to contribute to one or the other canonical predictors. Judgments were made on the basis of loading size and supplemented by univariate correlations with the criteria. Crops production was negatively associated with nondeath claims and accidental death, and was thus concluded to contribute to both a and b parameters.

Mining. Only one significant canonical variate (out of two possible for each analysis) emerged for mining data, which predicted accidental death. The noncanonical analysis showed significant effects for bifurcation by age ($p < .001$), the modulus term ($p < .001$), and metal mining as a more risky asymmetry group ($p < .10$).

Construction. Significant weights within the cusp model were obtained for the cubic potential ($p < .001$) and special construction as an asymmetry variable ($p < .10$). No bifurcation effect was found. The model could just as readily be represented as a fold catastrophe ($R^2 = .73$), but the weight of the evidence from other industries suggested that a common interpretation was more parsimonious.

Manufacturing. Significant weights within the cusp model were obtained for the cubic and quadratic potentials (both $p < .001$). Among the asymmetry variables, food, publishing (both $p < .05$), and electrical manufacturing were less risky, whereas stone ($p < .10$), primary metal ($p < .001$), and fabricated metal industries ($p < .05$) were more risky. Among the bifurcation tests, leather ($p < .01$), instrumentation ($p < .05$), and machinery manufacturing contributed to the negative gradient on the manifold.

Transportation. Only one significant weight was actually obtained, which was for the cubic function of nondeath claims. Its effect was quite large ($R^2 = .86$).

Wholesale Trades. Significant weights within the cusp model were obtained for the cubic ($p < .05$) and quadratic potentials ($p < .01$) on the second step of the forward entry. Introduction of gender as a bifurcation variable and durable goods as an asymmetry variable raised the R^2 greatly, but no significant weights were obtained, due to the very small sample size. In ordinary circumstances a regression with 12 cases would not be advised, but an exception was made here because each data point was based on voluminous data.

Retail Trades. Two significant canonical variates were obtained for retail trades. The first criterion was accidental death and the second was the difference between the two outcomes. All principal powers and bifurcation terms contributed significantly to the model. No significant asymmetry variables were found.

Service Organizations. Significant weights within the cusp model were obtained for the cubic and quadratic potentials ($p < .001$). Significant weights were obtained for gender as a bifurcation variable ($p < .05$), and educational services ($p < .001$) and membership organizations ($p < .05$) as less risky asymmetry variables.

Government. Two significant canonical variates were obtained for government groups. The first criterion was the sum of outcome differences, weighted $3.5 : 1$ in favor of nondeath claims. The second criterion was the difference between the outcomes. All principal powers and bifurcation terms were significantly correlated with either accidental death or nondeath claims.

Full Data Set. The cusp model for the full set of 484 risk categories contained significant weights for the cubic potential ($p < .05$), and bifurcation terms for gender ($p < .01$), leather manufacturing ($p < .05$), and machinery manufacturing ($p < .001$). Weights for asymmetry terms were significant for all industrial classes: agriculture ($p < .01$), mining ($p < .10$), construction ($p < .05$), manufacturing ($p < .10$), transportation ($p < .05$), wholesale trade ($p < .001$), retail trade ($p < .001$), finance ($p < .01$), and service industries ($p < .001$). Weights for asymmetry terms were significant for five additional industrial subgroups: primary metal manufacturing, fabricated metal manufacturing, educational services, membership organizations (all $p < .001$), and stone manufacturing ($p < .01$).

The noncanonical mushroom model showed significant weights for the cubic, quadratic, modulus (all $p < .05$), and bifurcation by age ($p < .001$); a significant weight for bifurcation by gender was not obtained, and collinearity with other terms in the model was suspected for why the gender effect did not show up in this instance. Significant weights for asymmetry terms were obtained for wholesale trades, retail, service industries, stone manufacturing, primary and secondary metals, educational services (all $p < .001$), special construction, banking, and membership organizations (all $p < .05$), and finance ($p < .10$).

Although the noncanonical mushroom was not better than the cusp model ($R^2 = .33$ vs. $.35$), the canonical mushroom was indeed better by a small margin (canonical $R^2 = .37$). Two significant canonical variates were obtained. The first canonical criterion was composed of nondeath claims, virtually by itself (Wilks' $\Lambda = .551$, $p < .001$). The second criterion was the difference between nondeath claims and accidental death (canonical $R^2 = .12$, $\Lambda = .877$, $p < .001$). Large coefficients were obtained for power potentials, bifurcation terms, and the modulus. All the asymmetry variables named in the earlier noncanonical analysis except stone manufacturing contributed to the first canonical variate. Stone manufacturing and crops production contributed to the second canonical variate.

Broad Trends. The first broad trend to emerge from the study was that the cusp model, as a simple nonlinear dynamic process, was a better descriptor of dispersions of risk across industries than a simple linear model. The cusp finding was true for all industrial classes together and for each industrial class individually. The largest cusp effect was obtained for service organizations, and the smallest effect was obtained for finance.

The mushroom catastrophe model did offer an improvement when outcomes for accidental death and nondeath claims were separated. The mushroom effect was true for all industrial classes together and for 6 out of 10 industrial classes. The largest mushroom effects were obtained for agricultural and government data. Data for two classes were insufficient to test for mushrooms. Risk dispersions in manufacturing and service industries were better classified as cusps. Figure 7.6 shows scatterplots of agricultural data, government data, and data for all industrial classes combined.

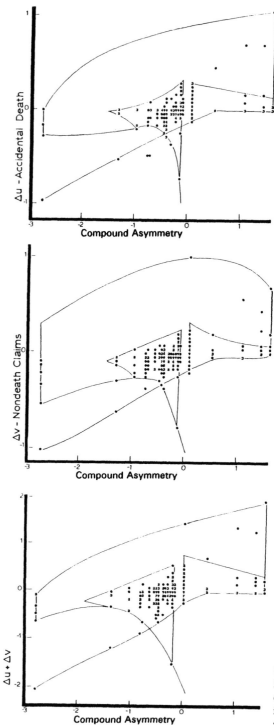

FIG. 7.6. Scatterplot of risk data for all 10 industrial classes, agriculture, and government, showing mushroom catastrophe response surface.

SUMMARY

Conventional approaches to accident modeling and explanation vary in complexity. Although nonlinear dynamics have mentioned only rarely in accident studies, they are apparent in many of the model structures and were discussed in the first section. A cusp catastrophe model of the accident process was next introduced in rudimentary form and the impact of group size as a bifurcation variable was considered. Small groups have an opportunity to attain zero-level accident rates that does not appear to be afforded to larger work groups. The essential recommendation is that work-group infrastructure should be developed to keep the ratio of safety-knowledgeable people to other workers at or below $17 : 1$.

The third section elaborated a full cusp model for safety climate, or safety culture, in which the control parameters were operator load and hazard levels, both of which were broadly defined. Safety management is a control mechanism both in real circumstances and as a bifurcating effect in the model. Tests of the cusp model in two situations showed that the model provides a good description of the accident process and affords a variety of qualitative recommendations that an organization can use to enhance its safety performance.

The next section contained a societal-level analysis of risk dispersions across all the major occupational categories in the United States using a large insurance database. It was probably true that finer definitions of occupational categories could have been useful. Nonetheless, cusp structure was found in all industrial classes. When the outcomes were more clearly separated between accidental deaths and nondeath insurance claims, mushroom catastrophe structure was observed. Mushroom structure was particularly strong in agriculture and government occupations.

8

Stress-Related Illness

The goal of this chapter is to extend the stress and accident concepts from the previous chapters to develop a model to describe the onset of stress-related illness. The first section summarizes some of the classic concepts of mathematical epidemiology and reinterprets them in terms of elementary catastrophe dynamics. The second section reviews some pertinent stress and accident concepts, and develops an interpretation of illness from the dynamics of the accident process.

In the course of developing the illness theory, the dynamics of the internal security subsystem are elaborated. The dynamics of the internal security subsystem are based in part on living systems theory and partly on the butterfly catastrophe model. The model for the internal security subsystem describes a mechanism by which an organism protects itself from environmentally based toxins or other health threats as well as from internal organ damage or similar health threats. Analogous mechanisms for the human individual and the organization are explored in this chapter; a national-level application of the model is considered in Chapter 10.

The third section reports an empirical investigation of conditions that promote the onset of stress-related illness among transit operators. The illnesses have a strong occupational linkage, and their dynamics follow closely the existing theories for occupational accidents and the internal security subsystem. The modeling approach regards illness as a basket of related outcomes. The model work is extended in the next section, where the onsets of seven illnesses are studied separately.

The final section extends the internal security subsystem to the organizational level of system analysis. Here the focus shifts from illness to an

232

organization's susceptibility to theft and espionage. Although it may appear that theft and medical illness are not related, they share some common dynamics and both involve stress concepts.

MATHEMATICS OF EPIDEMICS

Mathematical models have been used for over a century to describe and predict the course and extent of diseases. The underlying premise is that by identifying the mathematical functions, one may then acquire an understanding of the disease itself. In this section some classic epidemiology is abstracted from a longer survey by Fine (1979). The treatment is followed by a brief discussion of how catastrophe theory research has harnessed the concepts and, more poignantly, the application and results for medical disorders among transit operators.

Classical Epidemiology

Farr's (1840) formula was an example of the curve-fitting variety of mathematical modeling. Let there be a sequence of five successive, perhaps weekly, mortality levels x_1, x_2, x_3, x_4, x_5. Then:

$$K = (x_1/x_2)/(x_3/x_4) = (x_2/x_3)/(x_4/x_5) \tag{1}$$

Values of K remain constant throughout the course of an epidemic and are generally less than 1.

Hamer (1906) proposed a discrete time model in which the number of future casualties is a function of the present number of casualties, C_t, the number of susceptibles, S_t, and the epidemic threshold number of susceptibles, m:

$$C_{t+1} = C_t S_t / m \tag{2}$$

where t is equal to one incubation period. The innovative concept here was the "mass action principle," represented by the $C_t S_t$ element, which is essentially a mechanism of contagion. According to Fine (1979), the mass action concept was later incorporated into models built in the 1950s.

Ross (1916, 1917) contributed a series of continuous time models that also addressed the mass action concept. Equation 3 is representative:

$$\delta y / \delta t = ky(1 - y) \tag{3}$$

Brownlee's approach was also of the curve-fitting variety and was based on Farr's K. He discovered that

$$x = \exp(-At^2 + Bt + D) \tag{4}$$

defined the density of infected cases over time. Equation 4 is a normal family probability density function (pdf) (Brownlee, 1907). This conclusion allowed Brownlee to describe the course of many epidemics as symmetric normal or right-skewed normal functions over time. Equation 5 is Brownlee's discrete forecast:

$$C_{t+1} = C_t \, pq^t \tag{5}$$

where p is baseline infectivity, and q^t represents decay of infectivity over time. The general curve equation is:

$$C_t = C_0 \, p^t q^{t((t-1)/2)} \tag{6}$$

Brownlee's applications were based on the assumption of a symmetrical normal curve time series. Repetitive waves of infection showing right skew were fitted by two superimposed symmetrical normal distributions. With this technique it was possible to show that London summer diarrhea during the years 1860–1919 was a function of two infections, not just one (Brownlee & Young, 1922).

Several limitations of the Brownlee model were later uncovered. It did not include a provision for the number or proportion of susceptibles. Forecasts of casualties made before the epidemics had completed their course were inaccurate, although Farr obtained greater predictive accuracy. The exponential loss of infectivity over the course of an epidemic was interpreted by Brownlee as a mutation of the infecting agent taking place. The interpretation was later disproven. Brownlee overlooked alternative interpretations of pq^t, in that proportions and numbers of susceptibles vary through the course of the epidemic, as do the interactions between infected and noninfected subgroups (Fine, 1979).

Catastrophe Modeling of Epidemic Processes

Only a trivial rearrangement of terms is required to show that the Ross function for mass action (Equation 3) is structurally close to a fold catastrophe when set to its minimum:

$$ky^2 - ky = 0 \tag{7}$$

In statistical form, k is absorbed into the empirical weights. In Equation 7, y_1 substitutes for a, since the latter is a correlate of y_1 to the degree that the surface is not unfolded (a viable assumption for a fold model). Equation 7 is also a general logistic model when k is a control parameter. As k becomes sufficiently large, the number of people affected with the illness (or the rate of infection) changes from a fixed value to a periodically oscillating value. As k continues to increase, the infection level will become quasi-periodic during the period-doubling regime and eventually chaotic. At the present time, medically relevant bifurcation variables that could transform an infection rate all the way from stable to chaotic are not well known. It is left for future research to determine what sort of real conditions would promote such a destabilizing state of affairs.

Hamer's m is the epidemic threshold, which is the critical value in percent or number of population that must be infected before the epidemic actually "takes off." The critical threshold for any catastrophe is determined by setting the first derivative of the surface equation (or stochastic surface equation) to 0. Thus for a fold, the threshold is the point where $y = 0$. The cusp has two thresholds, one ascending and one descending; the latter denotes the decay and termination of an epidemic or catastrophic cycle:

$$\delta^2 y / \delta t^2 = 3y^2 - b = 0 \tag{8}$$

It can now be shown that the Hamer model is a cusp catastrophic process. First, cusp variables y and b are equal in meaning to C_t and S_t, respectively, from Equation 2. Second, modify Equation 2 into a difference equation by multiplying both sides by m and subtracting $C_t S_t$ from both sides:

$$mC_t - C_t S_t = 0 \tag{9}$$

Third, substitute Equation 8 for m:

$$3C_t^3 - 2C_t S_t = 0 \tag{10}$$

In practice the constants are then absorbed into the empirical weights.

Brownlee's twin infection problem appears to be a case of mushroom catastrophe rather than a cusp. The mushroom pdf is characterized by a steep peak followed by a skewed decline (which can look like a secondary mode), a long antimode, and a small recurrence. In principle, each of the two behaviors (diseases) may show the blast–cascade–plateau–antimode–aftershock pattern, or one behavior might show an inverted sequence of early warning, antimode, blast, and cascade (chapter 7). The summer diarrhea pattern (Brownlee & Young, 1922; Fine, 1979) showed the blast, cascade, and antimode; the aftershock appeared to be absorbed into the recurring blast. It is unclear at the present time, however, whether the secondary plateau that characterizes the mushroom pdf is structurally identifiable from the Brownlee data. The underdeveloped techniques for studying umbilic pdfs is probably the chief limitation, combined with underspecified control parameters. If it should be true that that secondary plateau cannot be isolated, then a wave crest or hair catastrophe model may be a better choice. Further research on twin infections should assess the relative merits of the elementary embolic group of models.

Because the Hamer, Ross, and Brownlee functions have been reasoned to be catastrophes or chaotic processes in disguise, and because their work proceeded from Farr's K, it should follow that K is a bifurcation index. To demonstrate, invert K such that, for four consecutive casualty rates, y,

$$K' = (y_4/y_3)/(y_2/y_1) \tag{11}$$

As before, K' is thought to remain constant throughout the time series, and hence the number of casualties for y_5 may be predicted given K' and the three previous values of y_i. When $K' = 1$, epidemic strength holds constant, as does the number of casualties expected. When $K' > 1$, sharp increases in casualties are expected or observed from one end of the series to another, followed by sharp decreases. When $K' < 1$, a decelerating series is taking place, gravitating to an asymptotic minimum. The functions of K' resemble the function of the b parameter of the cusp (Fig. 8.1).

The foregoing propositions regarding K' were verified empirically for biannual accidental death rates (rather than diseases) in the U.S. mining industry over the 1944–1973 period (Guastello & Dizadji, 1984). There were five separate types of mine involved (coal, limestone, gold and silver, copper, lead, and zinc), and thus 50 observations in the time series. A cusp model with time and K' as bifurcation parameters ($R^2 = .61$) was more accurate than the next best linear alternative ($R^2 = .42$). Contrary to expectations, K' fluctuated over time, but this aberration was interpreted as a property of the mining death phenomena rather than a property of K'.

Chaos, Medicine, and Psychiatry

Nonlinear dynamical systems theory (NDS) has found numerous applications in medical research, particularly on topics related to cardiology and neurology (Ditto, 1993). At the most simplistic level, the healthy heart emits a regular but complex rhythm. Cardiac arrhythmia is a destabilization of the healthy rhythm, which can further destabilize into chaos or death. Understanding electrocardiograms from a dynamics viewpoint

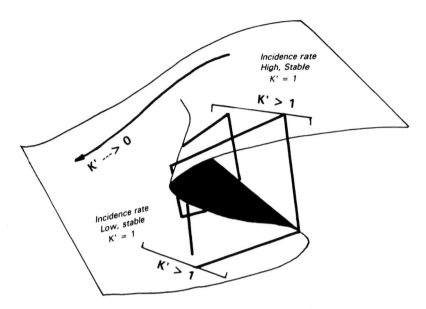

FIG. 8.1. Functions of Farr's K' shown as trajectories on the cusp response surface.

should eventually facilitate attempts to link disease-related variables to destabilizing dynamic scenarios. At the present time, however, the apparent dynamics of cardiac rhythm are more complex than the better known chaotic functions, and an iterative interplay between developments in NDS and medical theory can be anticipated for the next decade.

A similar principle is inherent in the neurological studies, although there is an apparently wider range of neurological events commanding attention. Neurons fire at regular intervals under specific conditions of stimulation. Neurotransmitter imbalances would alter the firing patterns, and a possible direction of study is to determine which chemical events translate into dynamical events, and how those connections could be translated into treatments with pharmaceutical agents (Ditto, 1993). Alternatively, studies of the behavior of sensory and motor nerves or tracts under varying stimulus conditions have been productive also. For instance, it is well known that many animals are extremely sensitive to low levels of environmental stimulation (by human standards). Douglass et al. (1993) discovered that the addition of small amounts of noise actually facilitates signal detection among crayfish. Noise may be experimentally introduced internally, under which condition no optimum level of noise has been determined, or externally to the stimulus itself, under which condition there is a point beyond which no further noise aids signal detection.

Cheng and Tong (1992) investigated the possible chaoticity of epidemic times series for monthly counts of measles in New York over the 1928–1963 period using nonlinear time series regression. They determined that no chaotic skeleton was inherent in the data, although previous work has suggested that the measles data reflected an embedding dimension between 5 and 7. Contemporary epidemic theory, however, has focused on methods of disease transmission, which could be caused by disruptions of environmental niches due to rapid urbanization in developing countries, or coevolutionary processes in disease functions (Levins et al., 1994). In the case of the latter, as medicine becomes more effective for knocking out most examples of a disease agent, the bacterium or virus mutates into something more resistant and more annoying to the human host. Evolutionary processes are considered in chapter 9.

The major psychoses have also attracted some attention, although little of that work has progressed beyond a few theoretical models. Of particular interest, however, are two approaches to bipolar (or manic-depressive) disorder. Scott (1985) used the cusp catastrophe to model the disorder where mania and depression formed the two stable states. Self-image constituted the bifurcation factor, such that a more rigid self-image would predispose the patient to greater mood swings. Anxiety was regarded as the asymmetry parameter, such that high anxiety was associated with the depressive pole. Abraham et al. (1990), who did not appear to have seen Scott's work, conceptualized bipolar disorder as a Lorenz attractor, which is of a similar level of dimensional complexity. The key difference is, however, that the Lorenz allows for small, chaotic variations in mood in either the manic or depressive state. The two control parameters were self-image again and rate of mood change. Rate was thought to act as a control parameter in a manner analogous to how the rate of change of a pendulum affects the position of the pendulum. One might surmise that neurochemical events would affect the rate function in the Lorenz interpretation or gradients in the cusp interpretation. Explicit reference to biochemical events was not apparent in either model. The depression model is loosely relevant to the studies of stress-related medical disorders that follow in this chapter.

Epidemic Modeling for Accidents

Kemp (1967) drew an important theoretical connection between mathematical models for disease epidemics and industrial accidents by sharing that accident distributions follow a contagious epidemic distribution when left uncontrolled. The model was

$$P_o = \exp[\lambda(e^{-\theta} - 1) - \phi] \tag{12}$$

where P_o is the probability of an accident occurring overall, λ is the number of "spells" during a given time period in which the operator's attentiveness is impaired, and θ is the probability of an accident outside a spell. Parameters λ, θ, and ϕ are Poisson distributed, and Equation 12 is a Poisson generalization of Poisson distributions.

Analysis of actual data showed that the model fit quite well, but Kemp (1967) cautioned that the model parameters were estimated after the accident series was collected. As with any forecasting model, it is assumed that future events will mirror past events in virtually every way that could have affected the observations that formed the basis of the forecasting model.

Virtually no research has surfaced in the accident literature to explain the psychological significance of the parameters in Equation 12 since Kemp (1967). The applicability of Poisson distributions to industrial accident data has been historically noted (Mintz & Blum, 1949). More germane to this exposition, however, is the presence of cusp-like characteristics in the Kemp model. First, there are two qualitatively different states of operator awareness which were thought to underlie two locally stable accident levels. The oscillation between the two alertness states appears to be a hysteresis effect. The term λ is a bifurcation parameter that describes the transition from a region of local stability (few oscillations per unit of time) to a region of global instability. Because θ is a probability, and thus a noninteger, it qualifies as a fractal.

The following sections of this chapter apply the dynamic principles of the cusp catastrophe to the onset of stress-related medical disorders. There is a close relationship between the stress model and premium work in which catastrophe models were applied to occupational accidents. Several qualitative variables are thought to contribute to the control parameters in both models. Both models share the cusp structure and its particular interpretation, or representation, of contagion.

STRESS-RELATED OCCUPATIONAL ILLNESS

The theory that emerged in the previous sections of this chapter that connected elementary epidemiological concepts, stress studies, and nonlinear dynamics has been tested empirically to a limited extent. The following study of stress-related illness among transit operators is a continuation of the accident analysis study reported in chapter 7.

The literature on stress is voluminous, as are the reviews. Therefore I only address literature that is most relevant to the present study. Stress is the nonspecific response of the organism to any environmental demand, according to Selye (1976); stress phenomena as they are known today encompass psychological consequences that might not be physically apparent. In accident investigations it has been useful to distinguish between *physical sources* of stress, such as noise, heat, cold, dust, and toxins, and *social sources*, such as traumatic life events and job-related matters (Guastello & Guastello, 1987b). Some types of stressors, such as crowding, are the combined results of closed physical space and reduced interpersonal distance (Oldham & Fried, 1987). Similarly, excess work load is usually regarded as a stressor, but is not easily classified as physical or social (or management-induced) due to the varieties of work that could exist.

Stress has a well-documented impact on work performance and on psychological and physical health. The three premier explanations for the work performance effects are adaptive cost, cognitive load, and learned helplessness (Cohen, 1980; Kantowitz & Sorkin, 1983). According to the adaptive cost explanation, a certain amount of "psychic energy" is bound up in adaptive strategies, thereby leaving less energy available for work. The cognitive load interpretation is based on the notion that humans have a relatively fixed amount of "mental workspace" with which to process information. Stress, in turn, results in lower work output because the worker is processing stressors for indications of imminent harm.

Learned helplessness theory (Seligman, 1972) is an explanation for many behavioral aspects of clinical depression as well as for the impact of stress on performance. Stressors have their most profound impact when they are unpredictable and uncontrollable. When humans and animals learn that a stressor they experience in one experimental situation cannot be controlled, they make relatively few attempts to control a stressor on a subsequent experimental task even though a means of control is available. Furthermore, people who have been exposed to uncontrollable stress are less likely to exhibit helping behavior to coworkers and give more electric shock to other experimental participants than those who were not subjected to uncontrollable stress (Cohen, 1980).

Anxiety is one of the principle psychological consequences of stress (Depue & Monroe, 1986; Quick & Quick, 1984). It is typically defined as irrational fear, or in terms of somatic complaints that do not go together medically, or both (Taylor, 1953). Chronic exposure to stress can result in a syndrome that is highly similar to clinical depression. It is not surprising, therefore, that stress reactions and depression share at least one ontological mechanism, that is, learned helplessness.

Stress affects health through two basic mechanisms, the immune system and the cardiovascular system. An overactive sympathetic nervous system results in overproduction of norepinephrine, epinephrine, growth hormone, prolactin, beta endorphin, or encephalon, which in turn has an immunosuppressant effect (Cohen & Williamson, 1991; Jemmott & Locke, 1984; O'Leary, 1990). Although it is also true that the body can withstand fluctuations in immune system activity without precipitating a disease, and although factors other than stress contribute to actual medical disorders, the stress–disease link is well documented.

With regard to sudden cardiac death, the role of stressors is not truly causal, but it is consistently precursory (Kamarck & Jennings, 1991). Vasoconstriction, caused by an overactive sympathetic nervous system, in turn produces high blood pressure. Hypertension becomes chronic when the individual is subjected to repeated stressors, such as there might occur in a dangerous occupation. Kidney failure and cardiac disorders are possible further outcomes (Quick & Quick, 1984). Leigh (1986) has begun to explore occupational linkages to cardiac health; these linkages may involve a wide range of stress and other variables.

Two lines of logic suggest that stress-dependent effects, notably accidents, are subject to a contagion-like escalation process (Guastello et al., 1985). One view addresses individual stress buildup, and the other addresses transpersonal stress buildup. With regard to the within-person view, stress is thought to be a predictor of accidents on the one hand (Levenson et al., 1983; McCarron & Haakonson, 1982), and a consequence on the other (Ersland et al., 1989; Weisaeth, 1989a, 1989b, 1989c). It only follows that each successive accident predisposes a person to greater amounts of risk for future calamities. With regard to transpersonal buildup, Holmes and Rahe (1967) showed that an individual's stress level can accumulate as a result of illnesses, accidents, or deaths of family members and friends. The learned helplessness research cited earlier describes another mechanism whereby stress spreads between coworkers.

The application of the cusp catastrophe model for stress-related occupational health disorders was an outgrowth of a larger study concerned with sources of stress that impact on transit operators and their work. The cusp model is developed next from two vantage points: cusp models for occupational accidents that have been empirically verified in the past, and theoretical applications of living systems theory to security subsystems in animal, human individual, organizational, and national levels of a system. Of concern here is the human individual internal security subsystem.

Accident Theory

There is growing awareness that accidents can be studied as if they were diseases (Bertazzi, 1989; Guastello, 1992b; Kemp, 1967; Leigh, 1986; Vilardo, 1988; Waller, 1987). Such epidemiological models would entail four major classes of ideas: background variables, trigger variables, a mechanism for contagion, and an overarching mathematical structure. In the cusp model for occupational accidents, accidents are interpreted as oscillations between two stable states: one with high risk where accidents occur, and one with low risk where accidents seldom occur. The asymmetry parameter, which is analogous to background variables, is composed of hazard and danger (severity of possible injury). The bifurcation parameter, which is analogous to trigger variables, is composed of safety management, stress, anxiety, and related variables (Guastello, 1988a, 1989, 1991b). As ambient hazards increase, the outcome (to an individual worker or a group of workers) does not change until a critical point is reached. Risk then increases suddenly and dramatically. The disparity of the difference in risk depends on the strength of the bifurcation parameter. If the hazard and danger levels are allowed to decrease, no change in risk level is observed until a different critical point is reached, at which time risk returns to its lower modal value. The model was shown in Fig. 7.4.

The mechanism for contagion is best shown in Fig. 8.1 by the oscillating path for $K' > 1$. The occurrence of an accident increases stress levels in the individual in question and in the immediate work group. Thus, with each successive accident, the control point veers further out along the manifold, instead of returning to its original position. Trajectories between the cusp point and the modes form gradients that can be defined behaviorally. If one observes the process of underlying a single accident, the equilibria represent either an accident or a lack of one. The gradients, then, represent underlying subcritical risk, perhaps expressed as the number of near-miss accidents. In a distribution of group accident rates, the gradients are observed as low and sometimes near-zero accident rates.

Security Subsystem for Human Individuals

Systems need protection from two types of hostile agents, those that attack the system from outside, and those that threaten the system from within. The security subsystem represents a special set of functions involving other parts of the system: information processing, the decider, boundaries, and the extruder. Disruptive agents and security subsystem components have been identified at the cellular, organ, organism, group, organizational, societal, and supranational level of analysis (Bosserman, 1982). An organismic level application is considered next. Organisms are at risk from hemorrhaging endo- and ectoparasites, anxiety, disruption with shock syndrome, antibodies, the immune response system as a whole, coagulation, and leukocyte production. Not all organisms have the same risk exposures.

It was possible to develop a butterfly catastrophe model for organism health based on four known dynamics of internal security subsystems (Fig. 8.2). First, internal security becomes more effective where systems must compete. Second, internal security efforts become more effective in a hostile environment. Third, security systems are ineffectual where they are either

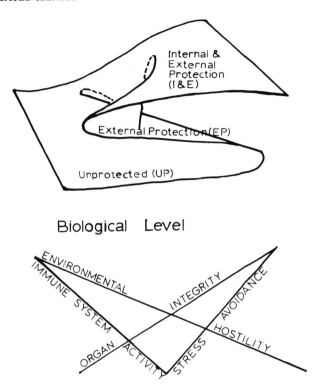

FIG. 8.2. Butterfly catastrophe model (sectioning) for the internal security subsystem at the organismic level of systems analysis. From Guastello (1988b). Reprinted with permission.

too loose or too rigid for their situational demands. Fourth, rigidity increases when the system contains pathologies (Bosserman, 1982). Three levels of health can be defined on the catastrophe response surface.

1. The system is protected from infections and the internal organs, circulatory systems, and so forth are intact.
2. The system is protected from infections from the outside, but organ integrity is compromised.
3. The system is threatened from both general sources of impairment (Guastello, 1988b).

The asymmetry parameter would be the hostility level of the environment in which the system is located. Environmental hostility would be measured in terms of the level of harm that could be induced to an organism by the presence of the bacterium, virus, or parasite or concentration thereof. The bifurcation parameter would be the level of immunological tolerance the system has for the hostile agent. Catastrophic reactions contain a reverse process under the hysteresis principle. On the one hand, high immunological activity in the presence of a moderate to high hazard level would result in maintaining system health, unless the hazard level increased markedly. On the other hand, high immunological activity in the presence of moderate to low biological hazard would result in an allergic condition.

The swallowtail parameter would be the health of the system's organ subsystems independent of the environmental agents. The amount of exposure to hostile environmental entities would appear on the butterfly parameter. In humans, the butterfly parameter would include stress management, where "stress" includes all types of stress described earlier. If stress is well managed, organ health and immunological balance work together to maintain system health overall. If stress is not well managed, any of four situations could result:

1. The organism would be led into unnecessary exposures to biological hazards, such that the immunological system would be inadequate.

2. The organism would be overexposed to physical or social stressors, making the organism susceptible to organ damage.

3. Continued exposure to stressors of physical or social origin has been found to result in a breakdown of immunological integrity, thus making the individual more susceptible to colds, flu, or other virus infections (Jemmott & Locke, 1984).

4. Any good management strategy can be carried to an extreme. Excessive harm avoidance could result in the system's inability to ward off disease, digest certain foods, or cope with stress situations in general.

The internal security model is summarized in Equation 13 and Fig. 8.2:

$$\Delta z = \beta_0 + \beta_1 z_1^5 + \beta_2 z_2^4 + \beta_3 (SA) z_1^3 + \beta (OI) z_1^2 + \beta_5 (IS) z_1 + \beta_6 (EH) \quad (13)$$

where z is a measure of system health, SA is stress avoidance, OI is organ integrity, IS is immune system activity, and EH is environmental hostility.

A corollary to the organismic security model can be stated, pertaining to cusp subsets of the model in Equation 13. First of all, it appears that disease contagion would follow catastrophic principles. Specifically, there are diseases that have serious health consequences, but for which there is no natural immunity. If we assume that the population of organisms is relatively healthy to begin with, the bifurcation and swallowtail functions are canceled, and only two outcome modalities are observed: healthy and infected organisms.

The empirical model is thus:

$$\beta z = \beta_0 + \beta_1 z_1^3 + \beta_2 z_1^2 + \beta_3(SA)z_1 + \beta_4(EH) \qquad (14)$$

where z is the normalized number of infected individuals in a relevant population, SA is stress avoidance, and EH is environmental hostility.

STRESS-RELATED ILLNESS AMONG TRANSIT OPERATORS

The theory that emerged in the previous sections of this chapter that connected elementary epidemiological concepts. stress studies, and non-linear dynamics has been tested empirically to a limited extent. The following study of stress-related illness among transit operators is a continuation of the accident analysis study reported in Chapter 7.

Method

Subjects. Subjects were 290 transit operators from a midwestern city. Of that number, 238 completed all the measures needed for this study. (The most frequently missing datum was the subject's age.) Each subject received a letter explaining the purpose of the study and a statement that the confidentiality of all responses was ensured. All data were collected on a voluntary and anonymous basis. Union assistants were available to assist operators in the completion of the survey.

Variables. The Occupational Hazards Survey (OHS) is a tool for diagnosing the causes of accidents, usually in manufacturing settings (Guastello & Guastello, 1987a, 1987b). In this study the OHS and the diagnostic paradigm were adapted for use with transit operators. Predictor variables were: danger ratings, transit experience and age, stress from physical sources, stress from social sources, anxiety, environmental hazards, and transit hazards. The OHS contained other scales that were not part of this study. Transit hazards included assaults and insults upon the operator and the need to reprimand passengers for various infractions of bus rules.

Criterion variables were transit accidents and medical disorders that are generally thought to be somewhat stress related (Quick & Quick, 1984): heart conditions, high blood pressure, kidney disorder, cancer, nervousness, insomnia, carpal tunnel, and ulcers. Operators were asked to check whether they had sought medical treatment for any of eight listed illnesses prior to their employment with the bus company. Next they were asked whether they had sought treatment for any of the eight illnesses after employment with the bus company. The total of preemployment illnesses comprised the Time 1 health measure. The total of illnesses that occurred in the 3 years prior to the survey comprised the Time 2 health measure.

Analyses. The cusp regression model (Equation 14) was then applied. The total of preemployment illnesses comprised y_1. Presence or absence of each of the eight illnesses was y_2. The location parameter was set equal to the lower limit of y, which was 0.00. The scale parameter was the estimated variation around the modes, which was calculated as follows. The two conceptual modalities were no health disorders and the presence of a disorder. The distribution of scores for the Time 1 and Time 2 health measures. The calculation of scale was

$$\sigma = \sqrt{\frac{\sum\sum (y_{m-}^{m+} - m_i)^2}{N - 1}} \tag{15}$$

where m_i is the modal value of y, which was either 0.00 or 1.00 for this problem, and y_{m-}^{m+} is the range of y in the neighborhood of m_i. For this problem, $y = 0$ for all cases in the neighborhood of $m_i = 0$, and $1 < y < 8$ in the neighborhood of $m_i = 1.00$. The sums of squares are summed over cases within modes, then summed over modes. The Time 1 estimate of scale was 0.327, and the Time 2 estimate was 0.827 (Table 8.1). Physical

TABLE 8.1
Distribution of Number of Stress-Related Illnesses Reported

Number	Frequency	
	Preemployment	Postemployment
0	223	138
1	38	80
2	9	21
3	3	19
4	2	9
5	0	3
6	0	1
7	0	0
8	0	0
Scale parameter[a]	0.327	0.872
N Reporting	265	271

[a]Based on $N = 271$.

stressors, social stressors, and anxiety were the hypothesized bifurcation variables. Age and experience, danger, environmental hazards, and transit hazards were tested as asymmetry variables.

Results

Control Models. The pre–post control regression model (per Equation 25 in chapter 3) was computed using the stepwise method of variable entry and a criterion of $p < .05$ to retain a variable in the model. There were four significant predictors: anxiety, age and experience, Time 1 illnesses, and social and job stress. The overall R^2 coefficient was .28 [$F(4, 233) = 22.29, p < .001$]. The qualitative hypothesis that stress and anxiety are associated with a nonspecific "basket" of disorders was upheld (Table 8.2).

The control difference regression model (per Equation 24 in chapter 3) was also computed using the stepwise method and variable entry criterion of $p < .05$. There were three significant predictors of change in the number of reported illnesses: anxiety, age and experience, and social and job stress. The overall R^2 coefficient was .24 [$F(3, 234) = 23.85, p < .001$]. These results were consistent with those obtained for the pre–post control model. A detail of regression results is given in Table 8.2.

Cusp Catastrophe Model. The cusp catastrophe model was built in a four-stage process that amounted to a hierarchical stepwise regression analysis. First, all variables from the hypothesized model were entered in a forward (or simultaneous) order: the cubic potential, the quadratic term, the bifurcation variables, and then the asymmetry variables. Second, all variables that did not have a significant weight in the model at $p < .10$ were eliminated. Third, more variables were entered to test the alternative hypotheses that the variables first thought to function as bifurcation variables would contribute to the asymmetry parameter, and that the variables first thought to function as asymmetry variables would contribute to the bifurcation parameter. Variables were once again entered in a forward order: those that remained at the second stage, new bifurcation variables, followed by new asymmetry variables. At the fourth stage of the analysis, variables that did not have a significant weight at $p < .10$ were removed. The final results are given in Table 8.2.

The overall R^2 for the cusp model was .70, or $R = .84$ [$F(6, 231) = 88.74, p < .001$]. Social and job stress was a significant contributor to the bifurcation parameter ($p < .10$). Age and experience ($p < .001$), anxiety ($p < .001$), and social and job stress ($p < .05$) were significant contributors to the asymmetry parameter.

Although the bifurcation effect was weaker than the other parts of the model, it made a significant contribution nonetheless. The combination of the cubic and quadratic terms together accounted for more variance

TABLE 8.2
Summary of Regression for Catastrophe and Control Models
Where Stress-Related Illnesses are Considered Collectively

Predictor	r	R (step)	R^2 (step)	t (weight)	F
Cusp model					
z_1^3	−.61	.61	.37	4.86****	
z_1^2	−.71	.77	.60	−6.69****	
z_1 *Social and job stress	.20	.77	.60	−1.77*	
Age and experience	.16	.79	.63	5.23****	
Anxiety	.24	.83	.69	5.34****	
Social and job stress	.20	.84	.70	2.46**	88.74****
Difference control					
Anxiety	.35	.35	.12	4.74****	
Age and experience	.25	.45	.20	5.00****	
Social and job stress	.28	.48	.23	2.90***	23.85****
All variables	—	.48	.23	—	9.21***
Pre–post control					
Anxiety	.36	.36	.13	4.92****	
Age and experience	.26	.46	.21	5.26****	
Time 1 illnesses	.19	.50	.25	3.43***	
Social and job stress	.29	.53	.28	3.17***	22.29****
All variables	—	.53	.28	—	10.76***

*$p < .10$. **$p < .05$. ***$p < .01$. ****$p < .001$.

($R^2 = .60$) than the quadratic term alone ($r^2 = .50$). Thus the model was classified as a cusp, and as such, there must be a bifurcation variable. Therefore, the decision to retain social and job stress as a bifurcation variable was further supported on logical grounds.

It was desirable to assess the stability of the regression results for the final cusp model. An ordinary cross-validation analysis was not attempted in which the sample of 238 would be divided into subgroups of 150 and 88 or some other similar split; the relatively few cases of people with preemployment stress-related illnesses and the weakness of the bifurcation effect suggested that smaller test samples would be inappropriate for this application. Therefore, a bootstrapping procedure was used instead. Fifty-five copies of the dataset were made to generate a sample of 15,590 cases (13,090 complete cases). Ten random samples of 200 cases were selected; the regression equation from the original sample was cross-validated on each of the 10 samples. The coefficients of cross-validation ranged from $r = .72$ to .84. The mean value was .79, and the median was .80. The cusp model was thus judged to be stable over repeated sampling.

The specific job and social stressors that were most often cited by the transit operators were change in working hours (59%), loss of sleep or change in sleeping hours (53%), and dubious job security in the sense that it had not improved recently (55%). This last survey item was negatively phrased to accommodate groups of workers in several industries whose job security was potentially precarious.

The specific anxiety symptoms that were most often cited were extreme fatigue (57%), migraine headache (42%), diarrhea or constipation (43%), and chronic back pain (46%). Anxiety was significantly correlated with the level of exposure to special transit hazards ($r = .41$). The most often cited transit hazards (which may also be considered as job-specific stressors) were insults from the passengers (52% reporting four or more instances in the prior 3 years), reprimanding passengers for radio playing (49%), smoking (50%), and loud talking. Also important were the incidence rates for breaking up fights among passengers (66% reporting at least one occasion in the prior 3 years), having to assist another operator in trouble (32%), and being attacked personally (28%). The final cusp model is shown in Fig. 8.3.

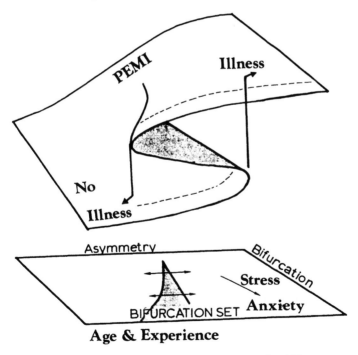

FIG. 8.3. Cusp catastrophe model obtained for stress-related illness among transit operators. (PEMI = Preemployment medical illness.) From Guastello (1992b). Reprinted with permission.

Discussion

The results of the study clearly upheld the central hypotheses that (a) stress contributed to a broad class of physical illnesses, (b) the stress and illnesses were occupational in origin, but not exclusively so, and (c) the relationship between qualitative variables and the onset of illnesses was cusp-catastrophic in nature. Anxiety, age, and experience as a transit operator played important roles in the model.

The overall R^2 for the cusp model was 2.5 times the size of the R^2 for the next best linear control model. The cubic and quadratic terms accounted for a large portion of the criterion variance. Bifurcation and asymmetry variables made unique contributions to the prediction of illnesses as well. The bootstrapping procedure that was used to cross-validate the cusp model showed that the median R^2 was .64 ($R = .80$) over 10 random samples, which in turn indicated that the results were stable over sampling variations.

The cusp model defined two stable states: presence or absence of an illness. Because there was no variability around the no-illness mode, the no-illness mode was a point-type equilibrium. The illness mode, however, was skewed so that the greatest density was around one illness, with progressively fewer cases reporting two to six illnesses. The illness equilibrium thus appears to be a strange attractor.

Anxiety, age and experience, and stressors function as background variables that govern the proximity of the control point (health of a person) to a threshold where a sudden change could take place. Stress also acted as a trigger variable. Because stress contributed to both asymmetry and bifurcation parameters, it is best regarded as a gradient variable. People under greater amounts of stress will become ill more gradually if they have been ill before, but they will become ill more suddenly if they had no prior history of stress-related medical disorder.

Although the cross-validation analysis showed that the obtained cusp model was stable over sampling variations, the specific model should not be generalized beyond transit operators and similar transportation workers. Limited use of the OHS with different organizations shows that the key predictors of accidents vary from place to place; all obtained models, however, proceed from the same general theory of safety climate. Similarly, a cusp model for the accident process that was obtained from mills and foundries (chapter 7) involved a different array of key variables from what was obtained from transit operators. One might anticipate that future research on stress and occupational health would show that stress-related illnesses would have different patterns of onset depending on the patient's occupation. The predictive power of the cusp model lies in its nonlinear mechanism which is, in effect, the "shape of the disease." In other words, there is an autonomous process taking place.

It was shown that the catastrophe models and other dynamical systems concepts are useful tools on account of their mathematical substance and implicit dynamical principles. The logic of these models, especially the relatively simple cusp, produced results that were consistent with early 20th century views of disease progress as well as with contemporary modeling work. Catastrophe models have been invoked in the past to explain the major psychoses (Scott, 1985) and anorexia and bulimia (Callahan, 1982). The cusp is an attractive model for bipolar disorder because it explains the fixed manic and depressed types through its equilibria and stability properties, and it explains the mood swings with the hysteresis principle. Schizophrenia also has cusp-like properties. Its potential for acute or chronic onset suggests that a bifurcation factor might distinguish the different types of morbidity. The nexus of self-starvation, gorging, and purging behaviors associated with anorexia and bulimia has been modeled by butterfly and higher order catastrophe models.

UNIQUE EFFECTS FOR SPECIFIC TYPES OF ILLNESS

On the basis of the findings just reported, it would be useful to develop specific accident and illness models from the point of view of particular occupational groups, as well as from the point of view of medical diagnosis. A medical research agenda should focus on medical history and test data that are specific to each stress-related illness. It would thus be useful to go beyond the "basket of illness" level of generalization to develop a family of models specific to each illness. Thus the goal of this section is to summarize the results of further study of specific stress-related illnesses among transit operators.

The sample and measurements were the same as those described earlier. The cusp model was specified by defining y_1 as the total number of stress-related illnesses reported as having occurred before employment with the bus company. The term y_2, however, was defined as the presence or absence of a particular disorder at the time of the survey. The two outcome measures were z-transformed separately at each point in time using the measure of scale described in Equation 15. Other details of the procedures for the regression analysis were the same as those used in the previous parts of the study.

Altogether there were seven cusp models tested. Cancer outcomes were not studied because of their low incidence rate in the sample (2%). All other incidence rates were 7% or higher. Table 8.3 summarizes the key findings. In all cases the cusp catastrophe model provided an interpretation of the illness patterns that was more accurate than the linear alternatives, based on the R^2 coefficients. Additional details of the statistical analysis can be found in Guastello (1992b).

TABLE 8.3
Summary of Results for Separate Stress-Related Illnesses

			R^2	
Illness	Asymmetry	Bifurcation	Cusp	P/P Linear
Nervousness	Age, experience Anxiety Transit hazards	Physical stress Social stress Anxiety	.81	.14
Insomnia	Anxiety Social stress	Anxiety Social stress	.77	.12
Ulcer	Age, experience Physical stress	Social stress	.76	.09
Kidney	Social stress	Anxiety Social stress	.77	.07
Blood pressure	Age, experience Anxiety	Danger	.79	.11
Heart	Anxiety	Social stress	.74	.06
Carpal tunnel	Danger Safety management	Safety management	.78	.10

Note. P/P Linear, pre–post linear control model.

Although the average accuracy level of the illness models was high, some models were qualitatively more complete than others. Treatment seeking for nervousness has the greatest number of variables associated with it. Transit hazards, age, and experience were the asymmetry variables. Physical stressors, social stressors and anxiety were the bifurcation variables. The weight was positive for anxiety and negative for physical and social stressors; that configuration was interpreted as meaning that it was not so much the amount of stress (as measured by the survey coding scheme) that triggered the illness but the strength of an individual's reaction to that amount of stress. The level of transit hazards that operator was subjected to plus the operator's age predisposed the operator to an increased susceptibility to stress.

A similar stress-anxiety mechanism was observed for kidney disfunction and insomnia. Overall danger level was the asymmetry variable in the kidney model. In the insomnia model, social stress and anxiety contributed to both parameters, suggesting that stress and anxiety form gradients on the cusp surface connecting the cusp point with the two attractors.

Physical and social stressors, age, and experience explained the outbreak of ulcers. Ulcers were triggered by social and job-related stress mostly among people who worked in physically uncomfortable environments, were older, and had been performing the job for a longer time.

High blood pressure was more age related than some of the other illnesses. It occurred among the more anxious operators and was triggered by danger levels. Anxiety and danger levels were, in turn, related to transit hazards and stressors such as nonstandard working hours, irregular eating and sleeping schedules (disregulation syndrome), poor job security, and inadequate lavatory facilities.

The model for heart disease showed that cardiac disorders were triggered by social and job-related stress, but an asymmetry variable was not found.

Danger level was a significant background variable in the model for carpal tunnel syndrome. Safety management contributed to both parameters. It was questionable whether the roles of danger and safety management were actually predictive or the result of hindsight bias on the part of the afflicted operators. If they were the result of hindsight bias, however, they would have been found more pervasively among the other illness models. Instead, danger was associated with one illness as an asymmetry variable and one other as a weak bifurcation effect. Safety management did not appear in any of the other illness models.

The model for carpal tunnel syndrome suggested some insights about the disorders that do not appear to have been considered in the past. Carpal tunnel syndrome is the result of prolonged exposure to intense vibration, often to the driver's wrist or seat. It now appears that operators under greater stress could be more susceptible to carpal tunnel, possibly because of a tendency to grip the steering wheel more tightly than other operators.

ORGANIZATIONAL SECURITY SUBSYSTEM

Organizations are susceptible not only to accident and health risks, but also to fire, industrial espionage, theft, and embezzlement. The organization can counteract disruptive forces by means of security guards and private detectives, alarms, vaults and locks, redundant procedures to enhance the reliability of internal control systems (checks and balances), and personnel selection techniques. The spectrum of system behavior is once again depicted as a butterfly catastrophe model. There are three stable states of system health. At one extreme, there is not protection against hostile intrusions into the systems. As a result, the system would be insufficiently bounded and unprotected from subterfuge from within. At the middle level, the system is protected from invasion, but not from hostile internal forces. At the other extreme, the system is protected from both internal and external disruptive influences (Fig. 8.4).

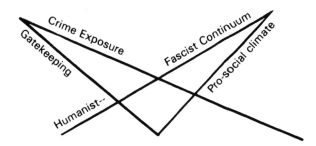

FIG. 8.4. Butterfly catastrophe bifurcation set (sectioning) for the internal security subsystems at the organizational level of systems analysis. Adapted from Guastello (1988b). Reprinted with permission.

The control parameters for the organizational security model are analogous to those that were defined earlier for the organismic system. The asymmetry parameter would be a measure of *environmental hostility*. At an earlier stage in the development of the organizational security theory, I suggested (Guastello, 1988b) that measurements of an individual's honesty or lack thereof may work as measures of environmental hostility. Unfortunately, psychological testing research has not been successful at isolating any such variable that had a relationship to actual behavior and that did not incur a significant social cost (Guastello & Rieke, 1991). A better definition for any asymmetry variable for an organizational level model should also be an organizational level variable. Environmental hostility would thus describe conditions to which the organization as a whole was susceptible, such as incidence rates of theft in a particular industry, market, or geographic area.

The presence of *external gatekeeping controls* would have the effect of bifurcating a global system into two local regions: the inside, which is protected from unwanted intrusions, and the outside, which contains the unwanted elements. Examples of gatekeeping controls would include the use of locks, surveillance equipment, security personnel, and reference checks on perspective employees. The bifurcation variable for the organizational model is, therefore, the stringency of gatekeeping controls. Controls are adaptive if they are relatively more stringent when the organization is exposed to moderate to high environmental hostility. Stringent gatekeeping controls create stronger boundaries between the organization and its environment.

The systems that are protected by gatekeeping controls can be further distinguished as belonging to two groups. One group is free from sources of danger or disruption originating from within. The other group does not have that level of security. The former type has a stronger climate for honesty, which would be fostered where individual members of the organization are basically honest, have a commitment to the organization, and perceive that the organization is treating them fairly. Ideally, there is an atmosphere of mutual trust between management and the employees. As a result, honesty and internal security are intrinsically motivated (Guastello, 1988b; Murphy, 1993).

When the swallowtail parameter is unfolded from the cusp, two stable modalities of behavior are defined, as described earlier, plus one unstable modality. The unstable situation is one where, at highly irregular times, people are expelled from the organization because of espionage or a similar transgression. Although the bifurcation parameter is represented by system boundaries, the swallowtail parameter is represented by the presence and *relative strength of the extruder system.*

The butterfly parameter defines the coaction of gatekeeping and climate factors. Gatekeeping and climate can be positive influences that work together, as just described. On the other hand, management could cause the two positive influences to work against each other by breaching the climate of mutual trust. Management can breach that trust by resorting to surveillance of its employees, intimidation interviewing, or requiring intrusive testing procedures. Relations would degenerate still further if employees were falsely accused of crimes against the organization. The relationship between the boundary, extruder, decider, and system outcomes in the organizational security model, therefore, is analogous to the relationship among extrinsic motivation, intrinsic motivation, and organizational climate relative to work performance in the butterfly catastrophe model of motivation in organizations (chapter 5).

Although it may be necessary for an organization to monitor its risk exposures, the key dynamic elements are the level of personal intrusiveness and interpersonal trust or distrust. Management's orientation to the use of security techniques, which defines the butterfly control parameter, is thus the *continuum between humanistic and fascistic styles.* Such a continuum in organizational management style was first observed and defined in political terms by Meltzer (1942). The labels *humanistic* and *fascistic* are loaded with Western value judgments. There are, however, some value-free properties that underlie the bipolar continuum. What we could think of as "humanistic" implies toleration of individual differences. Systems must be able to tolerate error and fluctuation in order for the system to adapt to environmental changes (Bosserman, 1982). Failure to tolerate individual differences in the long run results in overly rigid boundaries and an overactive extruder subsystem. Once system members who thought they were part of the organization are treated as outsiders, they become increasingly hostile and are in turn met with increased retaliation. This spiraling of antagonism is a Hopf bifurcation mechanism, but one of greater than usual complexity (Hopf bifurcations are typically associated with cusp-like processes).

SUMMARY

This chapter showed that many of the structural models used to define the progress of diseases since the turn of the last century displayed some significant nonlinear dynamics. Most dynamics were of a cusp-catastrophic nature, but fold catastrophe, logistic bifurcation, and umbilic dynamics were observed as well.

The supposition that accidents can be studied as if they were diseases, and vice versa, was supported empirically. Cusp models for stress-related illness among transit operators were similar to those obtained for occupational accidents for the same occupational group. Illness models varied somewhat depending on whether the focus of attention was on stress-related illnesses collectively or on specific illnesses.

The models for stress-related illnesses could be rationalized further from general systems theory concerning the internal security subsystem at the individual organismic level of analysis. It now appears that the obtained cusp models are subsets of a broader spectrum of possible outcomes that require a butterfly catastrophe model to describe.

The butterfly catastrophe model for an organism's security subsystem dynamics was reapplied to organizational security subsystem dynamics where industrial espionage and control of trade secrets, theft, and embezzlement were topics of concern. The set of control parameters for the organizational level model was strongly analogous to both the organism security subsystem model and the butterfly model of motivation in organizations.

9

The Evolution of Human Systems

This chapter is centered around the implications of NDS within the new thinking in evolutionary science that has developed in the past decade. The first section of this chapter begins with the essential concepts underlying Darwin's *Origin of Species*, which went unmodified for nearly a century. New paleontological findings suggest that the original theory of evolution had many loose ends, which are thought to be tied up in the new evolutionary paradigm. The new thinking in evolution is referred to as a paradigm by its central proponent because its dynamics extend well beyond the evolution of biological species into the evolution of human and social systems.

Not only do species survive through successful competition, but also through cooperation. The second section concerns the theory of competitive and cooperative games, which has a long history in conventional psychology of negotiation and conflict resolution, and which has a growing history in NDS as well. Of special concern is the evolutionary nature of gaming strategies, and more specifically, the evolution of sustainable cooperation. NDS also suggests some conflict resolution strategies that are, as yet, unknown to game theory.

The third section takes the combination of NDS and the new evolutionary thought in another direction toward population dynamics within and across spatial locations and the dynamics of urban development. The diffusion of attitudes can be represented in a similar fashion perhaps; attitude dynamics are considered in chapter 12. The fourth and fifth sections make an interesting leap from the dynamics of insect populations to workforce productivity. The fourth section proposes the theoretical framework for study. The range of possible outcomes are explored through simulations. The fifth section explores the same dynamics as they exist in the construction trades. It is proposed that personnel selection strategies, which represent one of many forms of "unnatural selection" in society, are not interminably adaptive. Rather, the continued application of a selection strategy in a workforce that has substantially changed may be no longer adaptive and may have perverse consequences for organizations.

Finally, the last section addresses principles of NDS economics that, for the most part, have been applied to security or commodity prices and natural resource dynamics. In those applications, both catastrophe and chaos dynamics are implicated. In the case of security prices, there is some debate as to whether chaos actually exists.

NEW EVOLUTIONARY PARADIGM

It would be valuable to begin with the essential principles of Darwin's (1859/1864) theory of evolution and to highlight some of its inherent problems that are addressed by the new evolutionary paradigm (Laszlo, 1987, 1991). The nature of evolution theory has itself evolved through theoretical and experimental progress over the last century (Good, 1986). In more recent times, computer simulation techniques, such as cellular automata, genetic algorithms, and evolutionary computations, have greatly assisted the exploration of evolutionary processes. Although simulations are imperfect representations of reality, they often provide better clues than the next best alternative—which is to wait 20 million years to find out what we want to know.

Biological Darwinism

Although genes were not discovered at the time of Darwin's major work, their discovery gave further credence to Darwin's principles. Thus, for all intents and purposes, the basic concept of genes is included in the following description of Darwinian evolutionary dynamics. Genes convey the essential biological information by which organizations reproduce themselves into similar organisms. Similar *genotypes* can give rise to a greater variety of *phenotypes*, or expressions of genetic material. There is natural variation in any species with respect to its possible genotypes and phenotypes.

Organisms must live in an environment to which they may be well suited (an *ecological niche*), or alternatively, the environment may be too hot, too cold, too wet, too dry. The environment may provide a sufficient quantity of food items for some organisms, but not for others. The environment may contain predatory organisms that eat other organisms. The reproduction speed of any organisms is going to be limited by its available food supply, on the one hand, and its own attractiveness as a food item to other organisms on the other hand.

Sometimes organisms expand their territories to new environments, or the environment itself changes drastically. Those species that adapt successfully to their new environments survive, and those that cannot adapt disappear. Environments were thought to change relatively slowly, as did the biological adaptation process. Successful biological adaptation was fueled by a process of *random variation and mutation*. Highly homogenous species have limited chances of survival if the environment changes beyond certain bounds. If a species contains sufficient variation, then its potential for survival in differentiating environments is enhanced. The environment thus selects the organisms that are best suited to exist within it.

A mutation is a more distinctive form of variation, and not readily perceived as an extreme form of an already existing species characteristic. Mutations were thought to occurs randomly. Mutations that enable survival within a hostile environment manage to spread throughout the population. Not all mutations have direct survival value, however. Computer simulations show that approximately 80% of reproductively neutral mutations that are introduced into a sexually reproducing population of constant size are lost in 90 generations. Approximately 18% of the mutations that persist are shared by 50% of the population (Ulam & Schrand, 1986). These findings provide a rough idea of the persistence and spread of a supposedly typical mutation.

Prey–predator relationships represent only one form of relationship between species. Alternatively, two or more species compete for scarce resources. The culminating principle behind random variation, natural selection, prey–predator relationships, and interspecies competition was *survival of the fittest*.

Ecological Systems

The survival of many species is sensitive to small purturbances, if not radical shifts, in their environments. An upset of one aspect of the environment has watershed effects on other aspects of the environment, as if the environments and species are organized into interlocking interdependent systems and *food chains*. Ecological disruption is usually the result of humans' irresponsible use of land for human enterprise, such as strip-mining, strip malls, overgrazing, slash-and-burn agriculture, and other real estate development that makes the land unusable for animals and plants for which that land was a natural habitat. Humans further interfere with the ecological balance by removing a natural predator, overhunting, or injecting pollutants into the food chain. In addition to the extinction of species, other perverse consequences of ecological disruption occur such as coyotes eating housepets in Southern California suburbs, or deer wandering in record quantities in suburban Milwaukee. The deer haven't eaten anything important, but last year, according to a flyer from my auto insurance company, there were 30,000 road accidents in Wisconsin involving deer–automobile conflicts.

Other ecological concerns have global importance. For instance, Antarctica is anything but a barren wasteland. There is a highly integrated and fragile food chain in existence there that is thought to critically affect the entire oceanic ecosystem (Laws, 1985). Antarctica is currently controlled by an international treaty that limits the use of the continent to scientific endeavors, and limits any political rights of nations with its representatives on the continent. When the treaty was up for renewal in 1991, there was a movement from some of the industrialized nations to allow petroleum extraction and mineral mining on the continent. Both operations would have devastating effects on the ecosystem, according to scientists.

Antarctica is also where we study the growing hole in the ozone layer of the atmosphere that is caused by fluorocarbon-based pollutants. One result of losing the ozone layer is that harmful solar radiation will penetrate to the earth's surface, giving rise to greater incidents of skin cancer. Humans' continual use of energy resources is discharging greater amounts of carbon dioxide into the atmosphere. As a result the planet is warming up. If the warming rate increases too far, the polar ice caps will melt, seas will rise, and many lowlands will become underwater Atlantises. The combined effects of planet warming and ozone depletion will turn much arable farm land into deserts.

Indeed, the global issues just outlined should serve to unite the nations of the earth behind a common cause of mutual survival. Is such human coordination and cooperation possible in a world where survival of the fittest is a dominant strategy? That question among many others leads to the social side of the new evolutionary paradigm.

Social Darwinism

In the late 19th century, when evolutionary concepts had circulated widely in intellectual communities, a sociological version of survival of the fittest emerged known as *social Darwinism*. The idea was that many of the social phenomena observed in that day, and that continue now, can be explained in terms of elementary Darwinian concepts (Richards, 1987). The rich, the poor, and the caste systems that relate them exist because some people are more fit to survive than others. Businesses compete, and some survive and grow whereas others fail. Individuals and institutions that adapt survive, and we know what happens to the others.

There were several flaws in social Darwinism. The first became apparent when free-market competition gave rise to major corporations that turned into major monopolies. Left uncontrolled, the monopolies manipulated the markets for products and services such that no newcomers could compete. Monopolies gave the corporations predatory advantage over all people who would purchase their goods, and the implications for economic and social control were obvious. The U.S. government responded with antitrust laws that prevented unfair monopolistic practices. A true social Darwinian might have simply remarked that the market needs to have competition, and that breaking up the monopolies was actually a Darwinian thing to do.

Another flaw pertained to its interpretation of socioeconomic disparity. Darwinian principles could be summoned to explain that the poor, sick, or others in society were intrinsically less fit than the rich and powerful. Such explanations served to justify the status quo and exploitive or predatory actions on the part of one part of society against another. The rise of labor unions in the United States, the communist revolution in Russia, and the inklings toward American communism in the early 1930s illustrated that the downtrodden were not so unfit as they might have appeared. New laws facilitated new programs to assist people in need. Such programs took the form of labor relations laws, welfare, unemployment compensation, and workman's compensation for industrial accident relief. Although popular in some circles, social Darwinism was never particularly deep as a philosophy or a movement in social science. It died an unremarkable death while biological Darwinism maintained its scientific respectability and won a few political battles, such as the famous Scopes Monkey Trial (detailed in Walker, 1990), with creationists who outlawed the teaching of evolution in some school districts.

Neither form of Darwinism addressed the fact that altruism exists in society: People do things for other people without repayment, at costs to themselves that sometimes involve their own lives, for no apparent reasons other than to do something for someone else or to save someone else's life. Parasitic and symbiotic relationships between organisms could be explained under the rubric of ecological niches, but there was no such explanation for real altruism.

The New Evolutionary Paradigm

Altruism represented a problem shared by both social and biological Darwinism. Two other deficits were the apparent discontinuity of evolutionary processes itself, and the anomalies that appear to exist in biochemical processes (Bocchi, 1991; Casti, 1989). Sociobiology theory (Wilson, 1975) proposed that there must be a gene for altruism somewhere. Unfortunately, the theory continued with a line of thought that all sorts of social behaviors were, at their roots, caused by genes. Virtually any social behavior could be explained that way, which is to say that genes did not explain much of any social behavior. The next innovation to explain altruism was the postulation of a selfish gene. Social behavior could then be explained as an interplay between selfish and altruistic genes. That was a little better, perhaps, but no such genes have ever been isolated.

Beyond altruism, there were two other problems with classical Darwinian evolution. In modern paleontology, the fossil records appear incomplete if classical theory were correct in saying that evolution is a slow and gradual process. Classical theory does not explain the gaps in the fossil records, which show striking changes in species arrays at relatively small increments of depth in the terrain from which they were excavated. Did the dinosaurs die suddenly? According to one theory, radical environmental shifts have occurred approximately once every 26 million years. A collision between the earth and a comet could have caused the skies to darken with soot, thus blocking the sunlight, stifling plant photosynthesis, and killing the dinosaurs' food supplies (Angier, cited in Good, 1986).

The disappearance of the dinosaurs was followed by the emergence, in undoubtedly a cascaded fashion, of many new species of mammals, birds, and marsupials, not to mention smaller reptiles. Many of those species have also fallen extinct. Paleontological research worldwide has turned up the disturbing trend that the disappearance of fauna was timed fairly closely to the appearance of humans in those regions of the world. Land use and predatory habits of people are the top explanations for species disappearance: The human impact was either direct through overhunting, or indirect through tampering with the food chains of those animals (Burney, 1993). New species do not appear to be emerging to replace the extinct ones. Within human paleontology, "missing links" between people and their primate predecessors are left as open spaces in the evolutionary family tree.

The third class of problems is observed at the biochemical level. It could not have been easy for life to emerge from the first primordial protein soup. DNA and RNA molecules, which are self-replicating, would have replicated randomly ad infinitum if there was not a further mechanism to encourage some patterns and not others. Something pseudo-random had to have been taking place.

Solutions

Having stated the problems, the solutions take the following forms. First, not all genes function alike. Some are replicators, which govern the replication process that is actually carried out by other genes. Replicators had to have existed in the early primordial soup to guide the reproduction of amino acid patterns in some of the directions they have obviously taken. A small mutation in the replicator function could have a dramatic impact on patterns of replication throughout the organism. A mutation at the right spot in the genetic system would cause a greater impact on the design of the organism than a slight change in one or two amino acids (Schuster, 1986). A concomitant mechanism is the autocatalytic biochemical reaction, where the presence of the right concentrations of certain sets of molecules automatically triggers the production of new species of molecule. Those new species that "cooperate" with the existing system most effectively remain inside the chemical reaction loop whereas others are excluded (Farmer et al., 1986).

Second, not all adaptation occurs through slow genetic mutation. Learning is a form of adaptation as well. An organism that adapts by learning to behave differently will survive where other organisms do not, and the adaptation permits the survival of the organism's genetic code. It is well known that the adaptive impact of learning can be massive. Third, the biological aspects of evolution were not in every way slow and continuous beyond the impact of the replicator functions. Some adaptations had a much greater impact than others. In humans, the ability to give birth to an offspring that is relatively undeveloped, compared to offspring of other species, was thought to be a major evolutionary Rubicon (Bocci, 1991).

Fourth, altruism is actually an aspect of a broader form of human adaptation, which is cooperation. Cooperation is just as adaptive as competition strategies and explains why people have been able to form societies and cultures and why some nonhuman species form cooperative clusters as well. Societies and cultures form mechanisms for transmitting the learned adaptations from one generation to the next. Societies, in turn, evolve and mutate, and their histories can be interpreted as results of cooperation and competition dynamics (Artigiani, 1991; Eisler, 1987, 1991; Eisler & Combs, 1992). Broad historical societal trends and implications of the new evolutionary viewpoint are considered in chapter 12.

GAME THEORY

A brief taxonomy of games would be useful. The first distinction is between the zero-sum, or noncooperative, game and cooperative games. In any game there are possible moves a player can make and possible outcomes from the moves. In a noncooperative game, the values of the possible outcomes for one player are opposite the values of those same outcomes for the competitor. One player's winnings are the other player's losses. Information is not typically shared by players in a noncooperative game, nor are binding agreements possible. A cooperative game is structured in such a way that outcomes could exist that provide maximum returns to both players if certain joint plays are made. In those cases information sharing is strategic, and binding agreements are possible (Zagare, 1984).

Sometimes games are played, or studied, in a finite series, where the game is played only once or played in a finite series. In some of the more interesting situations, the game is played an infinite number of times. When real humans are playing, "infinite" simply means that the game is played many times, but the players do not know when the series will end. In computerized simulations of the game, several hundred iterations can be played tirelessly.

Although it is possible to conceptualize a one-person game, where one player works against the environment, or a slot machine, more interesting games are the interactive types that require at least two players. Most of the known NDS applications to game theory revolve around two-person scenarios. Most of game theory is divided between two-person and three- or n-person games. The simplest games for two players are the 2×2 games, where each player has two options to consider.

Of the many ways of configuring 2×2 game, some have obvious and trivial outcomes, and others have no apparent solutions. Three are particularly dynamic and could lead to multiple outcomes, and thus have attracted considerable attention by theorists: the prisoners' dilemma, chicken, and battle of the sexes. Of the three games, the prisoners' dilemma has dominated the literature because it is the only game that explains the emergence of cooperation between players (Huberman & Glance, 1994).

A prisoners' dilemma game matrix appears in Table 9.1. In the classical scenario, two players are hypothetically arrested for armed robbery. The district attorney is trying to make a case against them but needs the cooperation and confession of at least one player in order to prosecute successfully. Thus a deal is offered to the players, each separately: If one confesses, or *defects*, before the other, the one who confesses gets off with a light sentence, whereas the one who does not confess receives the heavy

TABLE 9.1
Game Matrix for Prisoners' Dilemma

Player A	Player B	
	Cooperate	Defect
Cooperate	3, 3	4, 1
Defect	1, 4	2, 2

sentence. If both players *cooperate* with each other by not confessing, they stand a good chance of being found not guilty. If both players confess, their outcomes are only a little better than the worst possible sentence. The values in the table are values of the outcomes to each player, expressed as ranks. In any noncooperative game, the rational player will prefer the one of the four options that will maximize gains and minimize losses. If there is a play that satisfies this *maximin* principle, then an *equilibrium* occurs, which represents the play that both players will select. When the game is played repeatedly, players will choose one option more often than another, which becomes their *dominant strategy.* If one player knows another's dominant strategy, then strategic moves are made accordingly (von Neumann & Morgenstern, 1953). For instance, the cooperation strategy may work in the beginning of a series of games, but if a player learns that the odds of an opponent defecting are high, then a defect strategy will occur. Alternatively, in a finite game series where the end of the series is known to the players, the optimal strategy is to cooperate until the second to last round, then defect.

Players do not always maintain the same strategy throughout a series of games. Examples of one clear shift in a player's dominant strategy throughout a game series were just presented. Alternatively, however, players may use a *mixed strategy,* in which they switch strategies back and forth depending on the game matrix values or recent past experiences with other players. In cases of mixed strategies, the game matrix values for each player are not simply the values of payoffs such as in Table 9.1; rather, the values are expected odds of a strategy taking place multiplied by the valence of a particular outcome. Expectancies and valences were discussed in chapter 5 in the first section. The probabilistic interpretation of game values is most apparent when the game is played by multiple players simultaneously in infinite series. The case of simultaneous games in infinite series is more characteristic of societal processes than the one-shot game or a series for two players in a single continuous relationship.

Tit-for-tat (TFT) is a particular mixed strategy in which the player begins with cooperation and sustains cooperation until an opponent defects. A single defection is tolerable, but the TFT strategist will shift to defection in response to subsequent defections. TFT strategists may revert to cooperation with new players or in response to strategy changes toward cooperation from other parties. TFT is a relatively successful strategy in terms of a player being able to maximize outcomes over repeated plays (Casti, 1989). On the other hand, TFT is more complex than all-cooperation (all-C) or all-defection (all-D), and there may be a cost of complexity (COC) associated with operating a TFT policy (Hirshleiffer & Coll, 1988).

Not all games have equilibria, which are also known as *saddle points.* In NDS, saddles are not structurally stable. They attract players in some iterations of the game but may push them away after the play is made and the results are known. Saddles can be easily upset by changing the values of the game outcomes for the players. In more complex games involving two players and more than two options, or n players and n options, there may be more than one saddlepoint. Furthermore, there could be a saddle point among the saddle points, but there is never any guarantee that a real-world game will have such attractive solutions (Zagare, 1984).

NDS Approach to Gaming

The first bloc of theory was developed by Zeeman (1981) to express the competition between two species for scarce resources. The general model that found applicability to human games is:

$$\Delta p_s = kp_s(Y_s - M) \tag{1}$$

where Δp_s is the change in the proportion of players that use a particular strategy s, after execution of a strategy s (Hirshleiffer & Coll, 1988, p. 373), Y_s is the sum of payoffs to any player j for any strategy in the game matrix:

$$Y_s = \Sigma_j \ (p_j a_{aj}) \tag{2}$$

M is the mean payoff to all players in the "toy society,"

$$M = \Sigma_s \ (pY) \tag{3}$$

and k is the speed of response by a player to a play made by another player. Note that substitution of Equations 2 and 3 into 1 yields a set of logistic map trajectories.

Outbreak of Cooperation in Free-Form Iterated Gaming. Hirshleiffer and Coll (1988) used Equations 1–3 to generate computer simulations of simultaneous infinite series of prisoners' dilemma games. The goal of the project was to determine the conditions under which cooperation would evolve or go into extinction. In light of the importance of cooperation dynamics in any form of negotiation and in societal evolution (Combs, 1992), their gaming concept was highly interesting. Hirshleiffer and Coll's first scenario began with an iterated game where players began with a 50% representation of all-C strategy and a 50% representation of all-D. Cooperation began as the dominant strategy, but all-C and all-D came into balance by the 75th iteration, and cooperation became extinct thereafter; in the long run, all-D survived.

The second scenario played off TFT against all-D, which were initially represented at 50% each. Soon afterward, however, TFT became the surviving strategy and all-D went into extinction.

The third scenario was an iterated game of three strategies, all-C, all-D, and TFT, which were initially given 33–34% representation. All-D went into extinction, but TFT did not stabilize as a universal outcome. Rather, a balance was struck such that TFT occurred in two-thirds of the plays, and all-C occurred in the remaining third.

Hirshleiffer and Coll further noted that all-C could be viewed as a "parasitic" strategy because the TFT player bore the cost of complexity and the burden of punishment. The fourth scenario, therefore, explored what would happen when TFT had to pay a small COC. The game initialized with all-C at 45% representation, TFT at 45%, and all-D at 10%. The outcome was that all-D escalated to fixation, whereas TFT and C went into extinction.

The fourth scenario was repeated where a 10% error factor was introduced in TFT's judgment, such that cooperators might be falsely accused of defecting, or defectors might escape punishment. All-C went into extinction. As it was doing so, all-D became more common, as did TFT. TFT eventually dominated all-D.

The last scenario of interest here was the three strategy mix of all-C, all-D, and a new strategy of the punisher (P). P works like a "bounty hunter" by selectively seeking out and exploiting defectors while cooperating with everyone else. The results of the scenario were dependent on the sensitivity parameter k. When k was set to 0.18 or higher, the iterated game showed rapid oscillation in the numbers of all-C, all-D, and P plays, and the amplitudes of the oscillations expanded into chaos with no evolutionary equilibrium. When k was decreased to 0.05, and probabilities of strategies were initialized at all-C at 75%, all-D at 5%, and P at 20%, stability ensued.

Gaming in an Organizational Context. Huberman and Glance (1993) investigated the outcomes of iterated prisoners' dilemma games where the game rules were enhanced to reflect the type of outcomes associated with successful organizations. In their sets of cooperative games, the payoffs for players were rigged to reflect conditions where everyone shares in the group's outcomes, and all players must work to produce the outcome. In a perfectly cooperative game, all players have the same valuations of outcomes and experiences of the same costs.

The first of two situations Huberman and Glance (1993) studied concerned the role of group size in the relative rates of cooperation and defections. There was a critical group size below which only cooperation would occur. There was also an upper threshold of group size beyond which only defection would occur. Between the two thresholds, both outcomes were possible. The actual threshold values for group size that would apply to real life would depend on the game matrix involved. Also, although they did not discuss the point, critical values would appear to depend on the group's policy for responding to defects, based on the work of Hirshleiffer and Coll (1988).

In the second situation, Huberman and Glance (1993) considered the role of diversity on levels of cooperation within the hypothetical organization. Groups with high levels of diversity were defined as those where members do not value the inputs and outputs at the same levels. In a less dynamic version of diversity, a game matrix entry would take on a value of 10 ± 2, rather than a simple 10. In a more dynamic context, a group may be composed of factions who value a parameter at different levels, such as a packs of 3's, 4's, and 15's. In general circumstances, greater diversity can increase the chances of either sustainable cooperation or rampant defection.

It does appear that the two sets of findings by Huberman and Glance (1993) can be snapped together into a cusp catastrophe model, as shown in Fig. 9.1. The nature of the gaming situation is one where there are two distinct and potentially stable outcomes: cooperation and defection. The attractor areas on the cusp response surface represent asymptotic evolu-

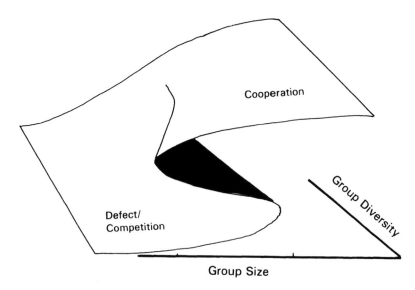

FIG. 9.1. Cusp catastrophe model for the outbreak of cooperation as a function of group size and diversity.

tionary fixations of one or the other strategy. The role of group size and the twin threshold finding strongly suggest that size functions as an asymmetry variable in this context. Diversity would act as a bifurcation variable because it predisposes the group toward stability in either direction. The view of diversity as a bifurcation variable would further imply that diverse groups contain greater levels of entropy in choice of dominant strategies precisely because the ability to locate an equilibrium is hampered by a variety of game matrices in play. Glance and Huberman (1993) continued their work with an exploration of how factions in organizations can be successfully managed; those ideas are considered in chapter 11.

Other Exotic Gaming Strategies. In one of the first applications of NDS to games in economics, Rand (1978) discovered the possibility of chaotic gaming strategies with complex two-person games. In those situations, there were three or four options available to each player, rather than two. Furthermore, the insets of 2 × 2 matrices represented different possible patterns of outcome values for the two players. In theory, the presence of local saddles within the insets predisposes the players to erratic shifts in strategies across a series of plays. The patterns of option choices over time, when drawn on the 3 × 3 or 4 × 4 game matrix, looked strikingly like the two-dimensional slices of the butterfly catastrophe bifurcation set shown in Fig. 2.17.

Applications to the Real World

The outcomes of computer-iterated games suggest some tempting applications to the real world matters of crime and punishment. Although the cat-and-mouse games that transpire between criminals and law enforcement provoke some interesting analogies to the results of iterated games, some further thought must be given to the limitations of the simulated results to the interpretation of any one particular policy (Rapoport, 1988). For instance, game matrix entries may not represent real matrix entries. Diversity in the valuation of options and outcomes changes results. Real games might not be 2 × 2 designs; a 2 × 2 game can be inset in larger games, and tunnel vision with respect to the scope of the game and the available plays can lead to hypothetical results that diverge greatly from truth (Rand, 1978; Zagare, 1984).

Most political events are actually 3-person or n-person games (Zagare, 1984). Game outcomes can be manipulated strongly by whether players express dominant strategies that sincerely reflect their valuations, or whether players deceive opponents by expressing valuations that are not true for them. Deceptions may be instantiated to create a coalition between to opponents for the eradication of a third.

Huberman and Glance (1994) raised yet another issue. Iterated computer games are developed in a way such that a round of games by a set of opponent pairs is taking place all at the same time. In the real world, the numerous game transactions are asynchronously timed. Huberman and Glance showed through computer simulation that a game situation that could produce a highly intricate pattern of cooperation and defection results when games were generated synchronously would produce a complete fixation to defection when the same games were played asynchronously.

Real People Playing Iterated Games. Richards (1990) studied the results of iterated prisoners' dilemmas with four pairs of real human players. The time series for the quantitative outcomes for each person in each game was analyzed using the Grassberger and Procaccia (1983) algorithm for measuring correlation dimension. Data for six out of eight players showed a chaotic regime with correlation dimensions between 1 and 2. There was no definable chaotic attractor for the other two players. The two nonchaotic players were paired with each other, as were the six chaotic players.

Implications that can be drawn from the study in light of the foregoing simulation results are, first, that chaotic regimes occur more readily than what initially appeared to be the case. The use of three separate fixed strategies may be one way to assure chaos in strategy adoption, but chaotic outcomes occur over time with simpler dynamics. Second, the similar regimes that emerged from pairs of players suggests that real human relations, which are often with the same people, take a different form from simulated pairwise players. Perhaps the player pairs learn each others' implicit gaming rules, which each player tries to anticipate.

Anticipation Strategies. Another whole aspect to gaming that has not been well represented in the NDS work to this point is the theory of moves (Brams, 1993). So far, iterated games have considered cases where players react to moves of other players. According to Brams, players of real-world games learn to anticipate each others' moves and choose strategies that maximize long-term returns. Politicians and chess players anticipate moves on a regular basis. Anticipating moves, however, requires that the player have a correct game matrix of utilities for the opponent as well as for himself.

Not understanding the opponent's rationality can lead to deadly miscalculations of moves. The negotiations between President Carter and Ayatollah Khomeini over the return of the hostages taken from the U.S. Embassy in Teheran in 1979 represent an example of such miscalculations, according to Brams (1993). Carter underestimated Khomeini's preference for a dominant strategy for obstinacy. His attempts to draw Khomeini into settling matters through negotiation met with no positive response and a botched military attempt at hostage rescue in 1980.

The hostage situation was drawn to a close with the return of the hostages on the day Ronald Reagan was inaugurated as President of the United States. It now appears, according to Brams (1993), that the release of the hostages was the result of a third-party play, in which agents for Ronald Reagan made a secret deal with Khomeini to delay the return of the hostages until after the 1980 election in which he won a landslide victory over Carter. Reagan won the election and the political kudos for releasing the hostages. Khomeini won an embarrassment at Carter's expense.

Blue Skies and Blue Loops

It is a well-accepted theme of negotiation that what is being negotiated is also negotiable. The nature of the game, the listing of option, and the number of players are all subject to negotiation—or so it would appear. Creative definitions of new options could make a critical difference in a game structure that has no equilibrium, or an unstable one, to one that has a stable solution. Two types of complex dynamics are considered next.

Blue Sky. The blue sky catastrophe is a catastrophic bifurcation in which a new attractor appears suddenly and shifts the configuration of a vector field. It begins with a vector field containing a saddle and a repellor. The saddle would represent the equilibrium position from a game in play. As with many real-life negotiations, one party is getting the proverbial short end of the stick. Player A, represented by the incoming arrow to the saddle in Fig. 2.22, is attracted to the exchange, perhaps out of necessity, but the exit from the transaction is not simple. The long loop around the repellor, denoting Player B, denotes a high cost of participating in the exchange. It would further appear that Player B is not equally affected by the costs incurred to A, and actually perpetrates the exchange in a bullying fashion.

The resolution of the blue sky takes place when a change in a critical control parameter is made, perhaps instantiated by Player A. The erstwhile game actually becomes a nongame or a trivial game. Player A passes through the point occupied by the saddle and goes directly to a stable periodic attractor around repellor force B. The result is a truly stable relationship whereby A does not enter the repellor field of B, but enters a stable orbit around B where the natural course of B's trajectories cannot avoid those of A. For example, if one organization, A, finds that it is too costly to trade with an organization in a foreign country, B, it may be worthwhile to set up an operation in B's country.

Another application of the blue sky concept would involve approach–avoidance dynamics. In that case, player A (same incoming arrow) is attracted to a saddle, where it encounters an obnoxious input from B. Perhaps B is interfering with the transactions of A with another party. A change in control parameter once again allows A to pass through the saddle and keep B contained. For instance, A might have sufficient power in a transaction to require its trading partner to keep B as far away as possible during the time of transaction.

Blue Loop. The blue loop dynamic is more complex than the blue sky because a third dynamic source, a fixed point, exists in the vector field. In this hypothetical gambit, an organization, A, is trying to establish a fixed and stable policy of some sort, but is receiving only mixed support from its constituency from within, or perhaps from its market outside. The opponent, constituency, or market (Player B in the previous nomenclature) is signified by the repellor force once again, and is sending its emissaries (trajectories) to trade (go to the saddle) with organization A.

The mixed support for A's policy or product is the result of the actions of a third party represented by the fixed point, or Player C. Player C is not only siphoning support of B away from A, but capitalizes on A's circuitous or costly exchange with B. The dynamic is concluded with the shift in a control parameter such that the fixed point is moved into the region of the saddle.

In a real-world situation, organization A might buy out B or vice versa. Alternatively, A might find a way to modify its policy or product offering to incorporate the most desirable features of its own ideas and those offered by C. In other words, A upstages C. The essential gambit underlying the blue loop annihilation, from A's vantage point, is to move C from a position that is beyond the control of A to a position where A can control the actions of C. The same move might be accomplished by A entering an entangling relationship with C, which would constrain certain actions of C.

SOCIOSPATIAL DYNAMICS

Applications of NDS to urban and regional systems date back to the 1970s. Much of the principal early work was based on catastrophe theory (Wilson, 1981), although the field expanded to include the study of chaotic and other nonlinear dynamics as well (Dendrinos & Mullally, 1985; Dendrinos & Sonis, 1990). Some of the more interesting recent work in that field, insofar as it pertains to the themes developed in this book, is considered next. This pertains to the evolution of urban patterns and population dynamics, which, in turn, have further relevance to the affairs of organizations in both the private and public sectors.

Urban Pattern Formation

Casetti and Krakover (1990) studied trends in population growth across the United States for the years 1950–1990 and forecasted growth rates into the year 2000. Negative population growth was anticipated for the northeastern quadrant of the country, which has been traditionally heavily industrialized. Similar deceleration was anticipated for the California seaboard, which was one of the fastest growing regions during the 1950–1970 era. The most rapid growth is expected to occur on the Washington–Oregon seaboard, inland across the southern regions of Idaho and Montana, and covering substantial sections of Wyoming and Utah. A second growth center will be in the sunbelt region; that trend will be an acceleration of a growth trend that began around 1980.

At a more general level of expression, the instantaneous growth rate (p) was a quartic polynomial function of time:

$$\ln(p) = B_0 + B_1 t + B_2 t^2 + B_3 t^3 + B_4 t^4 \tag{4}$$

($R^2 = .90$). One important result from the study was that actual growth-rate dynamics are complex nonlinear functions. Another interesting finding was that a bifurcation in national urban growth rates was anticipated, such that positive and negative growth rates were projected. Splitting in the direction of growth was not known until around 1970.

Population shifts between cities can occur slowly or rapidly. The rules of migration across a three-city system are based on the definition of cities as chaotic attractors (Dendrinos, 1991, p. 38), and could be rationalized from classical theories of population dynamics due to Malthus and to Volterra and Lotka:

$$X_{i,(t+1)} = F_{i(t)} / \Sigma F_{j(t)} \tag{5}$$

$$F_{i(t)} = A_i \, \Pi \, X_{j(t)a_{ij}} \tag{6}$$

In this system of two equations, the number of residents in a city i at one step ahead in time ($t + 1$) is a function of the city i at time t divided by the sum of function values for the other two cities. The function values are cross-products of the set of attractive attributes of city i (A_i), and the populations of the three cities each raised to a power a_{ij}. The exponent is a measure of interlocation elasticity caused by transportation accessibility and possibly other variables.

Migration in the three-city system is configured as a Mobius triangle. In the analysis of data, simultaneous migration trajectories were derived for fractional values of a_{ij} to explore the possible range of configurations of migration trajectories. Depending on values of a_{ij}, one might obtain fast or slow migrations, or competitive exclusivity around one city. Attractors may be periodic, quasi-periodic, chaotic, or funnel ring attractor patterns. A sampling of these outcomes appears in Fig. 9.2.

Morphegenesis of Cities

Nonlinear dynamics have also been used to explain the origin of cities, particularly within European history. The archeological records shows a hysteresis between urbanization and deconglomeration in many human settlements (Wilson, 1981). Initially, humans were relatively unsettled and roamed from one ecological niche to another in search of food supplies and safe places to live; perhaps there was some experimental agriculture for some of those groups. The protective value of highlands, which were also less arable, was initially preferred to the valleys. When suitable highlands had been exhausted through general population growth, the valleys near waterways were settled next. Arable land made agriculture more feasible and even profitable, and valleys became more attractive as settlement locations (Eisler, 1991).

As valleys became more densely populated, new commerce opportunities emerged that provided nonagricultural work. A competing gradient

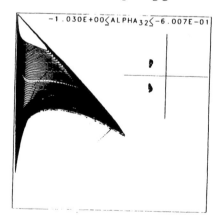

FIG. 9.2. Selected simulation results for population migration across a three-city system: (left) superimposition of dynamic trajectories, as parameter α_{21} changes within the range −0.86 to 0.5 in steps of 0.0028125; and (right) superimposition of dynamic trajectories as parameter α_{32} varies within the range −1.03 to −0.6007. From Dendrinos (1991). Reprinted with permission.

dynamic emerged, such that the two gradients were the effort–outcome ratio of farming and the effort–outcome ratio of urban activities. The relative favorability of the latter gave rise to urbanization, agglomeration of population, and more complex social and political infrastructures. These two gradient formed the basis of a cusp-catastrophic hysteresis between urbanization and ruralization (Rosser, 1992).

The next stage of urban development engendered a distinction between open and closed cities. As urban centers sprang up across Europe, a small amount of migration between them led to interurban trade relationships. Trade increased as transportation costs decreased. As transportation costs decreased, people could migrate to different cities on a relatively permanent basis. Interurban trade allowed the cities to sustain some of their cohesion, even though other dynamics might foster some migration back to the agricultural environment. An open city was one that continued to rely on the urban–agriculture gradient dynamics for its maintenance. A closed city was sustained by its interurban relationships, and experienced less migration to and from surrounding rural areas.

From the foregoing dynamics, it was possible to formulate a butterfly catastrophe model for urban development (Mees, 1975; Rosser, 1992). The three attractor states were the simple agrarian community, the presence of an open city, and the morphegenesis of a closed city. The four control parameters would therefore be the work–reward efficiency of agriculture, the work–reward efficiency of urbanization (gradient transformations), a bias factor represented by the relative strengths of the urban or agricultural sectors, and the transportation costs to other cities.

Suburban Decay and Urban Renewal

The dynamics depicted in Fig. 2.21 for an annihilation catastrophe describe the distribution of economic power throughout a metropolitan region under conditions of urban decay. The application is interesting not only for its impact on public sector organizations, but also because it represents dynamic environmental events to which other organizations are often forced to respond. The application begins with work initiated by Haag and Dendrinos (1983) on urban expansion, which I have followed through further evolutionary processes to explain urban renewal.

The dependent measure for the urban–suburban dynamic is the asking price (or bid price) for real estate properties. The control parameter is the demand for improved land, which is partially a result of an aversion to population density (Haag & Dendrinos, 1983). Initially, land development and migration trends emanate from the centrum outward. This movement may create a stable limit cycle in the form of a suburban ring. Alternatively, the limit cycle is not stable and the metropolis continues to expand. As wealth increases for individuals, they move to the suburbs to avoid the congestion, noise, and social problems of the city and to develop new real estate and communities. As capital investment moves out of the centrum, the separatrix expands, resulting in a more hostile urban environment. Businesses follow individual wealth to provide services to the outlying communities, to avail themselves of the professional labor supply who would prefer not traveling into the city, and to exchange outdated real estate for new.

The next logical step is to define what events would occur when a stable limit cycle has formed and a renewed demand for improved property occurs. First, the suburbs become aversively crowded. As urban residents move further from the center in search of better housing and other conditions, crime follows them out because there is little left worth stealing in the centrum. The two population forces (those from the limit cycle and those being repelled from the centrum) collide and the socioeconomic order self-destructs.

The annihilation process may not appear so discrete to the residents. The process takes place over a period of years in real time, and its distribution over real space is not uniform. As the centrum clears out, new opportunities emerge for real estate and business development. The centrum becomes an attractor force for economic concentration, professional activities, and condominium dwellers. People who did not complete the transition to the suburbs would be drawn back to the centrum, at least to the extent that appropriate jobs and housing became available. In other words, they return to the centrum to the extent that the attractor is sufficiently strong.

Throughout the process of urban decay and renewal, there is a myriad of business opportunities and decisions that could be made. The organization that clings to outdated locations and marketing concepts will self-destruct, either for lack of customers or clients or for lack of an appropriate labor supply. If it survives, it may not be well positioned to respond to the new economic demands when it does find itself again in the middle of an otherwise attractive field. Ultimately, the organization needs to read and interpret the environmental signs, rethink its current modes of behavior, and adapt successfully.

POPULATION DYNAMICS AND WORK FORCE
PRODUCTIVITY: THE POSSIBILITIES

Social scientists have expressed concern that the nation's workforce will change markedly by the year 2000 in terms of its available levels of work-related skills. Employers will have difficulty keeping a stable and qualified work force if the current trends continue, and the ultimate result will be a lower standard of living for everyone (Marshall, 1991). The problems posed to NDS are: To what extent and under what conditions will turbulent environmental conditions produce chaotic temporal fluctuations in an organization's human resource availability and its overall performance? How can this form of chaos be managed most appropriately?

The following thesis begins with a model for fluctuations in insect populations developed by May and Oster (1976), which is then applied to the human work force. In this section a set of scenarios based on varying model parameter values is explored that maps out the possible outcomes an organization could face. The next section examines the probabilities of any of those outcomes being true in the construction trades, which are particularly volatile. Analysis of constructed personnel data showed (Guastello, 1992c) that the insect population analogy is not at all absurd. Rather, it could serve as a general model for steady and volatile fluctuations in any population census.

Insect Populations

The equations for population dynamics (May & Oster, 1976) describe the number of individuals in two age classes observed in successive generations, based on their numbers at a previous generation, birth rate (b), survival rate (s), and a crowding factor (a). Let x_t represent the number of individuals (insects) in the young age class observed at generation t, and y_t the number of individuals in the older age class. Their numbers at a subsequent generation are given by:

$$y_{t+1} = sx_t \tag{7}$$

$$x_{t+1} = bN_t \, e^{(-aN_t)} \tag{8}$$

$$N_t = x_t + y_t \tag{9}$$

The model assumes that individuals at t do not survive to $t + 2$. The population is globally stable for $b < 8.95$, but crosses into Period 2 dynamics when $b > 8.95$. Local stability is observed for $8.95 < b < 14.5$, and period doubling is observed when $14.5 < b < 17$. Note that the precision associated with successive critical values of b decreases for this problem. Chaos in Period 3 begins when $b \cong 17$.

Workforce Dynamics

The model for insect population dynamics can be transformed into projections for quantities of people at two levels of skill: beginner (x) and advanced (y). Survival rate (s) represents the proportion of persons at x_t

that progress to y_{t+1} during a "hiring generation." Although a life generation can be hours, days, or weeks in insect time, a human life generation could vary from 15 to 40 years or more. A hiring generation can be defined in arbitrarily smaller units of time such as a year, or 4 years. The latter could be a reasonable choice because high school and college are typically 4-year periods; this interval is thus socially meaningful.

Birth rate (b) is the hiring rate per generation expressed as a ratio of persons hired to total persons currently employed. The crowding factor (a) represents an inhibition on actual hirings given an operational N, and b. Parameter a could perhaps represent the difficulty the organization could have in assimilating, training, and socializing new workers, or would represent a situation in the demand for an organization's products. Although there is a known connection between organizational subunit size and attitudes and work outcomes (Guastello, 1988), the causes and consequences of parameters b and a in human working population dynamics have never been directly addressed to date.

The concept of population dynamics used here considers the number of organisms (insects, humans) in one physical location representing an organization's workforce. It is not necessary to assume any special linkage between the spatial population dynamic and the temporal dynamic occurring in a limited space. The spatial dynamic is assumed to be slaved to the temporal dynamic. This is a convenient assumption, and the implications of it are discussed at the closing of the next section.

Slaving is the situation where a variable such as x_{t+1} is a function of x_t, and x_t is a function of one or more variables p, q, and r, such that the set $[p,q,r]$ is part of x_t. By simply saying that x_{t+1} is a function of x_t, the set $[p,q,r]$ is slaved to x_t. (This set of relationships is similar to, and actually a generalized case of, driver–slave relationships in coupled oscillator dynamics. Instead of one dynamic driving another to form a complex time series, we are looking at the relationship between a set and a subset). In the May–Oster dynamic model, survival rate s is slaved to the total population size N, but the completeness of the slaving process can be tested empirically (next section).

Prototype Simulations

The following seven simulations describe some plausible conditions of organizational population fluctuation. The first three describe growth conditions in Period 1 when the crowding parameter (a) is present or absent and when survival accumulates conditions where the pool of qualified applicants is shrinking dramatically. Period 2 dynamics are likely in one situation, whereas work force extinction is likely in another. The last two simulations illustrate some unusual growth conditions characteristic of small organizations in which period doubling and Period 3 chaos are observed. All simulations start with $x_1 = y_1 = 50$, and carry on until 15 hiring generations have elapsed. Once N_t has been calculated, it is a small matter to define a dichotomous performance variable z from x_t and y_t such that its variance is:

$$S_{z(t)}^2 = x_t y_t \, / \, (x_t + y_t)^2 \qquad (10)$$

It is fortunate that the May–Oster model is scale free, meaning that it is not necessary to operate further on z to correct for location and scale.

Scenario 1. The first simulation was based on $b = 1.0$, $s = 0.50$, and $a = 0.00$, and would represent a growth condition whereby the organization's hiring policy called for as many new employees per generation as there organizational members already, and only 50% of the beginner group survive to attain the advanced skill level. By setting $a = 0.00$, it is assumed that the crowding parameter either does not apply, or was absorbed into b or s; b and s remain constant throughout the 15 iterations. Thus Equation 8 simplifies to:

$$x_{t+1} = bN \qquad (11)$$

Curve A in the lower panel of Fig. 9.3 represents S_z^2 as a function of hiring generation. Variance starts at its maximum at Generation 1, drops to two-thirds its original value at Generation 2, increases at Generation 3, then drops slightly at Generation 4 and stabilizes. Low variance means an imbalance exists between beginner and advanced workers. When there are too many beginners, the work force is insufficiently skilled. When there are too many advanced workers, succession problems are imminent and may occur concurrently with dismantled training programs and unusually large (relative to competitors') wage and benefit costs. It is temporarily assumed (and explained eventually later) that a 50–50 split between advanced and beginner level workers is optimum. By the 15th iteration N increased from 100 to 7350.48.

Scenario 2. The second simulation was similar to the first except that $a = 0.001$. Curve B in Fig. 9.3 represents the population and variance function for Scenario 2. By the 15th iteration, N increased to only 395.02. The value S_z^2 dropped from .25 to .17 on the second iteration and bounced around .21 in iterations 3–8, than stabilized at .22.

Scenario 3. The third simulation (Fig. 9.3, curve C) was similar to the second, except that the restriction that advanced level employees expire after one generation was lifted. Advanced level employees were allowed

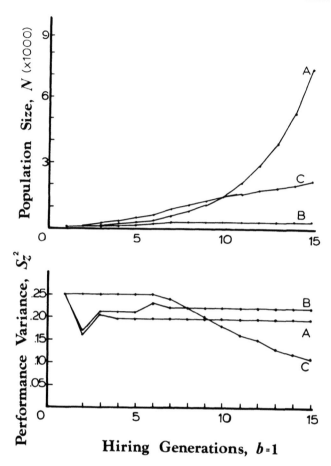

FIG. 9.3. Period 1 dynamics for population size and performance variance in Scenarios 1 (A), 2 (B), and 3 (C).

to remain in the work force for the full 15 iterations. The value of N increased from 100 to 2180.55 over 15 generations; S_z^2 remained at its maximum for 5 generations, then dropped steadily to .11 by the last iteration.

Scenario 4. Scenarios 4 and 5 simulated what could happen under conditions where the pool of qualified applicants shrinks such that the hiring goals exceed the number of qualified applicants. In Scenario 4, b = 10, s = .10, and a = .001. Here the organization hires at 10 times its current census although only 10% of beginners survive to a subsequent generation. Once again, advanced level workers do not survive to a subsequent generation. The graph of S_z^2 in Fig. 9.4 shows a drop from

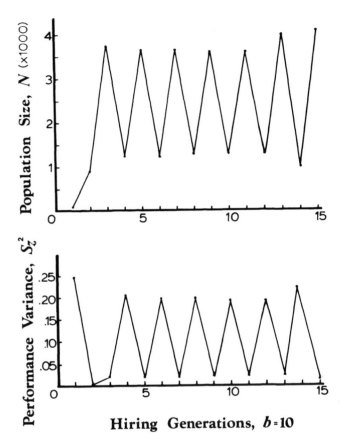

FIG. 9.4. Period 2 dynamics for population size and performance variance in Scenario 4.

.25 to less than .01 at the second generation. Iterations 3–15 show oscillations between two locally stable orbital attractors; one hovers around .22, and the other hovers around .02.

Scenario 5. In the fifth simulation (not shown in any figures), the organization only hires qualified applicants as they become available: $b = .50, s = .90, a = .001$. Here S_z^2 remained at its unrestricted maximum (.25), but N dropped to 6.54 by the fifth generation. The organization went into virtual extinction.

Scenario 6. The sixth scenario demonstrated the period doubling effect while making a transition to chaos ($b = 18, s = 1.0, a = .01$). The workforce exceeded 700 on Generations 2 and 11, and contracted to less than 25 at

Generations 4 and 13 (Fig. 9.5). The value of S_z^2 reached its maximum (.25) at Generations 4, 10, and 12, but dropped to less than .05 at 3, 5, 12, and 14.

The cycle of N in Scenario 6 is 9 generations long. Generations 1–4 and 10–13 from the "outer" cycle corresponding to any portion of Period 2 of the logistic map. Generations 5–9 and 14–18 form the "inner" cycle characteristic of the first episode of period doubling. (Generations 16–18 are not shown in Fig. 9.5.) The second doubling explains differences in the amplitude of N from Generation 6 compared to 8 and 9, and 5 compared to 7.

The pattern of S_z^2 over hiring generations is relatively chaotic, but not wholly unpredictable from knowledge of N_t. The S_z^2 takes on its maximum

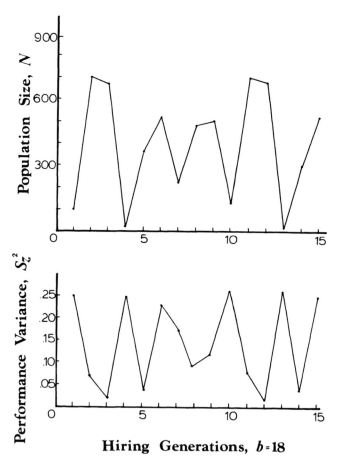

FIG. 9.5. Period doubling trends for population size and performance variance in Scenario 6.

value at Generations 1, 4, 10, and 13, which are the points where four lowest values of N_t are observed; S_z^2 takes on its lowest four values at Generations 3 and 12, which are coupled with two of the larger values of N_t. The apparent negative correlation between N and S_z^2 is only generalizable to limited ranges of b and t and should not be taken as a general rule connecting the two parameters.

Scenario 7. The seventh simulation demonstrated the chaotic fluctuations in N characteristic of Period 3 ($b = 22$, $s = 1.0$, $a = .01$). The workforce reached approximately 800 at Generations 3, 4, 12, and 13, but veered to near extinction at Generations 4 and 14 (Fig. 9.6). The average N over 15 generations was 433.19. The S_z^2 showed similar chaotic variation; S_z^2 never

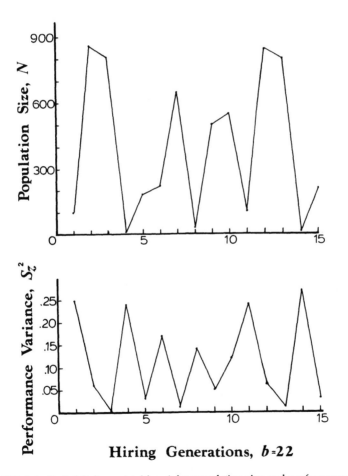

FIG. 9.6. Period 3 dynamics (chaos) for population size and performance variance in Scenario 7.

regained its maximum value but did reach .24 at Generations 4, 11, and 14.

Summary and Implications

The simulations showed that performance variance will be stable when Period 1 growth conditions are in effect, at least three hiring generations have elapsed since the starting conditions of maximum variance, or survival across a small number of generations is assumed. Performance variance will follow a saw-toothed function when Period 2 dynamics are in effect. Performance variance will decay when Period 1 growth conditions in effect, and when survival across a large number of generations is assumed. Performance variance will be chaotic as growth rate enters Period 3.

For purposes of illustrative simulations, it was necessary to assume that b, s, and t remained constant throughout the 15 hiring generations. If we assume a 4-year hiring generation, 60 years of exposure to constant values of b or s is more than any organization could expect. Thus if b and s are allowed to vary across generations, N and S_z^2 would be more chaotic than any of the scenarios indicated.

In assessing the impact of the model parameters on performance variance, only one type of criterion dynamic was assumed, namely, that an employee becomes more proficient at the job or the employee does not. If one assumes that the performance construct is continuously valued instead of dichotomous, and that other within-person fluctuations could occur, then performance variance would fluctuate more chaotically than the simulations showed.

The "law of requisite variety," which is well known in engineering circles and which appears to have taken its cue from basic evolutionary theory, states that the control of a system must be at least as complex as the system itself. This axiom has strong implications for the control of organizational workforce census, which is most often done through selection and training methods. The following remarks are specifically aimed at Scenario 4, which is perhaps the most likely scenario for the workforce shortage problem.

Performance variance is the primary concern for drawing implications for system control. If there is no variance, there is no control. If all employees are highly experienced "survivors" and perform accordingly, it will be impossible to find a variable that distinguishes them that could be used for personnel selection purposes. The substance of the variable is not important for the purposes at hand, although there is strong societal concern over the shrinking availability of strong educational skills. Similarly, if there is massive turnover among the surviving group, perhaps due to massive retirements incurred by a population bulge, and there is substantial replacement effort under way, variance will again be low, and it will not be possible to identify characteristics of successful employees until substantial time has elapsed. Of course, keeping "dead employees" in the database might provide a clue, but there is no guarantee that knowledge based on one generation would transfer well to another, in light of ambient societal evolution.

Training is another form of control. The simulations with the most volatile census and variance trends suggest that a complex strategy for using selection and training options needs to be developed. Perhaps the most alarming simulation was Scenario 5, where organizations insisted on using "tried and true" methods in the face of population shifts. Extinction was the final result.

POPULATION DYNAMICS AND WORKFORCE PRODUCTIVITY IN THE CONSTRUCTION TRADES

The goals of the next investigation were (a) to illustrate a practical application of population dynamics theory to a volatile industry, (b) to assess critical parameters when a management population control policy is in force, (c) to compare the results of a long-range management policy to a reactive policy, in the sense of anticipating moves in gaming, and (d) to consider the contribution of seasonal effects on the outcomes of those policies. The introduction of seasonal effects represents a problem in coupled oscillation.

The construction trades in Wisconsin have experienced the labor force problems explored earlier. A major slump in new home construction in 1980 caused a substantial number of tradesmen to find other work and discouraged new workers from entering those trades. A later boom in 1986–1988 created more of a demand for skills than there was a supply. The example considered here is that of an interior–exterior house painter who was having a significant difficulty maintaining a work crew of 15.

The data set consisted on census data for the housepainter over a 3-year period. The data were simulated on the basis of realistic constraints. Each frame of data represented a 1-week hiring generation consisted of new hires, the number of workers remaining from the previous week, the total number, and each of the foregoing counts from the previous week. Unconstrained nonlinear regression, as explained in Chapter 3, was used to estimate four parameters in Equation 12:

$$N_t = bN_{t-1} e^{(-aN)} + s_1 x_{t-1} + s_2 y_{t-1} \tag{12}$$

where b is the bifurcation parameter, a is the crowding parameter, s_1 is the survival rate of new hires to the second generation, and s_2 is the survival rate of the second generation to the third.

Any chaotic effect in the workforce population count, or lack thereof, will be filtered by the management strategy which is in place at the time. Such management strategies will serve, where applicable, to reduce uncertainty and thereby to provide the organization with a stable flow of workers. Indeed, management is expected, typically, to maintain a stable staff in spite of any chaotic events in the labor environment.

Sterman's (1988) beer distribution game illustrated how capable or inept typical managers are at maintaining a constant stock. The objective of the beer distribution game was to maintain a steady inventory of beer in spite of any random shock in the brewery supply or retail sales environments. Only 11% of gamers, none of which were trained in chaos theory, were successful at maintaining a reasonable inventory in the particularly challenging set of game parameters. "Reasonable" meant to not run out of beer and not to overflow the warehouse. Players who could not successfully control the inventory produced chaotic inventory histories (Mosekilde et al., 1991). In light of the past experimental results it was hypothesized that a greater index of bifurcation would be found under conditions of reactionary management.

Scenario Definitions

Long-Range Planning. The data set consisted of three sets (construction years) of 28 frames (weeks of work during the construction season) containing the census counts just described. The data were generated according to the following constraints:

1. The house painter must constrain the workforce to 10 except when the end of the season nears. He begins with himself and two senior works (partners) and hires the rest.

2. If he hires 10 new people a week, 7 are gone by the end of the week ($s_1 = .30$). The survival rate for advanced workers (s_2) was set at .33.

3. When the workforce exceeds 15 for 4 weeks in a row, hiring is cut to 5 per week until the work force falls below 15 for 1 week.

4. On Frames 20, 22, and 23 of each season, 4 students leave to return to school.

5. On Frame 24, the weekly hiring is cut to 5, either because the applicants are less available or because new work orders are slowing down.

6. The three seasons were generated according to the same rules, such that the seed values of a subsequent season were the final values of the previous season, and with the exception that random shock functions were added to the second and third seasons. In the second season, the

number of new hires was altered for 5 randomly selected frames in which the housepainter was short 1 new hire on three occasions and managed to hire one extra on two occasions. In the third season, 10 randomly selected frames were altered to represent random shock. In three cases the housepainter was short 2 hires, in three cases he was short 1, in two cases he hired 1 extra, and in two cases he hired 2 extra.

Reactive Management. Once again the data set consisted of three sets of 28 frames and the same variables as used in the previous scenario. Constraints 1, 4, 5, and 6 for long-range planning were the same in reactive management. The differences were as follows.

Constraint 2. Instead of hiring a steady 10 applicants per week, the housepainter hired as many as it took to get his workforce up to 15. He "knew" his s_1 rate was .30, so hired three times as many applicants as there were real openings. If he had no openings he did not hire.

Constraint 3. He could only hire a maximum of 10 per week, either because the applicant pool was limited or because he could not process any more new hires than 10. Random shock may cause the maximum number of new hires to reach 12, as provided by Constraint 6 above.

Data for the two conditions appear in Fig. 9.7. The long-term planning condition shows relatively small oscillations around one apparent attractor during the heavy season, and oscillations around a second attractor during the weeks in which the season was dying down. The reactive management condition shows relatively large oscillations, possibly between two attractors, throughout the series, with possible period doubling during the weeks in which the season was dying down. These interpretations of the time series were tested as hypotheses, discussed later.

Simulation Results

A summary of the nonlinear regression results for the two simulations appears in Table 9.2. The analytic strategy was to fit Equation 12 such that b, a, s_1, and s_2 were estimated regression parameters. For each simulation the R^2 for the nonlinear model was calculated along with R^2 for the pre–post linear control:

$$N_2 = B_0 + B_1 N_1 \tag{13}$$

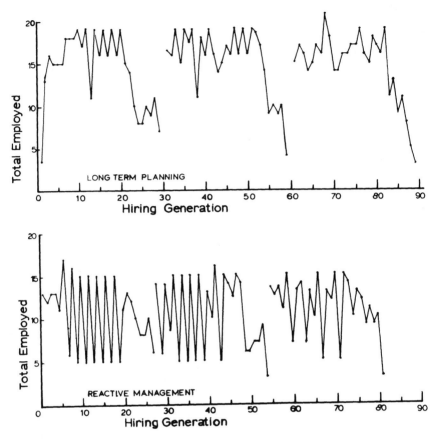

FIG. 9.7. Time series for housepainter's workforce size under conditions of long-range planning and reactive management.

Next, a seasonal difference operation, ∇, was defined to account for some of the remaining variance in the context of a moderator regression analysis:

$$N_2 = B_0 + B_1F + B_2\nabla + B_3\nabla^*F \qquad (14)$$

The difference operator was dichotomized such that 1 indicated that workers were returning to school (Frames 21–28) and 0 otherwise. The term F was equal to the right-hand side of Equation 12. A significant effect for ∇ and the moderator function would indicate that the function F was true only for the time frames not affected by the return to school and the slowdown of work, and that a coupled dynamic was obscuring the population dynamic function.

TABLE 9.2
Results of Nonlinear Regression and Comparison Analysis

| Model | R^2 | Parameters | | | |
		a	b	s_1	s_2
Long-range planning					
Nonlinear, all cases	.40**	−0.28*	1.915*	−0.015	0.380
Linear control	.40**				
Moderated seasonal	.62**				
Nonlinear, $\nabla = 0$	.32**	−0.06*	3.840*	−0.280	−0.360
Linear, $\nabla = 0$	.14*				
Reactive management					
Nonlinear, all cases	.22**	−0.16*	5.199*	−0.017	0.368
Linear control	.23**				
Moderated seasonal	.62**				
Nonlinear, $\nabla = 0$	.77**	−0.08*	7.120*	−0.512	−1.762
Linear, $\nabla = 0$	.57**				

*$p < .05$. **$p < .01$.

The Durbin–Watson statistic (DW) was applied to residuals of Equation 14 to determine its serial dependency among residuals that remained. A significant DW would indicate that some residual variance was not properly captured by the nonlinear function. The nature of the variance captured by a DW indicates sensitivity to initial conditions, such that errors introduced at one time frame would be carried through to later time frames.

Long-Range Planning. The nonlinear regression analysis for all 84 frames identified significant crowding and bifurcation parameters. The latter indicated that Period 1 dynamics were taking place. The R^2 for the model was .40, as was r^2 for the linear comparison. The results of the moderator regression analysis showed that both ∇ and ∇F made significant contributions to prediction, raising R^2 to .62. The seasonal trend tended to mask the underlying fractal function.

The value of DW was relatively large (2.59, $p < .05$), indicating that some serial dependency among residuals remained. The 10 frames with the largest standardized residuals were identified. All 10 could be explained by artificial circumstances that were unrelated to the pure function, F: Two frames were located at the start of a seasonal series. Three frames were located where the rule to cut or resume the hiring rate kicked in. Three frames were located where students returned to school, and two were located where random shocks were administered.

The nonlinear analysis was repeated for cases where $\nabla = 0$ only (57 frames). The R^2 dropped somewhat to .32, but r^2 for the linear comparison dropped further to .14. Thus, once the special seasonal differencing effect was removed, the nonlinear interpretation was 2.28 times as accurate as the linear alternative.

Reactive Management. The nonlinear regression analysis for all 84 frames identified significant crowding and bifurcation parameters. Although higher than the value obtained for long-range planning, $b = 7.120$ indicated that Period 1 dynamics were taking place. The linear comparison model was slightly more accurate ($r^2 = .23$). Moderator regression analysis for the seasonal difference operator showed significant effects of ∇ and ∇F, thus raising R^2 to .62 again. The DW (1.87) was not significant.

The nonlinear analysis was repeated for cases where $\nabla = 0$ only. The R^2 increased dramatically to .77. The linear comparison r^2 increased to .57. Thus when the effect of ∇ was removed, the nonlinear model was 1.35 times more accurate than the linear alternative. The bifurcation parameter now reached an all-time high of 7.12. The 95% confidence interval (6.17 $< b < 8.07$) showed that b did not cross the critical value of 8.95.

Dimensionality. The dimensionality for the attractors represented by the time series data was calculated as $e^a + 1$ (from chapter 3, Equation 55). The dimensionality of the first function for long-range planning was 1.76. When the seasonal oscillator was removed, dimensionality increased (because a was a negative number) to 1.94. For reactionary management, the dimensionality of the first function was 1.85, which increased to 1.92 when the seasonal effect was removed.

The conclusion from the dimensionality analysis was that the attractors (repellors) represented in the data were not chaotic because the Lyapunov exponents were negative. Indeed, theory predicted negative exponents because crowding would have a contracting impact, not an expanding one. Furthermore, the bifurcation parameter would be responsible for any periodicity or quasi-periodicity, and such was the case. Both functions qualified as fractal, because of their incomplete occupancy of two-dimensional space. The obtained dimension values were well within values expected for a system that was only beginning to veer into Period 2 dynamics.

Productivity Units. A productivity variable was finally created to augment the interpretation of the results. For each frame, productivity was valued as 2 units for each advanced worker plus 1 unit for each new worker. For long-range planning, the correlation between N_t and P_t was .92. The correlation between P_2 and N_1 was somewhat less ($r = .58$), but it indicated, nonetheless, that workforce size today was related to production tomorrow.

For reactive management, the correlation between N_t and P_t was still .92, but the correlation between P_2 and N_1 dropped to $-.38$. Thus, under conditions of reactive management, productivity takes a quasi-random walk with respect to workforce size. In days of old, this effect would have been interpreted as regression to the mean, but we now understand it to mean that there is a production attractor present, and reactive management keeps trying to steer into it, with difficulty. Increasing the size of the workforce does not alter the equilibrium level of production.

Interpretation

The contrast in results between long-range planning and reactionary management showed that with long-range tactics management obtained less instability than what was the case under reactionary tactics. Managers typically prefer business environments with less unnecessary instability. Economic observers have similarly extolled the virtues of thinking ahead over short-term reactions for years in the popular media. Now there is a new form of support for such an idea. There appeared to be one, apparently quasi-periodic, equilibrium point, which was the targeted staffing level of 15 workers in the long-range condition. In the reactionary condition, there appeared to be a single repellor point hovering around 10 workers. The impact of the repellor is more apparent when increased shock is introduced, as Fig. 9.7 shows.

In the reactive condition, the shocks that stood out in the long-range condition were not apparent. The shocks appeared to be incorporated into, rather than isolated from, the central logistic function. The data in Fig. 9.7 show an oscillation between the target value of 15 and a lesser value of 5 workers. The analysis showed, however, that the nonlinear process had not crossed into Period 2; a one-equilibrium interpretation is thus more correct than a two-equilibrium or period-doubling interpretation.

Chaotic functions require chaotic controllers. Fortunately, it appears that the workforce population dynamics are of a moderately benign type. Staffing of organizations with qualified personnel will require well-timed long-range plans for meeting human resource needs, selection decisions, and training. Poor timing would result in inadequate decision rules, hence poor hiring, overloaded training programs, and training programs that do not bridge the gap between the new hires' skill level and the skill level required for work.

Deskilling a job through technological advances may be an option, but the right technology might not be available at the right time. Deskilling may prove self-defeating in the long run, because the slow dynamics of societal development tend toward increased demands for human capability, not less. Deskilling efforts could widen the gap between availability of and demand for a skill. Lowering the demand for a skill encourages the skill to disappear.

CHAOECONOMICS

The relationships between NDS and economic theory have received considerable attention in recent years (Balasko, 1989; Brock, 1991; Brock et al., 1991; Gori et al., 1993; Peters, 1991; Priesmeyer, 1992; Rosser, 1991) although the roots of those connection trace back to early work on fractal geometry (Mandelbrot, 1960, 1962), catastrophe theory (Zeeman, 1974), and game theory (Rand, 1978). Conventional economic theory is based on the assumption that capital markets are essentially equilibrium-seeking, and deviations from apparent equilibrium can be rationalized as random walks that of no further theoretical consequence (Balasko, 1989; Peters, 1991). Conventional theory is bolstered by the efficient market hypothesis, which holds that all information that could affect the price of a commodity is quickly and efficiently translated into price adjustments. According to Peters (1991), no one really believes in the efficient market hypothesis in spite of its widespread assumption in conventional economic theory. Rather, information, when it is synthesized into a price adjustment, is not incorporated in a linear fashion, and the so-called random shocks are better understood as orderly fractal patterns (if that is not too much of an oxymoron). Rosser (1991) took matters several steps further by developing a general theory of economic discontinuities and instability.

The remainder of this section elaborates three themes that are directed at tying together the economic and political issues already introduced in this chapter with the ecological concerns raised in chapter 9. The first concerns the debate over whether chaosticity actually exists in capital markets. The apparent solution to the problem transits directly to the relationship between ecology and economics and the exploitation of public commodities. The third concerns the effectiveness of tariffs on economic control strategies, particularly because of their implications for labor, ecology, and both domestic and international policy. Those issues set the stage for the remainder of chapter concerning global social and economic unity—or chaos.

NDS and Capital Markets

Cusp Theories. The cusp model for stock market dynamics was first introduced by Zeeman (1974, 1977), was revised by Weintraub (1983), and served as a basis for later work connecting chaos and catastrophe dynamics

(Guastello, 1993b). In the original conceptualization, price changes can be smooth and continuous, or sudden and catastrophic, depending on the amount of speculative activity taking place in the market. The asymmetry parameter was excess demand for a commodity; price increases when demand exceeds supply, as in conventional economic theory. The bifurcation parameter governs the absolute size of the price fluctuation. When speculation levels (i.e., risk-taking behaviors) are low, price changes are smooth functions of demand. When speculation levels are high, however, a sudden price increase can be expected when demand increases, but a sudden and substantial price drop would be expected when demand subsides.

A crash in the Zeeman model is a sudden global (in the topological, not the geographical sense) drop in commodities prices of the type that occurred in 1929. A crash would occur when speculation trading dominates the market, and demand drops below a critical level. In 1929, demand dropped sharply because it was fueled by unrestricted and highly exposed credit policy. A drop in the world money supply shortened the available lendable cash in the United States, and banks began demanding payments on the debts outstanding.

Increasing demand causes prices to rise, which in turn causes demand to fall. Prices then stabilize at the high level. If demand increases without hesitation, there will be eventually no one left to buy. Those who made their purchases early in the price trajectory can realize the maximum profit by being the first ones to sell after stability has been reached. Prices will start to decline as more offers to sell are made. Those who were the latest to purchase would recognize the lack of growth potential or would prefer to stop losses. Thus a selling spree would ensue. The first sales go unnoticed as predictable profit-taking, and prices roll back a small amount, signaling imminent losses for the late arrivals. The selling becomes massive in an effort to stop losses, supply outstrips demand, and prices fall to bargain levels. Once prices have stabilized at the low price level, they may remain low, but could slowly slide upward toward value-fair levels if the speculative activity also subsides.

True stability in the Zeeman model is attained only when speculation dominates the market. Commodity trades that are based on financial certainties are represented by trajectories in the nonbifurcated portion of the surface. Although prices can fluctuate there also, they fluctuate around a highly unstable point; there is no attractor holding the prices in any sort of orbit.

Weintraub (1983) criticized the Zeeman model on a few economic points. First, the model was based on a retrospective view of history, and was not supported by a data analysis from either the distant past or from contemporary times when the credit and trading rules had changed. Second, the idea that true stability can only occur in a highly speculative market was absurd; stability is usually associated with "conservative" or "smart-money" value-based investments.

In revising the model, Weintraub (1983) noted that the excess demand dynamic that Zeeman proposed only holds true if prices are already in equilibrium. If trades are made when equilibrium has not been reached, which is usually the case, the equilibrium position shifts relative to what it would have been if those trades had not been made. The equilibrium shift occurs because the market is a complex system with feedback loops such that price movements signal other investors to rethink their strategies. Weintraub thus redefined the asymmetry parameter as the demand created by sound trading fundamentals of the stock.

Weintraub (1983) regarded the notion of chartists or speculators controlling the market as absurd. Rather, inflation is a more rigorous construct that affects the price of a stock and acts a bifurcation parameter. Inflation comes in two forms. Normal inflation is an increase in the money supply, caused by productivity of the economy at large. Abnormal inflation occurs when the increase in wages and prices exceeds the rate of increase that would be justified by real productivity. In the infamous spiral of inflation, the increased cost of living precipitates a demand for higher wages, which translates into higher prices, where prices are raised higher than what is required to meet the overhead expenses. The subsequent round of price increases precipitates an increased demand for wages, and the corporations record profit increases that are caused more by price-hiking on the products than by real growth in output or market expansion. The process is typically slow relative to the speed of stock transaction, but ultimately discomfort builds and perverse expectations increase with inflation. Strong perverse expectations push prices downward. A graphic of the Weintraub model with later embellishments (from Guastello, 1993b) appears in Fig. 9.8.

Multiple Basin Theory. In a series of mathematical proofs, Balasko (1978a, 1978b, 1978c, 1979a, 1979b) showed that the economy is made up of multiple equilibria, each of which resides in its own basin, or *envelope.* Each equilibrium is characterized by a commodity and a purchaser utility. Basins are contiguous, or tangential to each other, and fill the space defined by the global economy. Basins are arc-connected to each other, meaning that they contain a pathway that connects the basins (Balasko, 1978b). By knowing the number of basins, it is possible to know the equilibrium position of the global economy (Balasko, 1979b). In other words, the global economic effects that have been considered thus far are actually epiphenomena of multiple attractor dynamics.

Trajectories within the basin complex are thought to be reversible (diffeomorphic) when controlling parameters are reversed (Balasko,

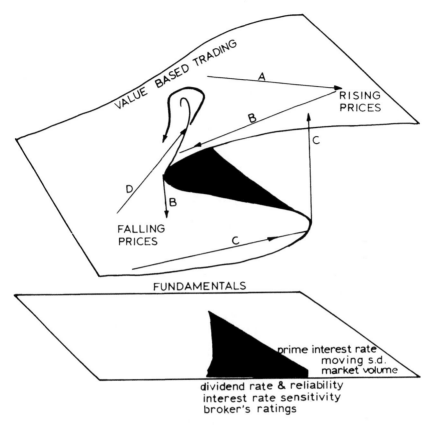

FIG. 9.8. Cusp catastrophe model for New York Stock Exchange prices.
From Guastello (1993b). Reprinted with permission.

1978a). In that sense, the attractors are not likely to be chaotic attractors.
In chaotic trajectories, two paths are not likely to be exact reversals of
each other. The multiple basin principle has at least three important
implications for NDS modeling of discontinuous market behavior. First,
given that two basins are tangential, they are largely separate in a manner
consistent with the bifurcation principle in catastrophe theory (Balasko,
1978b). Second, because trajectories within a basin are smooth, they can
be approximated by linear functions when observed locally. Indices of
nonlinear trajectories will be most apparent in the limited cases where a
trajectory between basins is observed. Third, the economy is not a single,
or even a double attractor basin, but a series of interlocked, albeit permeable, basins. As a result, global modeling of the economy in time series
would produce a deceiving picture of linearity in the sense that an array
of equilibria values observed at time t will be highly correlated with the

array of equilibria values at $t + 1$, such that the equilibria values will retain the same rank order with respect to each other.

Chaotic Behavior. Peters (1991) addressed the problem of nonlinear market dynamics from what is becoming a standard chaos theory approach. He analyzed time series of specific commodities and broader marker indices for the possible response of attractors, characterized the complexity of those (limit cycles versus chaotic attractors), and measured their dimensionality using both the Hausdoff and Lyapunov methods. Some commodities were more chaotic than others, and fractional dimensionality was apparent in some cases. Furthermore, chaosticity was thought to vary within a time series because of erratically generated news items and events that affect the autonomous price trajectories.

The matter of whether low-dimensional chaos exists in capital markets is controversial. Brock (1986) developed a diagnostic economic time series in which the time series is "bleached" to remove a linear effect, and the residuals are analyzed for chaos. The breaching process was based on the principle that the dimensionality of the residual time series should be equal to that of the function itself. Applications of the technique (Brock & Sayers, 1988) showed that the evidence for low-dimensional chaos was weak. Other researchers (summarized in Brock, 1991) obtained dimensionalities between six and seven. Theiler and Eubank (1993) showed that the bleaching process is no longer recommended, and that better estimates of dimensionality can be obtained by not using it.

The Crash of 1987. The various perspectives on market dynamics were eventually synthesized in a recent study (Guastello, 1993b) of market dynamic during the bull market of 1982, through the crash of 1987, and a few years afterward. The first part of the project was the development and test of the cusp model shown in Fig. 9.8. The database was composed of 65 to 72 NYSE common stocks, whose prices were taken on a quarterly basis. Analysis was repeated for each quarter where the data involved four consecutive quarterly price sets, producing three consecutive sets of difference scores.

The cusp model worked fairly well, with an average $R^2 = .94$, although the average R^2 for the linear pre–post model was .97. The R^2 for the cusp model was a little larger than the linear value in 7 out of 16 replications. The average cross-validity r^2 of the cusp model for two quarters ahead was .96.

Cusp and dimensionality analysis was conducted for consecutive difference scores taken just before and just after the crash of October 1987. The cusp versus linear comparison tipped in favor of the linear model ($R^2 = .93$ compared to .91). Application of the nonlinear regression technique (from chapter 3) on the same data produced a negative exponent, signifying that the process of a crash was not chaotic. The dimensionality was 0.92 and consistent with the cusp results.

In the final sequence of analyses, the multiple basin problem was attacked by correcting each stock in the database by its own value of location and scale, based on moving lower limits and moving standard deviation for the eight quarterly periods before the crash. Data were then analyzed for dimensionality during the quarter containing the crash and for periods afterward. During the crash itself, dimensionality was low again (1.46), but higher that what was previously observed, because the linear interlocking was removed. The greatest chaosticity, 5.70, was observed for the 2-year time gap between December 1988 and December 1990, when the data series terminated. Both functions were iterated backward to determine where the attractor centers were located. The centers turned out to be limit cycles that were located in the same (z-transformed) price range. There may have been chaos in trading patterns over the 3 years following the crash, but market fundamentals have not really changed.

The general conclusion from the study was, essentially, that everyone was correct in a way. Zeeman's cusp structure was essentially true, but obfuscated by other market dynamics. Weintraub's revisions made it better. Dimensionality was low or high depending on whether the multiple basin matter was corrected or ignored.

Of further importance, however, was where or when chaos would be observed. A crash is not chaos. It is an orderly and near-linear drop from one basin to another, characteristic of smooth mappings in the neighborhood of an attractor. The chaos occurred as time moved beyond the crash point and traders were trying to isolate new strategies and market meanings. Underlying the crashing and banging and noise, however, were essentially no changes in basin locations or structures. The Securities and Exchange Commission, however, did introduce some changes after the last crash: If the Dow Jones index drops more than 100 points in the course of a trading day, all trading is suspended for an hour. If it happens twice too close together, computer program trading is suspended.

Ecological Economics

The multiple basin concept can be regarded as a metaphor for ecological systems. Each product–price–consumer basin is essentially an organism–food–environment basin. If someone or something stumbles on control parameters that indicate a dynamic key, the organism skips to another basin and may make some adaptations. The saturation of a product within a market is comparable to running out of food (prey, customers). The adaptive response is to find another market and to adapt the product.

The evolution and adaptation principles are central in new theory concerning the economics of the firm (Hansen & Samuelson, 1988; Selten, 1991).

Having sketched the general metaphor, the topic should turn next to the economics of natural resources. Because humans pillage the planet for economic reasons, economics—somewhere—holds the key to reversing and revising consumption trends to keep the renewable resources renewed, and to preserve the nonrenewable resources to meet the needs of future generations.

Rosser (1991) illustrated the dynamics of natural resource economics, for which open sea fishing was used as the primary example, as a cusp catastrophe model. The model was based on the predator–prey dynamic, such that fishing leaves a sustainable population of fish on the upper sheet of the surface, but overfishing leaves an unsustainable population on the bottom sheet. The management trick is to establish a fishing level that is close to the critical threshold, at which the harvest is maximal short of ruining the future supply.

In practice, it is difficult to calculate the critical threshold for each economically interesting species due to many unknowns concerning the species' breeding habits, food supply, and competition dynamics with other species. In the Great Lakes, where the trout are stocked, the critical threshold might be ascertained by "surfing," which is, in essence, a trial-and-error procedure; in the event of an error, the pond can be restocked. In open waters, however, errors could mean indefinite disaster. A conservative shift too far from the threshold may be ecologically viable but may conflict with fishing economics. Fishing economics, like so many other industries, profits through economies of scale. Open sea fishing is often done by huge factory ships that clean and process the fish between the time at the fishing hole and the return to the port. Each fishing stop dredges huge quantities of fish, such that the sustainable population is likely to be bankrupted through routine visits. Large nets with small holes dredge fish that are too young, thus compromising the viability of the next generation of fish. Endangered species are dredged up along with the target species indiscriminately. Careful fishing, irrespective of the scale, requires time and attention, and time is money. Too bad for the fish.

SUMMARY

The new theories of evolution not only provide improved explanations for biological phenomena, but also extend to social developmental phenomena. A species adaptation can be fast as well as slow, and adaptations are as much a result of learning and behavior as they are of biological mutation and genetic mixing. The development of interpersonal exchange relationships and social institutions can explained from evolutionary dynamics, which are in turn explained by one or another aspect of NDS theory.

Relationships, cultures, and social institutions sustain or dissolve on the basis of two dynamics: that of cooperation, and that of competition through defection. Furthermore, it would appear that a group might have a competitive edge, relative to its general ability to survive, if its cooperation skills were developed. Studies of gaming strategies are often directed toward understanding how, and under what conditions, cooperative behaviors are going to spontaneously occur and sustain. The maintenance of cooperative strategies within a group appears to be the result of a nonlinear interaction between group size and diversity within the group.

The development of large-scale social structures such as cities and metropolitan regions can be explained to a point as end results of large-scale operation efforts. The issues become more complex, however, because the dynamics involve a new interplay between agglomeration and deglomeration, which is apparent from the development of agrarian communities into cities, and cities back into agrarian communities. Alternatively, cities form networks with other large cities through long-distance trading. Population migrations are the next likely result of yet another set of dynamics that explains migrations between cities and expansions of cities into suburban communities.

In addition to spatial population dynamics, there are yet other dynamics for birth and death trends. The final two sections of the chapter show that birth and survival dynamics can be viewed as analogies to the dynamics that describe the availability of skills needed to make a qualified workforce. Personnel selection is thus a form of "unnatural selection" process, and industrial training can be viewed as system for facilitating adaptation. Selection and training work together as controllers for instabilities in the supplies of human resources. It was shown through simulation that a selection and training strategy that was used successfully in the past may prove disastrous under some conditions of skills shortages. A complex strategy of allocating priorities toward selection or training is probably required to cope with unstable sources of skill supply. A modicum of long-range planning could seriously reduce the instabilities an organization experiences. Reactive strategies of management, "fire-fighting strategies," and short temporal term views of situations appear to excite instability, which could be desirable or not desirable, depending on what one wants to accomplish.

The economics applications began in one region of endeavor and crossed into the evolutionary subject matter. Securities markets are particularly interesting because they represent a microcosm of a broad range of real economic activities. There has been substantial debate regarding whether there is true chaos in commodities markets, but the foregoing research shows that both the pro and con positions have validity. A multiple basin effect appears to exert an apparently linear influence over an array of contiguous chaotic basin. Depending on how one defines the data analysis, either the broad effect or the local chaos will be dominant.

Finally, the economics of natural resource management purports to play havoc with the continuation of species. As food and other resource supplies dwindle unwittingly into extinction, economic and social instabilities become more likely. The next three chapters develop this theme, beginning with the study of creativity (chapter 10), and following with organization development (chapter 11), then political catastrophes and chaos, and issues in global economic development (chapter 12).

10

*Innovation, Creativity,
and Complexity*

It is possible to fill several pages with all the definitions of creativity that have been proposed over the years (Barron, 1988; Taylor, 1988). The definitions all appear to have similar elements in common: original ideas that have rarely been expressed before, integration of ideas into a unique synthesis, looking at problems in entirely new ways, discovery of entirely new problems, imagining a wide range of possible solutions to a problem or avenues to a solution, improvements over preexisting solutions if any had existed, and ultimately the feasibility and operational success of a particular solution. Simonton's (1988) definition is my personal favorite because of its use of NDS concepts: Creative solutions "reduce mental 'entropy' by joining configurations together into more comprehensive hierarchical formations," and the human intellect is programmed to self-organize its cognitions and emotions accordingly (p. 393).

The idea of a "solution" or "feasibility" take on different complexions depending on whether one is concerned with creativity in the arts, science, business, or social policy making. Science has evolved a rigid protocol for verification of theoretical ideas, which includes concepts such as statistical significance, goodness of fit or effect size, intensity, and extensiveness. True, those standards are often regarded as goals rather than characteristics of everything ever done.

In business, the solution often takes the form of "bottom line" issues such as revenue produced, litigation averted, or market share gained. As discussed in chapter 5, however, the level of objectivity one might observe in business conclusions may be deficient, but that is a different matter. Yet another paradox in objectivity is the choice that is often made between signs of success in the short term for one course of action and signs of success in the long term for other courses of action.

In the policymaking sector, the feedback loops are notoriously slow, as are the processes of perceiving the problem and suggesting some solutions. The bottom line, at least in some societies, is the vote, which means that, in the short term, the solutions do not have to work, they only have to look good. In the long term, however, the constituencies eventually figure out that their problems are only getting worse. Although political processes are not covered until chapter 12, it is useful to point out here that political systems need to develop creativity just as the other systems do.

Creativity has long been recognized as a vital resource for individual and collective survival, cultural development, and economic progress. Creativity research has thus centered on individual differences, group processes, and organizational and societal concerns; the conventional or pre-nonlinear approaches to the study of creativity are summarized in the first section of this chapter. The NDS perspectives on creativity cover the same wide range of territory and are presented in the next section. Some of the evolutionary dynamics that were covered in Chapter 9 have been incorporated into the current thinking on creative processes.

The third section builds on the recent NDS work to develop a high-dimensional mushroom catastrophe model for creative output. The mushroom structure is observed in creative output data through the curiously shaped frequency distribution associated with the mushroom catastrophe model (chapters 3 and 7). Thus, an interesting analogy can be drawn between creativity and accidents. In chapter 11 the mushroom catastrophe model is adapted further to a group problem-solving situation and accompanied by empirical tests of the model's validity.

The fourth section is a report of a new study in which nonlinear dynamics in a group problem-solving process was examined. The menu of constructs includes the role of feedback loops in a self-organization process, bifurcation, and instability. It was hypothesized that the change in creative output for a group member from one point in time to the next would follow a logistic map function where input from other group members and individual differences would act as bifurcation variables. The results of the study, which involved actual problem solving by 16 social scientists, substantiated the core dynamic concepts suggested by current nonlinear theory.

In the course of composing this chapter it was necessary to draw a line between creative problem solving in groups and some of the broader aspects of group dynamics, and between the relationships that exist between creativity in management and the broader aspects of NDS and management. Those broader issues are reserved for chapter 11.

CONVENTIONAL THEORY

During the last 20 years, approximately 3000 journal articles and several hundred books have been published on some aspect of creativity. It would be impossible to review all of them in such a short space, so the following summary is necessarily confined to the major ideas in the field, particularly those that affect the NDS models. Topics are divided by level of system complexity, and cover the individual, group, organizational, and societal levels of analysis.

Individual Differences

The following work on individual differences is segmented into cognitive, personality, and style issues. The topics are centered around the measurement of creativity, where much of the pertinent theoretical contributions has occurred.

Cognitive Concepts. Perhaps the largest single breakthrough in the study of mental abilities related to creativity was Guilford's discovery of the difference between convergent and divergent thinking in the early 1950s (Guilford, 1967). Conventional measures of intelligence (in the sense of IQ) typically measure *convergent* thinking, where "smart" means coming up with the correct solution (one best answer) to a problem, which could involve word definitions, logical deductive reasoning, numerical calculations, memory for long spans of senseless digits, assembling puzzle pieces, transcribing symbols from one system of notation to another, matching complex graphic figures, displaying common knowledge about the world, and similar exercises. *Divergent* thinking, on the other hand, is the set of abilities for generating many possible solutions to a problem, and most often takes the form of rearranging objects into many possible categorical schemes (*semantic fluency*), listing many possible adjectives for the cue noun (*ideational fluency*), and thinking up original uses for common objects (*originality*). Divergent thinking is also implicit in the ability to look at a hypothetical sociotechnical situation and imagine many possible consequences that would result if that situation were true (Guilford & Guilford, 1980). Substantial research has confirmed that convergent and divergent thinking are distinct forms of thought processes, such that ordinary intelligence is necessary but not sufficient for creative thought (Wallach & Wing, 1969).

There has been some debate as to whether creativity is a consistent outcome of divergent thinking ability or whether creative ability is situationally specific. The low and often nonsignificant correlations between divergent thinking skills and other indices of creative behavior (self-reports, judgments of creative work by so-called experts) that many researchers have reported has have been interpreted as support for the situational specificity view (Baer, 1993; Hocevar, 1981; Storfer, 1990). Recent work has shown, however, that measures of divergent thinking ability are correlated with creative output in seven out of eight different domains studied: visual arts, music, literature, science and engineering, business ventures, apparel design, and video and photography (Guastello et al., 1992; theater was the exceptional case, probably due to low involvement by the sample of undergraduates in that study). Furthermore, when measures of creative output in all the above domains, and collected across a wide sample of undergraduates and professionals in science and art, music, were factor analyzed, two correlated factors emerged. One factor contained all the arts, and the other contained science and business; the correlation between factors was .32 (Guastello & Shissler, 1994). The results of the study showed that people who make creative contributions in one domain often make creative contributions in other domains as well. Thus the situational specificity view can be comfortably refuted.

It should be noted that, in spite of the growing support for the generalizability of divergent thinking measures, there are some aspects of creativity that they do not measure, such as sensitivity to interesting problems, and the ability to reframe a problem in another fashion (Barron, 1988). Additionally, the commonality between creative output factors may be a result of more than common mental abilities. Personality and other factors can also be responsible, and are considered next.

Personality. The pertinent literature on personality and creativity centers around the trait theories of personality, which are distinct from psychodynamic and behavioral traditions. The psychodynamic approach to personality is primarily associated with the work of Freud and Jung, and is replete with thermodynamic metaphor. Unfortunately, an exposition of the relationships between those theories and NDS is beyond the scope of this book, but fortunately, Abraham et al. (1990) have covered the subject in detail. The behavioral approach is rooted in the learning theories covered in chapter 5.

A trait is a proclivity to act in a certain, consistent way, given a wide range of real-world circumstances. Behavior in any specific circumstance is going to be a result of the interaction between a person's traits and specific environmental circumstances. The English language contains several thousand words that can be used to describe a person. By confining one's focus to adjectives and eliminating near-duplicates and archaic words, the lexicon of trait words can be reduced to approximately 400, which personality research and factor analysis boil down further into 16 bipolar traits (Allport, 1937; Cattell et al., 1970), all of which pertain to the normal-range (as opposed to abnormal) personality. The 16 traits can be aggregated further into five second-order factors, four of which form axes of Jung's popular theory of psychological types (Conn & Rieke, 1994).

The 16-factor taxonomy of traits has been especially useful in the study of the personalities of creative professionals in art and science. It appears that all such creative people share a common personality profile. They are aloof rather than outgoing, abstract rather than concrete thinkers, dominant or assertive, serious as opposed to cheerful, nonconforming, socially bold rather than timid, sensitive, imaginative, experimentative and open-minded, and self-sufficient in that they would rather work alone rather than in groups (Cattell & Drevdahl, 1955; Cattell et al., 1970; Csikzentmihalyi & Getzels, 1973). The prototype profile was replicated 20 years later (Guastello & Shissler, 1994). Further analysis with an expanded sample containing more popular, rather than classical or fine, artists showed that contemporary artists were less aloof and serious than they used to be, and people who make creative contributions in multiple domains are more self-controlled or perfectionistic than less diversified people (Rieke, Guastello, & Conn, 1994).

Motivation and Style. According to Sternberg and Lubart (1991), creativity is the result of not only divergent thinking ability and personality traits, but also motivation, style, and cultural and environmental circumstances. The concept of motivation applied to creative work is not substantially different from the forms of motivation implicated in the butterfly catastrophe model of motivation in organizations; considerable effort must be channeled into a successful creative work. The process is sustained by strong intrinsic motivation, in the sense of both interest in the task and achievement motivation (McClelland, 1961). Recently there have been some negative findings reported concerning achievement motivation and creative output, and some situational moderators are thought to explain why that might be true (Guastello, 1993e). Communication factors within an organization are further thought to have a much stronger impact on creative output than motivational factors (Monge, 1992).

The two-factor structure of creative output (Guastello & Shissler, 1994) would appear to refute the situational specificity view of creative talent. At the same time, creative professionals still make choices as to how to invest their efforts when they pick careers and creative projects. According to the investment theory of creativity (Sternberg & Lubart, 1991), creative people experience a motivation comparable to that of the commodities investor, which is to buy at a low price and sell at a high price. A creative person's interests are best served by choosing projects that suggest the highest levels of payoff. What constitutes a desirable payoff may be fame for some, fortune for others, the experience of a great achievement, or perhaps a personal axe to grind.

Creative style appears to be a combination of cognitive talents and personality characteristics. The two recently proposed taxonomies (Byrd, 1986; Sternberg & Lubart, 1991) of style would appear to inspire some thoughtful new research. Both emphasize the propensity to take risks as an important feature of successful styles. In Sternberg and Lubart's scheme, styles can be further characterized as legislative, judicial, or executive in nature; the style names are analogous to the branches of government. Legislative types focus their energies on idea generation. Judicial types place greater emphasis on critical thinking about ideas and their implications and sorting out the best examples. Executive types are concerned with transiting ideas from the generation stage to their realization. On the one hand, executives will initiate big ideas, which they turn over to others for further work. One the other, executives keep the work process moving and solve problems related to any barriers to completion that might exist.

Byrd's (1986) scheme incorporates some similar thoughts, but organizes eight styles on a two-dimensional grid. The two axes are motivation and concern for creative work, and risk-taking tendency. The innovators would score high on both axes. Dreamers would score high on motivation for creativity, but low on risk taking. Critics would score high on risk taking but low on motivation for creativity. In the intermediate zones are people who like to plan alternative courses of action but seldom actually do anything, those that prefer to work with others' ideas and to make them a practical success, and the modifiers who make small but perhaps useful improvements over existing ideas. Also interesting are the synthesizers (high motivation, moderate risk), who specialize in combining ideas from several sources. As one might anticipate, people who characterize themselves as innovators or synthesizers also report greater rates of creative output (Guastello, 1993e).

Group Dynamics

The most widely shared perspective on creativity in groups centers around the brainstorming session (Osborn, 1953). The group, which is often composted of 6 to 10 people, proceeds through a sequence of stages in its quest for creative solutions to shared problems. The people begin by immersing themselves in the subject matter to become familiar with all the known ideas that could possibly be of value. Next, they generate ideas in a free-form discussion. At this stage it is essential for the group work in a positive atmosphere; discussants should encourage each other to talk and refrain from criticizing one another's ideas.

The third stage is an incubation stage where nothing appears to happen. Group members may break up into smaller groups or wander off individually for a while, or do or talk about other things. Something mysterious takes place in their minds, somehow, we hope, during that period. The result is a rash of insights that are expressed when the group reconvenes. During the second session, the goal is to pare down the inventory of ideas to the most workable courses of action. Participants are encouraged to build on each other's contributions and to combine ideas. Finally there are the elaborations, whistles and bells, and action plan, and feedback concerning the success of the solution.

The brainstorming process just described can apply equally well to individuals. Individual creative thinking appears to follow approximately the same pattern of immersion, idea generation, incubation, reformulation, and elaboration. They may talk to other people at different stages of the process. They may make several iterations through the process before they call the job finished. Major units of progress often occur suddenly, but not every act of insight is necessarily creative, and some creative works are not-so-suddenly created.

Recently there has been some expressed concern for the study of creative problem solving in groups (Gersick, 1988; van de Ven & Rogers, 1988). It appears that the entire structure of the group can evolve over repeated meetings, but identifiable patterns of development are still in their formative stages. One interesting view is that creativity is inherently a group or community process, in spite of the Western emphasis on individual effort. Modern Japanese schools now teach creativity and utilize group interaction techniques almost exclusively (Hunsaker, 1992). At the same time, some personality traits that are often associated with creative people predispose them not to participate in groups. The creatives are historically aloof or nonparticipative (16PF Factor A−). They prefer their own solutions to problems (16PF Factor Q2+), rather than to go along with the group's preferences.

Organizational Theory

The contemporary concerns with creativity at the organizational level of analysis center on two themes: the management of creativity, and creative management. The former concerns the best management strategies for a leader of a group of creative professionals, such as might be found in a research and development laboratory. The latter concerns the role of creativity in any sort of management objective.

Management of Innovation. The social climate that is most conducive to successful innovation is characterized by a positive emotional state, a concern for creativity, toleration of individual differences, a willingness to take risks, and support for half-baked ideas with goal of fully baking some of them (Isen et al., 1987; Pinchot, 1985; Siegel & Kaemerer, 1978). Small and growing firms are best served by moderate to large technological innovations combined with technical excellence to keep their competitive edge. Larger, more established organizations tend to concentrate on less dramatic modifications or product developments, in which the risks are smaller and the payoffs are often larger (Baba & Ziegler, 1985).

The classic managerial personality profile is similar to that of the creative person in several respects but substantially different in others. The two types are similar in that they are both dominant, social bold, and intelligent. They are different in that the typical manager is more rule-oriented, insensitive, pragmatic as opposed to imaginative, traditional or conservative, and prefers to work in groups (Cattell et al., 1970). There is thus plenty of opportunity to lock horns. According to Byrd (1986), an effective strategy for managers of creative units would involve knowing something about the creative styles of the group members. Modifiers and synthesizers are often the easiest for managers to get along with: They produce useful material but they are not too scary. Dreamers and copycats present performance problems and need to be motivated on the one hand and encouraged to take greater risks. Critics can be annoying and seldom have a better solution than the ones they criticize. Innovators are the most perplexing because they can divert substantial resources into projects that would require huge investments, are irregular about the timing of the delivery of their ideas, and put aside work requests for modest but necessary tasks.

Creative Management. The disparity between the classic profiles of managers and creative people has been narrowing somewhat in recent years. For instance, one variant on the managerial profile contains high scores on imagination and openness to experience. Such a person is likely to be a visionary-type manager (discussed later), or be the person most likely to acquire the greatest inventory of resources for a problem-solving team (Rieke et al., 1994). Furthermore, about 27% of managers would score high on both leadership potential (composite of personality trait scores) and creative potential, although only 7% would score high on both leadership potential and creative output.

By some ways of thinking, creative management should be the norm, not the special case. According to Bennis (1988), leaders of all types need to delegate more of their routine work to free up more time for creative thinking, vision, and direction of the whole organization or work unit. Unfortunately, those same leaders are often surrounded by an unconscious conspiracy on the part of the leader's administrative staff, society, and other vested interests to drown the leader in minutiae and thereby stifle any changes that would be made.

According to Sashkin (1984), leaders should gravitate to a visionary leadership style, which consists of three main components. The first is the ability to generate a clear, feasible, detailed, and imaginative vision for the organization and its future directions. The second is the communication of that vision to others in a form that motivates them to become involved with the vision. The third is to develop an organizational culture around that vision, the key feature of which is to allow the constituents to explore the vision in their own way and to make it their own through the decisions and programs they carry out. Although both versions of creative leadership have their enchanting sides, the lessons of NDS, considered in this chapter and in chapter 12, strongly suggest that vision is often blind or antithetical to real strategic management.

Societal Level

Two provocative societal viewpoints on creativity are considered next. One explains the origins of the creative personality as we now know it. The other concerns society's paradoxical stance toward innovation.

Creativity and Culture. Csikzentmihalyi and Getzels (1973) speculated that the distinguishing traits of creative people are the result of cultural norms. In ancient Egypt, according to their thesis, creativity in the arts was actively discouraged. Artists who continued to innovate (displayed imagination) would have needed to remove themselves from the rest of society, and hence the aloof, serious, and self-sufficiency characteristics were reinforced. They would have had to maintain links with their most open-minded contemporaries, who would not have been particularly upset by their disregard for societal norms. Artists of the early Renaissance mingled freely though society, but the push in the later period for continued creativity necessitated a social withdrawal for purposes of original thinking and not becoming unduly influenced by the trendiness of others. I should add further to the Renaissance story that there was a strong nonconformist theme in Galileo's work on the heliocentric universe. His challenge to socially approved dicta merited a down-home stake-burning, which was later commuted to a life sentence of house arrest (Zeeman, 1977).

In the 20th century, under the Stalin and Mao regimes of the Soviet Union and China, nonstatist works of literature and art were punishable. Thus innovative musicians such as Shostakovich had to give up 12-tone harmonic structure in favor of more conventional tonal structures that were more accessible to the masses. His innovative propensities resumed eventually in his *Tenth Symphony*, which more or less commemorated the death of Stalin. Statist art in China promoted a political agenda more deliberately, particularly in theater. Consider, for instance, now-classic operas such as *Red Guard for Women* and *The Red Lantern*, and a song that was popular about 15 years ago, *Oh How I Love to Carry Manure Up the Hill to the Collective!*

If the forces that shape creative behavior are cultural in origin, they appear to start working early in life. Torrance (1988) reported that sixth graders and military decision makers share the same strategies for stifling creative members of their groups: requiring the most creative person to work alone, pressuring that individual to leave the group, and appointing the most creative person in the group as leader.

Snow (1959) observed that there was evidence of two separate cultures among the creative professions in Britain in the 1950s. Scientists were unfamiliar with works of contemporary literature and art, although their interest in music was noted as an exception to that rule. Socially, little patience was expressed with each other's values—the scientists' pragmatism and the literary antisocial forms of self-expression.

According to Snow (1959), the schism between the artistic and scientific communities started with the industrial revolution, which was not developed by the educated community but by uneducated, although talented, pragmatists. These industrialists eventually realized that the continued propagation of wealth required the scientific education of subsequent generations. The industrial revolution represented a source of hope to the proletariat, who would have otherwise been destined to several more generations of low-technology agricultural labor. British scientists by 1959 had originated, more often than not, from proletariat backgrounds.

If one takes a more global view of 20th century movements in science and art, however, the relationship between science and art evolved as something more complex than mutual disinterest. The historical period 1890–1910 was a peak period of innovation as denoted by the record number of patents assigned by the U.S. Patent Office (McClelland, 1961). Some of the new inventions had serious implications for the arts. Photography and machine tools could fill the demand for representational works of painting and sculpture. Recorded music and cinema encroached on the domain of musical performance and theater, or provided new outlets for them, depending on one's point of view. Reacting to these innovations, art movements of the same period became less representational, and progressed through periods of "impressionism," "cubism," "dada," and "surrealism." These styles had counterparts in literature and music. Science fiction emerged as literature's way of leading science and industry.

The 1950s brought an artistic and scientific renaissance characterized by a postwar economic boom, a scientific race for space with the Soviet

Union, and a literary movement known as the "Beat Generation" (Kerouac, 1958). The Beat Generation encompassed novels, poetry, theater and jazz music. It was antiestablishment in its sentiments, as was its counterpart psychedelic movement a decade later. The latter occurred against a backdrop of social upheaval that was loosely centered around the Vietnam War.

The 1970s were characterized by a counterpart scientific movement as well, typified by the computer hackers (Turkle, 1984), whose culture centered around the community of users on a mainframe computer system. Their favorite arts were the music of Bach and science fiction novels. Their work reflected an interplay between science fiction and science fact; in their programs they constructed alternative realities based on any rules of order the programmer wished to entertain. For the arts, they developed music-writing and graphic programs that were new tools for the artists and musicians. Hackers had their own concepts of "elegant" and "beautiful" that influenced the development of their programs. Many large corporations eventually paid remarkable salaries to unconventional people who showed up to their offices perhaps once a week, and over whom they had little control, in order to access the new technologies.

Important realignments took place among science, business, and art. Until the early 20th century, business led science for its own interests. Art and business were largely divorced of each other until certain technologies became available that allowed for the mass production and mass marketing of artworks in the form of recordings, lithographs, and cinema. Art first led science in innovative thinking by reconceptualizing art, and later by accessing scientific innovations. The antiestablishmentarianism of the 1950s and 1960s caused a realignment of the interests in scientists and artists that has resulted in an economy composed of the innovative fringe, the establishment center, and market individualists who form coalitions with members of the fringe and the center.

Little Equilibria Mean a Lot. Haustein (1981) analyzed the forces that contributed to the history of innovation, mostly industrial, in East Germany. Two points emerged that are germane to the discussions at hand. First, the industrial innovations were marked by irregular patterns of growth. Innovative periods, when they occurred, were accompanied by a broader societal policy that supported further developments in education. Innovative periods were separated by times of little change when, presumably, the economy was assimilating the progress of the innovative period.

Baba and Ziegler (1985) noted similar patterns of change in U.S. industry, and in cultural (nonindustrial) change as well; they labeled the pattern *punctuated equilibrium* theory. The patterns of progress and stability can be further characterized by an interesting tension that appears to exist between the desire for creative production and the social progress it often entails and desire to prevent change or to minimize its impact. In other words, if society is not looking for something new, something new can be regarded as an annoyance. That brings us to Haustein's second point.

The size of an innovation and the size of the economic impact derived from it appear to be inversely related. Haustein (1981) scaled innovations on the basis of the industrial requirements to implement the novelty. At the small end of the spectrum, the new idea could be implemented with existing machinery, or with only small modifications of same. As ideas became larger, additional supplementary equipment and bureaucracy were needed to manage them. At the large end of the spectrum, entire new factories and equipment had to be designed to implement the new idea. Implementation costs were fairly well correlated with the scope of the idea. Thus big ideas, ironically, have small near-term benefit.

The lesson of Haustein's analysis is that it is often more profitable for an organization to strategically position itself as "Number Two" on the industrial playing field. Organization Number One develops an innovative new product from a set of successful and less viable ideas that could have taken any number of years to produce. It develops the new market for the product through extensive customer surveys, trade show exhibitions, and advertising. If the product is a success in the marketplace, Number Two jumps in and builds essentially the same product, but smaller and more cheaply. The "knock-off" process is formulaic and, compared to the agenda that faced Number One, requires only small amounts of creativity and risk.

DYNAMICAL PERSPECTIVES

Nonlinear dynamical systems theory has entered theories of creativity in several ways, which are reported next. The applications of NDS to creativity are once again ordered from the individual to the societal level of system complexity.

Cusp Models for Insight

A number of possible outcomes can occur when people try to solve original and difficult problems. They can stick with the problem and solve it, stick with the problem but not solve it, or escape from the situation. What is difficult for one person is not necessarily difficult for another, particular if one problem solver has encountered a similar problem before.

Boles (1990) used a pair of cusp catastrophe models to explain this range of outcomes. The unfolded region of the cusp manifold, which signifies discontinuous change, was used to distinguish between the sudden insight often associated with creative problem solving and traditional thinking; the latter takes place at the smooth side of the cusp response surface.

Here I should express a cautionary note that creative thinking and insight are not synonymous, although they often occur together. Not every insight is creative. Also, a routine problem for a creative person may have been creative at one time but no longer so, whereas the same problem may present a fresh challenge to another's creativity. The exposition is, nonetheless, provocative with the foregoing advisements in mind.

The first of two cusp models (Fig. 10.1, lower cusp) distinguishes between routine and creative problem solving in the class of situations where the problem is inescapable. Trajectory $a'-b'$ represents the smooth transition from an unsolved problem to a solved problem using algorithmic thought routines with all the needed data available. Trajectory $c'-d'$ represents a successful creative solution, which occurs when the problem solver's repertoire of responses and abilities are moderately high or high and the problem difficulty is also high. The limit cycles drawn at e' and f' represent fixated responding, which is likely to occur when the problem is not seen as relevant but is nonetheless inescapable.

A note should be interjected here: There is only one stable attractor on the lower sheet of the cusp, although it could very well be a limit cycle. The limit cycle is analogous to the colloquial expression "spinning one's wheels" when referring to repeated attempts at action that go nowhere.

The upper cusp in Fig. 10.1 covers the set of situations where the problem is escapable, meaning that the problem solver is at liberty to walk away from the problem and to choose another task. Here the two control parameters are frustration level and perceived importance of the problem. For frustrating situations that are not deemed to be especially important, the problem solver may gradually withdraw from the activity (trajectory $a-b$), sometimes after repeated attempts to solve the problem in the case of moderately important situations (*sharp escape*, $c-d$). The hysteresis pattern ($e-f-g-h$) is a repeated sharp escape reflecting repeated attempts at solution that meet with failure; this pattern suggests that the problem solver can recover from frustration, continues to work on the problem because of its importance, and has not received such a negative reinforcement from failure as to promote a permanent escape from the problem. Permanent escape would be characterized by an attractor on the upper sheet of the response surface.

Finally, Boles (1990) suggested that the two cusp models should be more properly visualized as a mushroom catastrophe, but modeling tech-

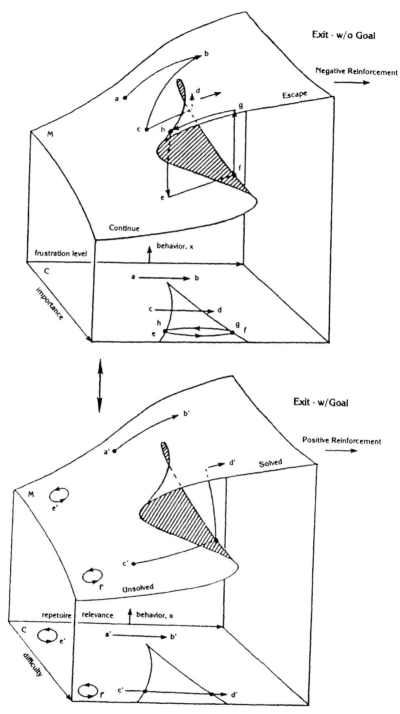

FIG. 10.1. Cusp models for insight. From Boles (1990). Reprinted with permission.

niques for the complex umbilic structure were not sufficiently developed. The next two sections show evidence that there is a mushroom structure underlying creative processes, but perhaps not in the form that Boles suggested. First of all, the mushroom contains a pair of stable states on one behavioral dimension—so far so good—but a stable–unstable combination on the second behavioral dimension. In the latter case I would suggest that the escape from the problem situation is the unstable outcome, because the problem solver, in principle, goes away and does not return. That would preclude a hysteresis mechanism that is shown on the upper cusp in Fig. 10.1, and would refine the hysteresis event as an outcome of what is now the lower cusp model.

A second problem with characterizing the two cusps as a mushroom is that the mushroom requires four control parameters, and the model contains five: two on each cusp, and one for the escapable–nonescapable distinction. My choice of an improvement would be to lose that distinction. Problems are escapable by simply not working on them (lower sheet, lower cusp). Not applying oneself to the problem may be maladaptive, but the outcome for all practical purposes is not different from repeated earnest attempts that fail.

Chance-Configuration Theory

According to Simonton (1988), there are four important aspects to creative work: the person, the product, the process, and persuasion. *Person* refers to the individual differences, already discussed at length. The *product* is the tangible result of one's work, such as a research paper, book, piece of music, sculpture, and so on. Nonlinear dynamics are intrinsic to the process and successful persuasion and form the core of the theory.

The dynamics of the creative process are analogous to those observed in natural variation and natural selection in Darwinian evolution. Creativity involves the successful capitalization on chance occurrences. According to Campbell (1960), successful creative products are closely linked to the ability to generate a large number of ideas. Ideas are configurations containing an even larger number of mental elements. Large numbers of mental elements are the result of an enriched home environment in a person's formative years and an enriched professional environment later on.

Self-organization occurs when the mental elements arrange themselves in configurations that are metaphorical to other ideas. Here striking similarities are observed between events that had hitherto been thought to be unrelated (Simonton, 1988). Once the problem solver has latched onto a cogent metaphor, additional idea elements are released to embellish the new concept. A subtle bifurcation appears to take place once self-organization occurs that separates ideas from those that are consistent with the metaphor and those that remain outside it.

Timing plays a crucial role in the communication and acceptance of an idea. Each member of the community must have a repertoire of shared mental elements. The community must be in a state of sufficient confusion (was Simonton thinking of *chaos* without saying so directly?) about a topic to make the new work worth the attention paid to it. The community must have reasonable consensus on the meanings of the symbols and idea elements. The thinker furthermore needs to translate the initial concept into a language readily understood by the community so that the community can "perform the reverse translation" (Simonton, 1988, p. 394–395).

When the innovation is too many steps ahead of its target audience or consumers, the strategic response is to cultivate taste, often by feeding the new idea to the public slowly and in pieces. Tastes mutate gradually when there is little deliberate attempt to modify them. A groping, trial-and-error, or learning by consuming strategy work efficiently when prices and product values are stable. When there is greater volatility (chaos) in price and value, consumption trends are more efficiently described by genetic algorithms; thus another echo of general evolution is taking place (McCain, 1992).

The use of NDS concepts in chance-configuration theory is literal, rather than figurative. Consider N as the number of mental elements giving rise to chance permutations that are precursory to successful products. If we assume that the elements are proportional to native mental abilities (divergent thinking, relevant personality traits), which are normally distributed, then the number of permutations e^N is definitely not normally distributed. Furthermore, if N is the number of contributions in a field, then about 50% of the contributions will be made by $N^{0.5}$ people, according to empirical evidence (Simonton, 1988). Thus the distribution of creative works per person is not normally distributed, but highly skewed with a long tail at the positive end. Functions of this type trace back to Lotka's (1926) work on population dynamics.

Productivity over a lifetime consists of two rates, ideation rate and elaboration rate, such that

$$p(t) = c \ (e^{-at} - e^{-bt})$$

where a is ideation rate, b is elaboration rate, and c is a function of a, b, and m, where m is lifetime creative potential (Simonton, 1989). Ideation and elaboration rates are germane to the field of specialization. Of additional interest is that the lifetime dynamics suggest that creative potential dissipates over a lifetime, but, because the rates of decay slow down considerably over time, a person in his or her final professional decade can produce as much as a person in the first decade of professional life.

Creativity in Strategic Management

Stacey (1992) appeared to agree with the visionary leadership theorist about the centrality of creativity in leadership. He arrived at sharply different conclusions, however, about the value of vision. This central thesis is that organizations exist in a turbulent and sometimes chaotic environment that is rife with instabilities. The organization that adapts successfully is one that can respond strategically to those instabilities. Successful strategic response requires free-flowing creative juices within the organization and a basic knowledge of NDS.

Creativity itself is conceptualized as a form of instability. A creative idea unleashed by one organization can upset a competitor's sense of homeostasis and complacency. Within an organization, the ideation process is chaotic, but output quantity and quality are affected by feedback channels. Copious feedback channels should extend among the problem solvers, the external environment, and up and down the management hierarchy. Feedback channels are, in effect, what produce the enriched professional environments that Campbell (1960) and Simonton (1988) wrote about.

Useful creative work could pop up at any time because of the chaotic nature of the idea generation process. Management should recognize that dynamic, go with the flow, and work to develop creative product when something of interest presents itself. In principle, therefore, every manager is a manager of an innovative unit. At the same time, however, management must call upon its problem-solving teams to respond swiftly and accurately to sudden environmental conditions. For the latter purpose, management needs to keep the creative forces in top running condition; feedback channels will not do much good if someone is not finding ways to use their contents.

Although visionary leadership may involve substantial creativity on the part of the leader, Stacey's (1992) problem with visionary leadership is precisely that visions stifle creativity in everyone else. A leader's plans for the organization's course of development may serve a valuable purpose initially, but a relentless implementation of that vision means a disregard for instabilities in the environment and a disregard for novel contribution from within the organization. Similarly, mission statements serve the purpose of keeping the status quo and do not allow a questioning of purpose.

The foregoing is not meant to encourage a fire-fighting approach to management. The fire-fighting approach is highly reactionary and abdicates the control over strategy to whatever the strongest sources of instability happen to be. Thus strategies are superior to either visions or fire fighting because there is both control and a mechanism for successfully modifying the strategy.

MUSHROOM CATASTROPHE DYNAMICS

Two lines of thinking have suggested that creative output could be a result of a mushroom catastrophe structure. Boles (1990) suggested that the two cusp models for creative output could be further organized into a parabolic umbilic model, and with a little twinking, the logic seemed to work. Lotka (1926) and Simonton (1988) observed that the distribution of creative output over people in a population is heavily skewed, with a long positive tail. Mushroom catastrophes have that characteristic but with additional detail.

Figure 10.2 is another example of the unusual skewed distribution for creative output. The measurement was the total creative output score on the Artistic and Scientific Activities Survey (ASAS; Guastello, 1991c). The ASAS was developed as a criterion in two recent studies (Guastello et al., 1992; Guastello & Shissler, 1994). It contains two types of items. The first type captures a rate of creative output. The items list possible artistic, scientific, or business activities, for which the subjects were to indicate whether they had engaged in any of those activities in the past 3 years. The scale ranged from 0 = not at all, to 4 = long-term commitment to that

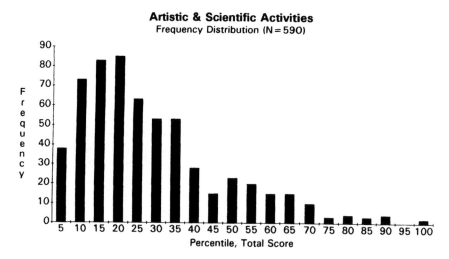

FIG. 10.2. Frequency distribution of creative output as measured by the Artistic and Scientific Activities Survey.

activity. The second types of item pertained to the publication of expressive work, and the scale ranged from 0 = not at all, to 4 = developing a career around that type of output.

The ASAS items are compiled into eight content domains and a total score. Total scores range from 0 to 84 (99th percentile), with a median of 22. The frequency distribution is skewed with a long positive tail. More importantly, the tail shows the blast–cascade–plateau–antimode–aftershock pattern associated with the mushroom catastrophe (chapter 7).

The factor analysis of ASAS scores showed that there were two underlying behavior factors, which were scientific and artistic output. The mushroom requires that there be an interaction between the two behaviors, and that interaction appeared to take the form of the correlation between the two factors. Not enough is known about ASAS data to say with assurance what qualitative variables contribute to the control parameters, but many of the theories discussed earlier suggest some clues: divergent thinking, personality, motivation (either to do creative work or the challenge levels of the applications), style, developmental, and environmental factors. Personality variables may be distributed over two or more control parameters.

Alternatively, the control parameters may be defined better in terms of feedback loops and relationships between the thinker and source of idea input. The topic requires further study before proposing a premature model.

CREATIVE PROBLEM SOLVING IN GROUPS

The following study investigated the role of feedback loops in creative production for a group of problem solvers. The goals were to asses the complexity of a nonlinear dynamic processes in creative output, particularly the relative amounts of stability and instability in the ideation process. The study also provided an opportunity to assess the relative contribution of feedback loops within a group and individual differences. It was also possible to identify mushroom probability density functions (pdfs) for output at both the individual and collective levels of analysis. Some plausible dynamic processes are discussed next, followed by some systematic observations of real problem solvers who communicated with each other over a computer system.

Creativity plays a role in Stacey's (1992) organizational theory in two ways. First, the organization needs to respond to sudden and unusual circumstances and instabilities in their environments. The stage must be set for creative and unusual response to emerge as soon as they are needed. When the organization is capable of responding adaptively, rather than with inertia, then we can say that *chaos causes creativity*.

The second role of creativity is in the spontaneous generation of ideas that could involve new business initiatives for the organization. Typically, spontaneous new ideas generate instabilities in the organization as they involve deviations from prior plans and redirection of energies from management's preset goals. It is a common, although unenlightened, management response to brush off new ideas as amusements or annoyances, but it is exactly this spontaneous process that eventually produces some very profitable disruptions. In that sense, we can say that *creativity causes chaos*. Societal trends show oscillations in innovative explosion and relative quietude. Imagine next that we have a system composed of three innovating sources, which could be organizations, cities, or groups. Zhang (1991) showed that a system consisting of three or more interacting oscillating innovation sources becomes chaotic in its diffusion of innovation from one source or site to another.

"Chaos" in reference to creativity is more than a handy metaphor. According to chance-configuration theory (Campbell, 1960; Simonton, 1988), creative products are the result of a random idea generation process. Greater quantities of ideas are generated from enriched personal and professional environments. Ideas recombine into configurations (self-organization) as part of the ideation process, where the creative thinker latches onto a new configuration and explores it as a solution to a problem. Once again, *chaos causes creativity*.

The enriched environment is just another example of the feedback channels that Stacey (1992) claimed as essential to successful creative efforts. Such channels run between the environment and problem solvers, among the problem solvers, and back and forth with other members of the organization who are in a position to do something about the idea.

The feedback channels that have been discussed to this point have all been positive feedback channels, meaning that as they become more frequent or more operative in some way, the ideation and self-organization processes are accelerated. There is also a negative feedback loop, which Greeley (1986) called the *bumper effect dynamic*. The bumper dynamic alters the problem solver if the line of thought is straying from its goal, or is otherwise not working. Apparently, many great thinkers in the past few centuries have reported the existence of such a mechanism operating in their thoughts and rooted to their aesthetic values. Some thinkers may report clear internal messages about the suitability of an end product, whereas others may experience a struggle with themselves over the judgment. Some thinkers have a strong feeling of physical effort when they have resolved the bumper dynamic conflict during the creative process, but others have not.

It may be difficult to prove the existence of a deep intrapsychic struggle, such as the bumper effect dynamic, that could take on so many forms.

It may be possible to observe groups of thinkers interacting, however. Living systems theory would suggest that if the bumper effect dynamic is real at the individual level of a system, there should be a group-level version of it as well. The signs, nonetheless, point to the importance of feedback channels in creative work.

An issue that emerges from the various NDS perspectives on creativity entertained so far is whether the creative process is dominated by stability or instability. Boles' (1990) cusp catastrophe models posited two sets of stable states: not solving the problem and solving it, and whether the problem solver continues working or escapes the problem. Further consideration of the ideas suggested that the escape result is an unstable outcome. Simonton (1988) characterized the ideation process as chaos-like at first, followed by self-organization when a new configuration makes a suitable metaphor for solving the problem.

The mushroom catastrophe model suggests that both stabilities and instabilities are at play, and that the system has a relatively high dimensionality (codimension six). High dimensionality is an important feature from a theoretical vantage point. According to the general (meta)theory and its application thus far, chaos leads to self-organization, and a creative self-organized system engenders more instability. It would follow that creative problem-solving groups are systems at the edge of chaos.

Actual control parameters for the mushroom model are not truly known, but numerous candidate variables have been suggested: divergent thinking, personality trait, style, motivation, where the latter could involve the problem solver's interest in the problem, personal motivation to do creative work, or reinforcement experience. Alternatively, control parameters could be defined in terms of feedback loops, their sources, and relative strengths.

Method

Participants in the study of group problem solving were 16 social scientists who were members of a professional organization that supported an electronic bulletin board (EBB) system. The acronym EBB is used here to refer generically to bulletin board, e-mail, or other specialized conferencing software. Their group discussions pertained to problems in general systems theories and their application. Although much is unknown about the participants, they all held advanced degrees and were employed as professors, consultants, and executives in the private and public sectors.

The discussions all began with an opening statement of the problem, from which the discussants were allowed to jump into the discussions at any time they chose and to respond in any way they chose with respect to content and length of response. Three intact discussions (the most recently completed discussions at the time of initiating the study) were studied, containing a total of 171 responses. Eleven of the 16 discussants participated in two or more discussions. The EBB software automatically recorded the date, time, and verbatim transcript of the participants' responses along with their names.

The dependent measure for the study was the number of lines of test for each response. A line was 60 characters wide. Partially complete lines at the end of paragraphs were counted as one line. Blank lines, signature lines (which were superfluous), and lines containing direct address only ("Joe, . . .") were not counted.

Two control parameters were studied: *cumulative elapsed response* and *personal response style*. Cumulative elapsed response was the total number of lines from all participants that intervened between two consecutive responses by a particular person. In the case of a person's first response in a discussion, cumulative elapsed response was the sum of all lines generated, including the moderator's statement, that elapsed before that person jumped into the discussion. Cumulative elapsed response was thus regarded as the total amount of feedback generated from the group.

A casual inspection of the raw data showed that cumulative elapsed response was itself quasi-periodic. If someone initiated an idea that attracted much attention, or triggered a self-organization process in the others somehow, the response was followed by a rash of elaborations and additional ideas from the group. Thus cumulative elapsed response between two consecutive responses by that initiator would be large. The "rash" reactions were interspersed with short questions requesting elaboration.

Cumulative elapsed response was hypothesized to function as a bifurcation effect, under the thinking that a greater number of transpiring ideas from the group at large would trigger a greater number of subsequent ideas from any one person. An increasing cumulative response would signify that the discussion was gaining momentum, such as would be the case if more people joined in. (EBB records showed that two to three times as many people monitored the discussions as participated in them directly.)

Personal response style was represented by the average response length contributed by a person whenever that person did respond. It was, in a sense, a "garbage can" variable that took into account individual verbosity, interest or preparedness for the topic, and available time or motivation to follow and to participate in the discussions. It was interpreted as a measure of effective individual involvement. Personal response style was also hypothesized to function as a bifurcation variable under the thinking that highly involved people would put forth a lot of effort and contribute more resource to the group than less involved people and would thus propel the discussion in the same way as cumulative elapsed response.

Structural Model

The progress of the group discussions was characterized as a logic map quadratic structure. Thus the emphasis was on the instabilities inherent in the ideation process. The model was further developed in a two-stage procedure. The Stage 1 hypothesis was:

$$\Delta z = B_0 + B_1 C z_1 + B_2 C z_1^2 \tag{1}$$

where z was response length corrected for location and scale, and C was cumulative elapsed response. Difference scores were taken over two consecutive responses from a particular person. For a person's initial response to a discussion, $z_1 = 0$. The State 2 hypothesis was:

$$\Delta z = B_0 + B_1 C z_1 + B_2 C z_1^2 + B_3 P z_1 + B_4 P z_1 \tag{2}$$

where P was personal response style. The terms C and P were also corrected for location and scale. The R^2 coefficients for Equations 1 and 2 were compared against those obtained for the respective linear difference models,

$$\Delta y = B_0 + B_1 C \tag{3}$$

$$\Delta y = B_0 + B_1 C + B_2 P \tag{4}$$

and linear pre–post models,

$$y_2 = B_0 + B_1 y_1 + B_2 C \tag{5}$$

$$y_2 = B_0 + B_1 y_1 + B_2 C + B_3 P \tag{6}$$

Results

The frequency distribution for response length for all 171 responses appears in Fig. 10.3. The distribution showed the characteristic mushroom structure with the blast occurring at 0–10 lines, the cascade in the region of 14–45 lines, the plateau at 50–95 lines, the antimode at 100–170 lines, and the aftershock at 175 lines.

The frequency distribution for total responses generated by the 16 participants over the three discussions appears in Fig. 10.4. Once again the distribution shows the characteristic mushroom structure, but less precisely so because of the much smaller number of data points. The blast occurred in the interval of (up to) 50 lines per participant, the cascade at 100–250 lines, the plateau at 250–600 lines, the antimode between 600 and 800 lines, and the aftershock at (up to) 850 lines.

Mushroom-Catastrophic PDF for
Response Length (N = 171)

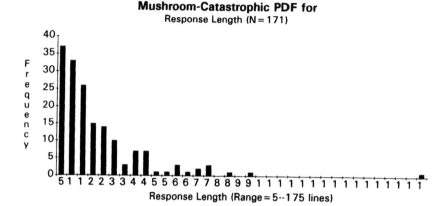

Response Length (Range = 5--175 lines)

FIG. 10.3. Frequency distribution of response length for 171 creative problem-solving responses in the EBB study.

Mushroom-Catastrophic PDF
Total Response per Participant

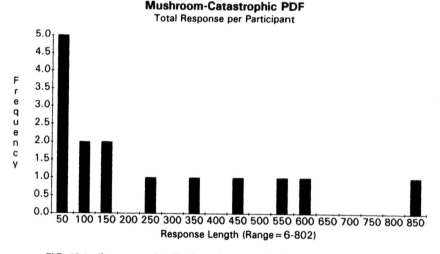

Response Length (Range = 6-802)

FIG. 10.4. Frequency distribution of response length for total responses generated by 16 participants in the EBB study.

Other descriptive statistics for the EBB variables are presented in Table 10.1. Ordinary analysis of variance showed that there were no significant differences on all but one of the measures across the three discussions. There was a small tendency for initial response in Discussion 2 to be longer than initial responses in the other discussions (previous response column, $p < .10$).

The regression results for the first stage of the structural analysis appear in Table 10.2. The nonlinear logistic model ($R^2 = .23$) was a substantially better fit for the data than either of the control models ($R^2 = .05, .06$). The

TABLE 10.1
Descriptive Statistics for EBB Variables

Discussion	Responses/ Person		Lines/ Response		Previous Response		Cumulative Elapsed	
	Mean	SD	Mean	SD	Mean	SD	Mean	SD
1	5.80	5.53	16.18	16.36	124.73	144.34	12.65	14.92
2	5.38	4.06	22.58	19.98	133.62	189.56	20.57	22.02
3	4.86	3.67	21.03	26.50	181.85	210.75	15.81	19.21
All	5.32	4.45	19.94	21.69	148.81	185.10	16.24	18.89

t-tests on both weights in the logistic model were significant. Thus it was possible to conclude that cumulative elapsed response had a bifurcating and destabilizing effect on creative output. The control-difference analysis showed, furthermore, that increase in response length by any person was significantly correlated with greater cumulative elapsed response. This result upheld the hypothesis that operating feedback channels enhance ideation.

The regression results for the second stage of the structural analysis appear in Table 10.3. The nonlinear logistic model improved markedly ($R^2 = .49$) with the introduction of the personal style variables, as did the pre–post control model ($R^2 = .22$). Significant weights were obtained for both personal response style variables. Some collinearity was observed between the C and P variables.

Additional regression analyses were carried out to determine that the complexity of the system was no greater than a quadratic function. The terms C and P made no additional impact on the results where they were treated as ordinary linear effects (or asymmetry parameters). An alternative logistic equation was tested where z_2 was, but the results were no better than the results obtained for the control models. The negative

TABLE 10.2
Summary of Regression for Stage 1, EBB Study

Independent Variable	r	$t(weight)$	R^2	F
Linear difference				
C	.21		.05**	
Linear pre–post				
C	.13	2.10*		
y_1	.15	2.30*	.05*	4.32
Logistic nonlinear				
Cz_1	−.20	4.43**		
Cz_1^2	−.37	6.37**	.23***	24.56

*$p < .05$. **$p < .10$. ***$p < .001$.

TABLE 10.3
Summary of Regression for Stage 2, EBB Study

Independent Variable	$t(weight)$	R^2	F
Linear difference			
P	1.19		
C	2.70*	.06**	4.75
Linear pre–post			
y_1	0.27		
C	1.25		
P	6.04	.22***	15.56
Logistic nonlinear			
Cz_1	1.67****		
Cz_1^2	−1.19		
Pz_1	−8.44***		
Pz_{12}	7.44***	.49***	39.46

*$p < .05$. **$p < .10$. ***$p < .001$. ****$p < .10$.

results for those analyses helped to eliminate some alternative dynamical structures for the group problem-solving discussions.

Figure 10.5 is a scatterplot of change in response length by cumulative elapsed response. The points form the characteristic pitchfork. Many data points surround the bifurcation point and follow the bifurcation gradients. The pattern appears to represent structural instability in the group's ideation process.

Discussion

The results showed that the sizes of responses varied considerably and were distributed as a mushroom pdf. Thus the dynamic that affects creative production in a group setting is similar to those encountered in individual analysis (e.g., Fig. 10.3). The control parameters are still unknown, but the logistic regression analysis suggested that feedback channels are essential to creative production, and that group and individual variables play approximately equal roles in the generation of ideas within a group context. The quadratic degree of complexity determined by the regression analysis showed that creative processes are instability producing, as was initially believed to be true.

There are implications for management, should it desire to enhance creative production:

1. Open all feedback channels so that information is communicated freely. Offering information on a "need to know" basis only is inappropriate as it stifles spontaneous action and the incubation process that is presumed to exist between the information input and creative output.

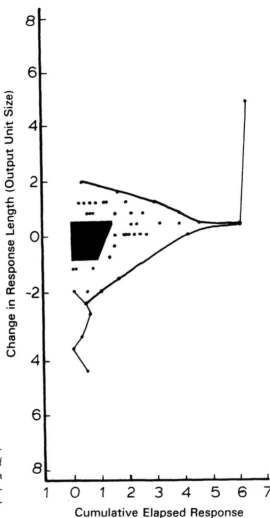

FIG. 10.5. Plot of change in response length (Δz) as a function of cumulative elapsed responses in the EBB study, showing bifurcation contours and greater instability when feedback level is small.

Censorship of information imposes configurations that may be misleading.

2. Promote and reinforce spontaneous idea generation processes. The presence of a highly communicative group heightens the ideation process.

3. Commit more time to creative thinking. Indulge activities whereby group members can hone their divergent thinking and problem formulation skills.

The implications for future research on NDS and creativity are numerous. New programs could be developed around several themes:

1. What specific roles do individual difference variables such as divergent thinking, problem definition and sensitivity, personality, style, and so forth play?
2. What makes a decent feedback channel, and in how many ways does the bumper effect occur?
3. Does the structure of the discussion question affect the patterns of response?
4. Do social aspects of individual or group behavior, rather than ideation behavior, affect idea production or the self-organization process?

SUMMARY

There are many sources of individual differences that contribute to creative output. As with most human talent, they begin with a genetic endowment that is cultivated by social forces. Evidence of the power of social forces is readily observed in group, organizational, and societal processes. Whether the potential for creative output is widely or narrowly distributed in the population is probably a matter of one's personal philosophy and any breakthroughs in educational technique that have yet to occur. What we can reasonably conclude, however, is that individuals' creative output is irregularly distributed according to a mushroom catastrophe dynamic, which is now believed to be epiphenomenal of one or more evolutionary mechanisms.

Virtually all known process dynamics concerning creativity and innovation are nonlinear: insight and tenacity, output over a professional lifespan, output over a professional cross section, the evolution of the creative personality, the impact of feedback channels in a group or organizational context, the economic assimilation of creative work, and organizational response to an already chaotic environment. Chaos and creativity have a mutual causation structure: Chaos promotes creativity. Creativity is self-organizational process that reduces complexity. Creative work induces more chaos in the social and economic environment. Thus creative systems exist at the edge of chaos.

Creative systems will thrive when feedback channels are open and widely interconnected. The process of configuring new idea elements has a contagious nature about it, which is to say that ideas diffuse throughout a group (or a society) and liberate other valuable ideas. Group dynamics and individual contributions appear to be of equal importance on the basis of the EBB study, which was the first study to make such a comparison.

11

The Dynamical Nature of
Organizational Development

Organizational development (OD) is a structured set of techniques for transforming an organization from one state of affairs to another. Often the motivation for change is to effect an improvement in the organization's human resource situation, its business posture, or both. Organizations often call in their development consultants when the business is not doing well financially, or when there is poor morale, confused work motivation, or perhaps excessive stress leading to burnout or high turnover.

Escape from disaster is not the only possible motivation for change. Organizations that are doing well financially can make an investment in whatever their consultants can contribute to human resource development. Alternatively, organizations may be growing rapidly, and need to rethink their internal workings to avoid liabilities that occur when many new people join the organization who do not really share the same history, or who are not well integrated into the networks of activities. Existing networks or patterns of activities are inevitably disrupted when many new people are implosively included in the organization.

Mergers and acquisitions cause disruption in both operations and human interactions. Jobs that are redundant between the two merging organizations are typically eliminated, and new interaction patterns need to be established. Other procedures used by one of the merging organizations are often supplanted by the other organization's procedures in order to attain standardization. On the human side, there are opportunities for stress, advancement, and fear of job loss. Motivation and morale can become salient concerns. It is difficult for an employee to be loyal to a company that is bought and sold by another like so many truckloads of pork bellies. Rapid changes in the external business environment generate opportunities for stress, conflict, or growth.

This chapter covers what OD actually meant historically, and what NDS has done to change it drastically. The first section describes the contributions of Lewin and others who made a foundational impact on OD thinking. The second section discusses the contrasts between the conventional and NDS approaches, with synopses of what theorists have contributed in this regard. The third section discusses views concerning evolutionary and revolutionary change, and their meaning to OD, with some empirical illustrations.

The group or team has long been regarded as the main building block of the organization and OD efforts. The fourth and fifth sections contain two original studies on chaos in production teams, and creativity in an interdisciplinary problem-solving team.

CONVENTIONAL APPROACH
TO ORGANIZATIONAL DEVELOPMENT

At the beginning of the 20th century there was no organizational science. Corporations grew so large in the United States that the government had to invent new laws to prevent unfair monopolistic practices. The growth of organizations was inextricably linked to parallel growth in science and technology, which brought us phonographs, telephones, typewriters, light bulbs, power plants, new tools for energy development, automobiles, airplanes, radios, camera and movies, and a couple of rockets.

Manufacturing processes were gaining momentum as well. Henry Ford developed assembly lines as tools for mass production. His contribution was built on a 40-year momentum of machine tooling and the concept of identical interchangeable parts. It was the Cadillac Motor Company that, just a few years before, astounded trade-show audiences by demonstrating that they could take three automobiles, disassemble them entirely, mix up the parts, and reassemble three fully functional vehicles.

Transportation-based products had enormous impact on the way business could be conducted. Innovations in transportation and telecommunications drastically reduced the costs associated with long-distance trade. Not only were there new things to make and buy, but new markets were shaping up as well.

In spite of the rapid growth of organizations, the human side of the enterprises reached new depths. From the workers' perspective, the rise of superindustrialization alienated workers from their means of production. The proportions of people who were employed by organizations and those who were self-employed became inverted. Production workers could work for low wages, but could not control the systems that produced the work or reaped the profits. Low wages meant more than barely meeting one's subsistence needs; they implied no hope for any change, because the economic system was designed to benefit those who already controlled it and who wanted to maintain that control indefinitely.

In response, labor unions allowed workers to use their collective power to do what no one worker could do alone, which was to buck the system, holding it hostage when necessary through strikes. Management, on the other hand, had no viable model from which to pattern its functions. The top two choices at the time were the Catholic Church and the military, both of which appeared to have different concerns and priorities. With the stage so set, Weber's sociology of organizations had much to contribute.

Bureaucracy as an Improvement

The notion of bureaucracy, in spite of its pejorative meaning today, was actually an improvement compared to the type of chaos that must have existed in the early part of the century. The bureaucracy concept separated work roles from actual people (Weber, 1947). An organization was a system of roles that people merely played out. The role was all-important, not its occupants, who were interchangeable parts. Each role had certain responsibilities attached to it, along with the authority to carry out those responsibilities. Decisions were standardized so that any role occupant could carry out the function without bothering upper management for a decision each time the decision was needed. The less mentally taxing the job, furthermore, the more interchangeable were the people.

Weber was responsible for two other ideas of enduring importance. One was the identification of organizational structures, as tall or flat, centralized or decentralized, span of control, size, and division of labor. Each aspect of structure has been subject to some form of study or idea for structural improvements in later decades.

The other was the concept of value-free sociology. Organizations and other human systems need to be studied dispassionately, and not from the vantage point of pet political theories. The capitalism–socialism dichotomy was very raw in the minds of many political observers. Social science, if it were to do anyone any good, should see the truth without biases that originate outside the legitimate theoretical framework. Perhaps Weber was taking his cue from the early days of physics and astronomy when the wrong idea could get a person burned at the stake. I will leave it as a playful debate question whether value-free social science is really possible.

The First OD Strategies

The first theories and approach to the study of organizational change did not emerge until about 30 years after Weber's theory of organizations. The human relations school of thought started during the 1930s, and culminated in the Lewin et al. (1939) studies of leadership styles and their impact on group dynamics. They discerned the autocratic, democratic, and laissez-faire leadership styles, all of which had different results on work teams. Of the three styles, the democratic style, which struck a balance between structured direction from leaders and participation from subordinates, was the most productive, produced the most positive morale and individual initiative, and produced the team most involved in its work. The themes of participation, structure, and consideration later permeated much of later leadership theory.

Three Phases of Change

Because it was possible to conclude that some leadership styles were better than others in most obvious ways, the next task was to transform entire organizations from whatever they were to something better. The process of organizational change, according to Lewin (1947, 1951), occurred in three major stages: *unfreezing, change,* and *refreezing.* During the unfreezing stage, the organization gets used to the idea that change is necessary. The organization, usually in concert with an OD consultant, identifies programs, procedures, and patterns of social relationships that need improvement. Barriers to change need to be discovered, and desired paths and goals need to be defined.

The repertoire of change techniques has grown since Lewin's first efforts. Initially there was the T-group, or sensitivity training group, in which participants learned something about themselves, human relations, and how they affect other people. Those elements of learning form a microlevel form of unfreezing. After the participants were thawed, the next part of the program was to learn new interpersonal skills, such as communication styles, person perception, and group leadership, to name a few. The final stage of sensitivity training was to reintegrate the new learning into one's permanent repertoire of social behaviors. Unfortunately, T-group training was not a smashing success most of the time, according to evaluation studies (Woodman & Sherman, 1980), because too often the T-group participants returned to environments where people behaved as they always did and supported the old, and usually deficient, social patterns.

Today's gamut of OD techniques includes team-building approaches, conflict resolution strategies, communication and human relations training of all sorts, the action research model, job redesign, and process consultation, to name some broad categories (French & Bell, 1990). Although some success with each of those techniques has been reported, the trend appears to be that when the evaluation methods are more rigorous, the odds are smaller that a favorable result will be obtained

(Terpstra, 1981; Woodman & Sherman, 1980). There is a substantial tendency for intervention techniques to be chosen on the basis of consultants' pet preferences, rather than on the basis of any well-known problem–solution linkages (Kegan & Rubinstein, 1973). Perhaps that finding is a result of the theory and knowledge base that practitioners have had to work with all along.

Process consultation (Bennis, 1988) is a technique whereby the consultant observes the processes that the organization exercises when it conducts its business, solves problems, and arrives at critical choices. Based on those observations, the consultant makes recommendations for changing those processes. The consultant is thus implicitly assuming that particular cause and effect linkages exist between process variables and organizational performance, and that by tweaking the process, performance will be proportionately tweaked as well. The thrust of the evaluation evidence is, however, that process consultation strategies are generally unsuccessful (Hackman, 1992).

To return to the broader theme, the refreezing part of the OD process is the phase where the newly formed patterns of behavior and social learning have become crystallized permanently, or stabilized, in the organization's behavior strategy. The organization is now capable of solving its own problems and no longer needs the consultant. The social science knowledge that has been acquired by the organization throughout the OD process has now been harnessed. The organization is now capable of solving its own problems self-sufficiently. The consultant then disengages, makes a graceful exist, and cashes the check before it bounces.

Assumptions of OD

How many industrial psychologists does it take to change a lightbulb? Just one, but the lightbulb has to *want* to change! The first assumption of OD is that the organization must want to change (French & Bell, 1990). Change cannot be induced from the outside. Change is the result of a collective will, and the consultants merely facilitate the efforts.

The second major assumption is that OD processes should be chosen for the organization's own good and not for extraneous reasons (recall the earlier mention of value-free). The entire organization is the client, not just the high-ranking official who pays the consultant. The consultant must often promote courses of action that are beneficial to the entire organization but that may conflict with the pet notions and values of some of the key people in the organization.

The third assumption is that OD is a joint effort between the organization and the consultant. Diagnoses are mutually defined, change procedures are mutually planned, and evaluations of activities are mutually formulated opinions. The consultant is not there to show off. The consultant is there to bring out the best in the people of the organization.

The Action Research Model

The action research model (French & Bell, 1990) is a meta-procedure, so to speak, for ascertaining diagnoses, formulating plans, and conducting evaluations of results. The core idea is that all the rigor usually associated with scientific work in applied settings should be incorporated in an OD change project as well. The action research model begins with a commitment to the OD effort from the organization, which should identify a team of its people to coordinate all internal activities of the project. Next, after explaining the project and its mission to everyone, the consultant utilizes standard tools such as surveys, meetings and discussions, one-on-one interviews, and so forth to obtain a picture of how the organization behaves, what the felt problems are, who feels that way, where the conflicts are, and so forth.

The process is replete with feedback meetings where the data are discussed, analyzed, interpreted, and argued. Eventually action planning occurs, which should be logically linked to the diagnostic findings. Throughout the process, the participants should discuss a simple sounding question, "How will we know that what we've done is a success?" The answer serves as the basis of evaluation studies later on, where the data collection, interpretation, discussion, and argument meetings are frequent and involve every possible relevant person in the organization.

Force Fields

Organizational development is not as simple as the 1–2–3 process it might appear to be. Change efforts often meet with barriers to change. Possible barriers are attitudes and behaviors that are so entrenched in the organization that localized change efforts are not sufficient to permanently effect change. Some organizational members have vested interests in the old ways of doing things, and any threats to those interests meet with active resistance, if not sabotage of the change efforts.

Other types of barriers may not be related to the willingness to change, but may be in conflict with regard to what the organization should change into. What we now recognize as an organizational culture might be a euphemistic way of saying that there is too much old baggage to move. Once again, vested interests could play insidious roles in the direction of change and the propagation of culture.

Lewin (1951) recognized that such conflicts arise in the course of an OD effort. He conceptualized those conflict dynamics as a force field. The

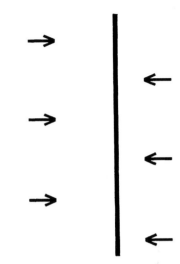

FIG. 11.1. Force field dynamics for organizational change in the conventional paradigm.

Pressure to change   **Resistance to change**

force field is composed of two types of forces: the pressure to change, and the resentence to change. When pressure to change exceeds resistance, then the forces of change prevail. If resistance prevails, no one is going anywhere. The force field concept is commonly depicted in a two-dimensional display using simple linear dynamics, as in Fig. 11.1.

CHAOS PARADIGM OF ORGANIZATIONAL DEVELOPMENT

According to Michaels (1993), OD as described earlier is extinct. He noted that major movements and approaches to OD have evolved over the years. By the early 1970s, OD espoused the societal value system of the 1960s, which might have been regarded as paradoxical in its twin objectives for human development and commercial viability. Shortly thereafter, OD thinking bifurcated into individualistic and groupist camps. The individualistic camp focused on human development in the sense of sensitivity training from a generation before. The groupist camp focused on teams, group interaction, and related ideas. Each camp later split between orientations toward process consultation and systems theory.

With enough splits, it would appear that chaos in OD is the logical next step, meaning that the practice of OD was in chaos. It would be logical, furthermore, that chaos theory would be the central set of concepts behind any new OD school of thought. Organizational development as we knew it was dead, but its death was a transition to the new chaos paradigm where all its best tricks would be regrouped and reinterpreted along with others that were germane to the new paradigm.

I should interject here that I received a survey in the mail a number of years ago from a research team whom I do not remember. The theme of the survey was to ascertain whether its respondents (howsoever we were defined) believed that the core concepts of OD were still alive, or whether OD had degenerated into a laundry list of localized disjointed programs. I endorsed the degenerate laundry list view because it seemed more accurate at the time. I would agree with Michaels, however, that NDS applications to organizational behavior should change that perception. NDS provides an alternative framework that integrates the most productive themes from past work with new ideas that explain phenomena that were apparently little understood.

Chaos Theory Principles in OD Practice

The first key principle of the chaos paradigm of OD is to invert the unfreeze–change–refreeze principle that has gone relatively unquestioned since Lewin first proposed it. In the new model, change is the steady state of affairs. Anything that appears frozen is just a temporary respite between bouts of change, which are primarily chaotic. Even where there is internal quietude, turbulence characterizes the external business environment, which itself is a source of chaotic behavior within the organization (Michaels, 1989). The attractors that underlie the turbulence are the sources of stability in an organization. To the untrained eye, the new model is paradoxical in its theme of stability through turbulence. A highly entrenched organizational culture, which is typically regarded as stable in the old-fashioned sense, continues to be viewed as a strong attractor force. Such rigid stability may be symptomatic of maladaptive behavior, however.

Effective organizational change cannot be effected by managerial mandates or through manipulative pseudo-participation opportunities. Such attempts are typically directed at stable attractor forces, which will respond rigidly, with obstinacy and stubbornness (Goldstein, 1994). Rather, an organization needs to be moved to a bifurcation point where its situation is unstable. Thereafter, change is possible.

An organization moves to its bifurcation point when its internal entropy level has increased sufficiently. The practitioner, therefore, needs to cultivate chaos into the system. Entropy levels can be raised by identifying diversities of opinions, rather than identifying group averages on survey variables, and spelling out the ranges of those diverse opinions; Goldstein (1988) named this technique *difference questioning*. There are other options for increasing entropy as well; considered next are neural net leadership, creativity enhancement, and techniques to further facilitate self-organization. When public attention is given to differing views and divergent information, the nature of those differences becomes amplified and their meanings are (perhaps) better understood (Wheatley, 1992).

Michaels (1991) introduced the concept of the *neural net organization*, which draws upon a metaphor with literal neural nets. Each member of the organization is a "neuron" that wants to be excited. To do so, it must connect with many other neurons in the organization, form as many different patterns of communication as possible, and thereby receive a comparable amount of stimulation. Interaction patterns should also be seen as transitory. They group and regroup. Adaptive teams are those that are continually adapting. It would appear, furthermore, from Huberman and Glance's (1993) work that sustainable cooperation within teams would result from a combination of sufficient diversity and a comfortable group or network size.

The dynamics of creative processes and their relationship to leadership were discussed extensively in chapter 10. For the present purposes it is only necessary to recall that creativity induces chaos and chaos induces creativity. Chaos and creativity are thus parts of a reciprocal dynamic, and self-organizational processes and communication links assist the transition from chaos to a creative work. The adoption of a management style that facilitates creative thinking within the organization is essential to successful strategic navigation of a turbulent business and social environment (Stacey, 1992).

Self-Organization and Sociotechnical Systems Theory

The self-organization principle was a key concept in the sociotechnical systems approach to organizational design and development, although the widespread importance of the dynamics was not well known until recently (DeGreene, 1990, 1991a, 1991b). The sociotechnical systems concept was first introduced by Trist and Bamforth (1951) and has become a salient viewpoint in organizational dynamics in the past decade. The core principle is that the division of labor in an organization is often based on a false rationality, where work is divided according to apparent natural divisions in the tasks and without regard for the human input. In sociotechnical systems approaches, however, the division of labor is rationalized from the viewpoint of human capabilities and efficient utilization of human talent. The best way to divide work is to gather a group of people who, in the aggregate, possess all the necessary skills and present them with the work objectives. Allow the workers to divide up the work and coordinate themselves around the work demands. After a little trial and error, they will land on a routine that accomplishes the work efficiently and equitably (French & Bell, 1990). The implicit participation in the work allocation would build further commitment to accomplishing the work well.

The sociotechnical systems idea gave rise to the concept of autonomous work groups in the 1980s. Supervisors still played a role, but that role was more confined to solving problems that affected the groups' relationships with other groups and the organization as a whole. In a study that addressed the differential levels of productivity in autonomous work groups, Rao et al. (1987) found that the more successful groups were less concerned about promotion opportunities and had supervisors oriented toward "consideration," or building interpersonal relationships, rather than "structure," or organizing the work of others.

Zimmerman and Hurst (1993, in press) have speculated that the self-organized work groups and neural-like networks might qualify as fractal-shaped configurations. A plausible line of future work on organizational structure might seek to determine whether an organization tends to generate a particular configuration of work teams and communication patterns, and whether those patterns are self-repeating throughout the organization.

DeGreene (1991a) merged some basic ideas from ergonomics and NDS to propose a new path for sociotechnical systems development. The design of jobs and equipment should be viewed as a coevolutionary process. Presently, although contemporary equipment manufacturing often reflects the cognitive capabilities and limitations of the end user, little information is reflected regarding the job the end user is trying to perform. As jobs evolve, equipment should evolve as well. Likewise, as new machine design ideas are proven to be worthy of adoption, the division of labor should adapt as well.

A certain amount of coevolution has already taken place in some industries. Jobs that required diverse skills, such as those found in the printing and publishing industry, have transformed with the aid of computer magic into one job—operating a computer program. What is wrong with this picture? In spite of the microlevel emphasis on flexible manufacturing and other computer-based innovation, the greater socioeconomic structure that contains all those activities appears to be gaining rigidity (DeGreene, 1991b). Symptoms of the rigidity trend include (but are not limited to) an overemphasis on money and profits on the part of U.S. corporations as a sole criterion of success, a shift from creativity and innovation to growth for its own sake, coalitions between government and business for the purposes of human exploitation, an unquestioning belief in the free-market system as something morally good, degeneration of social services and safety nets for people in need, and superficial quick-fix remedies to social problems that inevitably make matters worse (DeGreene, 1991b, p. 77).

Can Organizational Culture Be Changed?

There are three points of view on whether it is possible to change an organizational culture, according to Schein (1990). The anthropological view is that culture cannot be changed effectively, nor should one try to do so; there is an inherent belief in the stability of the "attractor." The business management view is that cultural change is not unusual at all. Strategic leaders, however, will capitalize on chance occurrences and dramatic events that could have a cultural impact and will follow up on those events with the right messages and action to promote continued change in the desired direction.

Wheatley (1992) made a similar observation about capitalizing on fortuitous chance events to effect cultural change. By doing so, the leadership is utilizing a feature of chaotic processes, which should be occurring in organizations, whereby a small deviation in behavior is rapidly amplified as it moves throughout the system.

From Wheatley's (1992) viewpoint, vision is an important component of a cultural change initiative. Once the organization has reached its bifurcation point, management needs to define attractors and make them strong enough to draw unstable "points" into their basins. Clear visions of the desired culture and goals are needed to define attractive objectives. As for inducing the change itself, it is preferable to let it happen, rather than to make it happen, for all the reasons suggested by Goldstein (1994).

Stacey (1992) differed on the matter of vision, as discussed earlier. Visionary leaders tend to invent immutable visions that no one is allowed to seriously alter or contradict. Vision can be a barrier to creative thinking, particularly when the organization needs to develop strategies in an environment that is fundamentally unstable. As for changing a culture, some cultures are more firmly ingrained than others. For those that are firmly ingrained, efforts are better spent developing creative potential and strategic managerial reactions to problem situations. Successive action might have an impact on the culture, but that should not be a primary concern. When cultures are less well ingrained, the capitalization on chance principle could work to effect change, but the change in culture might not stabilize and might change again when surprise events occur.

Total Quality Management

Total quality management (TQM) was a management philosophy (loose use of the word) or system developed by Deming (1986) in the late 1940s, the goal of which was to assist organizations to develop the quality of their products through logical and objective thinking, persistence, and effective use of the human element. On the logical side, the organization should strive to be a learning organization that objectively measures important features of its work, investigates deviations, and set goals to continually improve performance. Managers and quality specialists need to be firmly grounded in statistical techniques for manufacturing process control; statistical information gives exact feedback where needed. The concept of learning organization is considered further in the next section from a different perspective.

On the side of human systems, the typical emphasis in American organizations on individual performance issues should be disbanded in favor of group-centered definitions of work and outcomes. Most work is done by a group of interacting people and interacting groups, and the group phenomenon is greater, if not simply more interpretable, than the sum of the individual efforts. What we now know as self-organizing teams are responsible for the division of labor at a group level of analysis.

Dooley (1992; Dooley et al., 1993) identified several applications of chaos theory that appear in a true case of TQM. Both involve systems thinking. The concept of far-from-equilibrium conditions (high entropy) aptly describes the product quality crisis experienced by contemporary industries. Sensitive dependency (butterfly effect) emerges in three ways. In one sense, a small deviation in the manufacturing process translates into a bigger problem as the error travels through the system. In a second sense, TQM emphasizes the customer-driven organization in which the customer's feedback receives primary attention from the organization, which only exists to serve the customer. Small requests or suggestions from outside the organization should turn into important affairs for the organization as it strives to serve the customer better. Third, the continuous learning process keeps the organization's mind set in a less-than-equilibrium state, as it anticipates and eventually uses new information to redirect its actions.

Self-organization is an important part of TQM in two ways. One is in the ontogeny of teams, as expressed earlier. The other is in the customer–supplier networks that form after repeated successful interactions (Dooley, 1992). An organization's identity should not stop at its literal boundaries. It really includes a network of suppliers and customers with special needs and interrelationships. The members of such a network should be able to count on each other's product quality and primacy of customer service to sustain mutual growth. For self-organization to occur, however, an organization's boundaries must remain firm but permeable (Goldstein, 1994). In a similar vein, the organization has a coevolutionary relationship with its environment (Hurst & Zimmerman, 1993; Zimmerman, 1992).

One aspect of TQM appears to run contrary to NDS principles. The emphasis on statistical process control does not recognize that much variability in manufacturing processes is the result of deterministic chaos—complex differential equations—rather than noise or error in the usual statistical sense (Dooley et al., 1993). Hopefully the many sagas recounted in this book have dispelled the notion that NDS and statistical reasoning are incompatible. Rather, statistical reasoning must reach a new evolutionary stage.

Unfortunately, the evolutionary change and adaptation dynamic implicit in classical TQM and NDS may be undermined by sociopolitical forces. The ISO-9000 standards for product quality and occupational safety, which screen corporations seeking to sell their products in European Economic Community (EEC) countries, force organizations not only to develop statistical controls and quality program, but also to institutionalize those procedures for the review of ISO auditors. Thus stabilization is being forced where instability should reign. The Malcolm Baldrige National Quality Award offered in the United States to organizations who made superior strides in product quality serves a similar function (Dooley et al., 1993).

EVOLUTIONARY VERSUS REVOLUTIONARY CHANGE

The first model for describing organizational change processes through NDS theory was based on a contrast between evolutionary and revolutionary change (Bigelow, 1982). The contrast lent it self to modeling with a cusp catastrophe. The cusp model for organizational change appears in Fig. 11.2 and reflects updates and modifications to the original idea, based on progress in NDS theory in the last decade.

Response Surface

Classical biological evolutionary processes are relatively slow and progressive, and evolutionary change in organizations is no different. Each step in the change process is a logical outgrowth of the organization's state of development at a prior step in the change process. Examples of evolutionary change would include the use of new or improved personnel selection procedures or training programs, or growth in the organization's size in response to a steadily increasing demand for the organization's products.

A revolutionary change, in contrast, is relatively sudden. More importantly, however, the end result of change is qualitatively distinct from the starting situation. Revolutionary changes might involve a drastic change in the organization's structure from tall to flat, or centralized to decentralized. Other examples might occur in the course of mergers and

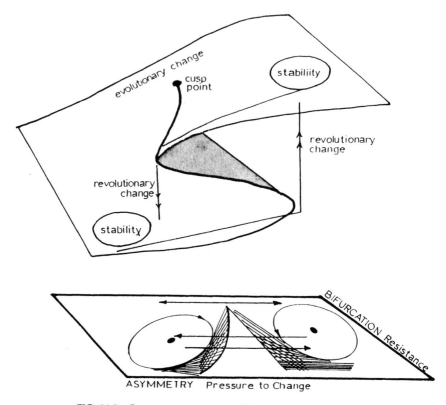

FIG. 11.2. Cusp catastrophe model for organizational change.

acquisitions where roles and cultures are reconstructed or amalgamated. In principle, some of the cultural changes or changes in business strategy that were discussed in the preceding section might qualify as revolutionary change, depending on how distinct the new ideas were from the prior state of the organization.

Ramaprasad (1982) observed that the distinction between evolutionary and revolutionary change may not be especially obvious. A long sequence of evolutionary changes could lead up to a large and dramatic change in the way an organization does business and in its profitability. A dramatic intervention, such as cultural change from traditional American versus Japanese-influenced management, could indeed be revolutionary or could make no impact at all. Revolutionary changes, Ramaprasad conjectured, were rare in the long run. His reasoning was based on an analogy with biological evolution, which, in his interpretation, showed that biological mutations were rare.

Miller (1984) acknowledged that small evolutionary changes could build up to a dramatic effect, but he noted some problems with

Ramaprasad's characterization of revolutionary change. It is necessary to separate the precursors of change from the change procedure itself and the effects of the change. Revolutionary change, as Miller and Freisen (1980) had explained previously, involved a reversal in direction from one organizational strategy to another. The impact or survival value of a particular example of such revolutionary change may be adaptive or not, depending on how well chosen it was to begin with.

In later work, Kets de Vries and Miller (1986) identified some pathological organizations that utilized revolutionary change strategies to their own disadvantage. The schizoid organization changed its procedures and strategies frequently without coherent reasoning for doing so, and often vacillated between some of those reversals. The result was an organization that kept its members continuously confused; it rendered itself incapable of taking any effective action because no one had a clear of what the policy of the week was supposed to be. Another pathological strategy was the dramatic organization that sized a new idea and ran with it without much deliberation. Those organizations were often successful, but only temporarily so. After an initial success, a repeat of the policy of radical change without deliberation could result in a failure that would negate any benefit accrued by the earlier success.

The synopsis of the dramatic organization does suggest that two other ideas Ramaprasad (1982) offered concerning revolutionary change should be given further consideration. Revolutionary change can be slow, rather than fast, as a result of two possible and distinct dynamics. In one case, the revolution appears sudden and dramatic, but it was actually brewing for an extended period of time. No one noticed what was happening until it happened. Thus an elbow-shaped trajectory has been drawn on the cusp response surface to reflect the slow revolution dynamic.

The other case of slow revolution is the result of a negative feedback loop that may be built into the organization's structure somehow. While a deliberate intervention is taking place, the negative feedback loop slows down the pace of change. Doing so allows the organization to assess the impact of what has been accomplished and to direct the change process as necessary. This negative feedback dynamic is an echo of the bumper effect dynamic, which was discussed in Chapter 10 in reference to creative processes. This concept is considered further in the next subsection, along with Bigelow's (1982) definitions of control parameters for organizational change.

Control Parameters

Cusp models contain two control parameters, which Bigelow (1982) defined as pressure to change (asymmetry) and resistance to change (bifurcation). Pressure to change will have a different effect on organizational behavior depending on the level of resistance. At low levels of resistance, pressure to change promotes a smooth and regular progression from one course of action to another. At high levels of resistance, however, the amount of pressure that would have otherwise resulted in change would probably not be enough. When pressure reaches a critical threshold, however, change is sudden. The result is a qualitative and discontinuous shift in organizational strategy.

Cusp functions are reversible. Organizational change, once it has occurred, may reverse itself if there is a substantial drop in the pressure that precipitated its change in the first place. The double-threshold function on the cusp surface indicates, however, that the critical point for changing back to the original form is located at a lower level of pressure that the critical point for making the change.

Resistance does not simply mean that forces exist that counteract efforts toward change as in Lewin's model, although Lewin's dynamic represents one way for events to turn out. Rather, greater levels of resistance predispose the organization to greater discontinuities of change, if the pressure to change is sufficiently strong. The resistance concept is closely analogous to the modulus of elasticity parameter in the Euler buckling model for structural beams and human performance under load. The "stiffer" the organization, the more likely it will be to "snap" when pressure becomes too great.

Often the pressures to change originate, at least in part, from environmental sources. The "stiff" response could easily translate into a significant financial failure, which a good many organizations would regard as a convincing form of pressure. The model does not specify the origins of all forms of pressure, only that they aggregate into one control parameter. The resulting pressure parameter and the resistance are the two control parameters most proximally related to actual change.

Gradients

Gradients on the cusp response surface are trajectories running between the bifurcation point and the attractor centers. Gradients represent transformations of the latent independent control parameters. One such gradient dynamic in organizational change model occurs where resistance to change could lead to financial impairment, which in turn would lead to increased pressure to change, as just discussed. At a more general level of definition, Lewin's (1951) vector field of opposing forces is now replaced by a field of diverging vectors that support the change or no-change attractor (DeGreene, 1978).

Another gradient behavior is shown in Fig. 11.2 as part of the slow revolution dynamic. In the case of the slow revolution, once it has built up sufficient momentum it could then encounter belated resistance, which would occur too late in the process to have much effect. Alternatively, the revolutionary change initiative might not meet with ideological obstinacy, but might experience some temporary challenges as the revolutionary forces dismantle the organizational machinery of the old system and instantiate the machinery of the new.

(Note: The word "machinery" in this context is a verbal convenience and is not meant to imply the type of mechanism encountered in classic Newtonian systems. Rather the idea of "soft machine," which was popular a couple decades ago, is more applicable, and denotes the flexible and organic human systems that ultimately make organizations function. It is plausible, however, that one class of organizational changes would involve the replacement of Newtonian-mechanistic management systems with something more amenable to the chaos paradigm!)

The slow revolution and rising economic pressure constitute two types of gradient dynamic favoring change to a particular attractor. The bumper effect dynamic, however, favors a gradient move back toward the previous state. A version of the bumper effect dynamic was also independently identified by Argyris and Schon (1978) in their concept of single- and double-loop learning, both of which are considered next. Both the bumper dynamic and double-loop concepts could promote much more than a dampening of change initiatives; they would challenge any particular change goal and possible suggest improved goal definitions. The dynamics of improving objectives are considered subsequently.

Single-loop learning, according to Argyris and Schon (1978), describes a sequence of events that connect a set of goals and objectives, an action plan, and results of those actions. The set of goals and objectives rests on a set of assumptions concerning cause-and-effect relationships among actions and events in the environments plus organizational values and other aspects of its culture. The single loop is a feedback between results and action that serves the purposes of reinforcing a current action plan or precipitating its modification to produce better results. The limitation of that form of learning is that the underlying assumptions and premises of the action plan are never questioned. Double-loop learning contains a second feedback loop from results to the set of goals, assumptions, and values. Not only can results of actions modify the action, but they can also modify an entire strategy for action, goals, and perhaps some aspects of a culture that promote dysfunctional strategies.

Logistic Map Dynamics

The next episode is an exploration into how the logistic map concept, if it were literally applied, might describe the pattern of events that could occur in an organizational change process. The logistic bifurcation that is thought to underlie the change processes extends the possible behavioral spectrum beyond the bipolar change area of the cusp response surface. The logistic map describes where chaos might actually occur, inasmuch as the chaos concept permeates the work of several contemporary theorists.

Many plausible paths for organizational change might be identified with a double-loop learning strategy. The logistic map with its multiple branches could show the relationship among some of those options. In such a scheme, the initial state of the organization could be depicted as a Period 1 stable state. Entropy might then increase as a combined result of inflowing information from the environment that induces pressure to change plus some of the dynamics of resistance. If so, the organization would eventually move toward an attractor that has been sighted on one or the other branches of the map in Period 2. Some forms of resistance may not arise from a disagreement that change is needed, but a reaction of "we don't want to do anything until we know what we're doing and consider our options," which is a fair enough initial response. Once action has been taken toward one attractor, feedback from the environment can sustain or not sustain that initiative.

In the event a path is not sustained, the organization may turn back before it is gripped in the attractor basin, or it may change its direction. Sometimes change is not reversible, as we have seen in many evolutionary dynamics, in which case entropy continues to increase until the organization reaches the next bifurcation point, where additional changes are made.

If we continue to extrapolate from within the logistic map dynamics, we could expect further bifurcations and choices that eventually lead to a regime of chaotic strategy. This condition might be likely if organizational units are in disagreement as to the right course of action, or believe that some potential courses of action might meet some objectives and not others. Crossing past the edge of chaos would soon induce a self-organization initiative. Instead of an organization bumbling through choice points and bifurcations endlessly while remaining intact itself, it would undergo a reconstruction of its internal organization to meet the demands of a complex situation it is trying to control; it controls through adaptation in this scenario.

Adaptive Responses from Savings and Loan Institutions

Gresov et al. (1993) began with the cusp model as initially defined by Bigelow (1982). They added a new concept of inertia to the model. In the business literature, inertia is commonly defined as the propensity not to act, usually because of an insensitivity to environmental conditions. Gersov et al. defined inertia as the slope of the tangent to the cusp surface, which is to say, the second derivative of the cusp potential function, or the first derivative of the response surface.

The organization they studied was a savings and loan institution in California. The organizational change behavior that formed the dependent measure was *response to competitive pressure*. Response was measured by four variances: growth rate as measured in dollar assets, percentage of assets invested in residential mortgages, percentage of brokered deposits, and sales volume of mortgages on the secondary market (Gresov et al., 1993, p. 197).

The two control parameters were organizational design and competitive pressure. Pressure was measured as the number of savings and loan institutions operating in California during a given time period. The three organizational design measures were chosen to reflect the potential for facilitating change or inflexibility toward change: organizational size as measured in dollar assets, years since the organization was incorporated, and its number of branch offices (Gresov et al., 1993, p. 197). Dollar values were corrected for inflation.

The measurements just described were taken at 26 repeated intervals over a 10-year period. Some observations were spaced semiannually, while others were spaced at quarterly intervals. No correction for time interval appeared to have been made. The GEMCAT method of latent variable extraction (Oliva et al., 1987) was used to extract weighted combinations of control and response (competitive response and inertia) variables.

Because GEMCAT does not provide a measure of fit between the latent control variables and the latent response surface, the connection controls with response and inertia was accomplished by graphical analysis. Plots of competitive pressure versus design in two dimensions (cusp bifurcation set) showed the greatest point density (of control parameter coordinates, not behavioral response) in the neighborhood of the no-change attractor. For Time Frames 1 through 9, pressure was low and design (resistance) was increasing. For Time Frames 9 through 12, pressure increased, such that the design-pressure coordinates blipped across the bifurcation set to the neighborhood of the change attractor. Pressure subsided in Time Frames 14–26; response reversed direction (Gresov et al., 1993, p. 200).

Reanalysis with Structural Equations

The trajectory of control parameter coordinates did not appear to show the same amount of stability around the change attractor as there was around the no-change attractor. Gresov et al. (1993) also presented a three-dimensional plot of their control parameters with their latent behavioral outcome measure, which in my opinion was curvilinear but not easily identified as a cusp (p. 204). Fortunately, Gresov et al. published their latent data points in a table, which facilitated my reanalysis of their data using both the cusp dynamic difference equation and the nonlinear regression methods.

For the competitive response dependent measure, an R^2 value of .40 ($p < .05$) was obtained for the cusp dynamic difference equation. Significant weights were obtained for the cubic potential ($p < .10$), the quadratic ($p < .05$), and the bifurcation parameter ($p < .001$). Because the output from GEMCAT analysis produced weighted, standardized scores on the latent variables, no further transformations of location or scale were used.

The linear control models for competitive response showed no significant effect for the linear difference model ($R^2 = .12$), but there was a significant effect for the pre–post control ($p < .01$) that was larger than that obtained for the cusp model ($R^2 = .58$). The one significant weight in the model was obtained for competitive response at Time 1. Although there was some evidence of cusp-like structure, an ordinary linear interpretation was more true.

The inertia variables was first tested as cusp with the same two control variables. The R^2 for the cusp was small (.16) and not significant, nor was the linear difference model ($R^2 = .02$). The linear pre–post model, on the other hand, was decidedly linear ($R^2 = .88$). There was one significant weight in the pre–post model that was obtained for inertia at Time 1. Because the cusp model was so much smaller and contained the quadratic term as a potential predictor, the acceleration or tangent-to-slope hypothesis was precluded.

Three models were tested by means of nonlinear regression. The first two specified roles for both control parameters, with design as a bifurcation effect:

$$z_2 = \theta_1 e^{[\theta_2 \times (design) \times z_1]} + \theta_3 \times (pressure) \tag{1}$$

$$z_2 = \theta_1 \times (design) \times e^{(\theta_2 z_1)} + \theta_3 \times (pressure) \tag{2}$$

The bifurcation models tested for possible chaotic effects on the competitive response criterion (z_i). In light of the previous results for inertia, no further analyses were conducted for that variable. Equations 1 and 2 were expected to show similar results, and they did. The R^2 values were .63 for Equation 1 and .64 for Equation 2. Significant weights were obtained for θ_1 and θ_2 in both models; θ_3 was not significant in either model.

Equation 3 was also tested to assess the dimensionality of the competitive response measure:

$$z_2 = \theta_1 e(\theta_2 z_1) + \theta_3 \times (pressure) + \theta_4 \times (design) \tag{3}$$

Pressure and design were introduced here to soak up some variance in hopes of obtaining a better estimate of θ_2. The term θ_1 was at first found to be not significant, so it was dropped and the remaining parameters were reestimated. Significant weights were obtained for θ_2 and θ_3 (pressure) but not for θ_4 with design. The resulting value of R^2 was .62, which was positive and indicated that an expanding, chaotic process was operating. The θ_2 translated into a Lyapunov dimension of 1.86.

The results of all the analyses were thoroughly consistent with each other. The cusp theory was broader than the actual dynamics taking place in the particular savings and loan company in the study. The actual dynamics were a little less than quadratic order. Design was a decent indicator of bifurcation, and, within the context of the original theory, did control the resistance to change in the form of competitive response. An approximately quadratic form should have one control parameter, and one was found; the pressure variable did not do much good. As for inertia, if the tangent-to-slope hypothesis were true, a linear function is exactly what would result from a quasi-quadratic response surface function.

It would appear, furthermore, that the dynamics of organizational change could be characterized as a sequence of initial stability, an excursion into instability, and a return to original form. Change had not stabilized. This trajectory is similar to the bumper loop trajectory shown in Fig. 11.2. Because the function was chaotic, in addition, it might be described by a Rossler attractor: chaotic with an unstable blip, followed by a return to the main "turntable" (Fig. 2.5).

A phase portrait of the competitive response measure is shown in Fig. 11.3. The behavior sequence begins in the dense region, spirals outward in a clockwise direction, makes a broad tour around the rim of a basin (a little dented perhaps), then loops into a rough "spindle" just before returning to the dense region. Perhaps if more savings and loan companies in the geographic region were available for study, it might have been possible to identify a second stable attractor occupied by some of them.

CHAOS IN THE PRODUCTION LINES

"Talk about chaos, you should see the place where *I* work!" is probably going through some of the readers' minds right about now. The question of interest here is whether the state of confusion that is commonly reported by workers everywhere, and called "chaos," resembles mathematical chaos.

The Chaos Exercise™ (Michaels, 1992) is a group dynamics simulation that was developed to provide its participants with an experience of chaotic change in the continuity of work flow. The players in the game are organized into production groups and management groups. The "organization" is viewed a complex system that exists within an environment that is generating spontaneous events that threaten the continuity or stability of production efforts. Each production team tosses a tennis ball to all its

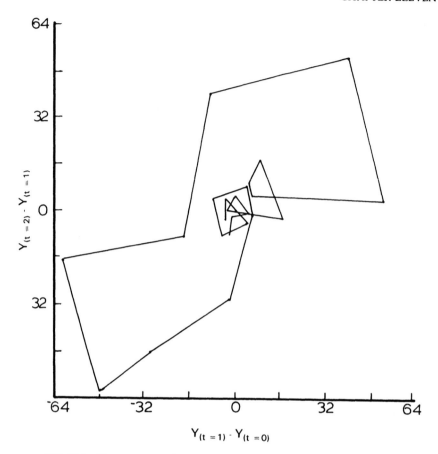

FIG. 11.3. Phase portrait of organizational change dynamics for a savings and loan institution.

members. Once a set of tosses is complete, the production teams send a different type of ball, called a "report ball," to the management group. The management group collects a set of report balls, one from each production team, tosses them among themselves and yells "Sale!" to signify that they "sold" a completed product. Meanwhile, the Gamemaster introduces unplanned events to help keep matters complicated.

Participants and Procedures

The participants were six industrial psychologists and seven graduate students in psychology who were participating in a continuing education seminar on organizational research and practice. Seven participants were male and six were female.

The "organization" in the exercise was configured into three production groups (four, four, and three players) and one management groups (three players). Players began with a "work and resource" load of one production ball per group and three report balls per group. During the first round of the game, which lasted 10 minutes, a second production ball was introduced at the 6-minute mark. Other "random" events that were introduced into the first round were a "power outage," an interchange of personnel, and a "tornado."

Between the first and second rounds of the game, a second set of report balls was distributed to each group. Management spent considerable time during the second round trying to sort the report balls to make a set, and the production groups experienced substantial downtime waiting for the report balls to be returned. Management was so overloaded (as determined by consensus of the players during debriefing) that they usually forgot to yell "Sale!" when they completed a set of production balls. The Gamemaster needed to remind them to record their sales on their tally sheets as well. The second round lasted 5 minutes, and a strike and second power outage were introduced as unplanned events by the Gamemaster.

Each group had a player who completed production reports for the group on a standardized tally sheet. The measurement taken was the number of toss cycles completed by the group during each 20-second interval of play. In principle, 30 data points should have been generated for each group during the first round, but actual quantities of points obtained were 23, 30, and 20 for Groups 1, 2, and 3, respectively. Group 3 recorded only one period of zero production at times when it experienced two such periods consecutively. Group 1 did not have a clue as to why their time intervals did not total 30. Data for Round 2 should have been organized into 15 intervals per group. Actual recorded results showed 6, 11, and 7 entries for Groups 1, 2, and 3, respectively.

The primary measurement in the exercise was the number of report balls generated by each group for each time interval. It became clear that this outcome was tainted with a form of error that is not normally assumed to exist in standard psychometric theory. The assumption in the standard theory is that error scores are uncorrelated with true scores, errors are normally distributed, and errors have a mean of 0.0 (Lord & Novick, 1968). The foregoing supposition regarding the nature of measurement error in the Chaos Exercise™ is readily assessed in the course of the nonlinear regression modeling (discussed in the next subsection) for the production data. Low R^2 coefficients for all nonlinear models would result if true psychometric noise were present. High R^2 coefficients would result if the error function were dependent on the true function and the hypothesized structural equation actually fit the data. In the Chaos Exercise™, measurement errors were epiphenomenal of the process itself, and were thus dependent on the true score and experimental context.

Analysis and Results

Remarks from the players during the game debriefing provided some insights into what took place during the administration of the Chaos Exercise™. First, the management group was the primary bottleneck that caused workers to wait idly until report balls were turned back. Second, excessive effort was expended by the "organization" in the reporting of work. Third, management did not consult with the worker groups when defining its intervention during the 10-minute lull between Rounds 1 and 2. Fourth, time was lost training new workers as a result of the career change manipulation. Fifth, there was no incentive to keep practicing skills while waiting for management to return report balls. If they had done so, the groups would have accumulated a warehouse full of unsold work. Sixth, the system prevented workers from performing to capacity.

Data from Rounds 1 and 2 (total of 96 points reported from three production groups), were analyzed separately, and the unequal time intervals were ignored. A simple nonlinear structural equation was tested using the nonlinear regression procedure explained in Chapter 3:

$$z_2 = e^{(\theta_1 z_1)} + \theta_2 \tag{4}$$

where z_1 and z_2 were production values for two consecutive periods of time. Equation 4 is a variant of Equation 53 in chapter 3, which contains an additional nonlinear regression weight preceding the exponential term. A simple linear alternative model was also tested where y_2 was predicted from y_1 only.

An R^2 coefficient of .91 ($p < .001$, $N = 72$ data points) was obtained for the Round 1 nonlinear model, which produced Equation 5 as a result:

$$z_1 = e^{(0.36 z_1)} + 0.81 \tag{5}$$

The dimensionality of the process was 1.43. The R^2 coefficient for the linear model was .18, which indicated a poorer fit compared to the nonlinear model.

Round 2 had the potential for introducing more chaos because of the larger number of report balls available for tossing to management. In practice, however, the Gamemaster noticed (as did the other players) that management became all the more confused and less timely about returning the report balls to the production teams. There appeared to be more waiting time, which was perforated by a shower of report balls from the production teams to management. In other words, production appeared more periodic in Round 2.

When Round 2 data were analyzed, an R^2 coefficient of .98 was obtained for nonlinear Equation 1, producing Equation 6:

$$z_2 = e^{(0.26z_1)} - 0.95 \tag{6}$$

The dimensionality of the process fell slightly to 1.30. The R^2 coefficient for the linear model was .01, which indicated no fit at all.

For both rounds, other, more complex models were tested, which included the difference between rounds as a possible bifurcation variable. The results of those efforts were not nearly as good as those reported earlier for an unbifurcated model.

Figures 11.4 and 11.5 are phase portraits of the production data for Groups 1 and 2 during Round 1. The axes are calibrated in raw score

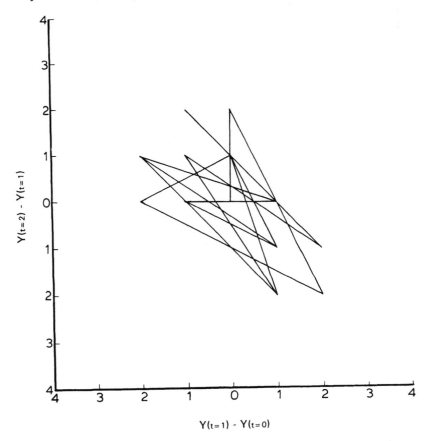

FIG. 11.4. Phase portrait of production trends for Group 1, Round 1, of the Chaos Exercise™.

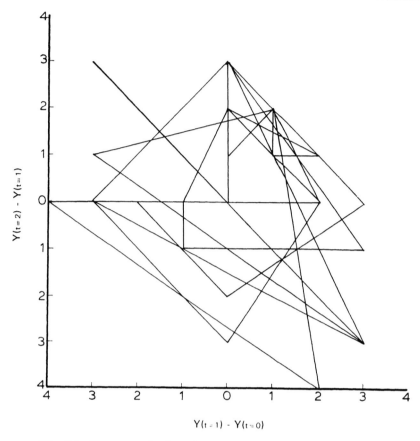

FIG. 11.5. Phase portrait of production trends for Group 2, Round 1, of the Chaos Exercise™.

units. The phase portrait for Group 3 during Round 1 just traced a diagonal from (–3,3) to (3,–3). If the extra zero-production time intervals had been correctly recorded, the trajectory would have traced a box around the diagonal with a cross intersecting at the origin.

Figure 11.6 shows the attractor basins for all groups combined for Rounds 1 and 2. Axes are calibrated in z-transformed units. Basins show three levels of density and illustrate the relative likelihood of finding any particular production rate pattern. The figures are based on Equations 5 and 6, which reflect functions that are optimally fitted to the data.

Discussion

Because the exponent was positive in both rounds of the game, it is possible to conclude that the Chaos Exercise™ did produce chaos in the mathematical sense. Thus the results support the general efficacy of the

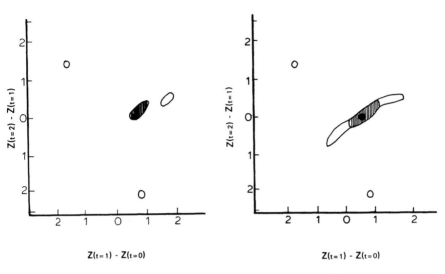

FIG. 11.6. Attractor basins for all groups in Chaos Exercise™ in Round 1 (left) and Round 2 (right).

chaos paradigm in organizational development. The dimensionality of the system was relatively low and, because it was less than 2.0, signified the possibility of the one control parameter. The control parameter is probably linked to the management bottleneck, but future research needs to assess that possibility directly.

The intervention between the two rounds of the game did not produce a change in the attractor's fractal dimension to any appreciable extent. The doubling of the number of report balls affected the scale parameter, rather than the complexity of the system. The nonlinear regression equation worked as expected when applied to the Chaos Exercise™ data. The group behavior was theoretically chaotic. The consistency between expected and obtained results supported the efficacy of the nonlinear regression procedure for the assessment of chaotic processes.

The attractors represented in the phase portraits of both the raw data and derived function also appear chaotic. At the present time there is no interpretation of what those intriguing geometries imply. It is plausible, however, that different configurations of management and production groups, group size, and countless other variables will eventually be found to explain why particular geometries are likely to occur.

Finally, the measurement errors associated with production reporting and time intervals were not the usual form of psychometric error, as denoted by the particularly high R^2 coefficient for the nonlinear model. The results further suggest that those measurement anomalies are epiphenomenal of the group production process, but further research efforts should attempt to separate actual dynamics from the reporting of same. The data collected following study of creative problem solving in an interdisciplinary team did not contain that particular quirk.

CREATIVE PROBLEM SOLVING
IN AN INTERDISCIPLINARY TEAM

Recent research reports have indicated a renewed interest in group processes. The thrust of the work has centered on whether groups are really more productive than individuals, particularly the best performing individual in the group. Often they are not, and insufficient group size (Dennis & Valacich, 1993), social loafing, negative social facilitation (Shepperd, 1993), and individual- rather than group-dependent task, reward, and feedback structures (Saavedra et al., 1993; Shepperd, 1993) are viable explanations for why that might be true.

Studies on group dynamics often use brainstorming output as a possible dependent measure. The present study draws on work begun in Chapter 10 that showed that creative output is a mushroom-catastrophic process, with the actual creative function occupying the unstable part function. The present study provided an opportunity to assess what was going on in the bistable part function and to capture an entire mushroom process.

Participants and Procedures

Participants were 55 students enrolled in industrial and other psychology classes, organized into seven groups of 7–9 (usually 8) players in a problem-solving simulation known as Island Commission (Gillan, 1989). All participants completed the 16PF Fifth Edition 3 weeks before the game.

Each game of Island Commission lasted 1.5 hours with instructions and debriefing. In the game, players took on roles of civic leaders on a small island that was located near a "friendly power." The group was presented with a budget that it needed to allocate to several interrelated and somewhat conflicting internal development projects. The game was played in four rounds of 16 minutes. At the beginnings of Rounds 2, 3, and 4, an information bulletin was presented to the players. Bulletins contained news that would affect, and often scramble, any tentative plans the group was in the process of making.

Videotapes of the games were analyzed to develop measures of nine group behaviors, defined below. The roster of behaviors was based on past group interaction research (e.g., Benne & Sheats, 1948; Bales, 1950). The definitions of the behaviors were influenced by the actual types of behaviors generated by the players.

Initiating occurred when a person made a statement that affected the line of thought in the subsequent stream of conversation. *Information seeking* usually took the form of a question, sometimes asking for clarification. *Information giving* responses presented information pursuant to an idea already started in the conversation (not an initiation) or in response to a question. *Clarifying* was an elaboration of an idea presented by the same or different person not more than a few statements previously.

Harmonizing sometimes took the form of a simple statement of agreement with a previous remark. At other times it took the form of active conflict resolution, but real ideological arguments broke out during the sessions studied.

Gatekeeping was a response that indicated that a line of conversation was getting off the track, or deviating from the goal, or confusing the issue at hand. Statements that were geared toward opening a channel of communication, either in content or form, were scored as initiation responses. *Following* responses usually denoted an agreement, but verbal or nonverbal gestures indicated that the speaker was following a line of thought and wanted to encourage it.

Tension relief took two basic forms. One was a remark that made some or all of the players laugh. Joining in the laughter also counted as a tension relief response. Another type of tension relief was a comment that broke an uncomfortable silence but did not have the initiating qualities of initiation responses defined earlier. The last category was *unclassified responses*, which did not fit into the foregoing categories or were unintelligible on the videotape.

Preliminary Analyses and Results

The first step in the analysis was to factor analyze the nine behavior measures. The maximum likelihood factor extraction method was used with direct oblimin (oblique) rotation; it was strongly suspected that there would be a significant correlation between the behavior factors. The routine extracted two factors (criterion eigenvalue = 1.00), and the correlation between them was .31. A criterion loading of .30 was used to interpret the factors. Factor 1 consisted of information seeking, information giving, clarifying, gatekeeping, initiating, and following. Factor 2 consisted of tension release, clarifying, initiating, harmonizing, and unclassified reponses.

The next step was to ascertain the relationship between personality traits and the behavior factors. Behavior factor scores were compiled by simply adding together the responses made in the categories that loaded on a particular factor. This factor score method involved no sample-specific weights that could have capitalized on a great deal of chance in a relatively small sample.

Bivariate correlation analysis using primary personality traits identified three significant traits for Factor 1: warmth and participativeness, social boldness, and unpretentiousness or a tendency to self-disclose. The multiple R^2 for this set of traits was .17. There were four primary personality traits associated with Factor 2, which were the same three traits associated with Factor 1 plus dominance or assertiveness. The multiple R^2 for this set of four traits was .18. Of additional interest, the Creative Potential trait composite (Rieke et al., 1994, and see chapter 10) was significantly correlated with Factor 2 ($r^2 = .10$, $p < .05$) but not with Factor 1. Factor 1 was interpreted as *general participation* (GP). Factor 2 was interpreted as *especially creative participation* (ECP).

Interaction Dynamics

It appears that group interaction behaviors self-organize around two main themes in a problem-solving context, GP and ECP. The ECP shared clarification and initiating behavior with GP. As an ECP behavior, clarification would take the form of creative elaboration; as a GP it would simply mean making oneself better understood by others. Similarly, initiating could be doing something that is obviously needed, but as an ECP it would take the form of a major insight, or a self-organization process, that sends the group off in a promising direction.

A bifurcation map of the separation of behaviors appears in Fig. 11.7. The next sequence of analyses was designed to identify whether temporal dynamics were occurring in either of the behavior constellations (GP or

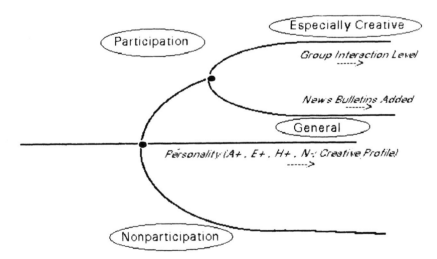

FIG. 11.7. Bifurcation diagram for group participation behaviors in the Island Commission simulation.

ECP), whether the group context or roles within groups influenced those dynamics, whether the mushroom catastrophe hypothesis was valid for the Island Commission application, and whether additional instabilities or chaotic components were also apparent.

Effect of News Bulletins and Different Problem-Solving Groups. Two hypotheses were tested. First, the news bulletins were hypothesized to affect the dynamics of role play by introducing a chaos-producing influence. If that were true, greater changes in group behavior, especially ECP, should occur over the four rounds of the game. Second, the impact of the news bulletins was hypothesized to occur as an interaction between round in the game and the actual game, because each group was composed of different people, whose collective response to the news bulletins would have a feedback-type impact on all other players in a particular group. Thus, a split-plot analysis of variance (ANOVA) was conducted where round of the game was the repeated factor, and group was the fixed factor. The main effect for game was not thought to have additional theoretical importance.

Analyses were conducted separately for GP and ECP. Results for GP showed a significant main effect for round of the game, or news bulletins ($F_{3,144} = 14.74$, $p < .001$). There was no main effect for game, but there was a significant bulletin-by-game interaction ($F_{18,144} = 2.12$, $p < .01$). Results of the analysis of ECP showed no significant main effect for round, but there was a significant bulletin-by-game interaction ($F_{18,144} = 2.59$, $p < .001$). A significant effect for game was also observed in the analysis of ECP ($F_{6,144} = 5.55$, $p < .001$), which was unexpected.

An inspection of the group means showed that GP increased after the first bulletin and maintained a constant level afterward. The ECP, however, did not change. It appears, therefore, that the instability produced by the news bulletins caused a lot more talk, but the actual engagement of creative forces was inconsistent.

In the bulletin-by-game interactions for ECP and GP, the actual nature of the trends was not important, but the observation that volatile inter-active trends did occur was important. The concept of sensitive dependency strongly suggested that the patterns the group formed earlier in the game would affect the reaction to a stimulus later, and each group might be reacting to a new bulletin differently each time they encountered one.

An additional multivariate ANOVA (MANOVA) was conducted to determine if the ECP trend by game could be related to any of the personality variables found earlier. That appeared to be true. There was no significant multivariate effect, or univariate effect for warmth, assertiveness, boldness, or self-disclosing tendencies. There was a significant univariate effect for creative potential, however ($F_{6,48} = 3.56$, $p < .01$). It appeared, through inspection of group means, that the highest and lowest scoring groups on creative potential were also the highest and lowest scoring groups on ECP.

Effect of Gaming Role. Players in Island Commission took on the role of a particular island dignitary, such as Director of Chamber of Commerce, Director of Community Development, General Manager of a manufacturing plant, Organizational Development consultant, and Council Member. Although most players later said that role name did not affect their play, a test was conducted to be sure that was true throughout the set of games. Some bulletin-by-round interaction could have occurred because some of the news bulletins made special mention of some of the island dignitaries' concerns, such as food production. In some of the games, the introduction of the bulletins was met with additional responses from a person supposedly playing a role that was implicated in the bulletin.

Once again a split-plot ANOVA was conducted for GP and ECP separately. The repeated effect was bulletin again, and the fixed effect was role (eight levels). Results for both GP and ECP showed no main effect for role. A bulletin-by-role interaction was observed for GP ($F_{21,141} = 177$, $p < .05$) only. This effect and lack of others indicated that some nominal contributions from players were introduced after news bulletins, but no major creative efforts resulted.

Mushroom Catastrophe Dynamics

In light of the mushroom catastrophe theory of creative processes in groups, summarized in chapter 10, it was hypothesized that the group participation efforts in the Island Commission would display mushroom structure. Figure 11.8 shows the frequency distribution for all responses of the 55 players (top panel), followed by distributions of GP (middle) and ECP (lower). The essential mushroom structure was apparent, but there did appear to be some added noise in the display.

The mushroom hypothesis was tested by polynomial canonical correlation analysis, using the following model from Equation 37 of chapter 3:

$$\gamma_1 \Delta u + \gamma_2 \Delta v = \beta_0 + \beta_1 v_1^3 + \beta_2 u_1^2 + \beta_3 u_1 v_1 + \beta_4 c u_1 + \beta_5 d v_1 + \beta_6 a + \beta_7 b$$

where u is the ECP, v is the GP, c is the average number of responses of any type per person in a game, d is the sequential round of the game from which the measurements were taken, a and b were collapsed into a unit-weight weighted composite of the four personality traits that were

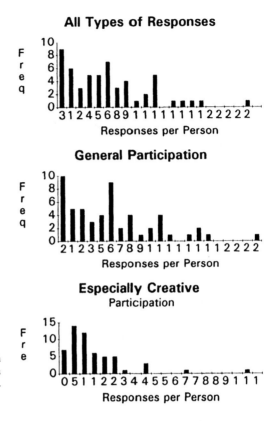

FIG. 11.8. Frequency distribution of group participation responses for all groups in the Island Commission simulation.

identified previously, and γ_i and β_i were regression weights. Parameter c thus represented a measure of group interaction density.

The hypothesized mushroom catastrophe model appears in Fig. 11.9. According to the model, the groups that interacted more, and thus emitted a greater total number of responses, would be those where individuals could produce increasing numbers of responses throughout the game. In other words, the group process would influence individual behavior. Location parameters of all variables were set to 0.00. Scale parameters were the ordinary standard deviations of variables observed in Round 1 only.

Difference scores were calculated for all people between successive rounds. There was a total of 165 data frames for the study. The initial multivariate test showed that there were canonical variates present in the data (Wilks $\Lambda = 0.49$, $F_{12,314} = 11.12$, $p < .001$), and two were extracted.

The composite criterion for the first canonical variate was composed of two parts Δu minus one part Δv. Significant canonical weights were observed for all terms in the model except dv_1 and the personality variable

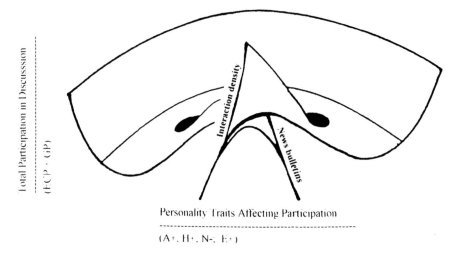

FIG. 11.9. Mushroom catastrophe model for results of the Island Commission experiment and dynamics analysis.

(canonical $r^2 = .47$, $p < .001$). The first canonical variate was thus composed of ECP, which was purged of any noncreative overlap with GP. All the essential components of the model were represented among the significant terms. The dv_1 was significantly correlated with the first canonical variate, but its effect in the model was apparently redundant with other terms already represented. The missing asymmetry variable does not alter the essential nonlinear structure.

The composite criterion for the second canonical variate was composed of almost equal parts Δu and Δv. Significant canonical weights were observed for dv_1 and the personality variable only (canonical $r^2 = .07$, $p < .10$). The second canonical variate was thus composed of all types of responses lumped together.

Ordinary polynomial regression was conducted for the two difference criteria separately. For change in ECP, R^2 was .38 ($p < .001$), and significant weights were observed for all terms except round (or new bulletins) as a bifurcation variable. For change in GP, $R^2 = .07$ ($p < .10$), and significant weights were observed for dv_1 and the personality asymmetry variable only. Other variants of the model were tested, such as reversing ECP and GP as the behavior with the cubic potential or reversing bifurcation parameters c and d. Neither manipulation resulted in an improved model.

Linear control models were calculated for each of the behavior criteria separately. For GP, the linear difference model was significant ($R^2 = .29$, $p < .01$). The control variables that were tested were bulletin, personality, and group response density, but only bulletin showed a significant weight in the model. For the pre–post linear control, R^2 was .65 ($p < .001$) with significant weights for bulletin, personality, and GP at Time 1. For ECP, the linear difference model was not significant ($R^2 = .03$). The pre–post linear model was significant ($R^2 = .46$) and slightly less than that obtained for the canonical mushroom. Weights in the linear pre–post model were significant for personality, group response density, and ECP at Time 1.

The conclusion from the mushroom analysis was that the results substantiated the mushroom structure on the basis of the first canonical variate, which was composed of both behaviors and the necessary power potentials and modulus term. The composition of the second canonical variate depicted the role of bulletins and personality as being more closely linked to GP, which was expected from the preliminary analyses.

Nonlinear Regression Analysis

The final set of analyses assessed the mushroom catastrophe structure using a different analytic approach. In principle, the nonlinear regression approach should corroborate the conclusion that creativity in a problem-solving group is a high-dimensional nonlinear process, with a response surface codimensionality close to that of the mushroom (i.e., five). Also, the presence of noninteger dimensionality could signify that additional instabilities were taking place that, on the one hand, were thought to exist on the basis of the frequency distributions discussed earlier, and on the other, could account for the moderate, rather than large, effect size for the mushroom model.

The hypothesized nonlinear regression model was an umbilic variant of the logistic hypothesis (Guastello, 1993a):

$$\gamma_1 u_2 + \gamma_2 v_2 = \theta_1 e^{(\theta_2 u_1)} + \theta_3 e^{(\theta_4 v_1)} \tag{7}$$

where γ_i are weights on the dependent measures and θ_i are nonlinear regression weights, and u is ECP and v is GP as before. For this application, the two behaviors were weighted as they had emerged from the first canonical variate of the mushroom catastrophe analysis. The final equation that resulted from the nonlinear regression analysis was:

$$1.09u_1 - 0.59v_1 = -.06e^{(0.94u_1)} + .01e^{(1.06v_1)} \tag{8}$$

with $R^2 = .49$ ($p < .001$). An expanded form of Equation 7 was also tested to determine whether the bifurcation variables in the study made any additional contribution to the model. Although R^2 increased to .51, there is considerable collinearity among the parameters tested. A frequency distribution of responses per person appears in Fig. 11.8 for all groups combined.

The dimensionality (D) of the process was calculated as:

$$D = e^{0.94} + e^{1.06} = 5.43 \qquad (9)$$

The dimensionality of the behavior was within the range expected for a mushroom dynamic. There was also a fractal character to the attractor system in the amount of 0.43 dimensions of expansion.

Discussion

The results obtained from the Island Commission experiment were consistent with theoretical expectations concerning the mushroom catastrophe structure. The group problem-solving behaviors could be reduced to two behaviors, GP and ECP. The GP and ECP illustrated the proper cubic and quadratic potentials with respect to a difference criterion composed of the two variables. The two outcomes showed interactive behavior as well. Interaction density was a strong bifurcation variable associated with ECP. News bulletins, represented by rounds of the game, was a weaker bifurcation variable associated with GP.

The personality variables at first distinguished active participants from less active participants on the basis of four traits: warmth and participativeness, assertiveness or dominance, social boldness, and self-disclosing tendencies. Assertiveness or dominance further distinguished people who gave more ECP responses than other players. Personality traits continued to play a small role in the nonlinear analyses that addressed how players' participation levels changed over time.

The role of group interaction density was essentially the same as the cumulative response variable in the EBB study in chapter 10. The amount of communication and idea generation by the group is intrinsic to an individual's creative output. The news about instability-producing events appeared to engender discussion but not creative initiatives. This finding was unexpected in light of the working axiom that creativity causes chaos and chaos causes creativity. It may be true that the link between the news event and creative initiatives is indirect and dependent on the intensity of the general discussion. This suggested relationship could be explored in other ways in future studies.

The Island Commission study corroborated Dennis and Valacich's (1993) results in a different form. Although Dennis and Valacich determined that larger group sizes resulted in a critical mass of thought that resulted in groups outperforming the most productive individuals, this study showed that groups with larger levels of output resulted in greater individual outcomes as well. The pair of findings lends further support to the NDS theory of creative processes, which holds that greater numbers and quality of communication channels and feedback links propel a successful creative process.

The presence of the personality influences strongly suggests that social loafing and group reward and task definition structures are not exhaustive explanations for why, historically, some groups have not performed as well as their most talented individuals. Future research should devote some attention to the nonlinear dynamics of group problem-solving processes where motivational variables have been manipulated. Indeed motivational variables were implicated in the process of creative production in chapter 5 but not followed up as yet. It would appear that stronger motivational pressures might cause a group's behavior spectrum to expand over the full range of the response manifold; higher R^2 values for the nonlinear structural models would then be likely.

SUMMARY

This chapter covered several perspectives on organizational development suggested from NDS theory. The sequence of unfreezing, change, and refreezing has been inverted to a worldview characterized by large and small levels of turbulence with stability as a temporary transitional state of affairs. The force field of change has been converted from opposing forces of pressure to change versus resistance to change, to sets of diverging gradients that travel from a bifurcation point to either an attractor representing the change goal or an attractor representing the starting state. An organization is moved toward change by first raising its entropy level, if circumstances have not already accomplished that. The organization then reduces entropy when it enters a new attractor regime characterized by new interpersonal structures, strategies for business plans, and possibly an overhaul in values or other aspects of culture.

Chaos-OD theorists have differences of opinion regarding the merits of visioning as a leadership technique. On the one hand, vision messages convey pictures of desirable attractor states. On the other, visions can induce tunnel vision in an organization whereby alternative action strategies and opportunities for new growth are overlooked or underappreciated. It may be true that vision is worthwhile so long as it remains contained within a creative process in the sense of visualizing solutions to problems, rather than as an axiom that has a restrictive effect on all possible future actions.

Sociotechnical systems theory, although it originated decades before the NDS approach to OD, was based squarely on the principle of self-organization. Self-organization is a natural process by which people form relationships to each other and to their tasks, and is the central "energy cell" that propels successful organizational change. It is also the same process that underlies the consolidation of ideas into creative solutions for organizational strategy and just about any place else when creativity is useful. The latest installment in the development of the sociotechnical systems theme occurs in the rethinking of TQM principles in terms of NDS principles.

Although the OD area of application contains a heavy dosage of theory that remains to be tested, empirical work available presently has confirmed and elaborated some of the key ideas. A study of corporate strategy development in a savings and loan company showed that the cusp catastrophe model for organizational change appears to have merit, but also that any one organizational change attempt might not occupy the full scope of the cusp manifold. The particular change event experienced by the savings and loan company represented a dabbling in a change strategy that did not stabilize. Results of the polynomial regression analyses confirmed that a cusp process was not better than a linear maintainstability explanation. Nonlinear regression showed that the process occupied more than one but less than two dimensions. The sign of the dimension value was positive, thus signifying a chaotic expansion.

Teams or groups have long been regarded as the building blocks of organizational change processes. A simulated group production situation showed that the groups' production trends were decidedly chaotic. The groups did not have trouble producing, but management showed severe difficulty with assimilating their work into "salable" units.

Group problem solving, finally, reflected the high-dimensional dynamic predicted from the mushroom catastrophe theory of creative processes started in chapter 10. The critical mass of ideas generated by the group was critical to the formulation of plans to develop the infrastructure of a small self-governing island. The creative process, which is central to an organization's ability to cope with a chaotically changing environment, is the result of a twin dynamic consisting of general communication and idea generation (GP) and a self-organizing process in which new directions in thought were undertaken and elaborated (ECP).

12

Chaos, Revolution, and War

The goal of this chapter is to extend the social theories, now heavily influenced by NDS, from the previous chapters to national and supranational systems. The first new observation is the unusual number of times books on sociopolitical or socioeconomic themes contain the word "chaos" in their titles. Examples include *Empire of Chaos* (Amin, 1992), which refers to the role of capitalism and world economy, *The Politics of Chaos* (Neatby, 1972), which concerns the politics of Canada in the 1930s, *Cocoa and Chaos in Ghana* (Mikell, 1989), which describes the social and economic turbulence in that country caused in part by its monocrop agricultural base, *Policies of Chaos* (White, 1989), concerning the politics of the People's Republic of China, and *Anarchy or Chaos* (Woodcock, 1944), which is a history of the major anarchistic political movements that were particularly influential in England. I discovered *Freedom Chooses Slavery* (d'Andrade, 1959) accidentally while chasing down another book in the library; chapter 1 was entitled, "Internal Well-being versus International Economic Chaos," and chapter 2, "Accident in the Life of the World."

The list of chaos-containing titles did not explicitly reference mathematical chaos theory, but the sheer weight of their numbers seems to be a scream for attention from a chaos scientist. Loye and Eisler (1987) noted similar themes in sociological works by Mumford, who referred to the "age of disintegration," by Drucker, who referred to the "age of discontinuity" (p. 54), and by Durkheim, who popularized the term *anomie*," which refers to "the psychological effects of the breakdown of norms and social expectations that characterize social chaos states" (p. 59). On an earlier occasion Loye (1977) suggested that these forms of social disintegration were the result of too much restraint, and I am reminded of the beam-buckling analogy to revolutionary change dynamic in the previous chapter.

All the works just mentioned have all influenced the composition of this chapter directly or indirectly. The first section of this chapter presents two NDS perspectives on revolution within a nation, and the next section presents NDS perspectives of wars between nations. The third section ponders the idea of the first world revolution and possibilities and liabilities of a world government.

PERSPECTIVES ON REVOLUTIONS

The growth of empires—Greek, Roman, Carthaginian, Persian—is well known, as is their disintegration. Disintegration of these and post-Medieval empires—Spanish, British, Dutch, Portuguese, Ottoman—appears to be marked by two common themes. When an empire has overexpanded, the ruling center is no longer responsive to the needs of the fringes, and it invites revolution from those territories; such revolts are predictable from the dynamics of attractor basins (Rosser, 1991). It also becomes vulnerable to assaults from competing empires. A second theme is that the massive expansion invites greater migration toward the center. Although its infrastructure differentiated and evolved accordingly (e.g., streets and sewers), Rome could not withstand the weight of the population and disintegrated; its population went from 1 million at its peak to around 30,000 a few centuries later (Artigiani, 1991).

Anarchy

Anarchy or Chaos (Woodcock, 1944) was written 20 years before Lorenz discovered the strange attractor, and the actual political movements based on anarchist political theory in Europe dated back to the 17th century. I found, nonetheless, that the core concepts were quite consistent with proper use of NDS concepts as we know them today, as well as with contemporary theory about the nature of revolutions.

Anarchy is not the Molotov-cocktail-throwing violence that it is often depicted as representing. On the contrary, the central themes have always revolved around peaceability and cooperation. The problem is that the rest of society does not leave such people alone for too long. Anarchy is a social system without a central government. There is no coercive participation in societal functions. Rather, anarchist societies are based on voluntary cooperation for the common good, and patterns of cooperation among people vary as needs vary. Many such fluid patterns can coexist at one point in time. Anarchy is thus the self-organization principle at work.

Conventional governments, in contrast, exist to maintain the stability of the socioeconomic order. Governments maintain negative feedback loops to prevent the disruption of the flow of wealth from the large percentage of proletariat (19th century word) to the small percentage of wealthy elite. When the distribution of wealth becomes too disparate, the potential for revolution increases, and is in turn met with counterrevolutionary suppression from the centralist forces.

War, according to Woodcock (1944), is just another way to curtail individual freedom. Those citizens who are not forced to fight are forced to work in munitions factories. If they are small business owners, their businesses have to be closed because of war obligations. That maneuver serves the interests of Big Money, who effectively eliminates competition in a broad range of business activities. Later research showed that nations with greater levels of civil liberty internally engage in fewer armed conflicts or wars (Rummel, 1983).

Armed revolution has, historically, been more of a failure than a success. The hegemonies that are overthrown become replaced by other hegemonies. Woodcock (1944) cited the French Revolution and its later politics as examples. Contemporary Latin America has many more such examples to its credit. The explosiveness of the Russian revolution was a curiosity that began with anarchist ideology, but adapted to meet particular situational requirements. Given the cycle of sustained poverty and indebtedness of the Russian peasant, the overthrow of the Czarist regime was more necessary than ideological purity. The lack of individual freedom that characterized the ensuing communist rule was based on two principles. First, in order for the revolution to work (it had failed once), energy could not be diverted from the common goal. Second, because the people never had individual freedom, they would not have any less under communism..

Juntas in Latin America

Heggen and Cuzan (1981) developed and tested a model for revolution in Latin American countries that was based on three interlocking control parameters: legitimacy, scope, and coercion. *Legitimacy* is the degree to which a government is recognized by the people as the correct and proper government; freely elected governments are viewed as more legitimate than those established by dictatorial military juntas (Cuzan, 1986). *Scope* is comparable to the organizational concept of span of control, which is the number of aspects of individual and business life that are controlled by the government. *Coercion* is the use of military to suppress revolutionary initiatives.

The relationships among the three parameters are nonlinear. Legitimacy increases as scope decreases. Coercion increases with increased scope to combat decreased perceptions of legitimacy. The highly coercive governments show less economic growth than others, perhaps because so much resource is devoted to suppressing the people. The governments' prerogatives are to maintain internal efficiency and to minimize social cost. *Internal efficiency* refers to the self-serving rewards of operating a government: salaries, grafts, perks, promoting a pet ideology. *Social costs* include taxes, confiscations, imprisonment, execution, or making people disappear mysteriously. As social cost increases, the risk of revolt increases, unless greater coercion is introduced to keep people in line (Heggan & Cuzan, 1981).

Violent revolution is typically undertaken by military organizations that dismantle the old machinery and establish themselves with sufficient coercive self-maintenance. Coercive tendencies threaten legitimacy. Stable growth requires a stable ratio of military personnel to the amount of fiscal expansion, where fiscal expansion is dollarized growth in scope in the form of taxation and spending. Lower ratios are required for stable democracies (Cuzan, 1986).

Adelman and Hihn (1982) developed a butterfly catastrophe model for the onset of juntas in Latin America, based on the political histories of 15 countries. The butterfly surface depicted three qualitatively different revolutionary outcomes: technocracy, compromise polyarchy, and consensus polyarchy. A *technocracy* is an elitist management system that is coupled with declining political participation. A *consensus polyarchy* is system of elected government officials that represent the different political interests of the nations. A *compromise polyarchy* has attributes of the two extremes and occupies the central sheet of the butterfly surface. A *popularist* government would be located on the same plane as the consensus polyarchy, but further off-center from the attractor and closer to the bifurcation set of the response manifold; popular governments have relatively high levels of political participation but run a high risk of authoritarian *coup d'état*. The three types of political outcomes are located on the unfolded side of the butterfly surface. Behind the point of degenerate singularity (butterfly point) is one type of outcome, which is a *closed hegemony*.

Transition between political forms begins with the asymmetry parameter, which is inequality of income. Inequality is greater for the technocracy, and least for the consensus polyarchy. The bifurcation parameter is education level. At lower income levels only modifications of the closed hegemony are possible. As the population becomes more educated, more diversified political forms are possible. The bias parameter was not specified for the model. The butterfly parameter controls whether the political shifts will be between the consensus polyarchy and technocracy only, or whether the middle sheet of the surface could open up. Change between the extreme forms would occur in countries that begin with low levels of political participation. Three-way change is likely when political participation is high.

Security Subsystem

The butterfly catastrophe model for the internal security subsystem that was developed at the organismic and organizational levels in chapter 8 can be transposed to the national level. The result is an explanation for how a national security system would respond to threats to its legitimacy (Guastello, 1988b).

Once again, the response surface depicts three behavioral modalities (Fig. 12.1). At the least effective level, the nation is susceptible to invasions by other nations and civil unrest from within. At the middle level, the nation is protected from invaders, but civil disorder is still a problem. Civil disorder would include political unrest and elevated crime levels. At the third level, the nation is reasonably free of civil disorder as well.

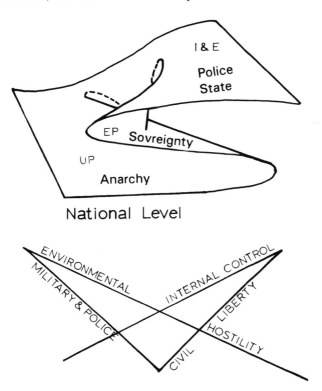

FIG. 12.1. Butterfly catastrophe model of the organizational security subsystem. From Guastello (1988b). Reprinted with permission.

Of course, "crime" is a relative term and can mean politicized behavior that the state does not approve of, mixed together with conventional crime against persons and property.

The control parameters are also analogous to controls for organismic and organizational levels. Once again, the asymmetry parameter represents *environmental hostility*, which is now defined in sociopolitical terms. The bifurcation parameter is composed of externally oriented defenses such as *military and intelligence capability*, and geographical boundaries. The swallowtail or bias parameter is the *police protection* that separates the civil unrest modality from the peaceful-normal modality. It is an extruder system that protects the society from undesirable elements occurring within its boundaries and operates on what is conventionally regarded as crime. Without it, life in the society becomes similar to the Old West United States as it was depicted in popular media. Hopf bifurcation or a similar dynamic operates here also. As crime escalates, so does the activity of the extruder system. The process is thus coevolutionary and akin to arms race dynamics (discussed in the next section). Although the extruder begins to operate within the society's libertarian conventions, overactivity produces greater error rates in this respect. Two surface gradients can be identified with this parameter. One protects civil liberty, and the other violates it, both with the intent of curbing hostility in the internal environment.

The butterfly parameter, *internal control*, governs the coaction of the boundary and extruder forces. The dynamic attribute of the system is the degree to which subsystems are turned against the resident populations by the decision-making subsystem. Such aberrant behavior would take a range of observable forms, from minor invasions of privacy to random police inspections and abridgements of First Amendment rights (of the U.S. Constitution). Police state conditions would be located on the open manifold side of the surface. Because the extrinsic rewards of enforced law and order occur at the expense of intrinsic rights (civil liberties), many citizens can be expected to also become dissidents according to the catastrophe-equity theory (Guastello, 1981); the overall status of the system would stabilize at the middle level. In the face of excessive amounts of civil unrest, the control point representing the system's security status moves toward the lowest fold line, at which the system is vulnerable to attack from outside forces.

Police states are stable. Their impact depends on whether one is describing "the land of the free and the home of the brave," a land of single-minded ideology where the needs of the state supersede any individual rights, or a "land of the slave and home of the wimp." The first case was described earlier. The third is where people do not care about their rights as long as some agency is protecting them from physical harm. In the second case, however, people agree that the needs of the state supersede the rights of individuals, and thus little or no hostility occurs in reaction to extruder activity.

The decider function can do more than simply increase or relax extruder activity. It can control hostility in the internal environmental by controlling the flow of information from which competitive ideologies could develop, and by removing any rights to keep and bear arms. It can control external sources of hostility through large defense budgets and military readiness, and by expanding its boundaries to envelop buffer states between its regular orders and its enemies.

The ideology factor can be built into the model as a fifth control parameter, thereby allowing a greater range of national situations. The model becomes a wigwam catastrophe, in which there are three stable modalities and one unstable condition. The three stable modalities are no protection, protection from external agencies only, and protection from internal and external agencies but with a low individual freedom. The unstable condition is one where there is protection from internal and external agencies and individual freedom is high. Thus civil liberty is fragile in a milieu of increasing hostility from internal or external sources.

Games, Attitudes, and Butterfly Models

As mentioned in chapter 9, cooperation is unlikely when large groups of diverse people are concerned. At the same time, the history of politics shows that groups of people are often organized into smaller, more homogeneous groups, and coalitions often form between the limited number of groups when there is a common basis of mutual cooperation. Indeed, some nations have governments structured as coalitions among nationally recognized political parties. As one example of a stable coalition in U.S. politics, the National Association for the Advancement of Colored People (NAACP) and the American Civil Liberties Union (ACLU) have often cooperated when issues of racial equality and constitutionally guaranteed liberty were a concern (Walker, 1990).

More general rules of cooperative coalition have emerged from the latest round of work from Glance and Huberman (1994). It appears that when a group of people is playing an iterative cooperation game, the state of mutual defection is not total and complete. Rather, there is some chaotic jitter around the equilibrium as players try to feel out the other players and predict their actions. When a player is given false information that other players will be cooperating with some adventure, which is akin to moving a control parameter past a critical value, one player will cooperate and by doing so attract other players to do the same. The interesting dynamic is, however, that once one person starts to cooperate the shift from noncooperation to cooperation is sharply discontinuous.

Glance and Huberman (1994) were developing a game-theoretical explanation for an old marketing trick known as social validity. By telling people that "everyone is doing it" someone will jump in and do it, which gives more credence to the continued claim that "everyone is doing it." The game model is the Unscrupulous Diner's Dilemma, in which the cost of a participation for an individual decreases as the number of participants increase. These gaming dynamics were taking place in East Germany when massive protests precipitated the downfall of the German Democratic Republic (DDR) in favor of German reunification. As more people joined the demonstrations, the risk of arrest declined. Different people had different thresholds for participation, but the total number of demonstrators grew to more than 500,000.

The spread of an attitude change is influenced by the physical distance between attitude sender and attitude receiver. An attitude derived from a next-door neighbor's actions would have greater impact than a message from a neighborhood across town (Glance & Huberman, 1994; Latané et al., 1994). The results of cellular automata simulations of spatial attitude spread and attitude stability are consistent with predictions from independently-drawn theories from social psychology (Nowak et al., 1990; Latané et al., 1994).

The suddenness of attitude change was addressed by Flay (1978). Although there has, of late, been more NDS work on attitude change (Eiser, 1994; Kaplowitz et al., 1983; Latané & Nowak, 1994), the essential principles do not appear to have changed appreciably. According to Flay, attitude change appears to require a butterfly catastrophe model to depict the convolutions already known from experimental social psychological research. The use of persuasive communications can induce attitude change (asymmetry), but is much less effective when the target person is strongly committed to a point of view (bifurcation). Some persuasive communications are more effective than others, not the least of which is the credibility of the source (bias).

Flay (1978) acknowledged that the butterfly factor was more conceptually fuzzy than the other three control parameters, but I think we can help him out here. The key feature of a butterfly model is that there are three stable states of attitude, which means that the broad theory is more complex than a simple attitude change such as cooperation or noncooperation, or political demonstration versus not. The middle sheet of a butterfly surface represents a compromise position between two extremes, which is, in principle, more stable than a saddle point. A compromise position may be viable when the issues concerning an attitude are complex. For instance, a political upheaval may occur due to combinations of social problems and economic problems. If a citizen is faced with a binary choice, two reasons to act are better than one or none. But if a citizen is trying to select a political candidate from an array of choices, a candidate in a compromise position might win the election. The fourth control parameter would be, therefore, the level of complexity, dissonance, and confusion among the political messages.

The translation of an attitude into action is another matter. The butterfly catastrophe model of equity in organizations. The equity model can be just as easily transformed into a butterfly model of equity in society with three qualitative behavior states. At one extreme, the citizen would participate in the social change and think up new ways to move it along. At the compromise position, the citizen would support the change with a vote when called upon to do so, but would remain passive, letting others do the thinking and most of the work. At the other extreme, the citizen would avoid or work against the change initiative either actively or passively.

The four gradients would be, from the citizen's viewpoint, the financial rewards of participation in the change such as promises of tax cuts that never arrive, costs of participation such as financial loss or loss of life, the positive value of the social principles typified by the revolutionary strategy, and the negative social backlash that could arise from participating in a movement that draws too much social disapproval. Each citizen would evaluate the same situation differently, which is where the diversity issue comes into play. The trick for the revolutionary hierarchy would be to define the revolution goals in terms of a stable position that could attract a coalition of supporters.

WAR

This section covers three nonlinear perspectives on war: repeated conflicts between nations, arms race dynamics, and the role of polarity in world conflict. The section concludes with new projections of polarity and international hostilities into the near future based on available theory and data.

Repeated Two-Nation Conflicts

Rummel (1987) built a butterfly catastrophe model to describe repeated hostilities between two nations; the discord between India and Pakistan over the 1948–1973 period was used as the illustrative example. According to the model, hostility and its opposite, cooperation, lie on a continuum, and some amount of conflict is always assumed. At one stable outcome state, the net result is nonviolent disagreements. At the middle sheet of the surface is scattered violence. At the bottom sheet is all-out war.

A butterfly model implies four control parameters, which are based on current political research. The asymmetry parameter reflects the imminent ability to engage in violence and is defined as the buildup of military resources and deployment of them along critical borders. The bifurcation parameter is the political gap between the two nations as measured by differences in political values within the nations, and the amount of disagreement the two nations displayed in their votes at United Nations meetings. The bias factor is joint freedom, which is an average of measures for the two countries during a particular year. Prior research (Rummel, 1983) showed that nations that promoted greater individual freedom for their citizens were less likely to engage in war.

The fourth control parameter (butterfly, d) in the theoretical model is *joint power projection*. Power projection is the ability for a nation to deliver a political or military assault on a nation of a given geographical distance. Because India and Pakistan are next-door neighbors, the operating geographical warring distance is 0.

The model was tested using the polynomial regression method for a butterfly catastrophe presented in chapters 3 and 5. The R^2 for the butterfly model depicting aggressions by India against Pakistan was .47, compared to a control linear R^2 of .14. The R^2 for the butterfly model depicting aggressions by Pakistan against India was .45 compared to .20 for the linear alternative. All weights in all models were significant, and encouraging for future modeling of war dynamics.

Arms Race Dynamics

At the end of World War II (1940–1945), the United States and its allies had defeated the armies of Japan and Nazi Germany, which had both embarked on programs for world domination. The United States had won a race against Germany to build the first nuclear bomb by a matter of months. Stockpiles of German V2 rockets, which were intended to transport nuclear bombs at long distances, were discovered in caves and brought back to the United States for closer analysis and eventual use in the first phases of the outer space exploration projects. Germany was defeated through conventional military strategies. Two atomic bombs were dropped from aircraft over Japan, exacting an unconditional surrender.

By the end of the war, U.S. armies were strewn all over the strategic points of the world. Allied armies met Soviet armies in Germany, and drew boundaries over the country and its capital city Berlin, such that three-quarters of each became Allied controlled and shortly thereafter placed under the autonomous rule of the Federal Republic of Germany. The remaining quarters of Germany and Berlin were Soviet controlled, and the German Democratic Republic was erect to govern there. The meeting of U.S. and Soviet armies proved uncomfortable; the Soviet Union established a political and military sphere of influence over the Eastern European nations. The United States promoted a relatively democratic government in Japan, cultivated capitalistic economic relationships with Japan, the Philippines, and West Germany, and kept its armies in place.

The United States and Soviet Union had created, perhaps without intention, a polarized world order. The Soviet Union soon developed nuclear capability, and the Cold War tension between the two nations began. Tensions were exacerbated by a third player, China, which revolutionized into its own brand of communism in 1949. To the U.S. military, communism was spreading according to the initial world view of Karl Marx. To the Soviet Union, the United States must have appeared as another threat in their historical chain. U.S. armies boxed them in on two sides, and we had already used an atomic bomb. The two nations thus engaged in a massive buildup of weaponry, including intercontinental ballistic missiles (ICBMs), so they could shoot nuclear material at each other over the North Pole, anti-ICBMs (ABMs) to knock out each other's ICBMs, and antisatellite missiles (ASATs) to knock out each other's ABMs. By the mid-1980s, each side had built up so many nuclear weapons they could each make the earth uninhabitable indefinitely.

The arms race reached still more absurd proportions when it was discovered that the Soviet Union was developing a killer satellite. The killer would be shot into orbit, cuddle up to an enemy satellite, and blow itself up. That launched a U.S. countereffort for the Strategic Defense Initiative (SDI, popularly known as "Star Wars" after a popular science fiction movie of the day), which was a highly costly space-based "defense" system that could knock out missiles from a satellite location, or knock out killer satellites.

It may not be surprising to learn that there was a high linear correlation ($r^2 = .82$) between U.S. military expenditures in one year and Soviet expenditures the next, and vice versa. Unfortunately, that value is inflated because it was based on an ordinary least squares model that did not take time dependence, or autocorrelation, or serial dependence among residuals into account. Not doing so could overestimate the true relationship between x and y by up to 300%. Thus, although there would still remain evidence of an arms race, the arms races are more of a function of autonomous buildup, or self-propelling policy, than they are a function of strategic realities of the two nations against each other (Ostrom, 1978).

Richardson (1960) developed a set of mathematical models that would describe nations' propensity to build armaments. The models turned out to be extensions of the logistic map, which Mayer-Kress (1992) explored through simulation. Equations 1 and 2 describe the armament expenditures for two nations x and y at two points in time t and $t + 1$:

$$x_{t+1} = x_t - k_{11}(x_t - x_s) + k_{12}y_t(1 - x_t) \tag{1}$$

$$y_{t+1} = y_t - k_{22}(y_t - y_s) + k_{21}x_t(1 - y_t) \tag{2}$$

where expenditures are expressed as fractions of available resource that would be appropriated to armaments. Parameters x_s and y_s are the countries' location parameters for armament supplies if no race were taking place. The coefficients k_{11} and k_{22} represent a force that controls the expenditures toward the prerace levels. Coefficients k_{12} and k_{21} represent the speed of the hostilities themselves. Analysis showed that a stable point could exist if k_{21} and k_{12} were kept low. If either value exceeded 3.0, however, the system would transit to chaos quickly, skipping the period doubling regime (pp. 157–158).

Similar dynamics would occur if both nations were operating under conditions of maximum allowable expenditures, x_m and y_m (p. 158):

$$x_{t+1} = x_t[-k_{11}(x_t - x_s) + k_{12}y_t](x_m - x_t) \tag{3}$$

$$y_{t+1} = y_t[-k_{22}(y_t - y_s) + k_{21}x_t](y_m - y_t) \tag{4}$$

A three-nation scenario is more complex, of course. The set of dynamic equations would look like:

$$x_{t+1} = x_t + [k_{11}(x_s - x_t) + k_{23}(y_t + z_t)](x_m - x_t) \tag{5}$$

$$y_{t+1} = y_t + [k_{22}(y_s - y_t) + k_{13}(x_t - z_t)](y_m - y_t) \tag{6}$$

$$z_{t+1} = z_t + [k_{33}(z_s - z_t) + k_{12}(x_t - y_t)](z_m - z_t) \tag{7}$$

The solution has multiple stable attractor basin, but they are disconnected, and interspersed with pockets of chaos (pp. 161–162). Transiting between basins could very likely be mistaken for an intention to actually use the weapons, which could then trigger a preemptive strike by another nation in the system.

Additional instabilities and variations could be built into any of the three systems just described. Hawks and doves, as political voting units, determine national policy more or less. Instabilities in national attitudes would further induce instabilities in arms procurements, if the shift was toward the hawk direction. Such instabilities could take the form of a preemptive strike, perhaps based on one side's miscalculations of their own might or exposure to danger. Alternatively, a nation would drive itself into bankruptcy trying to pay for the excess weaponry; the current states of the Soviet Union (that nation has dissolved) and U.S. (excessively debt-ridden by some standards) economies is evidence of the viability of this prospect. Stabilities may be induced by a turn toward the dove attitude, or a reduction in suspicion of the other nations, assuming that the estimations of the other side's hostile intentions were unrealistically high to begin with.

The arms race dynamic can be applied, with some conceptual adaptation, to the probability of a conventional military confrontation in a geographic area. Instead of using the purchase of arms as an index of intention, the deployment of those arms in the form of troop buildups and policing efforts could be studied instead. It is probably true that the k_{12} and k_{21} coefficients are high when measurable activity can be seen, in which case there is not much to simulate. The trick would be to predict locations where the beginnings of physical buildup dynamics would occur.

SDI proponents had claimed that the system would promote a transition to peace rather than escalate the likelihood of war. The modeling process begins with a two-nation Richardson model with fixed budgets. The model is then complicated to reflect inaccuracy in the programming of the missiles themselves and inaccuracy in the military intelligence of the conflicting nations about each other's expenditures (Saperstein & Mayer-Kress, 1988). Higher inaccuracy in the programming would result in a proportional increase in the number of warheads directed on one target and a reduction in the number of possible targets.

Further complexity was introduced to reflect the three different types of armaments involved: ICBMs, ABMs, and ASATs. The net results of the simulations showed that increasing accuracy or decreasing warheads would be paired with increased expenditures of defensive weapons. Either an offensive or defensive buildup would trigger an escalation of total arms to the point of an instability as described earlier. Large changes in the nations' military budgets would not affect the level of stability; they would only induce a shift in the portfolio of arms selected.

Polarity and War

The world wars involved two groups of nations working in opposition to each other. The Cold War took the same bipolar form with the intermittent contribution of China, which seemed to express distaste for both the United States and Soviet Union, on the one hand, and shared some military-political and economic interests with the United States and Soviet Union, respectively. The dynamics question is whether world polarity is a precondition of war, either directly or indirectly.

The realism of the polarity proposition became questionable after the dissolution of the Soviet Union. Instead of one nuclear-capable superpower leaving the playing field, the world suddenly acquired several new ones entering the field. Some were former Soviet states within whose boundaries the missile silos or manufacturing facilities resided before de-Sovietizing. Other nations of dubious political intentions may have purchased former Soviet materials. One might speculate that the two-titan system was more stable that the present situation.

If we imagine that the superpowers represent political, economic, or military spheres of influence, and consider that they interact on the military dimension (e.g., the Richardson equations), then we have a recipe for chaos. If the nations' political and economic strategies are not synchronized to neutralize or control military instability, then we have some frosting on the chaos cake. The remainder of this section addresses the issue of polarization as analyzed by political scientists, followed by a new NDS analysis of the same data.

Polynomial Structure. The importance of polarization was first brought to light by Wallace (1973), who developed statistical indices of polarity and war outcomes for the 1815–1964 period. His results showed "that war is more probable both at very low and at very high levels of polarization, while the chances of war are minimized by a moderately polarized alliance configuration" (p. 597, and Moul, 1993, p. 735). The U or V shape implied by that statement would imply a quadratic function, observed Moul (1993), but the most successful equation was a fourth-degree polynomial. Moul also noted several other problems with the data and analysis, such as a small sample size caused by aggregating data into 5-year intervals.

Moul rescored the years 1815–1976 on the polarization scale and six outcomes: the number of international wars, the number of interstate wars, the magnitude of international war, magnitude of interstate war, severity of international war, and the severity of interstate war. The polarization scale had a observed range from 1.00 to 3.56 where 1 represented bipolarity and 5 represented multipolarity. The 165 years were categorized into five ordinal categories, each 0.5 scale units wide. Mean war scores for the polarization categories of years were compared with ANOVA trend analysis. None of the curvilinear effects were significant.

Graphics of Moul's data, however, showed more variability for highly polarized year categories (1.00 to 2.5), and less variability for greater multipolarity years for the two measures of war magnitude. A less pronounced pattern showed up on the severity measures, and no such effect was apparent for the frequencies of wars. The pictorial trends thus suggested a bifurcation relationship between polarization and war, such that multiple outcomes were possible when the world was polarized, and a single stable outcome was likely when it was multipolarized.

Moul's data analysis contained polarization and war measures that were taken during the same year. No delay effects appeared to be taken into account. Fortunately, enough data were published to accommodate a reanalysis from an NDS point of view.

Reanalysis. Data for polarization were given by Moul (1993, pp. 746–747) in a table for each year separately. Aggregate data for the war measures were available on the basis of the polarization categories only; much of the variability due to a bifurcation effect could have been lost. Some aspects of nonlinear structure would thus be better assessed than the bifurcation effect. Data for the world wars were missing.

Based on the descriptions of the scales provided, I assigned values of 2.0 for the first 3 years of World War I before the United States entered it, and 1.5 after U.S. entry. World War II was scored as a 3.0 for the years before U.S. entry and 2.0 afterward. War measures were replaced by looking at the most severe average war scores in the five experimental categories, assuming an underlying Poisson distribution, the standard deviation of which would be the square root of the conditional means. One standard deviation was added for the first part of World War I, two standard deviations were added for the second part of World War I and the first part of World War II, and three standard deviations were added for the latter half of World War II. Data were lagged at 3 years, which was roughly half the duration of a world war. Four of the initial six war variables were used: magnitude of international war, magnitude of interstate war, severity of international war, and severity of interstate war.

The first analysis was to apply the nonlinear regression analysis for simple dimension analysis to polarization and the four war variables as in chapter 3, Equation 55:

$$z_2 = e^{(\theta_1 z_1)} + \theta_2$$

where lowest observed values were used as location parameters. Ordinary standard deviations were used as scale parameters for polarization and severity measures. Poisson-based standard deviations were used as scale parameters for war magnitude measures. The linear pre–post comparison model consisted of only one predictor variable, z_1. Only polarization showed a larger R^2 than the linear alternative. The next most complex model was tested where an unknown bifurcation constant was suspected to exist, using Equation 50 from Chapter 3:

$$z_2 = \theta_1 z_1 e^{(\theta_2 z_1)} + \theta_3$$

Results supported the nonlinear model for polarization and all wars measures, except that a tie was encountered in the case of severity of interstate war (Table 12.1).

TABLE 12.1
R^2 Coefficients for NDS and Linear Analysis of Polarization and War

Measure	Model of Chapter 3, Equation 53		Model of Chapter 3, Equation 51		Linear, R^2
	R^2	Dimension	R^2	Dimension	
Polarization	.62	1.45	.62	2.20	.61
Magnitude, international	.29	1.19	.41	1.94	.38
Magnitude, interstate	.30	1.21	.42	1.93	.40
Severity, international	.25	1.38	.25	2.13	.25
Severity, interstate	.23	1.35	.24	1.58	.22

Polarization could be represented in two equivalent ways. Without the free bifurcation parameter (Equation 8) the dimensionality was 1.45, but 2.20 when the bifurcation parameter was introduced (Equation 9):

$$z_2 = e^{(0.37z_1)} - 0.35 \tag{8}$$

$$z_2 = 0.41e^{(0.18z_1)} + 0.61 \tag{9}$$

Weights for all coefficients in Equations 8 and 9 were significant. The Lyapunov exponent was positive, which meant that the polarity function was expanding. Over time the shifts in polarity level were growing larger, and may continue to grow larger in the future.

The resulting function for magnitude of international war was

$$z_2 = 1.16z_1e^{(-0.06z_1)} + 1.11 \tag{10}$$

which showed a dimensionality of 1.94. The resulting function for magnitude of interstate war showed a dimensionality of 1.86:

$$z_2 = 1.11z_1e^{(-0.07z_1)} + 1.22 \tag{11}$$

Weights for all coefficients in Equations 10 and 11 were significant except for the constant in Equation 11. The Lyapunov values were negative, meaning that the magnitude of war has an inherent tendency to decay, perhaps because of a natural carrying capacity; people involved in a war may want it to end soon, or one side obliterates the other.

The results for the severity measures showed relatively low overall accuracy, and only a nominal advantage for the nonlinear interpretations. An attempt was made to assess logistic map models for the two magnitude measures with polarity as a criterion, but it was suspected in advance that the data aggregation might undermine such an analysis. That appeared to be the case, as linear models were stronger than the polynomial models. Of further interest, polarization did not have a significant weight in either linear model. The control difference models for the logistic map function were less accurate still, but significant correlations were observed between increased multipolarization and magnitude of international war ($r^2 = .07$, $p < .001$) and magnitude of interstate war ($r^2 = .09$, $p < .001$).

It would be hazardous to suggest that reliable forecasts could be made deep into the future on the basis of the past; any forecast assumes that the factors that influenced the past will not change in the future. On the other hand, Fig. 12.2 was created to see what the two polarization functions look like and how their predictions of the future might differ. The iterates of Equation 8, which are shown in original Wallace–Moul units, form an arc trajectory from 1974 that almost converges to an asymptote by the year 2016. The levels of multipolarization shown for the last entry are slightly higher than levels that existed in 1938–1939 and comparable to those that existed in 1899–1901. The iterates of Equation 9 show an initial depolarization, followed by a gravitation toward greater polarization than existed in 1961–1976, but not as extreme as 1950–1959.

It would appear, based on the equivalent accuracies of the two models, that the world met a choice point, or bifurcation point, a few years after

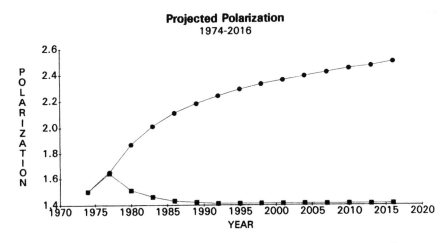

FIG. 12.2. Predicted values of international polarization (in original scale units) for the years 1976–2016, extrapolated from a reanalysis of data published in Moul (1993).

the Vietnam War. The events of history suggest that the multipolarized trajectory was the selection made by the world leaders. On the one hand, arms reduction discussions between the United States and Soviet Union progressed, albeit slowly. Also, new players emerged on the military scene in the Middle East who ostensibly did not prefer an alliance with either the United States or Soviet Union. The workers' revolt in Poland precipitated the dissolution of the Communist Bloc in Eastern Europe and later the Soviet Union itself. The SDI program, however, would have signaled a choice in the direction of polarization, because only two nations had the capability to shoot at anyone from beyond the skies; a stable polarization would have been ensured for many years to come. Fortunately, the SDI program did not have widespread popular support.

The iterates of Equation 10 for magnitude of war are shown in Fig. 12.3, and are scaled in moments. The projections show a decay function for hostilities from the 1974 level that does not bottom out by 2016. The last entry is comparable to the average hostility level of 1902–1911, 1920–1921, and 1938–1939; it is difficult to subjectively translate those figures into real terms. The U.S. experience was substantially different during each of those year groups. Because of the close similarity between Equations 10 and 11, iterates for magnitude of state wars are not shown.

Discussion. The analysis of the polarization and war data showed that a modest amount of chaotic behavior was taking place in polarization trends, but trends for magnitudes of war groped to fixed-point stability. The relationship between polarization and war does not appear to be direct, but polarization does suggest some possible scenarios by which

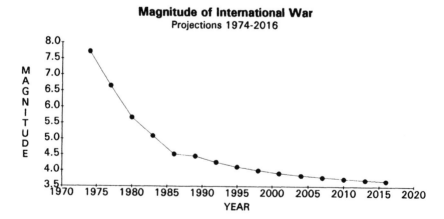

Magnitude of International War
Projections 1974-2016

FIG. 12.3. Predicted values of magnitude of war (in location- and scale-corrected units) for the years 1976–2016, extrapolated from a reanalysis of data published in Moul (1993).

war-related events could occur. Iterations of the obtained functions for polarization suggest that the events of the past set up a bifurcation map situation by which one of two historical paths may be played out. The events of history supported the path toward multipolarization with several militarily equivalent nations dominating world affairs. Iterations of the war magnitude function suggest that wars will become smaller, if not less frequent. Magnitude will reduce to a fixed lower limit, but will not disappear in the foreseeable future. The tenuousness of the future projections should be reemphasized.

At the same time, however, the bifurcation map function suggests that a sudden flip-flop from multipolarity to polarization is possible. The following section on sustainable economic development and world revolution plots some impending choice points in world affairs. Under some conditions a sudden polarization is possible.

SUSTAINABLE DEVELOPMENT AND WORLD REVOLUTION

The concept of sustainable development evolved from a controversial computer simulation study conducted by the Club of Rome (Meadows et al., 1972). *Limits to Growth* strongly suggested that unrenewable resources were being consumed at such a fast pace by the industrially advanced countries that soon there would be little left for the next generation or for other nations that hoped to develop economically. Furthermore, the world food supply was growing much more slowly than the increase in population, which also consumes natural resources. The recommendation was that industry should shift to a policy of zero economic growth, and that world citizens should limit their family sizes to two children for zero population growth.

As one might anticipate, the Club of Rome study was as popular as an icepick in the forehead. The economic establishment could not bear to think of zero economic growth. Zero population growth meant that a lot of consumer goods would not be bought, and was antithetical to the dictates of many religions as well. Obviously, neither recommendation has come to pass. The rich nations continue to enjoy economic growth while the developing nations of the Southern Hemisphere experience famine and disease, and natural resources such as the tropical rain forests are being whacked into toothpicks on a daily basis. Displaced peoples of the forest join the city, where they are accommodated with slums and unemployment (King & Schneider, 1991).

Critics of the Club or Rome report claimed the analysts underestimated the true availability of natural resources. They claimed, according to portrayals by King and Schneider (1991) and Rosser (1991), that the only way to solve the resource problems is to accelerate economic growth with the idea that economic growth will stimulate technologies with which to solve the problems of pollution, famine, and resource dependency. And if all else fails, we can mine the moon. King and Schneider replied, however, that the major contribution of *Limits to Growth* is not in its exact predictions, but in the use of futures forecasting to get a grip on what the future holds if certain global conditions persist; the tweaking of parameters for exactness is a much less important issue than the overall bleak picture that has more or less arrived. More importantly, the problems have not gone away.

Since the time of *Limits to Growth*, science, business, and government have reorganized their thinking toward the concept of sustainable development. The goal is to choose the right level of development that will maintain intergenerational equity, to maintain equity among the developed and undeveloped nations, and to consume renewable resources at a viable rate. These goals led to the Earth Summit conference in Rio de Janeiro in 1992 of world leaders who discussed a wide range of interrelated problems—public health, deforestation, environmental pollution, energy transmission, economic development, world hunger, and the rights of women, to mention a few—which took the form of the Agenda 21 document (United Nations, 1992). Agenda 21 outlined an action plan for solving the ecological and economic problems, "with the goal of establishing a new and equitable global partnership through the creation of new levels of cooperation among States, key sectors of societies and people, working toward international agreements which respect the interests of all and protect the integrity of the global environmental and developmental system, recognizing the integral and interdependent nature of the Earth, our home" (p. 9).

The preamble to Agenda 21 clearly reflected a consciousness of Earth as a complex system. Figure 12.4, from Mayer-Kress (1992), suggests how many of the key issues are interrelated in a general sense. All those ideas, in his opinion, are aspects of international security. The remainder of this section turns to the dynamics that are implicit in sustainable development.

The concept of sustainable development is, in some respects, an oxymoron. On the one hand, *sustainable* reflects notions of constancy or stability, whereas *development* represents instability and change. From an organizational theorist's viewpoint, transformations of the type that would change the world from its present state of affairs to one of sustainable development involve changing one or more, perhaps many, national cultures. Changing cultures often means not tampering with culture directly, but instead obviating barriers to change, and energizing corporations and governments to a point where change will indeed take place.

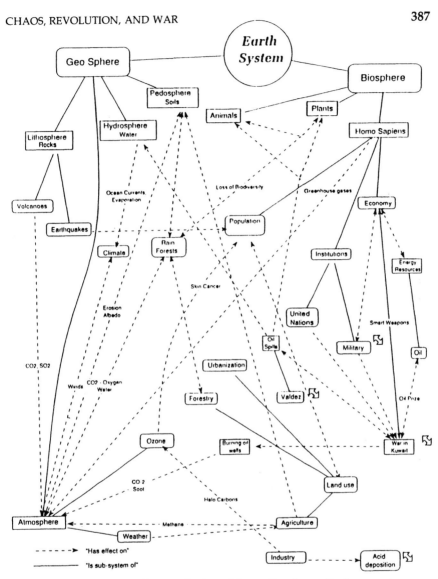

FIG. 12.4. A possible organization of international security issues suggested by Mayer-Kress (1992). Courtesy G. Mayer-Kress.

Punctuated Equilibria

Psychological theories of development are typically conceptualized as stage theories, which have several important characteristics (Fig. 12.5). Stage theories reflect a discontinuous qualitative change from one stage to another. Each person or entity progresses through an invariant sequence of stages, meaning that the order of the stages does not change.

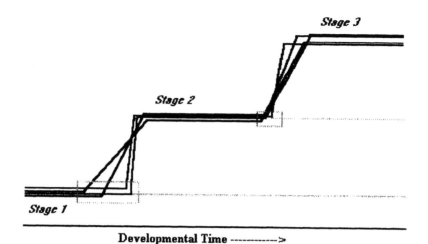

Stage 3

Stage 2

Stage 1

Developmental Time ------------>

FIG. 12.5. A punctuated equilibrium model for stages theories of human or social development.

Each stage is progressively more complex than the preceding stage, and subsumes all the cognitive and social structures of previous stages. The stage sequences for human psychological development are quasi-reversible, meaning that a person at a later stage of development has access to schemata found at an earlier stage.

Transition between stages is the result of an assimilation and accommodation dynamic. Assimilation reflects the system's drive toward stability. The system maintains its current structure, or level of complexity, for as long as circumstances will allow. When too many situations arise that are too complex to be handled adequately by an existing structure, an accommodation response takes place and the person transits to the next stage of development.

In NDS theory, the stair-step arrangement of developmental stages is essentially a punctuated equilibrium model. When events occur that seriously challenge the capabilities of the system, the system is increasing in entropy and reaching a far-from-equilibrium condition. Eventually, the system reaches a bifurcation point, which is a point of maximum instability, at which time the system either accedes quickly to its next stage of development, or retrenches to its former stage. Retrenchment usually means not solving one's problems and paying the consequences for not doing so. But even there, a qualitative shift has taken place from immaturity to arrested development.

The sequence of stages in Fig. 12.5 is drawn as a cord of several trajectories to indicate that broadly defined developmental stages are actually the result of several subprocesses, and that it is likely for development within each subprocess to be unsynchronized with development in other subprocesses (Thelen, 1992). In individual development, subprocesses would include cognitive complexity, emotional maturity, moral judgment, and social interactions. Societal subprocesses would include agriculture and technology, economics, government, transportation and communication, social services, health care, and ecological consciousness.

Criteria of Sustainability

The punctuated equilibrium model as presented thus far does not yet reflect the impact of any limits to growth that could be present in the system. It is thus worth questioning whether sustainable solutions for economic growth can exist at all. Dore and Ward (1994) began by defining sustainability as a situation where the growth in a consumption rate is zero and the depletion of relevant resources is zero. If consumption growth and resource renewal are occurring, then it is possible to identify two solutions for setting proper consumption rates for sustainability. One is a fixed-point attractor, and the other is a saddle point. The levels of consumption growth and resource renewal are higher for the saddle point than they are for the fixed point.

A likely path for future research is to apply the Dore and Ward (1994) general solution to real commodities. Beckenbach and Pasche (1994) started a similar line of investigation where economic activity is balanced against bioenvironmental criteria such as biodiversity impact and environmental damage levels.

Another distinct approach to defining sustainability that is currently being explored by internet study groups concerns distribution of the food supply. In principle, all people should have a secure, reasonably-priced food supply year round. Also, the agricultural producers should be able to extract a fair income that allows for maintenance of the farms, for suitable standards for farmers' living and health conditions, and for their participation in their culture. Conceivably, one might define similar criteria with respect to energy sources as well.

World Economy

The step function in Fig. 12.5 is actually a subset of events that have taken place in the development of world economy. Figure 12.6 is a more complete picture, modeled after the logistic map function. The world economy reached its first bifurcation point when it accommodated developments in physics, mathematics, and mechanics into the industrial revolution. Some nations were left behind. The next major bifurcation took place in this century as a result of many forms of scientific progress. The shift

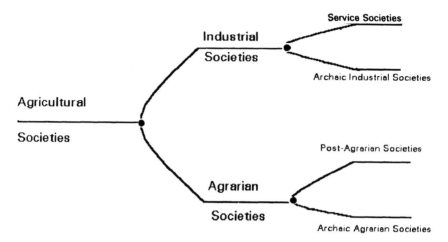

FIG. 12.6. Logistic model for world economic development. From Malaska (1991). Reprinted with permission.

transited the most developed nations into the service and information-based economy that is now familiar (Malaska, 1991).

Subtle patterns of development are thought to have also taken place within each stage of development. The stage begins with a period of extensive growth where resources are consumed to effect the transition. The stage culminates with intensive growth where the evolution is preoccupied with improving internal efficiency and reinvestment in itself (Malaska, 1989).

The new world economy is expected be coupled with a shift in dominances, according to King and Schneider (1991). In capitalist-centered economies, a shift in hegemonies is a natural decline. For instance, the debt structure of the United States is its major economic impairment, along with debts from Latin American countries that it has been forced to absorb, and military overload. The next hegemony, if past world history provides any clue, is the country with which the United States has the strongest economic ties, namely Japan. Japan would follow in the footsteps of Holland, Britain, and the United States, perhaps without the baggage of military expenses, and should expect challenges from China.

The hegemony of the center imperializes the periphery, which is the underdeveloped nations. The rich get richer and the poor get poorer. In the economics of free world trade, there will be competition between Latin America and Africa for tropical products. Nonelasticities of demand and lack of savings with which to invest in internal development would lead to a stable state, if not a further downward spiral, of impoverishment (Amin, 1992).

Tariffs are another problem. According to Bovard (1991), the U.S. tariff system is riddled with protectionism, classism, and capricious politicized disinterpretations of the existing tariff codes. The particular examples of tariffs and import bans may have a miniscule benefit for one U.S. industry, but larger detriments to others. "Any clothing or textile import from a Third World nation that amounts to 1% of the U.S. market for that product is almost automatically presumed to threaten the U.S. market" (p. 47). The War on Drugs became a new excuse for seizing imported merchandise without cause. For example, antiques were sawed in half to prove beyond a shadow of a doubt that no drugs were present. Thus Bovard characterized "fair trade" as "one of the greatest intellectual frauds of the twentieth century" (p. 1).

Assuming that other nations play similar tricks, it is possible that the newly ratified General Agreement on Tariffs and Trade (GATT) Treaty, which has hitherto fallen under the auspices of the United Nations, will serve to decomplexify tariff structure. The World Trade Organization operatives would mediate all standards for import duties, and would rule on allowable regulations concerning pollution and product safety. The current version of GATT and the history of the GATT agreement, which dates back to 1948, is severely biased against recognizing environmental concerns as a fair reason behind nations' tariff systems. Similarly, GATT rejects most human rights and work safety concerns as legitimate (child labor notably excepted) bases for capital flow and import regulations under the theme of "discrimination on the basis of means of production." At the same time, a revision of GATT is only a partial solution because the nature of effective tariff systems for curbing pollution and for preserving world resources without cheating remain a subject of debate (Dommen, 1993).

Some GATT watchers have reasoned that the GATT agreement will distribute wealth around the world better than it has before, but will have virtually no positive impact on the distribution of wealth within nations. Thus one might regard GATT as a coalition of the world's rich people against the world's poor people (Daly & Goodland, 1994; Ekins et al., 1994). Another concern is that the treaty would undermine sovereignty of nations, who would not be able to pass new laws concerning product safety or pollution control on goods regulated by GATT; the treaty would undermine the efforts of consumer activist groups in the United States as well.

The Onset of World Government

Social evolutionists are currently convinced that the panorama of world economies is at a bifurcation point that is an outgrowth of the unfolding that occurred over the eons. The latest phase of development accelerated in the past century and more so in the past decade (King & Schneider,

1991; Laszlo, 1991). A successful solution to the global economic dilemma will require new types of relationships among nations, allocation of capital to human resources within nations, and a central priority for creative processes for coping with systems at the edge of chaos (Artigiani, 1991; Malaska, 1991).

The edge of chaos is the next step in world social development, as typified by Period 3 of the logistic map. Each nation in our world system now will be shifting priorities and alliances with other nations in hopes of forming economic and political exchanges of mutual benefit. Each nation can be expected to define and refine its internal polities for economic growth and development many times in an almost schizoid fashion. Each successive failure will bring additional pressure to change direction in hopes of something new and successful.

Unstable coalitions among nations form at first, but self-organization occurs as winning combinations are found that reduce entropy and promote stability. Nations' internal development can be expected to undergo a similar self-organizational process as people, their industries, agriculture, and social systems respond to the changing environmental demands.

Another phase of the sustainable development problematique concerns the set of relationships that could exist between the developed countries and the least developed countries (LDCs). What were once local ecological problems have turned into macroecological problems, and the options for viable solutions are largely dependent on the economic viability of LDCs. Amin (1992) argued that the global economic trends now taking place are antithetical to the interests of the Southern Hemisphere's LDCs. He argued for delinking the LDC economies from those of the industrialized nations in order to promote a development of sustainable economic infrastructures in those countries. According to simulation studies (Lucas, 1988), a nation's initial economic wealth will be a key factor in determining its eventual wealth under conditions of globalization. In other words, the rich nations will become richer while the poor ones become poorer, which has been occurring progressively in the past few decades (Ekins et al., 1994). Amin (1992) suggested that future scenarios such as these set the stage for a North–South polarization that could possibly be accompanied by terrorist activity.

Clearly the need for a world cooperative effort has been apparent, but, as the edge of chaos draws near, two distinct classes of solutions will present themselves. One class of solutions will favor maintaining a version of the current world economic (dis)order under the guise of offering improvements. There are numerous examples in industry where the people who actually do the work are required to learn, to evolve, and to sustain progress, but the top management becomes further bent on standardization, rigidity, and maintaining its narrow view of the organization

(DeGreene, 1991b). Management has little tricks to maintain the status quo, which they call vision, or mission statements (Stacey, 1992), to name a couple. We could end up with an international fascist conspiracy based on self-centered financial concerns that undermines the sovereignty of nations and effects little progress. Such conditions would predispose the world to the scenario Amin (1992) suggested.

The other class of solutions will allow for novel self-organization of supranational systems. Supranational organization has already started among developed nations and has taken the form of trading blocks such as Japan/ASEAN, NAFTA, and GATT groupings. Some intermediary supranational organization is needed in Africa, according to King and Schneider (1991), because existing political boundaries were created at the convenience of European colonial powers. The existing states often merge diverge ethnic groups and split others, and cordon resources into control regions that do not constitute a viable economic base for the nation in question. Global policy suggestions from world leaders and the scientific elite need to be integrated with local initiatives where each nation or nation-group makes its own decisions about allocation of human capital and natural resources (Lemma, 1989; Loye & Eisler, 1987).

Creative thinking is the first step toward unleashing self-organization processes everywhere. To some extent self-organizational processes have already occurred with the rise of nongovernmental organizations for sustainable development (Lemma, 1989), urban gardening projects to enhance nutrition (Perkins, 1994), and the bioecological aspects of wetlands reclamation projects (Hey, 1994).

As the world gets smaller and larger scale international agreements take place, the presence of the United Nations as a form of world government becomes stronger. The United Nations maintains a theory of absolute sovereignty of participating nations, but that can be expected to break down as it tries to enforce GATT on nations with ideological disagreements. The United Nations has gone from a negotiating table for preventing and stopping war to one of active military interventions in Iraq and Somalia (Holmes, 1993).

Regarding freedom as we know it, there are opportunities, uncertainties, and challenges. If the United Nations has its way, the social and economic standing of women in underdeveloped countries will improve significantly, which is good. At the other end of the social systems perspective, however, a number of nations participating in the United Nations are not democracies as we are used to them in the United States (Holmes, 1993). There is, furthermore, a rising tide of nationalism and theocratic forms of government. The United States has, so far, played a central role in United Nations military expeditions, ostensibly because of its technological superiority. But a nation that plays "cop of the world" will be continually at war. In spite of my projections that the level of world war will drop, it will only reach a stable nonzero lower limit. Meanwhile, a nation continually at war will have labeled its young people the "cannon fodder of the world," which can only have a demoralizing effect. The financial costs will be paid by the U.S. public, and the legitimacy of the entire system will erode, along with civil liberty.

Unless something changes drastically. And where there is chaos, there is hope.

Epilogue:
Nothing Stops These Elephants

I refrained from summarizing the last chapter in hopes of gaining the momentum of a running start by summarizing everything else that transpired in this book. Evidence to support first premises of NDS, that seemingly random events are predictable with our new analytic concepts and mathematical models thereof, should be obvious by now. At the same time, some qualifications are in order. "Prediction" works well when modeling events over time when we have a whole event to look at. Prediction of future states is possible in the near term, but could decay rapidly as we try to extend further into the future. Part of the reason is that chaos itself is a state of relative unpredictability, but the presence of those times of unpredictability is predictable. Part of the limitation of future vision is that is assumes that future states will be based on the same dynamics that are operating in the present. Nowhere has such a guarantee ever been offered by anyone to anyone without crossing their fingers behind their backs. The limits of future vision were inherent in the concept of chaos from the outset and the nature of forecasting before chaos was ever conceptualized; it was not a discovery we actively pursued here. Rather, I am raising the issue to suggest that any elation about the new and useful insights into the dynamics of human social systems should be kept on a reasonable leash.

THE EMPIRICAL EVIDENCE

The support for any of the new theoretical developments come from logical connections between psychological (or other substantive) constructs, observations of behavior, and principles of NDS. In many places it was possible to conduct experiments and to evaluate results that could tell us how closely tied our imaginations were to reality. I have attempted to summarize results of as many empirical studies as possible by comparing linear and nonlinear models for the various applications contained in this book. Unfortunately, not all studies used data analysis techniques that provided a comparable comparisons. In cases where R^2 coefficients were used, however, it appears that the ratio of 2 : 1 against the accuracy of a linear model, which I cited in Chapter 1, still persists.

In making the reestimation, I lumped together R^2 coefficients from polynomial regression, nonlinear regression, and pseudo-R^2 procedures. No adjustments were made for sample size because of the variations in experimental design. Data for accidents in 10 industrial classes, stress-related illness, and stock market behavior were each treated as one pair of values. Behaviors that were judged to be decidedly not nonlinear (corporate inertia, severity of war) were not included. The actual average values of R^2 I arrived at were .57 for nonlinear models, with a range from .21 to .99, and an average of .30 for the best linear comparison, with a range from .05 to .96, or a ratio of 1.9 : 1. If the stock market data is eliminated as an unusual curiosity, the average values turn out to be .56 for nonlinear models, with no change in range, and .27 for the linear comparisons, with a range from .05 to .69, or a ratio of 2.1 : 1. If we look at pairwise ratios of R^2 coefficients from each experiment, the average ratio is 4.1 : 1 with a range from 1.04 : 1 to 9.50 : 1, not including the stock market data.

What explains the success of the nonlinear modeling efforts? Put simply, the NDS models provide better explanations for change than the best linear alternatives. More specifically, the nonlinearities that have been chronically missed in conventional psychological (and other social science) research are the result of manifolds created by bifurcations seen in the catastrophe models or in the logistic map path to chaos. Another major source of explanation is that the variance unaccounted for was never "random error" as previously thought. "Error" is better regarded as "noise," which is sometimes inextricably linked to the chaotic process, according to Abraham (1985). The inextricable link is translated (by way of an independent line of thought) into the distinction between dependent and independent error. Nonlinear models convert that dependent error into variance accounted for by an *appropriately chosen* model.

As for the 44% of variance still left unaccounted for, all the usual explanations why experimental results are imperfect apply, such as the imperfect operationalization of a theoretical concept into an experiment, definition of qualitative constructs, and real flaws in the measurement of those constructs. Simulation results (Guastello, 1992a) showed that complete and correct definition of variables assigned to control parameters can double the variance accounted and even change the degree of a germ polynomial; there is a complementarity among the parts of the models that produce the end result.

Two technical aspects of the polynomial and nonlinear regression methods could withstand some further work. One has to do the with specification of the scale parameter. Although the methods defined in Chapter 3 have served us well so far, there were also examples (accidents among transit operators) when a scale measure that was more exact than the standard deviation improved the results. The other alternative, which allows for automatic estimation of location and scale (Cobb & Zacks, 1985), involves estimating twice as many regression parameters to arrive at a model of the same complexity as the polynomial alternative to catastrophe modeling, and it has not been extended beyond cusps. The second method issue concerns time intervals. So far I have relied on naturally occurring time intervals, or those that have some meaning in the context of the problem under study. I suspect the next avenue of investigation is to determine optimal rules for specifying time intervals when the theory or the application does not offer a clue.

Several of the models considered here, and social implications drawn from them, remain untested in a direct and empirical manner. I do not see that to be a problem inasmuch as the theories I chose to present were well reasoned conceptually, on the one hand, and science is loaded with unfinished business on the other. I suspect the untested material can be seen in better light now than it was before, and that social scientists will be rolling up their sleeves to tackle the ones they consider their favorites.

The Network of Theories

The applications to work, organizations, and society at large spanned a wide range of topics at varying levels of living systems. We encountered the interface between humans and their nonliving environment at one extreme, and supranational systems at the other extreme. The presentation sequence followed the subject matter, rather than the system level, and the progression followed a zigzag path across systemic levels; there is probably a fractal in there somewhere. Some of the applications drew links between physical and biological organismic processes and human behavior at the individual, group, or societal levels of analysis. The cross-level mode of analysis brings further evidence that the NDS applications to substantive theories that looked defendable individually are all the more viable in light of their collective explanation for social phenomena.

So what have we learned about the psychology of work behavior? Quite a bit. The perception of stimuli from the nonliving environment was always regarded as a nonlinear process, but multidimensional stimuli were relatively intractable. We now know that stimuli have a destabilizing effect on a human perceptual system that is initially at rest, and the response to the stimuli can be modeled by a variant of the logistic map function. Complex stimuli and complex responses can now be handled though explosions of the same basic formula. Perceptions of ambiguous stimuli are eventually recognized as one or another stable perceptual pattern based on control parameters that underlie the configuration of the stimuli themselves. Complex social judgments—performance appraisals and jury decisions, which are analogous to many group decision situations—work according to essentially the same processes. Learning can be regarded as the process through which stable behavior patterns or knowledge patterns are formed.

We already knew that learning affected motivation and motivation affected learning, but NDS-based theories now regard motivation and learning as part and parcel of the same process. By coalescing the two we can explain, rather simply, the complex process by which a person is selected into the organization, motivated to learn what needs to be learned and to perform in a certain way. A large packet of motivational theories can be reduced to three control parameters of the butterfly model; ability, which is either innate or learned prior to entering the system, comprises the fourth. We can see the ramifications of the butterfly catastrophe model of motivation in organizations in studies of academic performance, human relations training, absenteeism, and turnover. Real-world work performance studies have taken fewer aspects of the model into account in any one study, but the results of performance analyses show that it too is decidedly nonlinear over time, with expected patterns of stability and instability.

The mirror image of motivation is stress, in the conventional negative sense of the word. We have seen performance fluctuate catastrophically in response to mental or physical fatigue, work load, or combinational effects of shift work, job difficulty, and management bumbling. If we make the work environment more hazardous, we can add accidents and stress-related health disorders to the list of catastrophic events. We can observe similar processes at the individual or group levels of analysis, and even at the societal level by way of the insurance database study. The connection between the control parameters in the accident process and those that affect stress-related health disorders opens up a wide area for utilizing NDS concepts for general medical and psychological epidemiology; indeed, the earliest mathematical epidemic functions appeared to have evolved logically into the NDS principles that we now invoke.

The science of biological evolution is itself evolving. Darwinian theory has joined forces with learning theory, if not complex systems theory as a whole. Living systems adapt. Those that adapt successfully take their genes along for the ride. Populations that are more variable stand a greater chance of recovery or adaptation from an environmental selection event. The same principle also implies, however, that clumsy human complex social systems will not be readily changed by operating on one of its characteristics at a time. Undesirable characteristics can just as easily become more formidable as they adapt to simple assaults; thus the diseases mutate in response to medicines, insects appear to thrive on insecticides, and criminals become craftier. (Crime issues were not considered explicitly here, but the extension to crime can be logically drawn.)

Evolution involves a process of self-organization by which genes, ideas, or social institutions aggregate into logical, self-sustaining, energy-efficient forms. Collections of individuals evolve into coordinated social units, which aggregate to agricultural settlements, and then into open cities, and then to closed cities that survive through their interactions with other cities. Human social organizations evolve through a dynamic of competition, which bears close resemblance to the dynamics of other animals in the food chain, and cooperation, which becomes more difficult to accomplish within large and diverse groups. But large-scale cooperation is not impossible if the efforts to enjoin cooperation are hierarchically organized and the payoff matrix is favorable. Various nonlinear dynamic models have been implicated by various theorists.

Personnel selection can be further viewed as a form of unnatural selection into the special organization and its culture. Through logistic map dynamics it can be shown how an organization might survive when its food supply (qualified job applicants) dwindles severely. The key here, as with other aspects of management, is to function as a chaotic controller.

The imbalances of the ecosystem are closely tied to natural resource economics. The model for stock market behavior, therefore, described the events of a public market, but at the same time described the general rules behind any market-product situation, which affects any organization that sells anything for a profit. It could represent the stability of a particular market or the stability of an entire global economy, with the multiple basin concept firmly attached, of course. As a general rule of social exchange, however, it would appear that the "economy" is really a two-domain concept involving the exchange of concrete goods, cash, services, and abstract principles, loosely associated with "freedom," "justice," "equality," and "democracy." What would necessarily result is a political economy version of the butterfly model of equity in organization; that idea needs to be developed further.

Creativity can be viewed as an individual, group, organizational, or society dynamic, and it may be artificial to separate the functions. Creative output appears to obey the same laws irrespective of the substance—arts, science, business. Chaos produces creativity, and creativity produces chaos. The creative process has a strong evolutionary explanation as a system at the edge of chaos where the self-organization process takes place when a workable idea is pulled together from elementary idea sources. Communication links facilitate the self-organizational process in much the same way as transportation allows relationships to build between cities. Creativity is a relatively high-dimensional system compared to other human systems that have been well studied.

Nonlinear dynamical systems theory has caused the rethinking of organizational change processes from stable–change–restabilize to a concept of continuous change that may be evolutionary or revolutionary. And a good deal of true chaos can occur before, during, and after the organizational change initiative. As a result, creativity enhancement should take a primary place on the list of management's "things-to-do" list. Rather than trying to make a change take place, the goal of changing, developing, or enhancing an organization's culture is best accomplished by relying on self-organizational processes. Sociotechnical systems theory has said so for years, but the analogy to other system dynamics was never as clear before as it is now.

The buckling of an elastic beam is a well-recognized classic of NDS application. Echos of the beam-buckling principle were seen in models for work performance under increased load, and in organizational change processes. Mathematical epidemic functions for diseases served as a basis for the development of a biological model for immunological activity, a link between occupational accident models and stress-related illness, and extensions to organizational security systems and national security systems. Underlying the organizational and national security systems is a control parameter of humanism versus fascism, or loose versus tight control, or rigidity versus flexibility, or the Euler modulus of elasticity all over again. An elasticity principle was observed as a bifurcation parameter in models for literal beam buckling, work performance under load, and organizational change, but in models for work motivation, organizational and national security it functions as a second bifurcation parameter, or a butterfly parameter, otherwise known as the elusive parameter d.

The national security subsystem is, of course, a government-centered point of view concerning national security issues. Population-centered views were considered as well. As it turned out, Adelman and Hihn (1982) and I ended up with a relatively similar spectrum of political outcomes, but the control parameters were defined from the vantage point of issues that matter to the people: educational level, equitable distribution of wealth, and political participation. Cuzan (1986) defined the critical controls in terms of financial responsibility, power legitimacy, and level of coercion. Altogether we are not a far cry different from the butterfly catastrophe model of equity in organizations. Butterfly-equity theory was, in its original form, rationalized from the viewpoint of signal detection psychophysics (Guastello, 1981). Not all cultural changes are revolutionary in the sense of violent overthrows. Some are revolutionary in a conceptual form, whereas others are evolutionary and not dissimilar to dynamics of the organizational change model.

War between two nations appears to work on a different dynamic from that of the political revolution. Arms race dynamics are more closely linked to predator–prey dynamics and an underlying logistic map function. Depending on the number of nations involved in the melee, logistic maps are coupled and compounded to represent the influences of all nations against each other; chaotic arms race buildups are inevitable and rapid given sufficient paranoia. If the arms race simulations were not convincing (they worked for me), my reanalysis of polarization and war dynamics should offer converging and consistent conclusions.

The events since 1815 set the world-full-of-nations up for a bifurcation point and branching pathway for future international affairs. The immanence of world government, world unity, world fascism, and world chaos is anyone's guess. The need for world cooperation to solve world problems is well understood, but the methods for making understanding real are not as well understood by the people in charge of things, or so it would appear. Complex systems cannot be effectively changed by simple, localized "band-aid" solutions to symptoms in isolation. The system will only evolve to maintain itself the way it is and make problems worse. Better, creative solutions to world dilemmas might thus arise from trying to solve several problems at once, and to look for a dynamical key that remedies the greatest number of problems with the smallest number of disruptions. Perhaps real change begins with improvements to everyone's work life at all levels of society. Perhaps the theories, models, and experiments that have been drawn together here will joggle a few useful thoughts in that direction.

THE BEGINNING.

References

Abelson, M. A. (1982). *Catastrophe theory model of the employee withdrawal process leading to job termination.* (Doctoral dissertation, Pennsylvania State University, 1981) *Dissertation Abstracts International, 42,* 3279A. (University Microfilms No. 81-29, 129).

Abraham, F. D., Abraham, R. H., & Shaw, C. D. (1990). *A visual introduction to dynamical systems theory for psychology.* Santa Cruz, CA: Aeriel.

Abraham, F. D., Kugler, P. N., Xie, M., Abraham, R. H., & Abraham, S. F. (1992, June). Dynamics, chaos bifurcation, self-organization, mind, conflict, insensitivity to initial conditions, time, unification/diversity, free-will, and social responsibility. In S. J. Guastello (Chair), *Chaos theory and social-organizational dynamics.* Symposium presented to the Fourth Annual Conference of the American Psychological Society, San Diego.

Abraham, R. H. (1985). Is there chaos without noise? In P. Fisher & W.R. Smith (Eds.), *Chaos, fratals, and dynamics. Lecture notes in pure and applied mathematics.* (Vol. 98, pp. 117–121). New York: Marcel Dekker.

Abraham, R. H., Shaw, C. D. (1992). *Dynamics, the geometry of behavior* (2nd edition). Reading, MA: Addison-Wesley.

Adams, J. S. (1965). Inequity in social exchange. In L. Berkowitz (Ed.), *Advances in experimental social psychology* (Vol. 2, pp. 265–299). New York: Academic Press.

Adams, J .S., & Friedman, S. (1976). Equity theory revisited: Comments and annotated bibliography. In L. Berkowitz & E. Walster (Eds.), *Equity theory: Toward a general theory of social interaction. Advances in experimental social psychology.* (Vol. 9, pp. 43–90). New York: Academic Press.

Adelman, I., & Hihn, J .M. (1982). Politics in Latin America. *Journal of Conflict Resolution, 26,* 592–620.

Agervold, M. (1976). Shiftwork: A critical review. *Scandinavian Journal of Psychology, 17,* 181–189.

Agu, M. (1983). A method for identification of linear or nonlinear systems with the use of externally applied random force. *Journal of Applied Physics, 54,* 1193–1197.

Akerstedt, T. (1977). Inversion of sleep-wakefulness pattern: Effects on circadian variations in psychophysical activation. *Ergonomics 10,* 459–474.

Allport, G. W. (1937). *Personality: A psychological perspective.* New York: Holt.

Amin, S. (1992). *Empire of chaos.* New York: Monthly Review Press.

402

Anderson, N. H., & Farkas, A. J. (1975). Integration theory applied to models of inequity. *Personality and Social Psychology Bulletin, 1*, 588–591.

Andreassi, J. L. (1980). *Psychophysiology*. New York: Oxford Press.

Argyris, C. (1976). *Increasing leadership effectiveness*. New York: Wiley.

Argyris, C., & Schon, D. (1978). *Organizational learning: A theory of action perspective*. Reading, MA: Addison-Wesley.

Arnold, V. I. (1974). Normal forms of functions in the neighborhoods of degenerate critical points. *Russian Mathematical Surveys, 29*, 10–50.

Arthur, W., Jr., & Doverspike, D. (1992). Locus of control and auditory selective attention as predictors of driving accident involvement: A comparative long studinal investigation. *Journal of Safety Research, 23*, 73–80.

Artigiani, R. (1991). Social evolution: A nonequilibrium systems model. In E. Laszlo (Ed.), *The new evolutionary paradigm* (pp. 93–129). New York: Gordon & Breach.

Ash, I. E. (1914). Fatigue and its effects upon control. *Archives of Psychology, 31*.

Atkinson, M. W. (1964). *An introduction to motivation*. Princeton, NJ: Van Nostrand.

Austin, J. T., Humphreys, L. G., & Hulin, C. L. (1989). Another view of dynamic criteria: A critical reanalysis of Barrett, Caldwell, & Alexander. *Personnel Psychology, 42*, 583–596.

Ayres, T. J. (1981). Catastrophe theory and brightness judgments. *Perception & Psychophysics, 29*, 407.

Baba, M. L., & Ziegler, B. P. (1985). Evolution and innovation in sociocultural systems: A punctuated equilibria model. In J. R. Nesselroade & A. von Eye (Eds.), *Individual development and social change: Explanatory analysis* (pp. 1–30). Orlando, FL: Academic Press.

Back, T., & Schwefel, H.-P. (1993). An overview of evolutionary algorithms for parameter optimization. *Evolutionary Computation, 1*, 1–24.

Baer, J. (1993). *Creative ability and divergent thinking: A task specific approach*. Hillsdale, NJ: Lawrence Erlbaum Associates.

Bahg, C. -G. (1990). Major systems theories throughout the world. *Behavioral Science, 35*, 79–107.

Baker, J. S., & Frey, P. W. (1980). A cusp catastrophe: Hysteresis, bimodality, and inaccessibility in rabbit eyelid conditioning. *Learning and Motivation, 10*, 520–535.

Balasko, Y. (1978a). Equilibrium analysis and envelope theory. *Journal of Mathematical Economics, 5*, 153–172.

Balasko, Y. (1978b). Economic equilibrium and catastrophe theory: An introduction. *Econometrica, 46*, 557–569.

Balasko, Y. (1978c). The behavior of economic equilibrium: A catastrophe theory approach. *Behavioral Science, 23*, 375–382.

Balasko, Y. (1979a). Economics with a finite but large number of equilibria. *Journal of Mathematical Economics, 6*, 145–147.

Balasko, Y. (1979b). Number and definiteness of economic equilibria. *Journal of Mathematical Economics, 6*, 215–225.

Balasko, Y. (1989). *Foundations of the theory of general equilibrium*. Orlando, FL: Academic Press.

Bales, R. F. (1950). *Interaction process analysis: A method for the study of small groups*. Chicago: University of Chicago Press.

Bandura, A. (1977). *Social learning theory*. Englewood Cliffs, NJ: Prentice-Hall.

Barrett, G. V., & Alexander, R. A. (1989). Rejoinder to Austin, Humphreys & Hulin: Critical reanalysis of Barrett, Caldwell, & Alexander. *Personnel Psychology, 42*, 597–612.

Barrett, G. V., Caldwell, M. S., & Alexander, R. A. (1985). The concept of dynamic criteria: A Critical reanalysis. *Personnel Psychology, 38*, 41–56.

Barron, F. (1988). Putting creativity to work. In R. J. Sternberg (Ed.), *The nature of creativity: Contemporary psychological perspectives* (pp. 76–98). Cambridge, MA: Cambridge University Press.

Bartley, S. H. (1976). Visual fatigue. In E. Simonson & P. C. Weiser (Eds.), *Psychological aspects and physiological correlates of work and fatigue* (pp. 155–175). Springfield, IL: Charles C. Thomas.

Beckenbach, F., & Pasche, M. (in press). Nonlinear ecological models and economic perturbation: Sustainability as a concept of stability corridors. In S. Faucheaux, D. Pearce, & J. L. R. Proops (Eds.), *Models of Sustainable Development.*

Benne, K. D., & Sheats, P. (1948). Functional roles of group members. *Journal of Social Issues, 4–5,* 41–49.

Benner, L., Jr. (1975). Accident investigation: Multilineal events sequencing methods. *Journal of Safety Research, 7,* 67–73.

Bennis, W. (1988). *Why leaders can't lead: The unconscious conspiracy continues.* San Francisco: Jossey-Bass.

Berliner, L. M. (1992). Statistics, probability, and chaos. *Statistical Science, 7,* 69–122.

Berringer, D. B. (1978). Collision avoidance response stereotypes in pilots and nonpilots. *Human Factors, 5,* 529–536.

Bertazzi, P. A. (1989). Industrial disasters and epidemiology. *Scandinavian Journal of Work and Environmental Health, 15,* 85–100.

Bigelow, J. (1982). A catastrophe model of organizational change. *Behavioral Science, 27,* 26–42.

Bills, A. G. (1931). Blocking: A new principle in mental fatigue. *American Journal of Psychology, 67,* 230–245.

Bocchi, G. (1991). Biological evolution: The changing image. In E. Lazlo (Ed.), *The new evolutionary paradigm* (pp. 33–54). New York: Gordon & Breach.

Boles, S. (1990). A model of routine and creative problem solving. *Journal of Creative Behavior, 24,* 171–189.

Bosserman, R. W. (1982). The internal security subsystem. *Behavioral Science, 27,* 95–103.

Bovard, J. (1991). *The fair trade fraud.* New York: St. Martin's Press.

Box, G. E. P., & Jenkins, G. M. (1970). *Time series analysis: Forecasting and control.* San Francisco: Holden-Day.

Brams, S. J. (1993). Theory of moves. *American Scientist, 81,* 562–570.

Breeden, J. L., Dinkelacker, F., & Hubler, A. (1990). Noise in the modeling and control of dynamical systems. *Physical Review A, 42,* 5827–5836.

Brock, W. A. (1986). Distinguishing random and deterministic systems. *Journal of Economic Theory, 40,* 168–195.

Brock, W. A. (1991). Causality, chaos, explanation, and prediction in economics and finance. In J. Casti & A. Karlqvist (Eds.), *Beyond belief: Randomness, prediction, and explanation in science* (pp. 230–279). Boca Raton, FL: CRC Press.

Brock, W. A., Hsieh, D. A., & LeBaron, B. (1991). *Nonlinear dynamics, chaos, and instability: Statistical theory and economic evidence.* Cambridge, MA: MIT Press.

Brock, W. A., & Sayers, C. (1988). Is the business cycle characterized by deterministic chaos? *Journal of Monetary Economics, 22,* 71–90.

Brown, J. S. (1948). Gradients approach to avoidance responses and their relation to motivation. *Journal of Comparative and Physiological Psychology, 41,* 450–465.

Brown, R. L., & Holmes, H. (1986). The use of factor-analytic procedure to assessing the validity of an employee safety climate model. *Accident Analysis and Prevention, 18,* 455–470.

Brownlee, J. (1907). Statistical studies in immunity: Theory of an epidemic. *Proceedings of the Royal Society of Edinburgh, 26,* 484–521.

Brownlee, J., & Young, M. (1922). The epidemiology of summer diarrhea. *Proceedings of the Royal Society of Medicine, 15,* 58–74.

Bryan, W. L., & Harter, N. (1897). Studies in the physiology and psychology of telegraphic language. *Psychological Review, 4,* 27–53.

Bryan, W. L., & Harter, N. (1899). Studies on the telegraphic language: The acquisition of a hierarchy of habits. *Psychological Review, 6*, 345–375.

Burney, D. A. (1993). Recent animal extinctions: Recipes for disaster. *American Scientist, 81*, 530–541.

Byrd, R. (1986). *The C & RT Index: The creatrix inventory.* San Diego: University Associates.

Caldwell, L. S., & Grossman, E. E. (1973). Effort scaling of isometric muscle contractions. *Journal of Motor Behavior, 5*, 9–16.

Callahan, J. (1980). Bifurcation geometry of E_6. *Mathematical Modeling, 1*, 283–309.

Callahan, J. (1982). A geometric model of anorexia and its treatment. *Behavioral Science, 27*, 140–154.

Campbell, D. T. (1960). Blind variation and selective retention in creative thought and in other knowledge processes. *Psychological Review, 67*, 380–400.

Campbell, D. T. (1977). *Manual for the Strong-campbell Interest Inventory.* Stanford, CA: Stanford University Press.

Campbell, J. P., & Pritchard, R. D. (1976). Motivation theory in industrial and organizational psychology. In M. D. Dunnette (Ed.), *Handbook of industrial and organizational psychology* (pp. 63–130). Chicago: Rand McNally.

Casdagli, M. (1992). Chaos and deterministic versus stochastic non-linear modeling. *Journal of the Royal Statistical Society, B, 54*, 303–328.

Casetti, E., & Krakover, S. (1990). The spatial distribution of the U.S. population: Estimates and extrapolations. *Socio-Spatial Dynamics, 1*, 139–160.

Casti, J. L. (1989). *Alternate realities: Mathematical models of nature and man.* New York: Wiley.

Casti, J. L. (1991). Chaos, Godel, and thuth. In J. L. Casti & A. Karlqvist (Eds.), *Beyond belief: Randomness, prediction and explanation in science* (pp. 280–327). Boca Raton, FL: CRC Press.

Cattell, J. M. (1886). The time it takes to see and name objects. *Mind, 11*, 63–65.

Cattell, R. B., & Drevdahl, J. E. (1955). A comparison of the personality profile (16PF) of eminent researchers with that of eminent teachers and administrators, and the general population. *British Journal of Psychology, 46*, 248–261.

Cattell, R. B., Eber, H. W., & Tatsuoka, M. M. (1970). *Handbook for the Sixteen Personality Factor Questionnaire.* Champaign, IL: Institute for Personality and Ability Testing.

Chatterjee, S., & Yilmaz, M. R. (1992). Chaos, fractals, and statistics. *Statistical Science, 7*, 49–121.

Cheng, B., & Tong, H. (1992). On consistent nonparametric order determination and chaos. *Journal of the Royal Statistical Society B, 54*, 427–449.

Clarke, D. H. (1962). Strength recovery from static and dynamic muscular fatigue. *Research Quarterly, 33*, 349–355.

Clarke, D. H., & Stelmach, G. E. (1966). Muscular fatigue and recovery curve parameters at various temperatures. *Research Quarterly, 37*, 468–479.

Cleary, T. A. (1968). Test bias: Prediction of grades of Negro and white students in integrated colleges. *Journal of Educational Measurement, 5*, 115–124.

Cobb, L. (1978). Stochastic catastrophe models and multimodal distributions. *Behavioral Science, 23*, 360–374.

Cobb, L. (1980). *Parameter estimation for the cusp catastrophe model: Programs and examples.* Charleston: Medical University of South Carolina.

Cobb, L. (1981a). Parameter estimation for the cusp catastrophe model, *Behavioral Science, 26*, 75–78.

Cobb, L. (1981b). Stochastic differential equations for the social sciences. In L. Cobb & R. M. Thrall (Eds.), *Mathematical frontiers of the social and policy sciences* (pp. 37–68). Boulder, CO: Westview Press & AAAS.

Cobb, L. (1981c). The multimodal exponential families of statistical catastrophe theory. In C. Taillie, G. P. Patil, & B. Baldessari (Eds.), *Statistical distributions in scientific work* (Vol. 4, pp. 67–90). Hingam, MA: Reidel.

Cobb, L., Koppstein, P., & Chen, N. H. (1983). Estimation and moment recursion relationships for multimodal distributions of the exponential family. *Journal of the American Statistical Association, 78,* 124–130.

Cobb, L., & Watson, B. (1980). Statistical catastrophe theory: An overview. *Mathematical Modeling, 1,* 311–317.

Cobb, L., & Zacks, S. (1985). Applications of catastrophe theory for statistical modeling in the biosciences. *Journal of the American Statistical Association, 78,* 124–130.

Cobb, L., & Zacks, S. (1988). Nonlinear time series analysis for dynamic systems of catastrophe type. In R. R. Mohler (Ed.), *Nonlinear time series and signal processing* (pp. 97–118). North Holland: Springer-Verlag.

Cohen, S. (1980). Aftereffects of stress on human performance and social behavior: A review of research and theory. *Psychological Bulletin, 88,* 82–108.

Cohen, S., & Williamson, G. M. (1991). Stress and infectious disease in humans. *Psychological Bulletin, 109,* 5–24.

Colquhoun, W. P. (1971). *Biological rhythms and human performance.* London: Academic Press.

Combs, A. (Ed.). (1992). *Cooperation: Beyond the age of competition.* New York: Gordon & Breach.

Conn, S. R., & Rieke, M. L. (Eds.). (1994). *The Sixteen Personality Factor Questionnaire: Fifth Edition Technical Manual.* Champaign, IL: Institute for Personality and Ability Testing.

Conrad, R. (1951). Speed and load stress in a sensorimotor skill. *British Journal of Industrial Medicine, 8,* 1–7.

Cortina, J. M. (1993). What is coefficient alpha? An examination of theory and applications. *Journal of Applied Psychology, 78,* 98–104.

Crawley, S. L. (1926). An experimental investigation of recovery from work. *Archives of Psychology, 85.*

Cronbach, L. J. (1951). Coefficient alpha and the internal structure of tests. *Psychometrika, 22,* 347–358.

Cronbach, L. J. (1976). Equity in selection: Where psychometrics and political philosophy meet. *Journal of Educational Measurement, 13,* 31–42.

Csikszentmihalyi, M., & Getzels, J. W. (1973). The personality of young artists: An empirical and theoretical exploration. *British Journal of Psychology, 64,* 91–104.

Cutting, J. E., & Garvin, J. J. (1987). Fractal curves and complexity. *Perception & Psychophysics, 42,* 365–370.

Cuzan, A. G. (1986). Fiscal policy, the military, and political stability in Iberoamerica. *Behavioral Science, 31,* 226–237.

Daly, H., & Goodland, R. (1994). An ecological economic assessment of deregulation of international commerce under GATT. *Ecological Economics, 9,* 73–92.

D'Amato, M. R. (1973). *Experimental psychology: Methodology, psychophysics, and learning.* New York: McGraw-Hill.

d'Andrade, J. F. (1959). *Freedom chooses slavery.* NewYork: Cowan-McCann.

Darlington, R. B. (1990). *Regression and linear models.* New York: Wiley.

Darwin, C. (1964). *On the origin of species.* Cambridge, MA: Harvard University Press. (Original work published 1859)

deCharms, R. (1968). *Personal causation.* New York: Wiley.

deCharms, R. (1976). *Enhancing motivation: Change in the classroom.* New York: Irvington.

deCharms, R., Carpenter, V., & Kuperman, A. (1965). The "Origin-Pawn" variable in person perception. *Sociometry, 28,* 241–258.

Deci, E. L. (1972). *Intrinsic motivation.* New York: Plenum.

Deese, J., & Hulse, S. H. (1967). *The psychology of learning* (3rd ed.). New York: McGraw-Hill.

DeGreene, K. B. (1978). Force fields and emergent phenomena in sociotechnical macrosystems: Theories and models. *Behavioral Science, 23,* 1–14.

DeGreene, K. B. (1990). The turbulent field environment of sociotechnical systems: Beyond metaphor. *Behavioral Science, 35,* 49–59.

DeGreene, K. B. (1991a). Emergent complexity and person-machine systems. *International Journal of Man–Machine Studies, 35,* 219–234.

DeGreene, K. B. (1991b). Rigidity and fragility of large sociotechnical systems: Advanced information technology, the dominant coalition, and paradigm shift at the end of the 20th century. *Behavioral Science, 36,* 64–79.

Deming, W. E. (1986). *Out of the crisis.* Cambridge, MA: MIT Press-CAES.

Dendrinos, D. S. (1991). Quasi-periodicity and chaos in spatial population dynamics. *Socio-Spatial Dynamics, 2,* 31–59.

Dendrinos, D. S., & Mullally, H. (1985). *Urban evolution: Studies in the mathematical ecology of cities.* Oxford: Cambridge University Press.

Dendrinos, D. S., & Sonis, M. (1990). *Turbulence and socio-spatial dynamics.* New York: Springer Verlag.

Dennis, A. R., & Valacich, J. S. (1993). Computer brainstorms: More heads are better than one. *Journal of Applied Psychology, 78,* 531–537.

Denny, V. E., Gilbert, K. J., Erdmann, R. C., & Rumble, E. T. (1978). Risk assessment methodologies: An application to underground mine systems. *Journal of Safety Research, 10,* 24–34.

Depue, R. A., & Monroe, S. M. (1986). Conceptualization and measurement of human disorder in life stress research: The problem of chronic disturbance. *Psychological Bulletin, 99,* 36–51.

Deutch, C. P. (1964). Auditory discrimination and learning: Social factors. *Merrill-Palmer Quarterly of Behavior and Development, 10,* 277–296.

Ditto, W. L. (Ed.). (1993). *Chaos in biology and medicine.* Proceedings of SPIE, No. 2036. Washington, DC: SPIE, The International Society for Optical Engineering.

Dittrich, J. E., & Carrell, M. R. (1979). Organizational equity perceptions, employees' job satisfaction, and department absence and turnover rates. *Organizational Behavior and Human Performance, 24,* 29–40.

Dommen, E. (Ed.). (1993). *Fair principles for sustainable development.* Brookfield, VT: Edward Elgar Publishing/United Nations.

Dooley, K. J. (1992, June). Total quality management and chaos theory. In S. J. Guastello, Chair, *Chaos theory and socio-organizational dynamics.* Symposium presented to the annual conference of the American Psychological Society, San Diego, CA.

Dooley, K. J., Johnson, T. L., & Bush, D. H. (1993, June). *Total quality management and the revolution in management paradigm.* Paper presented to the Continual Improvement Conference, Minneapolis, MN.

Dore, M. H. I., & Ward, A. J. (1994, October). *Modelling intertemporally sustainable development: A nonlinear approach.* Paper presented to the CASX Sustainable Development Forum II, Naperville, IL.

Douglas, M., & Wildavsky, A. (1982). *Risk and culture: An essay on the selection of environmental dangers.* Berkeley: University of California Press.

Douglass, J. K., Wilkens, L. A., & Moss, F. (1993). Noise assisted information transfer in crayfish mechanoreceptors: Stochastic resonance in a neuronal receptor. In W. L. Ditto (Ed.), *Chaos in biology and medicine* (pp. 152–161). Proceedings of SPIE, No. 2036. Washington, DC: SPIE, The International Society for Optical Engineering.

Drexler, J. A., Jr. (1977). Organizational climate: Its homogeneity within organizations. *Journal of Applied Psychology, 62,* 38–42.

Dureman, E. I., & Boden, C. (1972). Fatigue in simulated car driving. *Ergonomics, 15,* 299–308.

Dyer, L., & Parker, D. F. (1975). Classifying outcomes in work motivation research: An examination of the intrinsic-extrinsic dichotomy. *Journal of Applied Psychology, 60,* 455–458.

Edwards, J. E., & Waters, L. K. (1981). Moderating effect of achievement motivation and locus of control on the relationship between academic ability and academic performance. *Educational and Psychological Measurement, 41,* 585–587.

Edwards, W. (1981). Reflections on and criticisms of a highly political multiattribute utility analysis. In L. Cobb & R. M. Thrall (Eds.), *Mathematical frontiers of the social and policy sciences* (pp. 157–186). Boulder, CO: AAAS and Westview Press.

Eiser, J. (1994). *Attitudes, chaos, and the connectionist mind.* Cambridge, MA: Basil Blackwell.

Eisler, R. (1987). *The chalice and the blade.* San Francisco: Harper & Row.

Eisler, R. (1991). Cultural evolution: Social shifts and phase changes. In E. Laszlo (Ed.), *The new evolutionary paradigm* (pp. 179–200). New York: Gordon & Breach.

Eisler, R., & Combs, A. (1992). Cooperation, competition, and gylany: Cultural evolution from a new dynamic perspective. In A. Combs (Ed.), *Cooperation: Beyond the age of competition* (pp. 75–85). New York: Gordon & Breach.

Ekins, P., Folke, C., & Costanza, R. (1994). Trade, environment, and development: The issues in perspective. *Ecological Economics, 9,* 1–12.

Enzle, M. E., & Ross, J. M. (1978). Increasing and decreasing intrinsic interest with contingent rewards: A test of cognitive evaluation theory. *Journal of Experimental Social Psychology, 14,* 588–597.

Epstein, Y., & Karlin, R. A. (1975). Effects of acute experimental crowding. *Journal of Applied Social Psychology, 5,* 34–53.

Ersland, S., Weisaeth, L., & Sund, A. (1989). The stress upon rescuers involved in an oil rig disaster: "Alexander L. Kielland." *Acta Psyciatrica Scandinavica, 80* (355 Suppl.), 38–49.

Estes, W. K. (1950). Toward a statistical theory of learning. *Psychological Review, 57,* 94–107.

Evans, M. G. (1991). The problem of analyzing multiplicative composites. *American Psychologist, 46,* 6–15.

Fararo, T. J. (1978). An introduction to catastrophes. *Behavioral Science, 23,* 291–317.

Farmer, J. D., Ott, E., & Yorke, J. A. (1983). The dimension of chaotic attractors. *Physica D, 7,* 153–180.

Farmer, J. D., Kauffman, S. A., & Packard, N. H. (1986). Autocatalytic replication of polymers. *Physica D, 22,* 50–67.

Farr, W. (1840). Progress of epidemics. *Report of the Registrar General of England and Wales, 2,* 16–20.

Fazey, J. A., & Hardy, L. (1988). The inverted-U hypothesis: A catastrophe for sport psychology. *British Association of Sports Sciences Monograph, 1.* Leeds, UK: The National Coaching Foundation.

Feigenbaum, M. J. (1978). Quantitative universality in a class of nonlinear transformations. *Journal of Statistical Physics, 19,* 25–52.

File, Q. W., & Remmers, H. H. (1971). *Manual for How Supervise?* San Antonio, TX: Psychological Corporation.

Fine, P. E. M. (1979). John Brownlee and the measurement of infectiousness: An historical study in epidemic theory. *Journal of the Royal Statistical Society, A, 142,* 347–362.

Fishbein, M. (1967). Attitude and prediction of behavior. In M. Fishbein (Ed.), *Readings in attitude theory and measurement* (pp. 477–492). New York: Wiley.

Flay, B. R. (1978). Catastrophe theory in social psychology: Some applications to attitudes and social behavior. *Behavioral Science, 23,* 335–350.

Frederickson, P., Kaplan, J. L., Yorke, E. D., & Yorke, J. A. (1983). The Lyapunov dimension of strange attractors. *Journal of Differential Equations, 49,* 185–207.

French, W., & Bell, C., Jr. (1990). *Organization development* (4th Ed.). Englewood Cliffs, NJ: Prentice Hall.

Frey, P. W., & Sears, R. J. (1978). Model of conditioning incorporating the Rescorla-Wagner associative axiom, a dynamic attention process, and a catastrophe rule. *Psychological Review, 85,* 321–340.

Gardell, B., Aronsson, G., & Barkloff, K. (1982). *The working environment for local public transport personnel: Summary of a research report* (Tech. Rep.). University of Stockholm.

Geiser, R. L. (1976). *Behavior mod and the managed society.* Boston: Beacon Press.

Gersick, C. J. (1988). Time and transition in work teams: Toward a model of group development. *Academy of Management Journal, 31,* 9–41.

Gilden, D. L., Schmuckler, M. A., & Clayton, K. (1993). The perception of natural contour. *Psychological Review, 100,* 460–478.

Gillan, P. G. (1989). Island commission: Group problem solving. In J. Pfeiffer (Ed.), *Structured experiences in human relations* (Vol. 7, pp. 99–104). San Diego: J. Pfeiffer and Associates.

Gilmore, R. (1981). *Catastrophe theory for scientists and engineers.* New York: Wiley.

Girault, P. (1991). Attractors and dimensions. In G. Cherbit (Ed.), *Non-integral dimensions and applications* (pp. 60–82). West Sussex, UK: Wiley.

Glance, N. S., & Huberman, B. A. (1993). Organizational fluidity and sustainable cooperation. In K. Carley & M. Prietula (Eds.), *Computational organization theory.* Hillsdale, NJ: Lawrence Erlbaum Associates.

Glance, N. S., & Huberman, B. A. (1994). The dynamics of social dilemmas. *Scientific American, 270*(3), 76–81.

Glass, D. C. & Singer, J. E. (1972). *Urban stress: Experiments on noise and social stressors.* New York: Academic Press.

Glover, H. (1982). Four syndromes of post-traumatic stress disorder: Stressors and conflicts of the traumatized with special focus on the Vietnam Combat Veteran. *Journal of Traumatic Stress, 1,* 57–78.

Goldberg, A. I., Ezey, D. -E., & Rubin, A. -H. E. (1991). Threat perception and the readiness to participate in safety programs. *Journal of Organizational Behavior, 12,* 109–122.

Goldstein, J. (1988). A far-from-equilibrium approach to resistance to change. *Organizational Dynamics, 17,* 16–26.

Goldstein, J. (1994). *The unshackled corporation: Facing the challenge of unpredictability through spontaneous reorganization.* Portland, OR: Productivity Press.

Golembiewski, R. T. (1986). Contours in social change: Elemental graphics and a surrogate variable for gamma change. *Academy of Management Review, 11,* 550–566.

Good, I. J. (1986). (Neo)^n-Darwinism, *Physica D, 22,* 13–30.

Goodman, P., & Friedman, A. (1971). An examination of Adams' theory of inequity. *Administrative Science Quarterly, 16,* 271–288.

Gordon, J. E. (1978). *Structures, or why things don't fall down.* New York: Penguin.

Gori, F., Geronazzo, L., & Galeotti, M. (Eds.). (1993). *Nonlinear dynamics in economics and social sciences.* Berlin: Springer-Verlag.

Grassberger, P., & Proccaccia, I. (1983). Characterization of strange attractors. *Physics Review Letters, 50,* 346–349.

Greeley, L. (1986). The bumper effect dynamic in the creative process: The philosophical, psychological and neuropsychological link. *Journal of Creative Behavior, 20,* 261–275.

Green, D. M., McKay, M. J., & Licklider, J. C. R. (1988). Detection of a pulsed sinusoid in noise as a function of frequency. In J. A. Swets (Ed.), *Signal detection and recognition by human observers* (2nd ed., pp. 508–522). Los Altos, CA: Peninsula Publishing.

Greenwood, D. (1991). An overview of neural networks. *Behavioral Science, 36,* 1–33.

Gregson, R. A. M. (1988). *Nonlinear psychophysical dynamics.* Hillsdale, NJ: Lawrence Erlbaum Associates.

Gregson, R. A. M. (1992). *n-Dimensional nonlinear psychophysics.* Hillsdale, NJ: Lawrence Erlbaum Associates.

Gregson, R. A. M., & Harvey, J. P. (1992). Similarities of low-dimensional chaotic auditory attractor sequences to quasirandom noise. *Perception & Psychophysics, 51,* 267–278.

Gresov, C., Haveman, H. A., & Oliva, T. A. (1993). Organizational design, inertia, and the dynamics of competitive response. *Organization Science, 4,* 181–208.

Griggs v. Duke Power, 91 S. Ct. 849 (1971).

Grose, J. E. (1958). Depression of muscle fatigue curves by heat and cold. *Research Quarterly, 29,* 19–31.

Guastello, D. D., & Guastello, S. J. (1987a). A climate for safety in hazardous environments: A psychosocial approach (Rep. No. 2839). *Social and Behavioral Sciences Documents, 17,* 67.

Guastello, D. D., & Guastello, S. J. (1987b). The relationship between work group size and occupational accidents. *Journal of Occupational Accidents, 9,* 1–9.

Guastello, S. J. (1981). Catastrophe modeling of equity in organizations. *Behavioral Science, 26,* 63–74.

Guastello, S. J. (1982a). Moderator regression and the cusp catastrophe: Application of two-stage personnel selection, training, therapy, and policy evaluation. *Behavioral Science, 27,* 259–272.

Guastello, S. J. (1982b). Color matching and shift work: An industrial application of the cusp-difference equation. *Behavioral Science, 27,* 131–139.

Guastello, S. J. (1984a). Cusp and butterfly catastrophe modeling of two opponent process models: Drug addiction and work performance. *Behavioral Science, 29,* 258–262.

Guastello, S. J. (1984b). A catastrophe theory evaluation of a policy to control job absence. *Behavioral Science, 29,* 263–269.

Guastello, S. J. (1985a). Euler buckling in a wheelbarrow obstacle course: A catastrophe with complex lag. *Behavioral Science, 30,* 204–212(b).

Guastello, S. J. (1985b). Color matching and the weekly work cycle: An industrial application of the swallowtail-difference equation. *Behavioral Science, 30,* 213–218.

Guastello, S. J. (1986, April). *Butterfly catastrophe model of motivation in organizations: Evaluation of an introductory psychology course.* ERIC Resources in Education, (ERIC Document Reproduction Service No. Ed 263 846).

Guastello, S. J. (1987a). Catastrophe theory: Ten years of progress (Rep. No. 2790). *Social and Behavioral Science documents, 17,* 4.

Guastello, S. J. (1987b). A butterfly catastrophe model of motivation in organizations: Academic performance. *Journal of Applied Psychology, 72,* 165–182.

Guastello, S. J. (1987c). Catastrophe modeling of the accident process: Risk dispersion for ten industrial classes (Rep. No. 2817). *Social and Behavioral Sciences Documents, 17,* 41.

Guastello, S. J. (1988a). Catastrophe modeling of the accident process: Organizational subunit size. *Psychological Bulletin, 103,* 246–255.

Guastello, S. J. (1988b). The organizational security subsystem: Some potentially catastrophic events. *Behavioral Science, 33,* 48–58.

Guastello, S. J. (1989). Catastrophe modeling of the accident process: Evaluation of an accident reduction program using the Occupational Hazards Survey. *Accident Analysis and Prevention, 21,* 61–77.

Guastello, S. J. (1991a). *The comparative effectiveness of occupational accident reduction programs.* Paper presented to the International Symposium for Alcohol-related Accidents and Injuries, Yverdon-les-Bains, Switzerland.

Guastello, S. J. (1991b). Psychosocial variables related to transit accidents: A catastrophe model. *Work and Stress, 5,* 17–28.

Guastello, S. J. (1991c). *Artistic and Scientific Activities Survey.* Unpublished document.

Guastello, S. J. (1992a). Clash of the paradigms: A critique of an examination of the polynomial regression technique for evaluating catastrophe theory hypotheses. *Psychological Bulletin, 111,* 375–379.

Guastello, S. J. (1992b). Accidents and stress-related health disorders: Forecasting with catastrophe theory. In J. C. Quick, J. J. Hurrell, & L. M. Murphy (Eds.), *Work and well-being: Assessments and interventions for occupational mental health.* (pp. 252–269). Washington, DC: American Psychological Association.

Guastello, S. J. (1992c). Population dynamics and work force productivity. In M. Michaels (Ed.), *Proceedings of the Annual Conference of the Chaos Network: The Second Iteration* (pp. 120–127). Urbana, IL: People Technologies

Guastello, S. J. (1993a, June). Metaphors, Easter bunnies, and empirical verification of chaos theory applications in psychology. In F. Abraham (Chair), *Chaos theory: Secret sect for mathematical mystics versus popular multidisciplinary metamodeling paradigm.* Symposium presented to the American Psychological Society, Chicago.

Guastello, S. J. (1993b, August). *Catastrophe and chaos theory for NYSE stock prices: The crash of 1987 and beyond.* Paper presented to the annual conference of the Society of Chaos Theory in Psychology and the Life Sciences, Orillia, Ontario.

Guastello, S. J. (1993c). *Implications of recent legislation for pre-employment personality testing.* (Tech. Rep.). Champaign, IL: Institute for Personality and Ability Testing.

Guastello, S. J. (1993d). Do we really know how well our occupational accident prevention programs work? *Safety Science, 16*, 445–463.

Guastello, S. J. (1993e). *The assessment of creative potential with the 16PF: Artists, musicians, research scientists, and engineers.* (Tech. Rep.). Champaign, IL: Institute for Personality and Ability Testing.

Guastello, S. J., Bzdawka, A., Guastello, D. D., & Rieke, M. L. (1992). Cognitive abilities and creative behaviors: CAB-5 and consequences. *Journal of Creative Behavior, 26*, 260–267.

Guastello, S. J,. & Dizadji, D. M. (1984, May). *Catastrophe modeling of the accident process: Systemic control of risk in open pit and underground mines.* Paper presented to the Midwestern Psychological Association, Chicago.

Guastello, S. J., Dooley, K. J., Goldstein, J., & Abraham, F. D. (1993). *Nonlinear dynamics (chaos) for organizational theory and organizational development.* Unpublished manuscript.

Guastello, S. J., & Guastello, D. D. (1986). The relation between the locus of control construct and involvement in traffic accidents. *Journal of Psychology: Interdisciplinary and Applied, 120*, 293–298.

Guastello, S. J., & Guastello, D. D. (1988). *The Occupational Hazards Survey: Manual and case report.* Milwaukee, WI: Authors.

Guastello, S. J., Ikeda, M. J., & Connors, C. E. (1985). Stress, anxiety, errors, and accidents: A cyclic relationship. (Rep. No. 2725). *Psychological Documents, 15*, 26.

Guastello, S. J., & McGee, D. W. (1987). Catastrophe modeling of fatigue in physically demanding jobs. *Journal of Mathematical Psychology, 31*, 248–269.

Guastello, S. J., & Rieke, M. L. (1991). A review and critique of honesty test research. *Behavioral Sciences and the Law, 9*, 501–523.

Guastello, S. J., & Shissler, J. E. (1994). A two-factor taxonomy of creative behavior. *Journal of Creative Behavior, 28*, 211–221.

Guckenheimer, J., & Worfolk, P. (1992). Instant chaos. *Nonlinearity, 5*, 1211–1222.

Guilford, J. P. (1967). *The structure of intellect.* New York: McGraw-Hill.

Guilford, J. P., & Guilford, J. S. (1980). *Consequences: Manual of instructions and interpretations.* Orange, CA: Sheridan Psychological Services.

Haag, G., & Dendrinos, D. S. (1983). Toward a stochastic dynamical theory of location: A nonlinear migration process. *Geographical Analysis, 15*, 269–286.

Hackman, R. (1992, June). *Where the variance lives: Continuity and change in social behavior.* Paper presented to the annual conference of the American Psychological Society, San Diego, CA.

Haken, H. (1984). *The science of structure: Synergetics.* New York: Van Nostrand Reinhold.

Hamer, W. H. (1906). Epidemic disease in England: The evidence of variability and of persistency of type. *The Lancet, 2*, 733–739.

Hanges, P. J., Braverman, E. P., & Rentsch, J. R. (1991). Changes in raters' perception of subordinates: A catastrophe model. *Journal of Applied Psychology, 76*, 878–888.

Hansen, R. G., & Samuelson, W. F. (1988). Evolution in economic games. *Journal of Economic Behavior and Organization, 10,* 315–338.

Hardy, L. (1990). A catastrophe model of performance in sport. In J. G. Jones & L. Hardy (Eds.), *Stress and performance in sport* (pp. 81–106). Chichester, UK: Wiley.

Hardy, L. (1993). *A test of catastrophe models of anxiety and sports performance against multidimensional anxiety theory models using the method of dynamic differences.* Manuscript submitted for publication.

Hardy, L., & Parfitt, C. G. (1991). A catastrophe model of anxiety and performance. *British Journal of Psychology, 82,* 163–178.

Hardy, L., Parfitt, C. G., & Pates, J. (in press). Performance catastrophes in sport: A test of the hysteresis hypothesis. *Journal of Sports Sciences.*

Hartley, I. R., & Shirley, E. (1976). Color name interference at different times of the day. *Journal of Applied Psychology, 61,* 119–122.

Hausdorff, F. (1919). Dimension und ausseres mass. *Mathematical Annalen, 79,* 157–179.

Haustein, H. D. (1981). Human resources, creativity, and innovation: The conflict between Homo Faber and Homo Ludens. *Behavioral Science, 26,* 243–255.

Heinrich, H. W. (1931). *Industrial accident prevention.* New York: McGraw-Hill.

Heggen, R. J., & Cuzan, A. G. (1981). Legitimacy, coercion, and scope: An expansion path analysis applied to five Central American Countries and Cuba. *Behavioral Science, 26,* 143–152.

Heller, R. M., Guastello, S. J., & Aderman, M. (1982). Convergent and discriminant validity of psychological and objective indices of organizational climate. *Psychological Reports, 51,* 183–195.

Heneman, H. G. III, & Schwab, D. C. (1972). Evaluation of results on expectancy theory predictions of employee performance. *Psychological Bulletin, 78,* 1–9.

Henon, M. (1976). A two-dimensional mapping with a strange attractor. *Communications in Mathematical Physics, 50,* 69–77.

Henon, M., & Heiles, C. (1964). The applicability of the third integral of the motion: Some numerical experiments. *Astronomical Journal, 69,* 73–79.

Herzberg, F., Mausner, B., & Snyderman, D. (1959). *The motivation to work.* New York: Wiley.

Hey, D. (1994, March). *Wetland restoration: A sustainable solution to many water resource problems.* Paper presented to the Chicago Area Sigma Xi (CASX) Sustainable Development Forum, Chicago.

Hirshleiffer, J., & Coll, J. C. M. (1988). What strategies can support the evolutionary emergence of cooperation? *Journal of Conflict Resolution, 32,* 367–398.

Hocevar, D. (1981). Measurement of creativity: Review and critique. *Journal of Personality Assessment, 45,* 450–464.

Hofmann, D. A., Jacobs, R., & Baratta, J. E. (1993). Dynamic criteria and the measurement of change. *Journal of Applied Psychology, 78,* 195–205.

Holding, D. H. (1983). Fatigue. In G. R. J. Hockey (Ed.), *Stress and fatigue in human performance* (pp. 145–167). New York: Wiley.

Holmes, K. R. (1993). New world disorder: A critique of the United Nations. *Journal of International Affairs, 46,* 323–340.

Holmes, T. H., & Rahe, R. H., (1967). The Social Readjustment Rating Scale. *Journal of Psychosomatic Research, 11,* 213–218.

Hom, P. W., Hulin, C. L. (1981). A competitive test of the prediction of reenlistment by several models. *Journal of Applied Psychology, 66,* 23–39.

Hom, P. W., Katerberg, R., Jr., & Hulin, C. L. (1979). Comparative examination of three approaches to the prediction of turnover. *Journal of Applied Psychology, 64,* 280–290.

Huberman, B. A., & Glance, N. S. (1993). Diversity and collective action. In H. Haken & A. Mikhailov (Eds.), *Interdisciplinary approaches to nonlinear systems* (44–64). New York: Springer-Verlag.

Huberman, B. A., & Glance, N. S. (1994). Evolutionary games and computer simulations. *Proceedings of the National Academy of Sciences, 90,* 7716–7718.

Hubler, A. (1992). Modeling and control of complex systems. In L. Lam & V. Naroditsky (Eds.), *Modeling complex phenomena* (pp. 5–65). New York: Springer-Verlag.

Hull, C. L. (1943). *Principles of behavior.* New York: Appleton-Century-Crofts.

Hunsaker, S. L. (1992). Toward an ethnographic perspective on creativity research. *Journal of Creative Behavior, 26,* 235–241.

Hurst, D. K., & Zimmerman, B. J. (1993). *From life cycle to ecocycle: A new perspective on the growth, maturity, destruction and renewal of complex systems.* Working Paper No. 08–93. North York, Ontario: York University, Faculty of Administrative Studies.

Iaffaldano, J. M., & Muchinsky, P. M. (1985). The performance to satisfaction relationship: A causal analysis of stimulating and nonstimulating jobs. *Organizational Behavior and Human Performance, 22,* 350–365.

Isen, A. M., Daubman, K. A., & Nowicki, G. P. (1987). Positive affect facilitates creative problem solving. *Journal of Personality and Social Psychology, 52,* 1122–1131.

Ioteyko, J. (1920). *La fatigue* [Fatigue]. (2nd ed). Paris: Flammarion.

Jackson, E. A. (1991a). On the control of complex dynamic systems. *Physica D, 50,* 341–366.

Jackson, E. A. (1991b). Controls of dynamic flows with attractors. *Physical Review A, 44,* 4839–4853.

James, L. R,. & Jones, A. P. (1974). Organizational climate: A review of theory and research. *Psychological Bulletin, 81,* 1096–1112.

Jemmott, J., B., & Locke, S. E. (1984). Psychosocial factors, immunological mediation, and human susceptibility to infectious diseases: How much do we know? *Psychological Bulletin, 95,* 78–108.

Jiobu, R. M., & Lundgren, T. D. (1978). Catastrophe theory: A quasi-quantitative methodology. *Sociological Methods and Research, 7,* 29–54.

Johnson, T. L., & Dooley, K. J. (1994, June). *Looking for chaos in time series data.* Paper presented to the annual conference of the Society for Chaos Theory in Psychology and the Life Sciences, Baltimore.

Kahneman, D., & Tversky, A. (1979). Prospect theory: An analysis of decision under risk. *Econometrica, 47,* 253–291.

Kamarck, T., & Jennings, J. R. (1991). Biobehavioral factors in sudden cardiac death. *Psychological Bulletin, 109,* 42–75.

Kantowitz, B. H. (1985). Channels and stages in human information processing: A limited analysis of theory and methodology. *Journal of Mathematical Psychology, 29,* 135–174.

Kantowitz, B. H., & Sorkin, D. (1983). *Human factors: Understanding people-system relationships.* New York: Wiley.

Kaplowitz, S. A., Fink, E. L., & Bauer, C. L. (1983). A dynamic model of the effect of discrepant information on unidimensional attitude change. *Behavioral Science, 28,* 233–250.

Katzell, R. A. (1980). Work attitudes, motivation and performance. *Professional Psychology, 11,* 409–420.

Kasl, S. V., Chisholm, R. F., & Eskanazi, B. (1981). The impact of the accident at Three Mile Island on the behavior and well-being of nuclear workers. Part I: Perceptions and evaluations, behavioral responses, and work-related attitudes and feelings. *American Journal of Public Health, 71,* 472–483.

Kauffman, S. A. (1993). *The origins of order: Self-organization and selection in evolution.* New York: Oxford University Press.

Kegan, D. L., & Rubinstein, A. H. (1973). Trust, effectiveness, and organizational development. *Journal of Applied Behavioral Science, 9,* 498–513.

Kemp, C. D. (1967). On a contagious distribution suggested for accident data. *Biometrics, 23,* 241–255.

Keown, R. (1980). Catastrophe theory and law. *Mathematical Modeling, 1,* 319–329.

Kerouac, J. (1958, November). *Is there a Beat Generation?* Paper presented to the forum, "Is there a Beat Generation?" Brandeis University, Waltham, MA.

Kessler, R. C., & Greenberg, D. F. (1981). *Linear panel analysis.* New York: Academic Press.

Kets de Vries, M. R., & Miller, D. (1986). Personality, culture, and organization. *Academy of Management Review, 11,* 266–279.

King, A., & Schneider, B. (1991). *The first global revolution.* New York: Pantheon/Random House.

Kjellen, U. (1984a). The deviation concept in occupational accident control — I: Definition and classification. *Accident Analysis and Prevention, 16,* 289–306.

Kjellen, U. (1984b). The deviation concept in occupational accident control: Vol. 2. Data collection and assessment of significance. *Accident Analysis and Prevention 16,* 307–323.

Kjellen, U., & Hovden, J. (1993). Reducing risks by deviation control — A retrospection into a research strategy. *Safety Science, 16,* 417–438.

Kjellen, U., & Larsson, T. J. (1981). Investigating accidents and reducing risks: A dynamic approach. *Journal of Occupational Accidents, 3,* 129–140.

Kroll, W. (1981). The C. H. McCloy research lecture: Analysis of local muscular fatigue patterns. *Research Quarterly for Exercise and Sport, 52,* 523–539.

Kugiumtzis, D., Lillekjendlie, B., & Christophersen, N. (1994). *Chaotic time series, part I: Estimation of invariant properties in state space* (Tech. Rep.). University of Oslo, Department of Informatics.

Labouvie, E. W. (1980). Measurement of individual differences in intraindividual changes. *Psychological Bulletin, 88,* 54–59.

Landy, F. J. (1978). An opponent process theory of job satisfaction. *Journal of Applied Psychology, 63,* 533–547.

Larrain, M. (1991). Testing chaos and nonlinearities in T-bill rates. *Financial Analysts Journal, 47*(5), 51–62.

Larsson, T. J. (1993). Investigating accidents and reducing risks: A dynamic approach (Kjellen and Larsson, 1981): Its relevance for injury prevention. *Safety Science, 16,* 439–443.

Laszlo, E. (1987). *Evolution: The grand synthesis.* Boston: New Science Library, Shambhala.

Laszlo, E. (Ed.). (1991). *The new evolutionary paradigm.* New York: Gordon & Breach.

Latané, B., & Nowak, A. (1994). Attitudes as catastrophes: From dimensions to categories with increasing involvement. In R. R. Vallacher & A. Nowak (Eds.), *Dynamical systems in social psychology* (pp. 219–250). San Diego: Academic Press.

Latané, B., Nowak, A., & Liu, J. H. (1994). Measuring emergent social phenomena: Dynamism, polarization, and clustering as order parameters of social systems. *Behavioral Science, 39,* 1–24.

Lawler, E. E., III. (1973). *Motivation in work organizations.* Monterey, CA: Brooks/Cole.

Lawler, E. E., III, & Porter, L. W. (1967). The effect of performance on job satisfaction. *Industrial Relations, 7,* 20–28.

Laws, R. M. (1985). The ecology of the southern ocean. *American Scientist, 73,* 26–40.

Leary, M. R. (1990). Anxiety, cognition, and behavior: In search of a broader perspective. *Journal of Social Behavior and Personality, 5,* 39–44.

Leigh, J. P. (1986). Occupational hazards and heart attacks. *Social Science Medicine, 11,* 1181–1185.

Lemma, A. (1989). An agenda for action: Capacity building for self-reliant and sustainable development in Africa. In A. Lemma & P. Malaska (Eds.), *Africa beyond famine* (pp. 324–333). New York: Tycooly.

Leon, F. R. (1981). The role of positive and negative outcomes in the causation of motivational forces. *Journal of Applied Psychology, 66,* 45–53.

Levenson, H., Hirschfeld, M. L., Hirschfeld, A., & Dzubay, B. (1983). Recent life events and accidents: The role of sex differences. *Journal of Human Stress, 9,* 4–11.

Levins, R., Awerbuch, T., Brinkmann, U., Eckardt, I., Epstein, P., Makhoul, N., de Possas, C. A., Puccia, C., Speilman, A., & Wilson, M. E. (1994). The emergence of new diseases. *American Scientist, 82,* 52–60.

Lewin, K. (1947). Frontiers in group dynamics. *Human Relations, 1,* 5–41.

Lewin, K. (1951). *Field theory in social science.* New York: Harper & Row.

Lewin, K., Lippitt, R., & White, R. (1939). Patterns of aggressive behavior in experimentally created "social climates." *Journal of Social Psychology, 10,* 271–299.

Li, T.-Y., & Yorke, J. A. (1975). Period three implies chaos. *American Mathematical Monthly, 85,* 985–992.

Linn, R. (1986). Educational testing and assessment: Research needs and policy issues. *American Psychologist, 41,* 1153–1160.

Litwin, G. H., & Stringer, R. A. (1968). *Motivation and Organizational Climate.* (Tech. Rep.). Cambrige, MA: Harvard Business School.

Locke, E. A. (1976). The nature and causes of job satisfaction. In M. D. Dunnete (Ed.), *Handbook of industrial and organizational psychology* (pp. 1297–1350). Chicago: Rand McNally.

Locke, E. A., & Latham, G. P. (1990). Work motivation and satisfaction: Light at the end of the tunnel. *Psychological Science, 1,* 240–246.

Locke, E. A., Mento, A. J., & Katcher, B. L. (1978). The interaction of ability and motivation in performance: An exploration of the meaning of moderators. *Personnel Psychology, 31,* 269–280.

Lonero, L. P., & Clinton, K. M. (1993). *Methods to improve road user behavior.* Toronto: Road User Safety Office, Safety Planning and Policy Branch, Ministry of Transportation.

Lord, F. M., & Novick, M. R. (1968). *Statistical theories of mental test scores.* Reading, MA: Addison-Wesley.

Lorenz, E. N. (1963). Deterministic nonperiodic flow. *Journal of the Atmospheric Sciences, 20,* 130–141.

Lotka, A. J. (1926). The frequency distribution of scientific productivity. *Journal of the Washington Academy of Sciences, 16,* 317–323.

Loye, D. (1977). *The leadership passion: The psychology of ideology.* San Francisco: Jossey-Bass.

Loye, D., & Eisler, R. (1987). Chaos and transformation: Implications of nonequilibrium theory for social science and society. *Behavioral Science, 32,* 53–65.

Lu, Y.-C. (1976). *Singularity theory and an introduction to catastrophe theory.* New York: Springer-Verlag.

Lucas, R. E., Jr. (1988). On the mechanics of economic development. *Journal of Monetary Economics, 22,* 3–42.

Maehr, M. L., & Braskamp, L. A. (1986). *The motivation factor: A theory of personal investment.* Lexington, MA: Lexington.

Malaska, P. (1989). A conceptual framework for the self-reliant transformation of Africa. In A. Lemma & P. Malaska (Eds.), *Africa beyond famine* (pp. 291–323). New York: Tycooly.

Malaska, P. (1991). Economic and social evolution. The transformational dynamics approach. In E. Laslo (Ed.), *The new evolutionary paradigm* (pp. 131–155). New York: Gordon & Breach.

Malaviya, P., & Ganesh, K. (1976). Shift work and individual differences in the productivity of weavers in an Indian textile mill. *Journal of Applied Psychology, 61,* 774–776.

Malaviya, P., & Ganesh, K. (1977). Individual differences in productivity across type of work shift. *Journal of Applied Psychology, 62,* 527–528.

Mandelbrot, B. B. (1960). The Pareto-Levy law in income distribution. *International Economic Review, 1,* 79–106.

Mandelbrot, B. B. (1962). Sur certains prix speculatifs: Faits empiriques et modele base sur les processus stables additifs de Paul Levy. *Comptes Rendus, 254,* 3968–3970.

Mandelbrot, B. B. (1977). Fractals and turbulence: Attractors and dispersion. In P. Bernard & T. Raiu (Eds.), *Turbulence seminar Berkeley 1976/1977* (pp. 83–93). New York: Springer-Verlag.

Mandelbrot, B. B. (1983). *The fractal geometry of nature.* New York: Freeman.

Marks, E. S. (1935). Individual differences in work curves. *Archives of Psychology, 186.*

Marshall, R. (1991). America's choice. High skills or low wages. *Proceedings of the 1991 Spring Meeting of the Industrial Relations Research Association* (pp. 453–461). Madison, WI: Industrial Relations Research Association.

Mawhinney, T. C. (1979). Intrinsic X extrinsic work motivation: Perspectives from behaviorism. *Organizational Behavior and Human Performance, 24,* 411–440.

May, R. M. (1976). Simple mathematical models with very complicated dynamics. *Nature, 261,* 459–467.

May, R. M., & Oster, G. F. (1976). Bifurcations and dynamic complexity in simple ecological models. *American Naturalist, 110,* 573–599.

Mayer-Kress, G. (1992). Nonlinear dynamics and chaos in arms race models. In L. Lam & V. Naroditsky (Eds.), *Modeling complex systems* (pp. 153–186). New York: Springer-Verlag.

McCain, R. A. (1992, December). *Genetic algorithms, teleological conservatism, and the emergence of optimal demand relationships.* Paper presented to the Seminar on the Economics of the Arts, Venice, Italy.

McCarron, P. M., & Haakonson, N. H. (1982). Recent life change measurement in Canadian Forces pilots. *Aviation, Space and Environmental Medicine, 53,* 6–13.

McClelland, D. C. (1961). *The achieving society.* Princeton, NJ: Van Nostrand.

McClelland, D. C. (1970). The two faces of power. *Journal of International Affairs, 24,* 29–47.

McClelland, D. C. (1975). *Power: The inner experience.* New York: Irvington.

McClelland, D. C., Atkinson, J. W., Clark, R. A., & Lowell, E. L. (1953). *The achievement motive.* New York: Appleton-Century-Croft.

McClelland, D. C., & Boyatsis, R. E. (1982). Leadership motive pattern and long-term success in management. *Journal of Applied Psychology, 67,* 737–743.

McCormick, E. J. (1976). *Human factors in engineering and design* (4th ed.). New York: McGraw-Hill.

McCullers, J. C., Fabes, R. A., & Moran, J. D., III. (1987). Does intrinsic motivation theory explain the adverse effects of rewards on immediate task performance? *Journal of Personality and Social Psychology, 52,* 1027–1033.

McGrath, J. E. (1976). Stress and behavior in organizations. In M. D. Dunnette (Ed.), *Handbook of industrial and organizational psychology* (pp. 1031–1062). Chicago: Rand McNally.

McKendree, J., & Anderson, J. R. (1987). Effect of practice on knowledge and use of basic lisp. In J. M. Carroll (Ed.), *Interfacing thought: Cognitive aspects of human-computer interaction* (pp. 236–259). Cambridge, MA: MIT Press.

Meadows, D. H., Meadows, D. L., Randers, J., & Behrens, W. W., III (1972). *The limits to growth.* New York: Universe.

Mees, A. I. (1975). The revival of cities in medieval Europe. *Regional Science and Urban Economics, 5,* 403–425.

Meltzer, H. (1942). Exploring in humanizing relations of key people in industry. *American Journal of Orthopsychiatry, 12,* 517–528.

Meltzer, H., & Ludwig, D. (1968). Relationship of memory optimism to work competency and personality variables. *Journal of Applied Psychology, 52,* 423–428.

Metzger, A. M. (1994). Have subjects been shown to generate chaotic numbers? Commentary on Neuringer and Voss. *Psychological Science, 5,* 111–114.

Michaels, M. D. (1989). The chaos paradigm. *Organizational Development Journal, 7(2),* 31–35.

Michaels, M. D. (1991). Chaos constructions: A neural net model of organization. In M. D. Michaels (Ed.), *Proceedings of the First Annual Chaos Network Conference* (pp. 79–83). Savoy, IL: People Technologies.

Michaels, M. D. (1992). *The Chaos Exercise*™. Savoy, IL: People Technologies.

Michaels, M. D. (1993). Thoughts on the Organizational Development Institute's 25th anniversary. *Organizational Development Journal, 11(2),* 51–57.

Michalewicz, Z. (1993). A hierarchy of evolution programs: An experimental study. *Evolutionary Computation, 1*, 51–76.

Mikell, G. (1989). *Cocoa and chaos in Ghana.* New York: Paragon House.

Miller, D. (1984). The concept of revolutionary change: Rejoinder to Ramaprasad. *Behavioral Science, 29*, 274–275.

Miller, D., & Friesen, P. H. (1980). Momentum and revolution in organizational adaptation. *Academy of Management Journal, 23*, 591–614.

Miller, H. E., Katerberg, R., & Hulin, C. L. (1979). Evaluation of the Mobley, Horner, and Hollingworth model of employee turnover. *Journal of Applied Psychology, 64*, 509–517.

Miller, J. G. (1978). *Living systems.* New York: McGraw-Hill.

Miller, J. G., & Miller, J. L. (1990). Introduction: The nature of living systems. *Behavioral Science, 35*, 157–163.

Miller, J. L., & Miller, J. G. (1992). Greater than the sum of its parts 1. Subsystems which process both matter-energy and information: The reproducer, the boundary. *Behavioral Science, 37*, 1–38.

Miller, J. L., & Miller, J. G. (1993a). Greater than the sum of its parts II. Matter-energy processing subsystems: The ingestor, the distributor, the convertor, the producer, matter-energy storage, the extruder. *Behavioral Science, 38*, 1–72.

Miller, J. L. & Miller, J. G. (1993b). Greater than the sum of its parts II. Matter-energy processing subsystems: The motor, the supporter. *Behavioral Science, 38*, 151–188.

Mintz, A., & Blum, M. L. (1949). A re-examination of the accident proneness concept. *Journal of Applied Psychology, 33*, 195–221.

Mitchell, F. E. (1983). Letter to *Fortune*: Sex, insurance, and truth. *Fortune, 107(7)*, 21.

Mobley, W. H. (1977). Intermediate linkages in the relationship between job satisfaction and employee turnover. *Journal of Applied Psychology, 62*, 237–240.

Mobley, W. H. (1982). Some answered questions in turnover and withdrawal research. *Academy of Management Review, 7*, 111–117.

Mobley, W. H., Horner, S. O., & Hollingsworth, A. T. (1978). An evaluation of precursors of hospital employee turnover. *Journal of Applied Psychology, 63*, 408–414.

Monge, P. R. (1992). Communication and motivational predictors of the dynamics of organizational innovation. *Organization Science, 3*, 250–274.

Mosekilde, E., Larssen, E., & Sterman, J. (1991). Coping with complexity: Chaos in human decision making behavior. In J. Casti & A. Karlqvist (Eds.), *Beyond belief: Randomness, prediction, and explanation in science* (pp. 199–299). Boca Raton, FL: CRC Press.

Mosso, A. (1894). *La fatigue intellectuele and physique* (Mental and physical fatigue). Paris: Alcon.

Mosso, A. (1915). *Fatigue.* New York: Putnam.

Moul, W. B. (1993). Polarization, polynomials, and war. *Journal of Conflict Resolution, 37*, 735–748.

Muchinsky, P. M. (1990). *Psychology applied to work.* Belmont, CA: Brooks/Cole.

Muhlenbein, H., & Schlierkamp-Voosen, D. (1993). Predictive models for the Breeder genetic algorithm: I. Continuous parameter optimization. *Evolutionary Computation, 1*, 25–50.

Murphy, K. R. (1993). *Honesty in the workplace.* Belmont, CA: Brooks/Cole.

Narmour, E. (1992). The influence of embodied registral motion on the perception of higher-level melodic interpretation. In M. R. Jones & S. Hollaran (Eds.), *Cognitive bases of musical communication* (pp. 69–90). Washington, DC: American Psychological Association.

Natani, K. (1980). Future directions for selecting personnel. In T. S. Cheston & D. L. Winter (Eds.), *Human factors of outer space production* (pp. 25–63). Boulder, CO: AAAS & Westview Press.

National Safety Council. (1989). *Accident facts.* Chicago: National Safety Council.

Neatby, H. B. (1972). *The politics of chaos: Canada in the thirties.* Toronto: Macmillan.

Neuringer, A., & Voss, C. (1993). Approximating chaotic behavior. *Psychological Science, 4,* 113–119.

Newman, J. E. (1974). Predicting absenteeism and turnover: A field comparison of Fishbein's model and traditional job attitude measures. *Journal of Applied Psychology, 59,* 610–615.

Nicholson, N., Brown, C. A., & Chadwick-Jones, J. K. (1976). Absence from work and job satisfaction. *Journal of Applied Psychology, 61,* 728–737.

Nicholson, N., Wall, T., & Lischeron, J. (1977). The predictability of absence and propensity to leave from employees' job satisfaction and attitudes toward influence and decision-making. *Human Relations, 30,* 499–514.

Nicolis, G., & Prigogine, I. (1989). *Exploring complexity.* New York: Freeman.

Niefeld, M. R., & Poffenberger, A. T. (1928). A mathematical analysis of work curves. *Journal of General Psychology, 1,* 448–458.

Novick, M. R. (1980). Statistics as psychometrics. *Psychometrika, 45,* 411–424.

Novick, M. R., & Lewis, C. (1967). Coefficient alpha and the reliability of composite measurements. *Psychometrika, 32,* 1–13.

Nowak, A., Szamrej, J., & Latané, B. (1990). From private attitudes to public opinion: A dynamic theory of social impact. *Psychological Bulletin, 97,* 362–376.

Ohle, F., Dinkelacker, F., & Hubler, A., & Welge, M. (1990). *Adaptive control of chaotic systems.* (Tech. Rep. No. CCER-90-13). Urbana-Champaign: University of Illinois, Department of Physics, Beckman Institute.

Oldham, G. R., & Fried, Y. (1987). Employee reactions to workspace characteristics. *Journal of Applied Psychology, 72,* 75–80.

O'Leary, A. (1990). Stress, emotion and human immune function. *Psychological Bulletin, 108,* 363–382.

Oliva, T. A., & Capdevielle, C. M. (1980). Sussman & Zahler: Throwing the baby out with the bath water. *Behavioral Science, 25,* 229–230.

Oliva, T. A., Peters, M. H., & Murthy, H. S. K. (1981). A preliminary empirical test of a cusp catastrophe model in the social sciences. *Behavioral Science, 26,* 153–162.

Oliva, T. A., Desarbo, W. S., Day, D. L., & Jedidi, K. (1987). GEMCAT: A general multivariate methodology for estimating catastrophe models. *Behavioral Science, 32,* 121–137.

Organ, D. W. (1988). *Organizational citizenship behavior: The good soldier syndrome.* Lexington, MA: Lexington.

Orishimo, I., Sawada, K., & Togawa, Y. (1990). An invitation to the replicator equations. *Socio-Spatial Dynamics, 1,* 125–137.

Osborn, A. F. (1953). *Creative imagination: Principles and procedures of creative thinking.* New York: Schribner.

Osgood, C. E. (1949). The similarity paradox in human learning: A resolution. *Psychological Review, 56,* 132–143.

Ostrom, C. W., Jr. (1978). *Time series analysis: Regression techniques.* Beverly Hills: Sage, 1978.

Ott, E. (1981). Strange attractors and chaotic motions of dynamical systems. *Review of Modern Physics, 53,* 655–671.

Packard, N. H., Crutchfield, J. P., Farmer, J. D., & Shaw, R. S. (1980). Geometry from a time series. *Physics Review Letters, 45,* 712–716.

Packard, N. H., & Wolfram, S. (1985). Two dimensional cellular automata. *Journal of Statistical Physics, 38,* 901–946.

Pavlov, I. P. (1927). *Conditioned reflexes.* London: Oxford University Press.

Peitgen, H.-O., & Saupe, D. (Eds.). (1988). *The science of fractal images.* New York: Springer-Verlag.

Penrod, S., & Hastie, R. (1980). A computer simulation of jury decision making. *Psychological Review, 87,* 133–159.

Perkins, S. (1994, March). *Technical fixes and social systems.* Paper presented to the Sigma Xi Sustainable Development Forum, Chicago.

Peters, E. E. (1991). *Chaos and order in the capital markets*. New York: Wiley.

Peterson, J. L. (1981). *Petri net theory and the modeling of systems*. Englewood Cliffs, NJ: Prentice Hall.

Piaget, J. (1952). *Origins of intelligence in children*. New York: Norton.

Pickover, C. A. (1990). *Computers, pattern, chaos, and beauty: Graphics from an unseen world.* New York: St. Martin's Press.

Pidgeon, N. F. (1991). Safety culture and risk management in organizations. *Journal of Cross-Cultural Psychology, 22,* 129–140.

Pinchot, G., III. (1985). *Intrapreneuring: Why you don't have to leave the corporation to become an entrepreneur*. New York: Harper & Row.

Poffenberger, A. T. (1928). The effects of continuous work upon output and feelings. *Journal of Applied Psychology, 12,* 459–467.

Porter, L. W., & Lawler, E. E., III. (1965). Properties of organizational structure related to job attitudes and behavior. *Psychological Bulletin, 64,* 23–51.

Porter, L. W., Steers, R., Mowday, R., & Boulian, P. (1974). Organizational commitment, job satisfaction, and turnover among psychiatric technicians. *Journal of Applied Psychology, 59,* 603–609.

Poston, T., & Stewart, I. (1978a). *Catastrophe theory and its applications*. London, Pitman.

Poston, T., & Stewart, I. (1978b). Nonlinear modeling of multistable perception. *Behavioral Science, 23,* 318–334.

Premack, D. (1971). Catching up with common sense or two sides of a generalization: Reinforcement and punishment. In R. Glaser (Ed.), *The nature of reinforcement* (pp. 121–150). New York: Academic Press.

Priesmeyer, H. R. (1992). *Organizations and chaos*. Westport, CT: Quorum.

Pritchard, R. D., Campbell, K .M., & Campbell, D. J. (1977). Effects of extrinsic financial rewards on intrinsic motivation. *Journal of Applied Psychology, 62,* 9–15.

Quick, J. C., Hurrell, J. J., & Murphy, L. M. (Eds.). (1992). *Work and well-being: Assessments and interventions for occupational mental health*. Washington, DC: American Psychological Association.

Quick, J. C., & Quick, J. D. (1984). *Organizational stress and preventive management*. New York: McGraw-Hill.

Quinlan, M. (1988). Psychological and sociological approaches to the study of occupational illness: A critical review. *Australia and New Zealand Journal of Sociology, 24,* 189–207.

Ramaprasad, A. (1982). Revolutionary change and strategic management. *Behavioral Science, 27,* 387–392.

Rambo, W. W., Chomiak, A. M., & Price, J. M. (1983). Consistency of performance under stable conditions of work. *Journal of Applied Psychology, 68,* 78–87.

Ramsey, J. B. (1992). *Seasonal economic data as approximate harmonic oscillators* (Tech. Rep. No. 92-16). New York: New York University, C. S. Starr Center for Applied Economics.

Ramsey, J. B., & Keenan, S. (1993). *Forecastability of driven oscillators with noise* (Tech. Rep. #93-28). New York: New York University, C. V. Starr Center for Applied Economics.

Rand, D. (1978). Exotic phenomena in games and duopoly models. *Journal of Mathematical Economics, 5,* 173–184.

Rao, A., Thornberry, N., & Weintraub, J. (1987). An empirical study of autonomous work groups: Relationships between worker reactions and effectiveness. *Behavioral Science, 32,* 66–76.

Rapoport, A. (1988). Editorial comments on the article by Hirshleifer and Martinez Coll. *Journal of Conflict Resolution, 32,* 399–401.

Ratkowsky, D. A. (1990). *Handbook of nonlinear regression models*. New York: Marcel Dekker.

Rawlings, J. O. (1988). *Applied regression analysis: A research tool*. Pacific Grove, CA: Wadsworth & Brooks/Cole.

Rescorla, R. A., & Wagner, A. R. (1972). A theory of Pavlovian conditioning: Variations in the effectiveness of reinforcement and nonreinforcement. In A. H. Black & W. R. Prokasy (Eds.), *Classical conditioning II: Current research and theory* (pp. 64–99). New York: Appleton-Century-Crofts.

Richards, D. (1990). Is strategic decision making chaotic? *Behavioral Science, 35,* 219–232.

Richards, R. J. (1987). *Darwin and the emergence of evolutionary theories of mind and behavior.* Chicago: University of Chicago Press.

Richardson, L. F. (1960). *Arms and insecurity.* Pittsburgh: Boxwood.

Rieke, M. L., Guastello, S. J., & Conn, S. R. (1994). Leadership and creativity. In S. R. Conn & M. L. Rieke (Eds.), *The sixteen personality factor questionnaire: Fifth edition technical manual* (pp. 183–212). Champaign, IL: Institute for Personality and Ability Testing.

Rollins, R. W. (1990). *Chaotic dynamics workbench* [Software and manual]. New York: American Institute of Physics.

Ross, R. (1916). An application of the theory of probabilities to the study of a priori pathometry (Vol. 1). *Proceedings of the Royal Society, A, 92,* 204–230.

Ross, R. (1917). An application of the theory of probabilities to the study of a priori pathometry (Vol. 2). *Proceedings of the Royal Society, A, 93,* 225–240.

Rosser, J. B., Jr. (1991). *From catastrophe to chaos: A general theory of economic discontinuities.* Boston: Klewer.

Rosser, J. B., Jr. (1992). Morphogenesis of urban historical forms. *Socio-Spatial Dynamics, 3,* 17–34.

Rotter, J. B. (1966). Generalized expectancies for the internal versus external locus of control of reinforcement. *Psychological Monographs, 80.*

Rowe, W. D. (1977). *An anatomy of a risk.* New York: Wiley.

Rummel, R. J. (1983). Libertarianism and international violence. *Journal of Conflict Resolution, 27,* 27–71.

Rummel, R. J. (1987). A catastrophe theory model of the conflict helix, with tests. *Behavioral Science, 32,* 241–266.

Saari, J. (1992). Successful implementation of occupational health and safety programs in manufacturing for the 1990s. *International Journal of Human Factors in Manufacturing, 2,* 55–66.

Saavedra, R., Earley, C., & Van Dyne, L. (1993). Complex interdependence in task-performing groups. *Journal of Applied Psychology, 78,* 61–72.

Saks, M. (1976). The limits of scientific jury selection: Ethical and empirical. *Jurimetrics Journal, 17,* 3–22.

Saleh, S. D., & Grygier, T. G. (1969). Psychodynamics of intrinsic and extrinsic job orientation. *Journal of Applied Psychology, 53,* 446–450.

Saperstein, A. M., & Mayer-Kress, G. (1988). A nonlinear dynamical model of the impact of SDI on the arms race. *Journal of Conflict Resolution, 32,* 636–670.

Sashkin, M. (1984). *The leader behavior questionnaire.* King of Prussia, PA: Organization Design and Development.

Schein, E. H. (1990). Organizational Culture. *American Psychologist, 45,* 109–119.

Schmidt, F. L. (1992). What do data really mean? Research findings, meta-analysis and cumulative knowledge in psychology. *American Psychologist, 47,* 1173–1181.

Schmidt, F. L., & Hunter, J. E. (1981). Employment testing: Old theories and new research findings. *American Psychologist, 36,* 1128–1137.

Schneider, B., & Reichers, A. E. (1983). On the etiology of climates. *Personnel Psychology, 36,* 19–39.

Schuster, P. (1986). Dynamics of molecular evolution. *Physica D,* 100–119.

Scott, D. W. (1985). Catastrophe theory applications in clinical psychology: A review. *Current Directions in Psychological Research and Reviews, 4,* 69–86.

Seber, G. A. F., & Wild, C. J. (1989). *Nonlinear regression.* New York: Wiley.

Seligman, M. P. (1975). *Helplessness: On depression, development and death.* San Francisco: Freeman.

Selten, R. (1991). Evolution, learning and economic behavior. *Games and Economic Behavior, 3,* 3–24.

Selye, H. (1976). *Stress in health and disease.* Boston: Butterworths.

Sheppard, B. N., & Minton, J. W. (1986). Research on procedural justice: Implications for industrial relations. In B. D. Dennis (Ed.), *Proceedings of the thirty-ninth annual meeting of the Industrial Relations Research Association* (pp. 368–374). Madison, WI: Industrial Relations Research Association.

Shepperd, J. A. (1993). Productivity loss in performance groups: A motivation study. *Psychological Bulletin, 113,* 67–81.

Sheridan, J. E. (1980). Catastrophe model of employee turnover among hospital nursing staff. In *Proceedings of the Academy of Management,* (pp. 161–165, expanded edition).

Sheridan, J. E. (1985). Catastrophe model of employee withdrawal leading to low job performance, high absenteeism and turnover during the first year of employment in an organization. *Academy of Management Journal, 28,* 88–109.

Sheridan, J. E., & Abelson, M. A. (1983). Cusp catastrophe model of employee turnover. *Academy of Management Journal, 26,* 418–436.

Sheridan, J. E., & Vredenburgh, D. J. (1978). Usefulness of leadership behavior and social power variables in predicting job tension, performance and turnover of nursing employees. *Journal of Applied Psychology, 63,* 89–95.

Shipley, P. (1987). The management of psychosocial risk factors in the working environment: UK law compared. *Work & Stress, 1,* 43–48.

Siegel, S. M., & Kaemmerer, W. G. (1978). Measuring the perceived support for innovation in organizations. *Journal of Applied Psychology, 63,* 553–563.

Simonton, D. K. (1988). Creativity, leadership, and chance. In R. J. Sternberg (Ed.), *The nature of creativity: Contemporary psychological perspective* (pp. 386–426). New York: Cambridge University Press.

Simonton, D. K. (1989). Age and creative productivity: Nonlinear estimation of an information processing model. *International Journal of Aging and Human Development, 29,* 23–37.

Skinner, B. F. (1938). *The behavior of organisms.* New York: Appleton-Century-Crofts.

Skinner, B. F. (1948). *Walden Two.* New York: Macmillan.

Skinner, B. F. (1971). *Beyond freedom and dignity.* New York: Knopf.

Slocum, J. W. (1971). Motivation in managerial levels: Relationship of need satisfaction to job performance. *Journal of Applied Psychology, 55,* 312–316.

Smale, S. (1964). Diffeomorphisms with many periodic points. In S. S. Cairns (Ed.), *Differential and Combination Topology Symposium in Honor of Marston Morse* (pp. 63–80). Princeton, NJ: Princeton University Press.

Smetana, J. G., & Adler, N. E. (1980). Fishbein's value X expectancy model: An examination of some assumptions. *Personality and Social Psychology Bulletin, 6,* 89–96.

Smith, J. Q. (1980). The prediction of prison riots. *British Journal of Mathematical and Statistical Psychology, 30,* 151–160.

Snow, C. P. (1959). *The two cultures.* London: Cambridge University Press.

Society of Actuaries. (1982). *Transactions: 1980 Reports of mortality and morbility experience.* Chicago: Author.

Solomon, R. L. (1980). The opponent process theory of acquired motivation: The costs of pleasure and the benefits of pain. *American Psychologist, 35,* 691–712.

Solomon, R. L., & Corbit, J. D. (1973). An opponent process of motivation II: Cigarette addiction. *Journal of Abnormal Psychology, 81,* 158–171.

Solomon, R. L., & Corbit, J. D. (1974). An opponent process theory of motivation I: Temporal dynamics of affect. *Psychological Review, 81,* 119–145.

Stacey, R. D. (1992). *Managing the unknowable: Strategic boundaries between order and chaos.* San Francisco: Jossey-Bass.

Starch, D., & Ash, I. E. (1917). The mental curve of work. *Psychological Review, 24,* 391–402.

Steers, R. M., & Rhodes, S. R. (1978). Major influences on employee attendance: A process model. *Journal of Applied Psychology, 63,* 391–407.

Sterman, J. (1988). Deterministic models of chaos in human behavior: Methodological issues and experimental results. *System Dynamics Review, 4,* 148–178.

Sternberg, R. J., & Lubart, T. I. (1991). An investment theory of creativity and its development. *Human Development, 34,* 1–31.

Stevens, S. S. (1951). Mathematics, measurement, and psychophysics. In S. S. Stevens (Ed.), *Handbook of experimental psychology* (pp. 1–50). New York: Wiley.

Stewart, I. N. (1980). Catastrophe theory and equations of state: Conditions for butterfly singularity. *Mathematical Proceedings of the Cambridge Philosophical Society, 88,* 429–499.

Stewart, I. (1989). *Does God play dice: The mathematics of chaos.* Oxford: Basil Blackwell.

Stewart, I. N., & Peregoy, P. L. (1983). Catastrophe theory modeling in psychology. *Psychological Bulletin, 94,* 336–362.

Storfer, M. D. (1990). *Intelligence and giftedness: The contributions of heredity and early environment.* San Francisco: Jossey-Bass.

Stroop, J. R. (1935). Studies of interference in serial verbal reactions. *Journal of Experimental Psychology, 18,* 643–662.

Surry, J. (1969). *Industrial accident research: A human engineering appraisal.* Toronto: Labor Safety Council, Ontario Ministry of Labor.

Sussmann, H. J., & Zahler, R. S. (1978a). Catastrophe theory as applied to the social and biological sciences. *Synthese, 37,* 117–216.

Sussmann, H. J., & Zahler, R. S. (1978b). A critique of applied catastrophe theory in the applied behavioral sciences. *Behavioral Science, 23,* 383–389.

Ta'eed, L. K., Ta'eed, O., & Wright, J. E. (1988). Determinants involved in the perception of the Necker cubes: An application of catastrophe theory. *Behavioral Science, 33,* 97–115.

Tasto, D. L., Colligan, M. J., Skjel, E. W., & Polly, S. J. (1978). *Health consequences of shift work.* Washington, D.C.: United States Department of Health, Education and Welfare: National Institute for Occupational Safety and Health. United States Government Printing Office.

Taylor, C. W. (1988). Various approaches to and definitions of creativity: In R. J. Sternberg (Ed.), *The nature of creativity: Contemporary psychological perspectives* (pp. 386–426). Cambridge, MA: MIT Press.

Taylor, H. C., & Russell, J. T. (1939). The relationship of validity coefficients to the practical effectiveness in selection: Discussion and tables. *Journal of Applied Psychology, 23,* 565–578.

Taylor, J. A. (1953). A personality scale of manifest anxiety. *Journal of Abnormal and Social Psychology, 48,* 285–290.

Terpstra, D. E. (1981). Relationship between methodological rigor and reported outcomes in organizational development evaluation research. *Journal of Applied Psychology, 66,* 541–543.

Theiler, J., & Eubank, S. (1993). Don't bleach chaotic data. *Chaos, 3,* 771–782.

Thelen, E. (1992). Development as a dynamic system. *Current Directions in Psychological Science, 1,* 189–192.

Thom, R. (1975). *Structural stability and morphogenesis.* New York: Benjamin-Addison-Wesley.

Thom, R. (1983). *Mathematical models of morphogenesis.* New York: Halsted.

Thompson, J. M. T. (1982). *Instabilities and catastrophes in science and engineering.* New York: Wiley.

Thompson, J. M. T., & Stewart, H. B. (1986). *Nonlinear dynamics and chaos.* New York: Wiley.

Thorndike, E. L. (1911). *Animal intelligence.* New York: Macmillan.

Thrall, R. M., Cardus, D., & Fuhrer, M. J. (1981). Multicriterion decision analysis. In L. Cobb and R. M. Thrall (Eds.), *Mathematical frontiers of the social and policy sciences* (pp. 131–156). Boulder, CO: AAAS and Westview Press.

Tindale, R. S., & Nagao, D. H. (1986). An assessment of the potential utility of "Scientific Jury Selection:" A "thought experiment" approach. *Organizational Behavior and Human Decision Processes, 37,* 409–425.

Toffoli, T., & Margolus, N. (1987). *Cellular automata machines: A new environment for modeling.* Cambridge, MA: MIT Press.

Toffoli, T., & Margolus, N. (1990). Invertible cellular automata: A review. *Physica D, 45,* 229–253.

Tolman, E. C. (1932). *Purposive behavior in animals and man.* New York: Century.

Tong, H. (1990). *Non-linear time series: A dynamical system approach.* Oxford, UK: Oxford University Press.

Torrance, E. P. (1988). Creativity as manifest in testing. In R. J. Sternberg (Ed.), *The nature of creativity: Contemporary Psychological Perspectives* (pp. 43–75). New York: Cambridge University Press.

Townsend, J. T., & Busemeyer, J. R. (1989). Approach-avoidance: Return to dynamic decision behavior. In C. Izawa (Ed.), *Current issues in cognitive processes: The Tulane Floweree Symposium on Cognition* (pp. 107–133). Hillsdale, NJ: Lawrence Erlbaum Associates.

Travis, C. B., McLean, B. E., & Ribar, C. (Eds., 1989). Environmental toxins: Psychological, behavioral, and sociocultural aspects, 1973–1989. *Bibliographies in Psychology, No. 5.* Washington, DC: American Psychological Association.

Trist, E., & Bamforth, K. (1951). Some social and psychological consequences of the longwall method of coal getting. *Human Relations, 4,* 3–38.

Turkle, S. (1984). *The second self: Computers and the human spirit.* New York: Wiley.

Ueda, Y. (1993). *The road to chaos.* Santa Cruz, CA: Ariel Press.

Ulam, S., & Schrandt, R. (1986). Some elementary attempts at numerical modeling of problems concerning rates of evolutionary processes. *Physica D, 22,* 4–12.

United Nations. (1992). *Agenda 21: Programme of action for sustainable development.* New York: United Nations.

van de Ven, A. H., & Rogers, E. M. (1988). Innovations and organizations: Critical perspectives. Special issue: Innovative research on innovations and organizations. *Communication Research, 15,* 632–651.

Verhaegen, P. (1993). Absenteeism, accidents and risk-taking: A review ten years later. *Safety Science, 16,* 359–367.

Vilardo, F. J. (1988). The role of the epidemiological model in injury control. *Journal of Safety Research, 19,* 1–4.

Vinchur, A. J., Schippmann, J. S., Smalley, M. D., & Rothe, H. F. (1991). Productivity consistency of foundry chippers and grinders: A 6-year field study. *Journal of Applied Psychology, 76,* 134–136.

von Bertalanffy, L. (1968). *General systems theory.* New York: Braziller.

von Neumann, J., & Morgenstern, O. (1953). *Theory of games and economic behavior.* Princeton, NJ: Princeton University Press.

Vroom, V. H. (1964). *Work and motivation.* New York: Wiley.

Wahba, M. A., & House, R. J. (1974). Expectancy theory in work and motivation: Some logical and methodological issues. *Human Relations, 27,* 121–147.

Walker, J. I., & Cavenar, J. (1982). Vietnam veterans: Their problems continue. *Journal of Nervous Mental Disorder, 170,* 174–179.

Walker, S. (1990). *In defense of American liberties.* New York. Oxford.

Wallace, M. D. (1973). Alliance, polarization, cross-cutting, and international war, 1815–1964: A measurement procedure and some preliminary evidence. *Journal of Conflict Resolution, 17,* 575–604.

Wallach, M. A., & Wing, C. W. (1969). *The talented student: A validation of the creativity-intelligence distinction.* New York: Holt.

Waller, J. A. (1987). Injury as disease. *Accident Analysis and Prevention, 19,* 13–20.

Walster, E., Berscheid, E., & Walster, G. W. (1973). New direction in equity research. *Journal of Personality and Social Psychology, 25,* 151–176.

Wandell, B. A. (1982). Measurement of small color differences. *Psychological Bulletin, 89,* 281–302.

Wanous, J. P. (1980). *Organizational entry: Recruitment, selection, and socialization of newcomers.* Reading, MA: Addison-Wesley.

Ward, L. M., & West, R. L. (1994). On chaotic behavior. *Psychological Science, 5,* 232–236.

Waters, L. K., & Roach, D. (1979). Job satisfaction, behavioral intention, and absenteeism as predictors of turnover. *Personnel Psychology, 32,* 393–397.

Watson, C. J. (1981). An evaluation of some aspects of the Steers and Rhodes model of employee attendance. *Journal of Applied Psychology, 66,* 385–389.

Watson, J. B., & Rayner, R. (1920). Conditioned emotional responses. *Journal of Experimental Psychology, 3,* 1–14.

Weber, M. (1947). *Theory of economic and social organization.* New York: Oxford University Press.

Weinland, J. P. (1927). Variability of performance in the curve of work. *Archives of Psychology, 30.*

Weintraub, E. R. (1983). Zeeman's unstable stock exchange. *Behavioral Science, 28,* 79–83.

Weisaeth, L. (1989a). A study of behavioral responses to an industrial disaster. *Acta Psyciatrica Scandinavica, 80* (355 Suppl.), 13–24.

Weisaeth, L. (1989b). The stressors and the post-traumatic stress syndrome after an industrial disaster. *Acta Psychiatrica Scandinavica, 80* (355 Suppl.), 25–37.

Weisaeth, L. (1989c). The importance of high response rates in traumatic stress research. *Acta Psychiatrica Scandinavica, 80* (355 Suppl.), 131–137.

Welford, A. T. (1980). Relationships between reaction time, fatigue, stress, age, and sex. In A. T. Welford (Ed.), *Reaction time* (pp. 321–354). New York: Academic Press.

Wernimont, P. F. (1972). A systems view of job satisfaction. *Journal of Applied Psychology, 56,* 173–176.

Westheimer, G. (1991). Visual discrimination of fractal borders. *Proceedings of the Royal Society of London: Series B, Biological Sciences, 243,* 215–219.

Wheatley, M. J. (1992). *Leadership and the new science.* San Francisco: Berrett-Kohler.

White, L. T., III (1989). *Policies of chaos: The organizational causes of violence in China's cultural revolution.* Princeton, NJ: Princeton University Press.

Wiggins, S. (1988). *Global bifurcations and chaos.* New York: Springer-Verlag.

Wilson, A. G. (1981). *Catastrophe theory and bifurcations: Applications to urban and regional systems.* Berkeley, CA: University of California Press.

Wilson, E. (1975). *Sociobiology.* Cambridge, MA: Harvard University Press.

Wilson, G. T., & Davison, G. C. (1971). Processes of fear reduction in systematic desensitization. *Psychological Bulletin, 76,* 1–14.

Wojtezak-Jaroszowa, J. (1978). *Physiological and psychological aspects of night and shift work.* Washington, DC: United States Department of Health, Education, and Welfare: National Insitute for Occupational Safety and Health, United States Government Printing Office.

Wolf, A., Swift, J. B., Swinney, H. L., & Vastano, J. A. (1985). Determining Lyapunov exponents from a time series. *Physica D, 16,* 285–317.

Wolfram, S. (1983). Statistical mechanics of cellular automata. *Review of Modern Physics, 55,* 601–644.

Wolfram, S. (1986). Outline. In S. Wolfram (Ed.), *Theory and applications of cellular automata* (pp. 1–4). Singapore: World Scientific.

Woodcock, A. E. R., & Davis, M. (1978). *Catastrophe theory.* New York: Avon.

Woodcock, G. (1944). *Anarchy or chaos*. London: Freedom Press.

Woodman, R. W., & Sherman, J. J. (1980). The role of team development in organizational effectiveness: A critical review. *Psychological Bulletin, 88*, 166–186.

Wright, D. J. (1983). Catastrophe theory in management forecasting and decision making. *Journal of the operational Research Society, 34*, 935–942.

Wymore, A. W. (1967). *A mathematical theory of systems engineering*. New York: Wiley.

Yee, H. C., Sweby, P. K., & Griffiths, D. F. (1991). Dynamical approach study of spurious steady-state numerical solutions of nonlinear differential equations I: The dynamics of time discretization and its implications for algorithm development in computational fluid dynamics. *Journal of Computational Physics, 97*, 249–310.

Yelen, D. R. (1980). A catastrophe model for the effects of a response set on a discrimination task. *Perception & Psychophysics, 28*, 177–178.

Yerkes, R. M., & Dodson, J. D. (1908). The relationship of strength of stimulus to rapidity of habit formation. *Journal of Comparative Neurology and Psychology, 18*, 459–482.

Zagare, F. C. (1984). *Game theory: Concepts and applications*. Beverly Hills, CA: Sage.

Zedeck, S. (1977). An information processing model and approach to the study of motivation. *Organizational Behavior and Human Performance, 18*, 47–77.

Zeeman, E. C. (1974). On the unstable behavior of stock exchanges. *Journal of Mathematical Economics, 1*, 39–49.

Zeeman, E. C. (1976a). Catastrophe theory. *Scientific American, 234*, 65–83.

Zeeman, E. C. (1976b). A mathematical model for conflicting judgments caused by stress applied to possible misestimation of speed caused by alcohol. *British Journal of Mathematical and Statistical Psychology, 29*, 19–32.

Zeeman, E. C. (1977). *Catastrophe theory: Selected papers, 1972–1977*. Reading, MA: Addison-Wesley.

Zeeman, E. C. (1981). Dynamics of evolution of animal conflicts. *Journal of Theoretical Biology, 89*, 249–270.

Zeeman, E. C., Hall, G., Harrison, P. J., Marriage, H., & Shapland, P. (1976). A model for institutional disturbance. *British Journal of Mathematical and Statistical Psychology, 29*, 66–80.

Zeiler, M. D., & Solano, N. J. M. (1982). Responses and pauses: Discrimination and a choice catastrophe. *Journal of the Experimental Analysis of Behavior, 37*, 223–231.

Zhang, W.-B. (1991). Economic growth, creativity and spatial diffusion of knowledge. *Socio-Spatial Dynamics, 2*, 19–30.

Zimmerman, B. J. (1992). *Chaos and self-renewing organizations: Designing transformation processes for co-evolution*. Working Paper No. 29–92. North York: ONT: York University, Faculty of Administrative Studies.

Zimmerman, B. J., & Hurst, D. K. (1993). Fratals: A lens to view organizational change, learning, and leadership. *The Chaos Network, 5*(1), 1–5. (Available from People Technologies, Savoy, IL 61874)

Zohar, D. (1980). Safety climate in industrial organizations: Theoretical and applied implications. *Journal of Applied Psychology, 65*, 96–102.

Author Index

Subject Index

A

Ability, 126–128, 141, 151
Absenteeism, 130–132, 148–151, 156–158
Absolute threshold, 100–102
Academic performance, 154–156, 158–160
Accidents, 205–231, 241–242, 367
  control of, 206–217, 220–221
Adaptation, 143, 181, 259–260, 297–341
Adverse impact, 126–127
Agriculture, 227, 389
Alienation, 163–167, 367
Anarchy, 367–369
Annihilation, 46–48, 275–276
  blue loop, 47–48, 272
Anomie, *see* Alienation
Anticipation strategies, 270–271
Anxiety, 178, 193–195, 213–215, 221, 242
Approach-avoidance, 149–150
Artistic and Scientific Activities Survey, 318–319
Arms race, 376–379
Attitude, 128–136, 374–375
Attractor, 12–14, 336
  basin, 13, 26, 274–296, 339, 354–355
  chaotic (strange), 16–25, 50, 250
  fixed point, 13, 23, 46, 250
  Henon, 20–22, 92
  limit cycle, 13, 23, 46–50
  Lorenz, 18–19, 51, 92

quasi-periodic, 16
repellor, 15, 46–48, 170
Rossler, 19–20, 92, 349
saddle, 15–16, 23, 47–49, 255–256, 269, 379
Asymmetry, 35
Autocratic style, 332, *see also* fascistic style
Autonomous process, 45, 250

B

Bifurcation, 21, 24–29, 44, *see also* Catastrophe theory
  catastrophic, 25, 46–48, 271–272, 275–276
  explosive, 25, 272
  Hopf, 25, 47, 255
  logistic map, 26–28, 31–32, 46, 84, 86–89, 160, 235, 269, 278–285, 321–327, 345–346, 363, 389–390, 392
  Neimark, 25
  parameter, 25, 35
  point, *see* singularity
  subtle, 25–26
Boundary (-ies), 45, 242, 340
Brainstorm, 306–307, 356
Buckling, Euler, 196–197, 368
Bumper effect dynamic, 320, 328, 343, 349
Bureaucracy, 331

435